THE LOSS OF
THE TITANIC

D1388242

WALTHAM FOREST LIBRARIES

904 000 00261866

About the Authors

Lawrence Beesley was a science teacher, journalist and author who survivied the sinking of the *Titanic*. He was born in Wirksworth, Derbyshire. Beesley's book about his experience, which was published just nine weeks after the disaster, was a huge success. During the filming of *A Night to Remember*, Beesley famously gatecrashed the set during the sinking scene, hoping to 'go down with the ship' that time. But he was spotted by the director, who vetoed this unscheduled appearance, due to actors' union rules.

Nicholas Wade is the science correspondent for the *New York Times* and is the grandson of Lawrence Beesley He lives in New Jersey, USA.

THE LOSS OF THE TITANIC

'I Survived the TITANIC'

LAWRENCE
BEESLEY

AMBERLEY

Cover illustrations: Front: Olympic, Titanic's near-identical sister ship. © Jonathan Reeve JR2214f140 1912.

Waltham Forest Libraries	
904 000 00261866	
Askews & Holts	16-Apr-2013
910.9163 BEE	£9.99
3852536	

Originally published in 1912 as *The Loss of the RMS Titanic: Its Story and Its Lessons*

This edition first published 2013

Amberley Publishing
The Hill, Stroud,
Gloucestershire, GL5 4EP

www.amberleybooks.com

Copyright © The Estate of Lawrence Beesley, 1912, 1979, 2011, 2013

The right of Lawrence Beesley to be identified as the Author of this work has been asserted in accordance with the Copyrights, Designs and Patents Act 1988.

ISBN 978 1 4456 1383 3 paperback
ISBN 978 1 4456 0785 6 ebook

All rights reserved. No part of this book may be reprinted or reproduced or utilised in any form or by any electronic, mechanical or other means, now known or hereafter invented, including photocopying and recording, or in any information storage or retrieval system, without the permission in writing from the Publishers.

British Library Cataloguing in Publication Data. A catalogue record for this book is available from the British Library.

Typesetting and Origination by Amberley Publishing. Printed in the UK.

Contents

Preface to Centenary Edition

On 10 April 1912, my grandfather Lawrence Beesley boarded a ship in Southampton, bound for New York. He had paid £13 for a second class ticket, and planned to visit his youngest brother Arthur, then living in Toronto.

Five days later, he became one of the few men to escape from a historic disaster, the sinking of the *Titanic* after it brushed against an iceberg while running at full speed. Arriving in New York he wrote, in six weeks, an account that vividly described the drama of his escape, the terrible fate of those unable to find space on a lifeboat, and the technical and managerial flaws that contributed to the accident.

His book, *The Loss of the RMS Titanic,* is a classic account of disaster at sea. It has been constantly in print because of the intense interest the tragedy aroused. A luxury liner, built with advanced technology and carrying wealthy and famous passengers, had met with unparalleled disaster on its maiden voyage. Of its 2,223 passengers and crew, 1,517 perished. But the tragedy was no act of God. It was through human folly that the

Titanic carried too few lifeboats, that she was not properly equipped to spot icebergs at night, and that her captain drove her at full speed while ignoring several warnings of an ice field in her path. The catastrophe was a monument to the destruction that can be brought about by technology and miscalculation, presaging the even greater disaster from the same cause that was to break out two years later in the First World War.

My grandfather was an ordinary individual caught in the throes of a historic event. But he was not a passive agent in his survival. Had he not been keenly aware of his surroundings, and kept his head during a few crucial minutes, he would have perished as did 92 per cent of the male passengers travelling in second class.

Lawrence Beesley was born on 31 December 1877, in Wirksworth, Derbyshire. It was in this ancient town that Richard Arkwright, the inventor of the water frame and other cotton-processing machines, and a pioneer of the Industrial Revolution, built one of his first factories. Lawrence's father, Henry Beesley, was a disciplinarian who often beat his children, and they in turn showed him respect rather than affection. Henry was the manager of the Arkwright bank in Wirksworth. That was not his only association with the Arkwright family. After Henry's death in 1907, Lawrence learned that his father was the illegitimate son of Albert Arkwright, Richard Arkwright's great-grandson who lived at the Gate House in Wirksworth. Henry's mother, Anne Wigley, was the daughter of a gardener on the Arkwright estate.

Lawrence was educated at Cambridge University where he studied science and discovered a species of algae, named *Ulvella beesleyi*. While still an undergraduate he married Gertrude Cecile Macbeth with whom he had a son, Alec. (Alec grew up to be an accountant, then married Dodie Smith, a playwright and author of *I Capture the Castle* and *The Hundred and One Dalmations*.)

My grandfather graduated with first class honours in natural science and decided to become a science teacher. His first job was teaching back home at Wirksworth, and he then moved to Dulwich College in London. Around this time he developed a keen interest in Christian Science. This was a perhaps surprising departure for a science teacher, given that Christian Scientists assign priority to spiritual healing over scientifically based medicine. In 1909 he resigned from Dulwich College and set up practice in London as a Christian Science healer.

During the *Titanic*'s voyage, my grandfather took a keen interest in every detail of the ship, noticing for instance that it listed slightly to port, and that vibration increased as the ship picked up speed during the night of 14 April. The deadly brush with the iceberg was imperceptible to the passengers, but Lawrence was at once alert when the propellers stopped and he climbed from his cabin to the top deck to see what had happened.

His escape, according to his account, evidently lay in his thinking differently from the crowd. The *Titanic* hit the iceberg at 11.40 p.m. on 14 April, and sank at 2.20 a.m. the following morning. The enormous ship was turning at the moment of impact and avoided a head-on collision, only to have an underwater extension of the iceberg incise a 300-foot gash in its metal walls. The *Titanic* was designed to stay afloat with four of its forward sections flooded, but could not sustain the compromise of six.

Shortly after midnight, barely twenty minutes later, Captain Smith ordered the lifeboats to be readied, presumably because he realised that the ship would founder. This knowledge was not shared with the passengers. Probably to prevent panic, they were left in ignorance that the ship was doomed and that there were not enough lifeboats.

The first public hint of this impending tragedy came when the crew ordered men and women to be separated, a strong pointer that women and children would be given priority in leaving the ship. A rumour went around the starboard side of the ship that all men were to be taken off on the port side, and almost all the men on deck crossed over to port. Only Lawrence and two others remained on the starboard side of the ship. Then, as he watched a lifeboat full of women being lowered to the sea, a crew member called up from the boat, asking Lawrence if there were any women left on his deck. When he said no, the crew member said, 'Then you had better jump.' My grandfather was thus able to step clear of the stricken ship.

So what made Lawrence stay starboard, a decision which led to his survival, when almost all the other men went portside to their perdition? The explanation he gives in his book is not entirely satisfying. 'I can personally think of no decision arising from reasoned thought that induced me to remain rather than to cross over,' he writes. Perhaps anticipating the reader's thought that some conscious decision would be required to avoid following the crowd, he adds a further sentence, which also falls short of providing an illuminating explanation: 'But while there was no process of conscious reason at work, I am convinced that what was my salvation was a recognition of the necessity of being quiet and waiting in patience for some opportunity of safety to present itself.'

While many passengers were at first reluctant to leave the ship, Lawrence had noticed early on that something was seriously amiss. As he ran down a flight of stairs shortly after the collision, he writes, he felt 'a curious sense of something out of balance and of not being able to put one's feet down in the right place.' Later, when the crew took the drastic step of separating wives from their husbands, Lawrence perhaps grasped the implication that there were not enough lifeboats. If so, he may have concluded that being among a throng of men offered the lowest chance of survival and he would therefore be better off away from the crowd. But he would perhaps have been unwilling to describe such a cold calculation in print, even though it would not have been unethical; his place in the lifeboat was not obtained at anyone else's expense.

An extraordinary postscript to Lawrence's narrative relates to the receipt he received after checking his valuables with the *Titanic*'s purser. The receipt, which looks like one half of a baggage label, was before him as he wrote his book. It bore the words 'White Star Line, RMS *Titanic*' and the number 208. The other half of the label was attached to the envelope holding his money. 'Along with other similar envelopes it may still be intact in the safe at the bottom of the sea,' Lawrence wrote.

One day in May 1995 I received a call from a historian, Michael A. Findlay, who was examining the artefacts recently salvaged from the *Titanic*'s wreck site. One of them was a label with the words 'White Star Line, RMS *Titanic*, 208.' Mr Findlay had recognised it as the match to my grandfather's receipt. Along with other documents it had been removed from the purser's safe and stuffed into a Gladstone bag.

I don't know what became of the receipt that remained in Lawrence's possession. Its counterpart, buried for more than eighty years in 12,500 feet of water 400 miles off the coast of Newfoundland, was evidently in the safer place.

On his return from the United States Lawrence resumed his career as a Christian Science practitioner. He joined the Psychical Research Society. His first wife, Gertrude, had died in 1906 and in 1919 he married his second wife, Muriel Greenwood, formerly Brownjohn. Muriel had three daughters before her marriage to Lawrence – Vera, Dinah and my mother Laurien. But Laurien always said that Lawrence was her biological father, and I see no reason to doubt her.

Besides the similarities of their looks and first names is the fact that Lawrence assigned Laurien the same birthday as his – 31 December – which she believed was not the true date, although probably close to it. After his marriage to Muriel, Lawrence had two more children with her, Waveney and Hugh.

Lawrence was not an ideal father. He was estranged from his son Alec, who felt his father neglected him. My mother, whose spelling was always idiosyncratic, often complained that Lawrence failed to provide a proper education, taking his children to the golf course when they should have been in school.

He made them participate in another of his hobbies, the chasing of fires. At the first sound of the fire alarm he would pile all the children into his car and take off after the fire engine. The firemen were not really happy with his attentions. But they could not dismiss him as a mere nuisance after an occasion when they arrived at the scene of the fire to find their hose was missing. This vital piece of equipment had dropped off the fire engine during its journey. A few minutes later Lawrence and family drove up along with the hose that they had retrieved along the way.

Lawrence eventually gave up his Christian Science practice and reverted to education. In 1934 he bought and ran a school in Bexhill for boys aged five to fourteen. It was at this school that my father Michael arrived as a tutor and where he met my mother Laurien. Both were interested in the stage. Laurien had begun a promising acting career and Michael had written several plays, one of which was to have been performed in London but production was cancelled on the outbreak of the Second World War.

Michael's relationship with his father-in-law was not one of unalloyed respect. He used to tell the story of how Lawrence, as headmaster of the school, decided one day to embark on a series of Sunday sermons about the Ten Commandments. Michael wondered if Lawrence had realised he would soon need to explain what adultery was to his innocent young charges. He need not have worried. When the seventh Sunday came around, Lawrence blandly announced that he was about to talk of a grave sin, that of adulteration, as in watering down the milk. Reflecting on Lawrence's personal situation with respect to the Commandment's actual words, Michael had serious difficulty during the sermon in maintaining the composure expected of a junior master.

Lawrence was often consulted by historians arguing over the events of the *Titanic*'s sinking and by film-makers re-enacting them. On one occasion he and Laurien were invited to the film set of *A Night to Remember*, a 1958 docudrama based on a book of the same title by Walter Lord. For some reason Lawrence decided that it was not enough merely to observe the re-enactment of the great drama of which he had been part. He managed to infiltrate himself and Laurien into the crowd of extras who were milling about on a life-size model of the *Titanic* constructed in a field in the Pinewood Studios. Unwisely, he pushed his way to the front of the mob of stricken passengers just before the cameras were about to roll and was spotted by the director. Over the megaphone came an invitation for Mr Beesley and his daughter kindly to leave the set immediately.

Laurien dryly recounted this episode in a preface she contributed to a paperback reissue of her father's book. The preface is unusually well written and I suspect may have been edited by a friend of hers, the novelist Julian Barnes. In describing Lawrence's undignified eviction from the set, Laurien (or Julian) wrote, 'And so, for the second time in his life, my father found himself leaving the deck of the *Titanic* in a hurry.'

Lawrence never gave up his interest in spiritual matters. I recall him showing me both his microscope and his Ouija board. He also took up dousing, or water-divining. Even as a boy of fourteen, I was surprised that so many underground torrents apparently coursed beneath his suburban garden, prompting his forked stick to twitch upward every dozen or so steps he took.

Lawrence died on 14 February 1967 at the age of eighty-nine. His book on the *Titanic* is his enduring achievement.

Of his children, Alec died in 1987, three years before Dodie. Of his daughters Dinah and Waveney, the mothers of large and happy families, Dinah is still going strong at the age of 99 but Waveney died in 2011. My mother Laurien died in 2009 after a long illness. Vera, the eldest sister, died in childhood. Hugh was killed in the Second World War after the plane he was flying was lost at sea off the coast of West Africa.

'The pleasures of the joyful heart hang by a single, silken thread,' wrote the Persian poet Hafez. The lives of Lawrence's many descendants hang by a slender strand that could so easily have been broken, his escape against heavy odds from an overwhelming disaster. Here follows his account, as clear and compelling as on the day it was written a century ago.

Nicholas Wade
31 October 2011

I am indebted for many facts and dates given here to Pat Cook of Houston, a *Titanic* expert and author of *The Annotated 'Loss of the SS Titanic'*, a privately printed monograph.

Preface to the 1912 Edition

The circumstances in which this book came to be written are as follows. Some five weeks after the survivors from the *Titanic* landed in New York, I was the guest at luncheon of Hon. Samuel J. Elder and Hon. Charles T. Gallagher, both well-known lawyers in Boston. After luncheon I was asked to relate to those present the experiences of the survivors in leaving the *Titanic* and reaching the *Carpathia*.

When I had done so, Mr Robert Lincoln O'Brien, the editor of the *Boston Herald*, urged me as a matter of public interest to write a correct history of the *Titanic* disaster, his reason being that he knew several publications were in preparation by people who had not been present at the disaster, but from newspaper accounts were piecing together a description of it. He said that these publications would probably be erroneous, full of highly coloured details, and generally calculated to disturb public thought on the matter. He was supported in his request by all present, and under this general pressure I accompanied him to Messrs. Houghton Mifflin Company, where we discussed the question of publication.

Messrs. Houghton Mifflin Company took at that time exactly the same view that I did, that it was probably not advisable to put on record the incidents connected with the *Titanic*'s sinking: it seemed better to forget details as rapidly as possible.

However, we decided to take a few days to think about it. At our next meeting we found ourselves in agreement again – but this time on the common ground that it would probably be a wise thing to write a history of the *Titanic* disaster as correctly as possible. I was supported in this decision by the fact that a short account, which I wrote at intervals on board the *Carpathia*, in the hope that it would calm public opinion by stating the truth of what happened as nearly as I could recollect it, appeared in all the American, English, and Colonial papers and had exactly the effect it was intended to have. This encourages me to hope that the effect of this work will be the same.

Another matter aided me in coming to a decision – the duty that we, as survivors of the disaster, owe to those who went down with the ship, to see that the reforms so urgently needed are not allowed to be forgotten.

Whoever reads the account of the cries that came to us afloat on the sea from those sinking in the ice-cold water must remember that they were addressed to him just as much as to those who heard them, and that the duty, of seeing that reforms are carried out devolves on every one who knows that such cries were heard in utter helplessness the night the *Titanic* sank.

I

Construction and Preparations
for the First Voyage

The history of the RMS *Titanic*, of the White Star Line, is one of the most tragically short it is possible to conceive. The world had waited expectantly for its launching and again for its sailing; had read accounts of its tremendous size and its unexampled completeness and luxury; had felt it a matter of the greatest satisfaction that such a comfortable, and above all such a safe boat had been designed and built – the 'unsinkable lifeboat' – and then in a moment to hear that it had gone to the bottom as if it had been the veriest tramp steamer of a few hundred tons; and with it fifteen hundred passengers, some of them known the world over! The improbability of such a thing ever happening was what staggered humanity.

If its history had to be written in a single paragraph it would be somewhat as follows:

The RMS *Titanic* was built by Messrs. Harland & Wolff at their well-known ship-building works at Queen's Island, Belfast, side by side with her sister ship the *Olympic*. The twin vessels marked such an increase in size that specially laid-out joiner and boiler shops were prepared to aid in their construction, and the space usually taken up by three building slips was given up to them. The keel of the *Titanic* was laid on 31 March 1909, and she was launched on 31 May 1911; she passed her trials before the Board of Trade officials on 31 March 1912, at Belfast, arrived at Southampton on 4 April and sailed the following Wednesday, 10 April with 2,208 passengers and crew, on her maiden voyage to New York. She called at Cherbourg the same day, Queenstown Thursday, and left for New York in the afternoon, expecting to arrive the following Wednesday morning. But the voyage was never completed. She collided with an iceberg on Sunday at 11.45 p.m. in Lat. 41° 46′ N. and Long. 50° 14′ W., and sank two hours and a half later; 815 of her passengers and 688 of her crew were drowned and 705 rescued by the *Carpathia*.

Such is the record of the *Titanic*, the largest ship the world had ever seen – she was three inches longer than the *Olympic* and one thousand tons more in gross tonnage – and her end was the greatest maritime disaster known. The whole civilised world was stirred to its depths when the full extent of loss of life was learned, and it has not yet recovered from the shock. And that is without doubt a good thing. It should not recover from it until the possibility of such a disaster occurring again has been utterly removed from human society, whether by separate legislation in different countries or by international agreement. No living person should seek to dwell in thought for one moment on such a disaster except in the endeavour to glean from it knowledge that will be of profit to the whole world in the future. When such knowledge is practically applied in the construction, equipment, and navigation of passenger steamers – and not until then – will be the time to cease to think of the *Titanic* disaster and of the hundreds of men and women so needlessly sacrificed.

A few words on the ship's construction and equipment will be necessary in order to make clear many points that arise in the course of this book. A few figures have been added which it is hoped will help the reader to follow events more closely than he otherwise could.

The considerations that inspired the builders to design the *Titanic* on the lines on which she was constructed were those of speed, weight of displacement, passenger and cargo accommodation. High speed is very expensive, because the initial cost of the necessary powerful machinery is enormous, the running expenses entailed very heavy, and passenger and cargo accommodation have to be fined down to make the resistance through the water as little as possible and to keep the weight down. An increase in size brings a builder at once into conflict with the question of dock and harbour accommodation at the ports she will touch: if her total displacement is very great while the lines are kept slender for speed, the draught limit may be exceeded. The *Titanic*, therefore, was built on broader lines than the ocean racers, increasing the total displacement; but because of the broader build, she was able to keep within the draught limit at each port she visited. At the same time she was able to accommodate more passengers and cargo, and thereby increase largely her earning capacity. A comparison between the *Mauretania* and the *Titanic* illustrates the difference in these respects:

	Displacement	Horse power	Speed in knots
Mauretania	44,640	70,000	26
Titanic	60,000	46,000	21

The vessel when completed was 883 feet long, 92 $^1/_2$ feet broad; her height from keel to bridge was 104 feet. She had 8 steel decks, a cellular double bottom, 5 $^1/_4$ feet through (the inner and outer 'skins' so-called), and with bilge keels projecting 2 feet for 300 feet of her length amidships. These latter were intended to lessen the tendency to roll in a sea; they no doubt did so very well, but, as it happened, they proved to be a weakness, for this was the first portion of the ship touched by the iceberg and it has been suggested that the keels were forced inwards by the collision and made the work of smashing in the two 'skins' a more simple matter. Not that the final result would have been any different.

Her machinery was an expression of the latest progress in marine engineering, being a combination of reciprocating engines with Parsons's low-pressure turbine engine – a combination which gives increased power with the same steam consumption, an advance on the use of reciprocating engines alone. The reciprocating engines drove the wing-propellers and the turbine a mid-propeller, making her a triple-screw vessel. To drive these engines she had 29 enormous boilers and 159 furnaces. Three elliptical funnels, 24 feet 6 inches in the widest diameter, took away smoke and water gases; the fourth one was a dummy for ventilation.

She was fitted with 16 lifeboats 30 feet long, swung on davits of the Welin double-acting type. These davits are specially designed for dealing with two, and, where necessary, three, sets of lifeboats – i.e., 48 altogether; more than enough to have saved every soul on board on the night of the collision. She was divided into 16 compartments by 15 transverse watertight bulkheads reaching from the double bottom to the upper deck in the forward end and to the saloon deck in the after end, in both cases well above the water line. Communication between the engine rooms and boiler rooms was through watertight doors, which could all be closed instantly from the captain's bridge: a single switch, controlling powerful electro-magnets, operated them. They could also be closed by hand with a lever, and in case the floor below them was flooded by accident, a float underneath the flooring shut them automatically. These compartments were so designed that if the two largest were flooded with water – a most unlikely contingency in the ordinary way – the ship would still be quite safe. Of course, more than two were flooded the night of the collision, but exactly how many is not yet thoroughly established.

Her crew had a complement of 860, made up of 475 stewards, cooks, etc., 320 engineers, and 65 engaged in her navigation. The machinery and equipment of the *Titanic* was the finest obtainable and represented the last word in marine construction. All her structure was of steel, of a weight, size, and thickness greater than that of any ship yet known: the girders, beams, bulkheads, and floors all of exceptional strength. It would hardly seem necessary to mention this, were it not that there is an impression among a portion of the general public that the provision of Turkish baths, gymnasiums, and other so-called luxuries involved a sacrifice of some more essential things, the absence of which was responsible for the loss of so many lives. But this is quite an erroneous impression. All these things were an additional provision for the comfort and convenience of passengers, and there is no more reason why they should not be provided on these ships than in a large hotel. There were places on the *Titanic*'s deck where more boats and rafts could have been stored without sacrificing these things. The fault lay in not providing them, not in designing the ship without places to put them. On whom the responsibility must rest for their not being provided is another matter and must be left until later.

When arranging a tour round the United States, I had decided to cross in the *Titanic* for several reasons – one, that it was rather a novelty to be on board the largest ship yet launched, and another that friends who had crossed in the *Olympic* described her as a most comfortable boat in a seaway, and it was reported that the *Titanic* had been still further improved in this respect by having a thousand tons more built in to steady her. I went on board at Southampton at 10 a.m. Wednesday 10 April, after staying the night in the town. It is pathetic to recall that as I sat that morning in the breakfast room of a hotel, from the windows of which could be seen the four huge funnels of the *Titanic* towering over the roofs of the various shipping offices opposite, and the procession of stokers and stewards wending their way to the ship, there sat behind me three of the *Titanic*'s passengers discussing the coming voyage and estimating, among other things, the probabilities of an accident at sea to the ship. As I rose from breakfast, I glanced at the group and recognised them later on board, but they were not among the number who answered to the roll-call on the *Carpathia* on the following Monday morning.

Between the time of going on board and sailing, I inspected, in the company of two friends who had come from Exeter to see me off, the various decks, dining-saloons and libraries; and so extensive were they that it is no exaggeration to say that it was quite easy to lose one's way on such a ship. We wandered casually into the gymnasium on the boatdeck, and were engaged in bicycle exercise when the instructor came in with two photographers and insisted on our remaining there while his friends – as we thought at the time – made a record for him of his apparatus in use. It was only later that we discovered that they were the photographers of one of the illustrated London papers. More passengers came in, and the instructor ran here and there, looking the very picture of robust, rosy-cheeked health and 'fitness' in his white flannels, placing one passenger on the electric 'horse', another on the 'camel', while the laughing group of onlookers watched the inexperienced riders vigorously shaken up and down as he controlled the little motor which made the machines imitate so realistically horse and camel exercise.

It is related that on the night of the disaster, right up to the time of the *Titanic's* sinking, while the band grouped outside the gymnasium doors played with such supreme courage in face of the water which rose foot by foot before their eyes, the instructor was on duty inside, with passengers on the bicycles and the rowing-machines, still assisting and encouraging to the last. Along with the bandsmen it is fitting that his name, which I do not think has yet been put on record – it is McCawley – should have a place in the honourable list of those who did their duty faithfully to the ship and the line they served.

2

From Southampton to the Night of the Collision

Soon after noon the whistles blew for friends to go ashore, the gangways were withdrawn, and the *Titanic* moved slowly down the dock, to the accompaniment of last messages and shouted farewells of those on the quay. There was no cheering or hooting of steamers' whistles from the fleet of ships that lined the dock, as might seem probable on the occasion of the largest vessel in the world putting to sea on her maiden voyage; the whole scene was quiet and rather ordinary, with little of the picturesque and interesting ceremonial which imagination paints as usual in such circumstances. But if this was lacking, two unexpected dramatic incidents supplied a thrill of excitement and interest to the departure from dock. The first of these occurred just before the last gangway was withdrawn – a knot of stokers ran along the quay, with their kit slung over their shoulders in bundles, and made for the gangway with the evident intention of joining the ship. But a petty officer guarding the shore end of the gangway firmly refused to allow them on board; they argued, gesticulated, apparently attempting to explain the reasons why they were late, but he remained obdurate and waved them back with a determined hand, the gangway was dragged back amid their protests, putting a summary ending to their determined efforts to join the *Titanic*. Those stokers must be thankful men today that some circumstance, whether their own lack of punctuality or some unforeseen delay over which they had no control, prevented their being in time to run up that last gangway! They will have told – and will no doubt tell for years – the story of how their lives were probably saved by being too late to join the *Titanic*.

The second incident occurred soon afterwards, and while it has no doubt been thoroughly described at the time by those on shore, perhaps a view of the occurrence from the deck of the *Titanic* will not be without interest. As the *Titanic* moved majestically down the dock, the crowd of friends keeping pace with us along the quay, we came together level with the steamer *New York* lying moored to the side of the dock along with the *Oceanic*, the crowd waving 'goodbyes' to those on board as well as they could for the intervening bulk of the two ships. But as the bows of our ship came about level with those of the *New York*, there came a series of reports like those of a revolver, and on the quay side of the *New York* snaky coils of thick rope flung themselves high in the air and fell backwards among the crowd, which retreated in alarm to escape the flying ropes. We hoped that no one was struck by the ropes, but a sailor next to me was certain he saw a woman carried away to receive attention. And then, to our amazement the *New York* crept towards us, slowly and stealthily, as if drawn by some invisible force which she was powerless to withstand. It reminded me instantly of an experiment I had shown many times to a form of boys learning the elements of physics in a laboratory, in which a small magnet is made to float on a cork in a bowl of water and small steel objects placed on neighbouring pieces of cork are drawn up to the floating magnet by magnetic force. It reminded me, too, of seeing in my little boy's bath how a large celluloid floating duck would draw towards itself, by what is called capillary attraction, smaller ducks, frogs, beetles, and other animal folk, until the menagerie floated about as a unit, oblivious of their natural antipathies and reminding us of the 'happy families' one sees in cages on the seashore. On the *New York* there was shouting of orders, sailors running to and fro, paying out ropes and putting mats over the side where it seemed likely we should collide; the tug which had a few moments before cast off from the bows of the *Titanic* came up around our stern and passed to the quay side of the *New York*'s stern, made fast to her and started to haul her back with all the force her engines were capable of; but it did not seem that the tug made much impression on the *New York*. Apart from the serious nature of the accident, it made an irresistibly comic picture to see the huge vessel drifting down the dock with a snorting tug at its heels, for all the world like a small boy dragging a diminutive puppy down the road with its teeth locked on a piece of rope, its feet splayed out, its head and body shaking from side to side in the effort to get every ounce of its weight used to the best advantage. At first all appearance showed that the sterns of the two vessels would collide; but from the stern bridge of the *Titanic* an officer directing operations stopped us dead, the suction ceased, and the *New York* with her tug trailing behind moved obliquely down the dock, her stern gliding along the side of the *Titanic* some few yards away. It gave an extraordinary impression of the absolute helplessness of a big liner in the absence of any motive power to guide her. But all excitement was not yet over: the *New York* turned her bows inward towards the quay, her stern swinging just clear of and passing in front of our bows, and moved slowly head on for the *Teutonic* lying moored to the side; mats were quickly got out and so deadened the force of the collision, which from where we were seemed to be too slight to cause any damage. Another tug came up and took hold of the *New York* by the bows; and between the two of them they dragged her round the corner of the quay which just here came to an end on the side of the river.

We now moved slowly ahead and passed the *Teutonic* at a creeping pace, but notwithstanding this, the latter strained at her ropes so much that she heeled over several degrees in her efforts to follow the *Titanic*: the crowd were shouted back, a group of gold-braided officials, probably the harbour-master and his staff, standing on the sea side of the moored ropes, jumped back over them as they drew up taut to a rigid line, and urged the crowd back still farther. But we were just clear, and as we slowly turned the corner into the river I saw the *Teutonic* swing slowly back into her normal station, relieving the tension alike of the ropes and of the minds of all who witnessed the incident.

Unpleasant as this incident was, it was interesting to all the passengers leaning over the rails to see the means adopted by the officers and crew of the various vessels to avoid collision, to see on the *Titanic*'s docking-bridge (at the stern) an officer and seamen telephoning and ringing bells, hauling up and down little red and white flags, as danger of collision alternately threatened and diminished. No one was more interested than a young American kinematograph photographer, who, with his wife, followed the whole scene with eager eyes, turning the handle of his camera with the most evident pleasure as he recorded the unexpected incident on his films. It was obviously quite a windfall for him to have been on board at such a time. But neither the film nor those who exposed it reached the other side, and the record of the accident from the *Titanic*'s deck has never been thrown on the screen.

As we steamed down the river, the scene we had just witnessed was the topic of every conversation: the comparison with the *Olympic–*

Hawke collision was drawn in every little group of passengers, and it seemed to be generally agreed that this would confirm the suction theory which was so successfully advanced by the cruiser *Hawke* in the law courts, but which many people scoffed at when the British Admiralty first suggested it as the explanation of the cruiser ramming the *Olympic*. And since this is an attempt to chronicle facts as they happened on board the *Titanic*, it must be recorded that there were among the passengers and such of the crew as were heard to speak on the matter, the direst misgivings at the incident we had just witnessed. Sailors are proverbially superstitious; far too many people are prone to follow their lead, or, indeed, the lead of anyone who asserts a statement with an air of conviction and the opportunity of constant repetition; the sense of mystery that shrouds a prophetic utterance, particularly if it be an ominous one (for so constituted apparently is the human mind that it will receive the impress of an evil prophecy far more readily than it will that of a beneficent one, possibly through subservient fear to the thing it dreads, possibly through the degraded, morbid attraction which the sense of evil has for the innate evil in the human mind), leads many people to pay a certain respect to superstitious theories. Not that they wholly believe in them or would wish their dearest friends to know they ever gave them a second thought; but the feeling that other people do so and the half conviction that there 'may be something in it, after all,' sways them into tacit obedience to the most absurd and childish theories. I wish in a later chapter to discuss the subject of superstition in its reference to our life on board the *Titanic*, but will anticipate events here a little by relating a second so-called 'bad omen' which was hatched at Queenstown. As one of the tenders containing passengers and mails neared the *Titanic*, some of those on board gazed up at the liner towering above them, and saw a stoker's head, black from his work in the stokehold below, peering out at them from the top of one of the enormous funnels – a dummy one for ventilation – that rose many feet above the highest deck. He had climbed up inside for a joke, but to some of those who saw him there the sight was seed for the growth of an 'omen', which bore fruit in an unknown dread of dangers to come. An American lady – may she forgive me if she reads these lines! – has related to me with the deepest conviction and earnestness of manner that she saw the man and attributes the sinking of the *Titanic* largely to that. Arrant foolishness, you may say! Yes, indeed, but not to those who believe in it; and it is well not to have such prophetic thoughts of danger passed round among passengers and crew: it would seem to have an unhealthy influence.

We dropped down Spithead, past the shores of the Isle of Wight looking superbly beautiful in new spring foliage, exchanged salutes with a White Star tug lying-to in wait for one of their liners inward bound, and saw in the distance several warships with attendant black destroyers guarding the entrance from the sea. In the calmest weather we made Cherbourg just as it grew dusk and left again about 8.30, after taking on board passengers and mails. We reached Queenstown about 12 noon on Thursday, after a most enjoyable passage across the Channel, although the wind was almost too cold to allow of sitting out on deck on Thursday morning.

The coast of Ireland looked very beautiful as we approached Queenstown Harbour, the brilliant morning sun showing up the green hillsides and picking out groups of dwellings dotted here and there above the rugged grey cliffs that fringed the coast. We took on board our pilot, ran slowly towards the harbour with the sounding-line dropping all the time, and came to a stop well out to sea, with our screws churning up the bottom and turning the sea all brown with sand from below. It had seemed to me that the ship stopped rather suddenly, and in my ignorance of the depth of the harbour entrance, that perhaps the sounding-line had revealed a smaller depth than was thought safe for the great size of the *Titanic*: this seemed to be confirmed by the sight of sand churned up from the bottom – but this is mere supposition. Passengers and mails were put on board from two tenders, and nothing could have given us a better idea of the enormous length and bulk of the *Titanic* than to stand as far astern as possible and look over the side from the top deck, forwards and downwards to where the tenders rolled at her bows, the merest cockleshells beside the majestic vessel that rose deck after deck above them. Truly she was a magnificent boat! There was something so graceful in her movement as she rode up and down on the slight swell in the harbour, a slow, stately dip and recover, only noticeable by watching her bows in comparison with some landmark on the coast in the near distance; the two little tenders tossing up and down like corks beside her illustrated vividly the advance made in comfort of motion from the time of the small steamer.

Presently the work of transfer was ended, the tenders cast off, and at 1.30 p.m., with the screws churning up the sea bottom again, the *Titanic* turned slowly through a quarter-circle until her nose pointed down along the Irish coast, and then steamed rapidly away from Queenstown, the little house on the left of the town gleaming white on the hillside for many miles astern. In our wake soared and screamed hundreds of gulls, which had quarrelled and fought over the remnants of lunch pouring out of the waste pipes as we lay-to in the harbour entrance; and now they followed us in the expectation of further spoil. I watched them for a long time and was astonished at the ease with which they soared and kept up with the ship with hardly a motion of their wings: picking out a particular gull, I would keep him under observation for minutes at a time and see no motion of his wings downwards or upwards to aid his flight. He would tilt all of a piece to one side or another as the gusts of wind caught him: rigidly unbendable, as an aeroplane tilts sideways in a puff of wind. And yet with graceful ease he kept pace with the *Titanic* forging through the water at twenty knots: as the wind met him he would rise upwards and obliquely forwards, and come down slantingly again, his wings curved in a beautiful arch and his tail feathers outspread as a fan. It was plain that he was possessed of a secret we are only just beginning to learn – that of utilising air-currents as escalators up and down which he can glide at will with the expenditure of the minimum amount of energy, or of using them as a ship does when it sails within one or two points of a head wind. Aviators, of course, are imitating the gull, and soon perhaps we may see an aeroplane or a glider dipping gracefully up and down in the face of an opposing wind and all the time forging ahead across the Atlantic Ocean. The gulls were still behind us when night fell, and still they screamed and dipped down into the broad wake of foam which we left behind; but in the morning they were gone: perhaps they had seen in the night a steamer bound for their Queenstown home and had escorted her back.

All afternoon we steamed along the coast of Ireland, with grey cliffs guarding the shores, and hills rising behind gaunt and barren; as dusk fell, the coast rounded away from us to the north-west, and the last we saw of Europe was the Irish mountains dim and faint in the dropping darkness. With the thought that we had seen the last of land until we set foot on the shores of America, I retired to the library to write letters, little knowing that many things would happen to us all – many experiences, sudden, vivid and impressive to be encountered, many perils to be faced, many good and true people for whom we should have to mourn – before we saw land again.

There is very little to relate from the time of leaving Queenstown on Thursday to Sunday morning. The sea was calm – so calm, indeed, that very few were absent from meals: the wind westerly and south-westerly – 'fresh' as the daily chart described it – but often rather cold, generally too cold to sit out on deck to read or write, so that many of us spent a good part of the time in the library, reading and writing. I wrote a large number of letters and posted them day by day in the box outside the library door: possibly they are there yet.

Each morning the sun rose behind us in a sky of circular clouds, stretching round the horizon in long, narrow streaks and rising tier upon tier above the skyline, red and pink and fading from pink to white, as the sun rose higher in the sky. It was a beautiful sight to one who had not crossed the ocean before (or indeed been out of sight of the shores of England) to stand on the top deck and watch the swell of the sea extending outwards from the ship in an unbroken circle until it met the skyline with its hint of infinity: behind, the wake of the vessel white with foam where, fancy suggested, the propeller blades had cut up the long Atlantic rollers and with them made a level white road bounded on either side by banks of green, blue, and blue-green waves that would presently sweep away the white road, though as yet it stretched back to the horizon and dipped over the edge of the world back to Ireland and the gulls, while along it the morning sun glittered and sparkled. And each night the sun sank right in our eyes along the sea, making an undulating glittering pathway, a golden track charted on the surface of the ocean which our ship followed unswervingly until the sun dipped below the edge of the horizon, and the pathway ran ahead of us faster than we could steam and slipped over the edge of the skyline – as if the sun had been a golden ball and had wound up its thread of gold too quickly for us to follow.

From 12 noon Thursday to 12 noon Friday we ran 386 miles, Friday to Saturday 519 miles, Saturday to Sunday 546 miles. The second day's run of 519 miles was, the purser told us, a disappointment, and we should not dock until Wednesday morning instead of Tuesday night, as we had expected; however, on Sunday we were glad to see a longer run had been made, and it was thought we should make New York, after all, on Tuesday night. The purser remarked: 'They are not pushing her this trip and don't intend to make any fast running: I don't suppose we shall do more than 546 now; it is not a bad day's run for the first trip.' This was at lunch, and I remember the conversation then turned to the speed and build of Atlantic liners as factors in their comfort of motion: all those who had crossed many times were unanimous in saying the *Titanic* was the most comfortable boat they had been on, and they preferred the speed we were making to that of the faster boats, from the point of view of lessened vibration as well as because the faster boats would bore through the waves with a twisted, screw-like motion instead of the straight up-and-down swing of the *Titanic*. I then called the attention of our table to the way the *Titanic* listed to port (I had noticed this before), and we all watched the skyline through the portholes as we sat at the purser's table in the saloon: it was plain she did so, for the skyline and sea on the port side were visible most of the time and on the starboard only sky. The purser remarked that probably coal had been used mostly from the starboard side. It is no doubt a common occurrence for all vessels to list to some degree; but in view of the fact that the *Titanic* was cut open on the starboard side and before she sank listed so much to port that there was quite a chasm between her and the swinging lifeboats, across which ladies had to be thrown or to cross on chairs laid flat, the previous listing to port may be of interest.

Returning for a moment to the motion of the *Titanic*, it was interesting to stand on the boat deck, as I frequently did, in the angle between lifeboats 13 and 15 on the starboard side (two boats I have every reason to remember, for the first carried me in safety to the *Carpathia*, and it seemed likely at one time that the other would come down on our heads as we sat in 13 trying to get away from the ship's side), and watch the general motion of the ship through the waves resolve itself into two motions – one to be observed by contrasting the docking-bridge, from which the log-line trailed away behind in the foaming wake, with the horizon, and observing the long, slow heave as we rode up and down. I timed the average period occupied in one up-and-down vibration, but do not now remember the figures. The second motion was a side-to-side roll, and could be calculated by watching the port rail and contrasting it with the horizon as before. It seems likely that this double motion is due to the angle at which our direction to New York cuts the general set of the Gulf Stream sweeping from the Gulf of Mexico across to Europe; but the almost clock-like regularity of the two vibratory movements was what attracted my attention: it was while watching the side roll that I first became aware of the list to port. Looking down astern from the boat deck or from B deck to the steerage quarters, I often noticed how the third class passengers were enjoying every minute of the time: a most uproarious skipping game of the mixed-double type was the great favourite, while 'in and out and roundabout' went a Scotchman with his bagpipes playing something that Gilbert says 'faintly resembled an air'. Standing aloof from all of them, generally on the raised stern deck above the 'playing field', was a man of about twenty to twenty-four years of age, well-dressed, always gloved and nicely groomed, and obviously quite out of place among his fellow passengers: he never looked happy all the time. I watched him, and classified him at hazard as the man who had been a failure in some way at home and had received the proverbial shilling plus third class fare to America: he did not look resolute enough or happy enough to be working out his own problem. Another interesting man was travelling steerage, but had placed his wife in the second cabin: he would climb the stairs leading from the steerage to the second deck and talk affectionately with his wife across the low gate which separated them. I never saw him after the collision, but I think his wife was on the *Carpathia*. Whether they ever saw each other on the Sunday night is very doubtful: he would not at first be allowed on the second class deck, and if he were, the chances of seeing his wife in the darkness and the crowd would be very small, indeed. Of all those playing so happily on the steerage deck I did not recognise many afterwards on the *Carpathia*.

Coming now to Sunday, the day on which the *Titanic* struck the iceberg, it will be interesting, perhaps, to give the day's events in some detail, to appreciate the general attitude of passengers to their surroundings just before the collision. Service was held in the saloon by the purser in the morning, and going on deck after lunch we found such a change in temperature that not many cared to remain to face the bitter wind – an artificial wind created mainly, if not entirely, by the ship's rapid motion through the chilly atmosphere. I should judge there was no wind blowing at the time, for I had noticed about the same force of wind approaching Queenstown, to find that it died away as soon as we stopped, only to rise again as we steamed away from the harbour.

Returning to the library, I stopped for a moment to read again the day's run and observe our position on the chart; the Rev. Mr Carter, a clergyman of the Church of England, was similarly engaged, and we renewed a conversation we had enjoyed for some days: it had commenced with a discussion of the relative merits of his university – Oxford – with mine – Cambridge – as world-wide educational agencies, the opportunities at each for the formation of character apart from mere education as such, and had led on to the lack of sufficiently qualified men to take up the work of the Church of England (a matter apparently on which he felt very deeply) and from that to his own

33

work in England as a priest. He told me some of his parish problems and spoke of the impossibility of doing half his work in his church without the help his wife gave. I knew her only slightly at that time, but meeting her later in the day, I realised something of what he meant in attributing a large part of what success he had as a vicar to her. My only excuse for mentioning these details about the Carters – now and later in the day – is that, while they have perhaps not much interest for the average reader, they will no doubt be some comfort to the parish over which he presided and where I am sure he was loved. He next mentioned the absence of a service in the evening and asked if I knew the purser well enough to request the use of the saloon in the evening where he would like to have a 'hymn sing-song'; the purser gave his consent at once, and Mr Carter made preparations during the afternoon by asking all he knew – and many he did not – to come to the saloon at 8.30 p.m.

The library was crowded that afternoon, owing to the cold on deck, but through the windows we could see the clear sky with brilliant sunlight that seemed to augur a fine night and a clear day tomorrow, and the prospect of landing in two days, with calm weather all the way to New York, was a matter of general satisfaction among us all. I can look back and see every detail of the library that afternoon – the beautifully furnished room, with lounges, armchairs, and small writing- or card-tables scattered about, writing-bureaus round the walls of the room, and the library in glass-cased shelves flanking one side, – the whole finished in mahogany relieved with white fluted wooden columns that supported the deck above. Through the windows there is the covered corridor, reserved by general consent as the children's playground, and here are playing the two Navatril children with their father – devoted to them, never absent from them. Who would have thought of the dramatic history of the happy group at play in the corridor that afternoon! The abduction of the children in Nice, the assumed name, the separation of father and children in a few hours, his death and their subsequent union with their mother after a period of doubt as to their parentage! How many more similar secrets the *Titanic* revealed in the privacy of family life, or carried down with her untold, we shall never know.

In the same corridor is a man and his wife with two children, and one of them he is generally carrying: they are all young and happy: he is dressed always in a grey knickerbocker suit – with a camera slung over his shoulder. I have not seen any of them since that afternoon.

Close beside me – so near that I cannot avoid hearing scraps of their conversation – are two American ladies, both dressed in white, young, probably friends only: one has been to India and is returning by way of England, the other is a school teacher in America, a graceful girl with a distinguished air heightened by a pair of *pince-nez*. Engaged in conversation with them is a gentleman whom I subsequently identified from a photograph as a well-known resident of Cambridge, Massachusetts, genial, polished, and with a courtly air towards the two ladies, whom he has known but a few hours; from time to time as they talk, a child acquaintance breaks in on their conversation and insists on their taking notice of a large doll clasped in her arms; I have seen none of this group since then. In the opposite corner are the young American kinematograph photographer and his young wife, evidently French, very fond of playing patience, which she is doing now, while he sits back in his chair watching the game and interposing from time to time with suggestions. I did not see them again. In the middle of the room are two Catholic priests, one quietly reading – either English or Irish, and probably the latter – the other, dark, bearded, with broad-brimmed hat, talking earnestly to a friend in German and evidently explaining some verse in the open Bible before him; near them a young fire engineer on his way to Mexico, and of the same religion as the rest of the group. None of them were saved. It may be noted here that the percentage of men saved in the second class is the lowest of any other division – only 8 per cent.

Many other faces recur to thought, but it is impossible to describe them all in the space of a short book: of all those in the library that Sunday afternoon, I can remember only two or three persons who found their way to the *Carpathia*. Looking over this room, with his back to the library shelves, is the library steward, thin, stooping, sad-faced, and generally with nothing to do but serve out books; but this afternoon he is busier than I have ever seen him, serving out baggage declaration forms for passengers to fill in. Mine is before me as I write: 'Form for nonresidents in the United States. Steamship *Titanic*: No. 31444, D,' etc. I had filled it in that afternoon and slipped it in my pocketbook instead of returning it to the steward. Before me, too, is a small cardboard square: 'White Star Line. RMS *Titanic*. 208. This label must be given up when the article is returned. The property will be deposited in the Purser's safe. The Company will not be liable to passengers for the loss of money, jewels, or ornaments, by theft or otherwise, not so deposited.' The 'property deposited' in my case was money, placed in an envelope, sealed, with my name written across the flap, and handed to the purser; the 'label' is my receipt. Along with other similar envelopes it may be still intact in the safe at the bottom of the sea, but in all probability it is not, as will be seen presently.

After dinner, Mr Carter invited all who wished to the saloon, and with the assistance at the piano of a gentleman who sat at the purser's table opposite me (a young Scotch engineer going out to join his brother fruit-farming at the foot of the Rockies), he started some hundred passengers singing hymns. They were asked to choose whichever hymn they wished, and with so many to choose, it was impossible for him to do more than have the greatest favourites sung. As he announced each hymn, it was evident that he was thoroughly versed in their history: no hymn was sung but that he gave a short sketch of its author and in some cases a description of the circumstances in which it was composed. I think all were impressed with his knowledge of hymns and with his eagerness to tell us all he knew of them. It was curious to see how many chose hymns dealing with dangers at sea. I noticed the hushed tone with which all sang the hymn 'For those in peril on the Sea'.

The singing must have gone on until after ten o'clock, when, seeing the stewards standing about waiting to serve biscuits and coffee before going off duty, Mr Carter brought the evening to a close by a few words of thanks to the purser for the use of the saloon, a short sketch of the happiness and safety of the voyage hitherto, the great confidence all felt on board this great liner with her steadiness and her size, and the happy outlook of landing in a few hours in New York at the close of a delightful voyage; and all the time he spoke, a few miles ahead of us lay the 'peril on the sea' that was to sink this same great liner with many of those on board who listened with gratitude to his simple, heartfelt words. So much for the frailty of human hopes and for the confidence reposed in material human designs.

Think of the shame of it, that a mass of ice of no use to anyone or anything should have the power fatally to injure the beautiful *Titanic*! That an insensible block should be able to threaten, even in the smallest degree, the lives of many good men and women who think and plan and hope and love – and not only to threaten, but to end their lives. It is unbearable! Are we never to educate ourselves to foresee such dangers and to prevent them before they happen? All the evidence of history shows that laws unknown and unsuspected are being discovered day by day: as this knowledge accumulates for the use of man, is it not certain that the ability to see and destroy beforehand the threat of danger will be one of the privileges the whole world will utilise? May that day come soon. Until it does, no precaution too rigorous can be taken, no safety appliance, however costly, must be omitted from a ship's equipment.

After the meeting had broken up, I talked with the Carters over a cup of coffee, said goodnight to them, and retired to my cabin at about quarter to eleven. They were good people and this world is much poorer by their loss.

It may be a matter of pleasure to many people to know that their friends were perhaps among that gathering of people in the saloon, and that at the last the sound of the hymns still echoed in their ears as they stood on the deck so quietly and courageously. Who can tell how much it had to do with the demeanour of some of them and the example this would set to others?

3

The Collision and Embarkation in Lifeboats

I had been fortunate enough to secure a two-berth cabin to myself – D 56 – quite close to the saloon and most convenient in every way for getting about the ship; and on a big ship like the *Titanic* it was quite a consideration to be on D deck, only three decks below the top or boat deck. Below D again were cabins on E and F decks, and to walk from a cabin on F up to the top deck, climbing five flights of stairs on the way, was certainly a considerable task for those not able to take much exercise. The *Titanic* management has been criticised, among other things, for supplying the boat with lifts: it has been said they were an expensive luxury and the room they took up might have been utilised in some way for more life-saving appliances. Whatever else may have been superfluous, lifts certainly were not: old ladies, for example, in cabins on F deck, would hardly have got to the top deck during the whole voyage had they not been able to ring for the lift-boy. Perhaps nothing gave one a greater impression of the size of the ship than to take the lift from the top and drop slowly down past the different floors, discharging and taking in passengers just as in a large hotel. I wonder where the lift-boy was that night. I would have been glad to find him in our boat, or on the *Carpathia* when we took count of the saved. He was quite young – not more than sixteen, I think – a bright-eyed, handsome boy, with a love for the sea and the games on deck and the view over the ocean – and he did not get any of them. One day, as he put me out of his lift and saw through the vestibule windows a game of deck quoits in progress, he said, in a wistful tone, 'My! I wish I could go out there sometimes!' I wished he could, too, and made a jesting offer to take charge of his lift for an hour while he went out to watch the game; but he smilingly shook his head and dropped down in answer to an imperative ring from below. I think he was not on duty with his lift after the collision, but if he were, he would smile at his passengers all the time as he took them up to the boats waiting to leave the sinking ship.

After undressing and climbing into the top berth, I read from about quarter past eleven to the time we struck, about quarter to twelve. During this time I noticed particularly the increased vibration of the ship, and I assumed that we were going at a higher speed than at any other time since we sailed from Queenstown. Now I am aware that this is an important point, and bears strongly on the question of responsibility for the effects of the collision; but the impression of increased vibration is fixed in my memory so strongly that it seems important to record it. Two things led me to this conclusion – first, that as I sat on the sofa undressing, with bare feet on the floor, the jar of the vibration came up from the engines below very noticeably; and second, that as I sat up in the berth reading, the spring mattress supporting me was vibrating more rapidly than usual: this cradle-like motion was always noticeable as one lay in bed, but that night there was certainly a marked increase in the motion. Referring to the plan, it will be seen that the vibration must have come almost directly up from below, when it is mentioned that the saloon was immediately above the engines as shown in the plan, and my cabin next to the saloon. From these two data, on the assumption that greater vibration is an indication of higher speed – and I suppose it must be – then I am sure we were going faster that night at the time we struck the iceberg than we had done before, i.e., during the hours I was awake and able to take note of anything.

And then, as I read in the quietness of the night, broken only by the muffled sound that came to me through the ventilators of stewards talking and moving along the corridors, when nearly all the passengers were in their cabins, some asleep in bed, others undressing, and others only just down from the smoking room and still discussing many things, there came what seemed to me nothing more than an extra heave of the engines and a more than usually obvious dancing motion of the mattress on which I sat. Nothing more than that – no sound of a crash or of anything else: no sense of shock, no jar that felt like one heavy body meeting another. And presently the same thing repeated with about the same intensity. The thought came to me that they must have still further increased the speed. And all this time the *Titanic* was being cut open by the iceberg and water was pouring in her side, and yet no evidence that would indicate such a disaster had been presented to us. It fills me with astonishment now to think of it. Consider the question of list alone. Here was this enormous vessel running starboard-side on to an iceberg, and a passenger sitting quietly in bed, reading, felt no motion or list to the opposite or port side, and this must have been felt had it been more than the usual roll of the ship – never very much in the calm weather we had all the way. Again, my bunk was fixed to the wall on the starboard side, and any list to port would have tended to fling me out on the floor: I am sure I should have noted it had there been any. And yet the explanation is simple enough: the *Titanic* struck the berg with a force of impact of over a million foot-tons; her plates were less than an inch thick, and they must have been cut through as a knife cuts paper: there would be no need to list; it would have been better if she had listed and thrown us out on the floor, for it would have been an indication that our plates were strong enough to offer, at any rate, some resistance to the blow, and we might all have been safe today.

And so, with no thought of anything serious having happened to the ship, I continued my reading; and still the murmur from the stewards and from adjoining cabins, and no other sound: no cry in the night; no alarm given; no one afraid – there was then nothing which could cause fear to the most timid person. But in a few moments I felt the engines slow and stop; the dancing motion and the vibration ceased suddenly after being part of our very existence for four days, and that was the first hint that anything out of the ordinary had happened. We have all 'heard' a loud-ticking clock stop suddenly in a quiet room, and then have noticed the clock and the ticking noise, of which we seemed until then quite unconscious. So in the same way the fact was suddenly brought home to all in the ship that the engines – that part of the ship that drove us through the sea – had stopped dead. But the stopping of the engines gave us no information: we had to make our own calculations as to why we had stopped. Like a flash it came to me: 'We have dropped a propeller blade: when this happens the engines always race away until they are controlled, and this accounts for the extra heave they gave'; not a very logical conclusion when considered now, for the engines should have continued to heave all the time until we stopped, but it was at the time a sufficiently tenable hypothesis to hold. Acting on it, I jumped out of bed, slipped on a dressing gown over pyjamas, put on shoes, and went out of my cabin into the hall near the saloon. Here was a steward leaning against the staircase, probably waiting until those in the smoke room above had gone to bed and he could put out the lights. I said, 'Why have we stopped?' 'I don't know, sir,' he replied, 'but I don't suppose it is anything much.' 'Well,' I said, 'I am going on deck to see what it is,' and started towards the stairs. He smiled indulgently at me as I passed him, and said, 'All right, sir, but it is mighty cold up there.' I am sure at that time he thought I was rather foolish to go up with so little reason, and I must confess I felt rather absurd for not remaining in the cabin: it seemed like making a needless fuss to walk about the ship in a dressing gown. But it was my first trip across the sea; I had enjoyed every minute of it and was keenly alive to note every new experience; and certainly to stop in the middle of the sea with a propeller dropped seemed sufficient reason for going on deck. And yet the steward, with his fatherly smile, and the fact that no one else was about the passages or going upstairs to reconnoitre, made me feel guilty in an undefined way of breaking some code of a ship's regime – an Englishman's fear of being thought 'unusual', perhaps!

I climbed the three flights of stairs, opened the vestibule door leading to the top deck, and stepped out into an atmosphere that cut me, clad as I was, like a knife. Walking to the starboard side, I peered over and saw the sea many feet below, calm and black; forward, the deserted deck stretching away to the first class quarters and the captain's bridge; and behind, the steerage quarters and the stern bridge; nothing more: no iceberg on either side or astern as far as we could see in the darkness. There were two or three men on deck, and with one – the Scotch engineer who played hymns in the saloon – I compared notes of our experiences. He had just begun to undress when the engines stopped and had come up at once, so that he was fairly well-clad; none of us

43

could see anything, and all being quiet and still, the Scotchman and I went down to the next deck. Through the windows of the smoking room we saw a game of cards going on, with several onlookers, and went in to enquire if they knew more than we did. They had apparently felt rather more of the heaving motion, but so far as I remember, none of them had gone out on deck to make any enquiries, even when one of them had seen through the windows an iceberg go by towering above the decks. He had called their attention to it, and they all watched it disappear, but had then at once resumed the game. We asked them the height of the berg and some said one hundred feet, others, sixty feet; one of the onlookers – a motor engineer travelling to America with a model carburetter (he had filled in his declaration form near me in the afternoon and had questioned the library steward how he should declare his patent) – said, 'Well, I am accustomed to estimating distances and I put it at between eighty and ninety feet.' We accepted his estimate and made guesses as to what had happened to the *Titanic*: the general impression was that we had just scraped the iceberg with a glancing blow on the starboard side, and they had stopped as a wise precaution, to examine her thoroughly all over. 'I expect the iceberg has scratched off some of her new paint,' said one, 'and the captain doesn't like to go on until she is painted up again.' We laughed at his estimate of the captain's care for the ship. Poor Captain Smith! – he knew by this time only too well what had happened.

One of the players, pointing to his glass of whiskey standing at his elbow, and turning to an onlooker, said, 'Just run along the deck and see if any ice has come aboard: I would like some for this.' Amid the general laughter at what we thought was his imagination – only too realistic, alas! for when he spoke the forward deck was covered with ice that had tumbled over – and seeing that no more information was forthcoming, I left the smoking room and went down to my cabin, where I sat for some time reading again. I am filled with sorrow to think I never saw any of the occupants of that smoking room again: nearly all young men full of hope for their prospects in a new world; mostly unmarried; keen, alert, with the makings of good citizens. Presently, hearing people walking about the corridors, I looked out and saw several standing in the hall talking to a steward – most of them ladies in dressing gowns; other people were going upstairs, and I decided to go on deck again, but as it was too cold to do so in a dressing gown, I dressed in a Norfolk jacket and trousers and walked up. There were now more people looking over the side and walking about, questioning each other as to why we had stopped, but without obtaining any definite information. I stayed on deck some minutes, walking about vigorously to keep warm and occasionally looking downwards to the sea as if something there would indicate the reason for delay. The ship had now resumed her course, moving very slowly through the water with a little white line of foam on each side. I think we were all glad to see this: it seemed better than standing still. I soon decided to go down again, and as I crossed from the starboard to the port side to go down by the vestibule door, I saw an officer climb on the last lifeboat on the port side – number 16 – and begin to throw off the cover, but I do not remember that anyone paid any particular attention to him. Certainly no one thought they were preparing to man the lifeboats and embark from the ship. All this time there was no apprehension of any danger in the minds of passengers, and no one was in any condition of panic or hysteria; after all, it would have been strange if they had been, without any definite evidence of danger.

As I passed to the door to go down, I looked forward again and saw to my surprise an undoubted tilt downwards from the stern to the bows: only a slight slope, which I don't think anyone had noticed – at any rate, they had not remarked on it. As I went downstairs a confirmation of this tilting forward came in something unusual about the stairs, a curious sense of something out of balance and of not being able to put one's feet down in the right place: naturally, being tilted forward, the stairs would slope downwards at an angle and tend to throw one forward. I could not see any visible slope of the stairway: it was perceptible only by the sense of balance at this time.

On D deck were three ladies – I think they were all saved, and it is a good thing at least to be able to chronicle meeting someone who was saved after so much record of those who were not – standing in the passage near the cabin. 'Oh! why have we stopped?' they said. 'We did stop,' I replied, 'but we are now going on again.' 'Oh, no,' one replied; 'I cannot feel the engines as I usually do, or hear them. Listen!' We listened, and there was no throb audible. Having noticed that the vibration of the engines is most noticeable lying in a bath, where the throb comes straight from the floor through its metal sides – too much so ordinarily for one to put one's head back with comfort on the bath, – I took them along the corridor to a bathroom and made them put their hands on the side of the bath: they were much reassured to feel the engines throbbing down below and to know we were making some headway. I left them and on the way to my cabin passed some stewards standing unconcernedly against the walls of the saloon: one of them, the library steward again, was leaning over a table, writing. It is no exaggeration to say that they had neither any knowledge of the accident nor any feeling of alarm that we had stopped and had not yet gone on again full speed: their whole attitude expressed perfect confidence in the ship and officers.

Turning into my gangway (my cabin being the first in the gangway), I saw a man standing at the other end of it fastening his tie. 'Anything fresh?' he said. 'Not much,' I replied; 'we are going ahead slowly and she is down a little at the bows, but I don't think it is anything serious.' 'Come in and look at this man,' he laughed;

'he won't get up.' I looked in, and in the top bunk lay a man with his back to me, closely wrapped in his bedclothes and only the back of his head visible. 'Why won't he get up? Is he asleep?' I said. 'No,' laughed the man dressing, 'he says – '. But before he could finish the sentence the man above grunted: 'You don't catch me leaving a warm bed to go up on that cold deck at midnight. I know better than that.' We both told him laughingly why he had better get up, but he was certain he was just as safe there and all this dressing was quite unnecessary; so I left them and went again to my cabin. I put on some underclothing, sat on the sofa, and read for some ten minutes, when I heard through the open door, above, the noise of people passing up and down, and a loud shout from above: 'All passengers on deck with lifebelts on.'

I placed the two books I was reading in the side pockets of my Norfolk jacket, picked up my lifebelt (curiously enough, I had taken it down for the first time that night from the wardrobe when I first retired to my cabin) and my dressing gown, and walked upstairs tying on the lifebelt. As I came out of my cabin, I remember seeing the purser's assistant, with his foot on the stairs about to climb them, whisper to a steward and jerk his head significantly behind him; not that I thought anything of it at the time, but I have no doubt he was telling him what had happened up in the bows, and was giving him orders to call all passengers.

Going upstairs with other passengers – no one ran a step or seemed alarmed – we met two ladies coming down: one seized me by the arm and said, 'Oh! I have no lifebelt; will you come down to my cabin and help me to find it?' I returned with them to F deck – the lady who had addressed me holding my arm all the time in a vice-like grip, much to my amusement – and we found a steward in her gangway who took them in and found their lifebelts. Coming

47

upstairs again, I passed the purser's window on F deck, and noticed a light inside; when halfway up to E deck, I heard the heavy metallic clang of the safe door, followed by a hasty step retreating along the corridor towards the first class quarters. I have little doubt it was the purser, who had taken all valuables from his safe and was transferring them to the charge of the first class purser, in the hope they might all be saved in one package. That is why I said above that perhaps the envelope containing my money was not in the safe at the bottom of the sea: it is probably in a bundle, with many others like it, waterlogged at the bottom.

Reaching the top deck, we found many people assembled there, – some fully dressed, with coats and wraps, well-prepared for anything that might happen; others who had thrown wraps hastily round them when they were called or heard the summons to equip themselves with lifebelts – not in much condition to face the cold of that night. Fortunately there was no wind to beat the cold air through our clothing: even the breeze caused by the ship's motion had died entirely away, for the engines had stopped again and the *Titanic* lay peacefully on the surface of the sea – motionless, quiet, not even rocking to the roll of the sea; indeed, as we were to discover presently, the sea was as calm as an inland lake save for the gentle swell which could impart no motion to a ship the size of the *Titanic*. To stand on the deck many feet above the water lapping idly against her sides, and looking much farther off than it really was because of the darkness, gave one a sense of wonderful security: to feel her so steady and still was like standing on a large rock in the middle of the ocean. But there were now more evidences of the coming catastrophe to the observer than had been apparent when on deck last: one was the roar and hiss of escaping steam from the boilers, issuing out of a large steam pipe reaching high up one of the funnels: a harsh, deafening boom that made conversation difficult and no doubt increased the apprehension of some people merely because of the volume of noise: if one imagines twenty locomotives blowing off steam in a low key it would give some idea of the unpleasant sound that met us as we climbed out on the top deck.

But after all it was the kind of phenomenon we ought to expect: engines blow off steam when standing in a station, and why should not a ship's boilers do the same when the ship is not moving? I never heard anyone connect this noise with the danger of boiler explosion, in the event of the ship sinking with her boilers under a high pressure of steam, which was no doubt the true explanation of this precaution. But this is perhaps speculation; some people may have known it quite well, for from the time we came on deck until boat 13 got away, I heard very little conversation of any kind among the passengers. It is not the slightest exaggeration to say that no signs of alarm were exhibited by anyone: there was no indication of panic or hysteria; no cries of fear, and no running to and fro to discover what was the matter, why we had been summoned on deck with lifebelts, and what was to be done with us now we were there. We stood there quietly looking on at the work of the crew as they manned the lifeboats, and no one ventured to interfere with them or offered to help them. It was plain we should be of no use; and the crowd of men and women stood quietly on the deck or paced slowly up and down waiting for orders from the officers.

Now, before we consider any further the events that followed, the state of mind of passengers at this juncture, and the motives which led each one to act as he or she did in the circumstances, it is important to keep in thought the amount of information at our disposal. Men and women act according to judgement based on knowledge of the conditions around them, and the best way to understand some apparently inconceivable things that happened is for anyone to imagine himself or herself standing on deck that night. It seems a mystery to some people that women refused to leave the ship, that some persons retired to their cabins, and so on; but it is a matter of judgement, after all.

So that if the reader will come and stand with the crowd on deck, he must first rid himself entirely of the knowledge that the *Titanic* has sunk – an important necessity, for he cannot see conditions as they existed there through the mental haze arising from knowledge of the greatest maritime tragedy the world has known: he must get rid of any foreknowledge of disaster to appreciate why people acted as they did. Secondly, he had better get rid of any picture in thought painted either by his own imagination or by some artist, whether pictorial or verbal, 'from information supplied'. Some are most inaccurate (these, mostly word-pictures), and where they err, they err on the highly dramatic side. They need not have done so: the whole conditions were dramatic enough in all their bare simplicity, without the addition of any high colouring.

Having made these mental erasures, he will find himself as one of the crowd faced with the following conditions: a perfectly still atmosphere; a brilliantly beautiful starlight night, but no moon, and so with little light that was of any use; a ship that had come quietly to rest without any indication of disaster – no iceberg visible, no hole in the ship's side through which water was pouring in, nothing broken or out of place, no sound of alarm, no panic, no movement of anyone except at a walking pace; the absence of any knowledge of the nature of the accident, of the extent of damage, of the danger of the ship sinking in a few hours, of the numbers of boats, rafts, and other lifesaving appliances available, their capacity, what other ships were near or coming to help – in fact, an almost complete absence of any positive knowledge on any point. I think this was the result of deliberate judgement on the part of the officers, and perhaps it was the best thing that could be done. In particular, he must remember that the ship was a sixth of a mile long, with passengers on three decks open to the sea, and port and starboard sides to each deck: he will then get some idea of the difficulty presented to the officers of keeping control over such a large area, and the impossibility of anyone knowing what was happening except in his own immediate vicinity. Perhaps the whole thing can be summed up best by saying that, after we had embarked in the lifeboats and rowed away from the *Titanic*, it would not have surprised us to hear that all passengers would be saved: the cries of drowning people after the *Titanic* gave the final plunge were a thunderbolt to us. I am aware that the experiences of many of those saved differed in some respects from the above: some had knowledge of certain things, some were experienced travellers and sailors, and therefore deduced more rapidly what was likely to happen; but I think the above gives a fairly accurate representation of the state of mind of most of those on deck that night.

All this time people were pouring up from the stairs and adding to the crowd: I remember at that moment thinking it would be well to return to my cabin and rescue some money and warmer clothing if we were to embark in boats, but looking through the vestibule windows and seeing people still coming upstairs, I decided it would only cause confusion passing them on the stairs, and so remained on deck.

I was now on the starboard side of the top boat deck; the time about 12.20. We watched the crew at work on the lifeboats, numbers 9, 11, 13, 15, some inside arranging the oars, some coiling ropes on the deck – the ropes which ran through the pulleys to lower to the sea – others with cranks fitted to the rocking arms of the davits. As we watched, the cranks were turned, the davits swung outwards until the boats hung clear of the edge of the deck. Just then an officer came along from the first class deck and shouted above the noise of escaping steam, 'All women and children get down to deck below and all men stand back from the boats.' He had apparently been off duty when the ship struck, and was lightly dressed, with a white muffler twisted hastily round his neck. The men fell back and the women retired below to get into the boats from the next deck. Two women refused at first to leave their husbands, but partly by persuasion and partly by force they were separated from them and sent down to the next deck. I think that by this time the work on the lifeboats and the separation of men and women impressed on us slowly the presence of imminent danger, but it made no difference in the attitude of the crowd: they were just as prepared to obey orders and to do what came next as when they first came on deck. I do not mean that they actually reasoned it out: they were the average Teutonic crowd, with an inborn respect for law and order and for traditions bequeathed to them by generations of ancestors: the reasons that made them act as they did were impersonal, instinctive, hereditary.

But if there were anyone who had not by now realised that the ship was in danger, all doubt on this point was to be set at rest in a dramatic manner. Suddenly a rush of light from the forward deck, a hissing roar that made us all turn from watching the boats, and a rocket leapt upwards to where the stars blinked and twinkled above us. Up it went, higher and higher, with a sea of faces upturned to watch it, and then an explosion that seemed to split the silent night in two, and a shower of stars sank slowly down and went out one by one. And with a gasping sigh one word escaped the lips of the crowd: 'Rockets!' Anybody knows what rockets at sea mean. And presently another, and then a third. It is no use denying the dramatic intensity of the scene: separate it if you can from all the terrible events that followed, and picture the calmness of the night, the sudden light on the decks crowded with people in different stages of dress and undress, the background of huge funnels and tapering masts revealed by the soaring rocket, whose flash illumined at the same time the faces and minds of the obedient crowd, the one with mere physical light, the other with a sudden revelation of what its message was. Everyone knew without being told that we were calling for help from anyone who was near enough to see.

The crew were now in the boats, the sailors standing by the pulley ropes let them slip through the cleats in jerks, and down the boats went till level with B deck; women and children climbed over the rail into the boats and filled them; when full, they were lowered one by one, beginning with number 9, the first on the second class deck, and working backwards towards 15. All this we could see by peering over the edge of the boat deck, which was now quite open to the sea, the four boats which formed a natural barrier being lowered from the deck and leaving it exposed.

About this time, while walking the deck, I saw two ladies come over from the port side and walk towards the rail separating the second class from the first class deck. There stood an officer barring the way. 'May we pass to the boats?' they said. 'No, madam,' he replied politely, 'your boats are down on your own deck,' pointing to where they swung below. The ladies turned and went towards the stairway, and no doubt were able to enter one of the boats: they had ample time. I mention this to show that there was, at any rate, some arrangement – whether official or not – for separating the classes in embarking in boats; how far it was carried out, I do not know, but if the second class ladies were not expected to enter a boat from the first class deck, while steerage passengers were allowed access to the second class deck, it would seem to press rather hardly on the second class men, and this is rather supported by the low percentage saved. [While steerage passengers did find their way to other decks than their own, there is good evidence that some means were adopted to prevent them wandering at will to every part of the ship. An officer was stationed at the head of the stairs leading from the steerage deck to prevent steerage passengers climbing up to decks above – perhaps to lessen the possibility of a rush for the boats. Presently the boat to which he was assigned was being filled, and seeing it ready to go down, he said, 'There goes my boat! But I can't be in two places at the same time, and I have to keep this crowd back.']

Almost immediately after this incident, a report went round among men on the top deck – the starboard side – that men were to be taken off on the port side; how it originated, I am quite unable to say, but can only suppose that as the port boats, numbers 10 to 16, were not lowered from the top deck quite so soon as the starboard boats (they could still be seen on deck), it might be assumed that women were being taken off on one side and men on the other; but in whatever way the report started, it was acted on at once by almost all the men, who crowded across to the port side and watched the preparation for lowering the boats, leaving the starboard side almost deserted. Two or three men remained, however: not for any reason that we were consciously aware of; I can personally think of no decision arising from reasoned thought that induced me to remain rather than to cross over. But while there was no process of conscious reason at work, I am convinced that what was my salvation was a recognition of the necessity of being quiet and waiting in patience for some opportunity of safety to present itself.

Soon after the men had left the starboard side, I saw a bandsman – the cellist – come round the vestibule corner from the staircase entrance and run down the now deserted starboard deck, his cello trailing behind him, the spike dragging along the floor. This must have been about 12.40 a.m. I suppose the band must have begun to play soon after this and gone on until after 2 a.m. Many brave things were done that night, but none more brave than by those few men playing minute after minute as the ship settled quietly lower and lower in the sea and the sea rose higher and higher to where they stood; the music they played serving alike as their own immortal requiem and their right to be recorded on the rolls of undying fame.

Looking forward and downward, we could see several of the boats now in the water, moving slowly one by one from the side, without confusion or noise, and stealing away in the darkness which swallowed them in turn as the crew bent to the oars. An officer – I think First Officer Murdock – came striding along the deck, clad in a long coat, from his manner and face evidently in great agitation, but determined and resolute; he looked over the side and shouted to the boats being lowered: 'Lower away, and when afloat, row around to the gangway and wait for orders.' 'Aye, aye, sir,' was the reply; and the officer passed by and went across the ship to the port side.

Almost immediately after this, I heard a cry from below of, 'Any more ladies?' and looking over the edge of the deck, saw boat 13 swinging level with the rail of B deck, with the crew, some stokers, a few men passengers and the rest ladies – the latter being about half the total number; the boat was almost full and just about to be lowered. The call for ladies was repeated twice again, but apparently there were none to be found. Just then one of the crew looked up and saw me looking over. 'Any ladies on your deck?' he said. 'No,' I replied. 'Then you had better jump.' I sat on the edge of the deck with my feet over, threw the dressing gown (which I had carried on my arm all of the time) into the boat, dropped, and fell in the boat near the stern.

As I picked myself up, I heard a shout: 'Wait a moment, here are two more ladies,' and they were pushed hurriedly over the side and tumbled into the boat, one into the middle and one next to me in the stern. They told me afterwards that they had been assembled on a lower deck with other ladies, and had come up to B deck not by the usual stairway inside, but by one of the vertically upright iron ladders that connect each deck with the one below it, meant for the use of sailors passing about the ship. Other ladies had been in front of them and got up quickly, but these two were delayed a long time by the fact that one of them – the one that was helped first over the side into boat 13 near the middle – was not at all active: it seemed almost impossible for her to climb up a vertical ladder. We saw her trying to climb the swinging rope ladder up the *Carpathia*'s side a few hours later, and she had the same difficulty.

As they tumbled in, the crew shouted, 'Lower away'; but before the order was obeyed, a man with his wife and a baby came quickly to the side: the baby was handed to the lady in the stern, the mother got in near the middle and the father at the last moment dropped in as the boat began its journey down to the sea many feet below.

4

The Sinking of the *Titanic*, Seen From a Lifeboat

Looking back now on the descent of our boat down the ship's side, it is a matter of surprise, I think, to all the occupants to remember how little they thought of it at the time. It was a great adventure, certainly: it was exciting to feel the boat sink by jerks, foot by foot, as the ropes were paid out from above and shrieked as they passed through the pulley blocks, the new ropes and gear creaking under the strain of a boat laden with people, and the crew calling to the sailors above as the boat tilted slightly, now at one end, now at the other, 'Lower aft!' 'Lower stern!' and 'Lower together!' as she came level again – but I do not think we felt much apprehension about reaching the water safely. It certainly was thrilling to see the black hull of the ship on one side and the sea, seventy feet below, on the other, or to pass down by cabins and saloons brilliantly lighted; but we knew nothing of the apprehension felt in the minds of some of the officers whether the boats and lowering-gear would stand the strain of the weight of our sixty people. The ropes, however, were new and strong, and the boat did not buckle in the middle as an older boat might have done. Whether it was right or not to lower boats full of people to the water, – and it seems likely it was not, – I think there can be nothing but the highest praise given to the officers and crew above for the way in which they lowered the boats one after the other safely to the water; it may seem a simple matter, to read about such a thing, but any sailor knows, apparently, that it is not so. An experienced officer has told me that he has seen a boat lowered in practice from a ship's deck, with a trained crew and no passengers in the boat, with practised sailors paying out the ropes, in daylight, in calm weather, with the ship lying in dock – and has seen the boat tilt over and pitch the crew headlong into the sea. Contrast these conditions with those obtaining that Monday morning at 12.45 a.m., and it is impossible not to feel that, whether the lowering crew were trained or not, whether they had or had not drilled since coming on board, they did their duty in a way that argues the greatest efficiency. I cannot help feeling the deepest gratitude to the two sailors who stood at the ropes above and lowered us to the sea: I do not suppose they were saved.

Perhaps one explanation of our feeling little sense of the unusual in leaving the *Titanic* in this way was that it seemed the climax to a series of extraordinary occurrences: the magnitude of the whole thing dwarfed events that in the ordinary way would seem to be full of imminent peril. It is easy to imagine it – a voyage of four days on a calm sea, without a single untoward incident; the presumption, perhaps already mentally half realised, that we should be ashore in forty-eight hours and so complete a splendid voyage – and then to feel the engine stop, to be summoned on deck with little time to dress, to tie on a lifebelt, to see rockets shooting aloft in call for help, to be told to get into a lifeboat – after all these things, it did not seem much to feel the boat sinking down to the sea: it was the natural sequence of previous events, and we had learned in the last hour to take things just as they came. At the same time, if anyone should wonder what the sensation is like, it is quite easy to measure seventy-five feet from the windows of a tall house or a block of flats, look down to the ground and fancy himself with some sixty other people crowded into a boat so tightly that he could not sit down or move about, and then picture the boat sinking down in a continuous series of jerks, as the sailors pay out the ropes through cleats above. There are more pleasant sensations than this! How thankful we were that the sea was calm and the *Titanic* lay so steadily and quietly as we dropped down her side. We were spared the bumping and grinding against the side which so often accompanies the launching of boats: I do not remember that we even had to fend off our boat while we were trying to get free.

As we went down, one of the crew shouted, 'We are just over the condenser exhaust: we don't want to stay in that long or we shall be swamped; feel down on the floor and be ready to pull up the pin which lets the ropes free as soon as we are afloat.' I had often looked over the side and noticed this stream of water coming out of the side of the *Titanic* just above the waterline: in fact so large was the volume of water that as we ploughed along and met the waves coming towards us, this stream would cause a splash that sent spray flying. We felt, as well as we could in the crowd of people, on the floor, along the sides, with no idea where the pin could be found – and none of the crew knew where it was, only of its existence somewhere – but we never found it. And all the time we got closer to the sea and the exhaust roared nearer and nearer – until finally we floated with the ropes still holding us from above, the exhaust washing us away and the force of the tide driving us back against the side – the latter not of much account in influencing the direction, however. Thinking over what followed, I imagine we must have touched the water with the condenser stream at our bows, and not in the middle as I thought at one time: at any rate, the resultant of these three forces was that we were carried parallel to the ship, directly under the place where boat 15 would drop from her davits into the sea. Looking up we saw her already coming down rapidly from B deck: she must have filled almost immediately after ours. We shouted up, 'Stop lowering 15,' (In an account which appeared in the newspapers of 19 April I have described this boat as 14, not knowing they were numbered alternately.) and the crew and passengers in the boat above, hearing us shout and seeing our position immediately below them, shouted the same to the sailors on the boat deck; but apparently they did not hear, for she dropped down foot by foot – twenty feet, fifteen, ten, – and a stoker and I in the bows reached up and touched her bottom swinging above our heads, trying to push away our boat from under her. It seemed now as if nothing could prevent her dropping on us, but at this moment another stoker sprang with his knife to the ropes that still held us and I heard him shout, 'One! Two!' as he cut them through. The next moment we had swung away from underneath 15, and were clear of her as she dropped into the water in the space we had just before occupied. I do not know how the bow ropes were freed, but imagine that they were cut in the same way, for we were washed clear of the *Titanic* at once by the force of the stream and floated away as the oars were got out.

I think we all felt that that was quite the most exciting thing we had yet been through, and a great sigh of relief and gratitude went up as we swung away from the boat above our heads; but I heard no one cry aloud during the experience – not a woman's voice was raised in fear or hysteria. I think we all learnt many things that night about the bogey called 'fear', and how the facing of it is much less than the dread of it.

The crew was made up of cooks and stewards, mostly the former, I think; their white jackets showing up in the darkness as they pulled away, two to an oar: I do not think they can have had any practice in rowing, for all night long their oars crossed and clashed; if our safety had depended on speed or accuracy in keeping time it would have gone hard with us. Shouting began from one end of the boat to the other as to what we should do, where we should go, and no one seemed to have any knowledge how to act. At last we asked, 'Who is in charge of this boat?' but there was no reply. We then agreed by general consent that the stoker who stood in the stern with the tiller should act as captain, and from that time he directed the course, shouting to other boats and keeping in touch with them. Not that there was anywhere to go or anything we could do. Our plan of action was simple: to keep all the boats together as far as possible and wait until we were picked up by other liners. The crew had apparently heard of the wireless communications before they left the *Titanic*, but I never heard them say that we were in touch with any boat but the *Olympic*: it was always the *Olympic* that was coming to our rescue. They thought they knew even her distance, and making a calculation, we came to the conclusion that we ought to be picked up by her about two o'clock in the afternoon. But this was not our only hope of rescue: we watched all the time the darkness lasted for steamers' lights, thinking there might be a chance of other steamers coming near enough to see the lights which some of our boats carried. I am sure there was no feeling in the minds of anyone that we should not be picked up next day: we knew that wireless messages would go out from ship to ship, and as one of the stokers said: 'The sea will be covered with ships tomorrow afternoon: they will race up from all over the sea to find us.' Some even thought that fast torpedo boats might run up ahead of the *Olympic*. And yet the *Olympic* was, after all, the farthest away of them all; eight other ships lay within three hundred miles of us.

How thankful we should have been to know how near help was, and how many ships had heard our message and were rushing to the *Titanic*'s aid. I think nothing has surprised us more than to learn so many ships were near enough to rescue us in a few hours.

Almost immediately after leaving the *Titanic* we saw what we all said was a ship's lights down on the horizon on the *Titanic*'s port side: two lights, one above the other, and plainly not one of our boats; we even rowed in that direction for some time, but the lights drew away and disappeared below the horizon.

But this is rather anticipating: we did none of these things first. We had no eyes for anything but the ship we had just left. As the oarsmen pulled slowly away we all turned and took a long look at the mighty vessel towering high above our midget boat, and I know it must have been the most extraordinary sight I shall ever be called upon to witness; I realise now how totally inadequate language is to convey to some other person who was not there any real impression of what we saw.

But the task must be attempted: the whole picture is so intensely dramatic that, while it is not possible to place on paper for eyes to see the actual likeness of the ship as she lay there, some sketch of the scene will be possible. First of all, the climatic conditions were extraordinary. The night was one of the most beautiful I have ever seen: the sky without a single cloud to mar the perfect brilliance of the stars, clustered so thickly together that in places there seemed almost more dazzling points of light set in the black sky than background of sky itself; and each star seemed, in the keen atmosphere, free from any haze, to have increased its brilliance tenfold and to twinkle and glitter with a staccato flash that made the sky seem nothing but a setting made for them in which to display their wonder. They seemed so near, and their light so much more intense than ever before, that fancy suggested they saw this beautiful ship in dire distress below and all their energies had awakened to flash messages across the black dome of the sky to each other; telling and warning of the calamity happening in the world beneath. Later, when the *Titanic* had gone down and we lay still on the sea waiting for the day to dawn or a ship to come, I remember looking up at the perfect sky and realising why Shakespeare wrote the beautiful words he puts in the mouth of Lorenzo:

Jessica, look how the floor of heaven
Is thick inlaid with patines of bright gold.
There's not the smallest orb which thou behold'st
But in his motion like an angel sings,
Still quiring to the young-eyed cherubims;
Such harmony is in immortal souls;
But whilst this muddy vesture of decay
Doth grossly close it in, we cannot hear it.

But it seemed almost as if we could – that night: the stars seemed really to be alive and to talk. The complete absence of haze produced a phenomenon I had never seen before: where the sky met the sea the line was as clear and definite as the edge of a knife, so that the water and the air never merged gradually into each other and blended to a softened rounded horizon, but each element was so exclusively separate that where a star came low down in the sky near the clear-cut edge of the waterline, it still lost none of its brilliance. As the earth revolved and the water edge came up and covered partially the star, as it were, it simply cut the star in two, the upper half continuing to sparkle as long as it was not entirely hidden, and throwing a long beam of light along the sea to us.

In the evidence before the United States Senate Committee the captain of one of the ships near us that night said the stars were so extraordinarily bright near the horizon that he was deceived into thinking that they were ships' lights: he did not remember seeing such a night before. Those who were afloat will all agree with that statement: *we* were often deceived into thinking they were lights of a ship.

And next the cold air! Here again was something quite new to us: there was not a breath of wind to blow keenly round us as we stood in the boat, and because of its continued persistence to make us feel cold; it was just a keen, bitter, icy, motionless cold that came from nowhere and yet was there all the time; the stillness of it – if one can imagine 'cold' being motionless and still – was what seemed new and strange.

And these – the sky and the air – were overhead; and below was the sea. Here again something uncommon: the surface was like a lake of oil, heaving gently up and down with a quiet motion that rocked our boat dreamily to and fro. We did not need to keep her head to the swell: often I watched her lying broadside on to the tide, and with a boat loaded as we were, this would have been impossible with anything like a swell. The sea slipped away smoothly under the boat, and I think we never heard it lapping on the sides, so oily in appearance was the water. So when one of the stokers said he had been to sea for twenty-six years and never yet seen such a calm night, we accepted it as true without comment. Just as expressive was the remark of another – 'It reminds me of a bloomin' picnic!' It was quite true; it did: a picnic on a lake, or a quiet inland river like the Cam, or a backwater on the Thames.

And so in these conditions of sky and air and sea, we gazed broadside on the *Titanic* from a short distance. She was absolutely still – indeed from the first it seemed as if the blow from the iceberg had taken all the courage out of her and she had just come quietly to rest and was settling

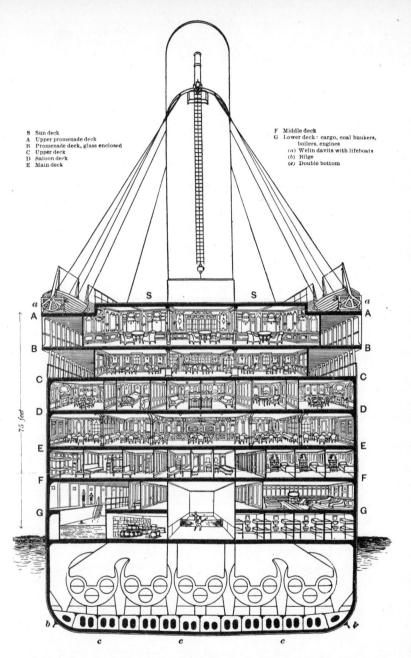

S Sun deck
A Upper promenade deck
B Promenade deck, glass enclosed
C Upper deck
D Saloon deck
E Main deck

F Middle deck
G Lower deck: cargo, coal bunkers,
    boilers, engines
    (a) Welin davits with lifeboats
    (b) Bilge
    (c) Double bottom

1. Transverse amidship section through the *Titanic* showing the various decks of the ship, the indoor squash court, swimming pool and third class living quarters. This was reproduced in the 1912 edition of Lawrence's book.

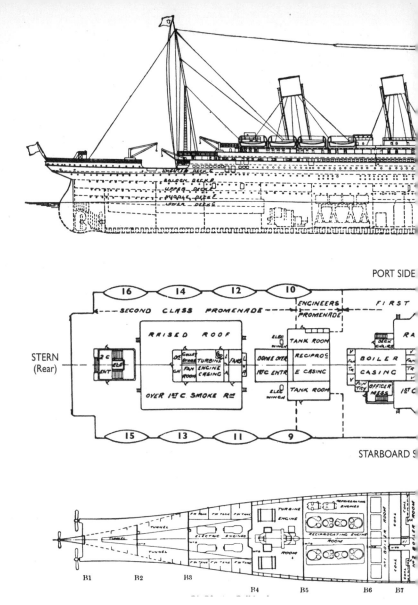

Top page spread: 2. Longitudinal section of the *Titanic* from the Harland & Wolff blueprints *c.* 1911. Bridge deck B through to lower deck G are marked.

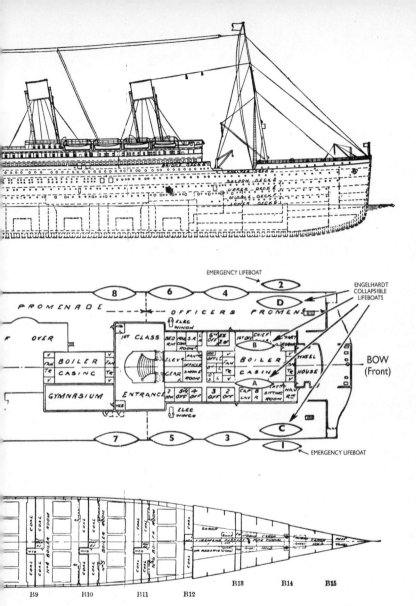

Middle page spread: 3. Plan of the boat deck of the *Titanic* showing the position of all 20 lifeboats, 1 to 16 and collapsibles A, B, C & D.
Above: 4. Plan of the Tank Top of the *Titanic* showing the 15 transverse bulkheads of the ship's hull which created 16 compartments, each of which could be isolated from the adjoining compartment by a watertight door.

5. *Titanic* passing through Belfast Lough en route to the Irish Sea for her trials, 2 April 1912.

bottom page spread: 6. *Titanic*'s near miss with the SS *New York* shortly after departing from Southampton on her maiden voyage, noon Wednesday 10 April. Lawrence was out on deck to witness the incident: 'It gave an extraordinary impression of the absolute helplessness of a big liner in the absence of any motive power to guide her.'

Above: 7. The *Titanic* ablaze with lights heading out of Cherbourg harbour on 10 April. Lawrence Beesley: 'In the calmest weather we made Cherbourg just as it grew dusk and left again about 8.30 p.m., after taking on board passengers and mails.'

Right: 8. Captain of the *Titanic*, Edward Smith.

Left: 9. View of the forecastle. Lawrence: 'All the boats were lowered and sent away by about a.m. and by this time the ship was very low in the water, the forecast deck completely submerged, and the sea creeping steadily up to the bridge and probably only a few yards away.'

Below: 10. *Titanic*'s near-identical sister ship, *Olympic*. This shows the layout of the forward starboard lifeboats, from left to right in this picture, 7, 5, 3, with 1 next, and C just visible behind lifeboat 1. Note the proximity to the bridge. Collapsible lifeboat A is not visible but is stowed alongside the funnel

Above: 11. Promenade deck which ran nearly the whole length of the ship. Many female passengers were loaded into lifeboats from this deck.

Right: 12. Forward starboard boat deck. On Good Friday, 5 April 1912, the liner was thrown open to the public for the day in Southampton. This was the only occasion the ship was dressed overall in flags. The lifeboats shown are 3 (nearest), 5 and 7. In the distance can be seen lifeboats 9, 11, 13 (the lifeboat Lawrence escaped on) and 15. The exit onto the boat deck from the gym and grand staircase is opposite lifeboat 7.

Left: 13. After deck *Olympic* 1911. View towards the decks at the stern of the ship. Helen Bishop (lifeboat 7) describes the last moments of the *Titanic*: 'When the forward part of the ship dropped suddenly at a faster rate so that the upward slope became marked there was a sudden rush of passengers on all decks toward the stern. It was like a wave. We could see the great black mass of people in the steerage sweeping to the rear part of the boat... Then it began to slide gently downwards. Its speed increased as it went down head first, so that the stern shot down with a rush. We could see the people packed densely in the stern till it was gone.'

Below: 14. *Olympic*, showing the layout of the rear starboard lifeboats, from left to right in this picture 15, 13 (which Lawrence left *Titanic* on), 11 and 9

above: 15. Rear starboard boat deck and the second class promenade area. The lifeboats shown are 15 (nearest), 13, 11 and 9. Lawrence: 'I was now on the starboard side of the top boat deck; the time about 12.20 a.m. We watched the crew work on the lifeboats, numbers 9, 11, 13, 15, some inside arranging the oars, some coiling ropes on the deck, the ropes which ran through the pulleys to lower to the sea, others with cranks fitted to the rocking arms of the davits. As we watched, the cranks were turned, the davits swung outwards until the boats hung clear of the edge of the deck. Just then an officer came along from the first class deck and shouted above the noise of escaping steam, "All women and children get down to deck below and all men stand back from the boats." The men fell back and the women retired below to get into the boats from the next deck.'

right: 16. Four decks of *Olympic*. Note the stairs from the deck used by steerage passengers up to the lower promenade deck. Lawrence: 'Looking down astern from the boat deck or from the deck to the steerage quarters, I often noticed how the third class passengers were enjoying every minute of the time... [an] interesting man was travelling steerage, but had placed his wife in the second cabin: he would climb the stairs leading from the steerage to the second deck and talk affectionately with his wife across the low gate which separated them. I never saw him after the collision, but I think his wife was on the *Carpathia*. Whether they ever saw each other on the Sunday night is very doubtful: he would not at first be allowed on the second class deck, and if he were, the chances of seeing his wife in the darkness and the crowd would be very small, indeed. Of all those playing so happily on the steerage deck I did not recognise many afterwards on the *Carpathia*.'

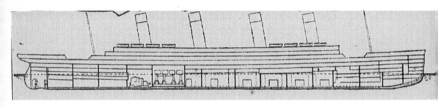

Top spread: 17. Cutaway drawing of *Titanic* reproduced in newspapers in late April 1912.

Above: 18. Contemporary drawing of *Titanic* showing her 15 transverse bulkheads.

Below: 19. *Titanic* in Belfast Harbour.

20. *Titanic* proceeding down Southampton Water on its maiden voyage, 10 April. Although *Titanic* was the most luxurious ship in the world she carried 20 lifeboats, enough for 1,178 passengers. On her maiden voyage to New York she was carrying over 2,200 people.

21. Forward first class grand stairway immortalised in the *Titanic* film. The top landing led out directly onto the boat deck. Elizabeth Shutes, lifeboat 3: 'How different are these staircases now! No laughing throng, but on either side stand quietly, bravely, the stewards, all equipped with the white, ghostly life preservers.'

22. Bedroom of the parlor suite on board *Titanic*.

23. First class dining room (or dining saloon).

24. This photograph from the *Olympic* reveals how the first class smoking room on the *Titanic* would have looked.

Opposite page: 25. An over-dramatic depiction of the *Titanic* striking the iceberg head on. From a French journal, April 1912. Lawrence complained of the inaccurate potrayal of the disaster in the newspapers of the time.

Above: 26. A contemporary illustration of *Titanic*'s hull being struck below the waterline by the underwater mass of the iceberg. A more accurate portrayal of the collision.

Below: 27. Cartoon from a 1912 newspaper about the *Titanic* disaster showing the despair of wives being physically parted from their husbands by the crew and put aboard the lifeboats. Lawrence witnessed just such a drama: 'Two women refused at first to leave their husbands, but partly by persuasion and partly by force they were separated from them and sent down to the next deck.'

28. Lawrence: 'I think there can be nothing but the highest praise given to the officers and crew above for the way in which they lowered the boats one after the other safely to the water; it may seem a simple matter, to read about such a thing, but any sailor knows, apparently, that it is not so. An experienced officer has told me that he has seen a boat lowered in practice from a ship's deck, with practiced sailors paying out the ropes, in daylight and has seen the boat tilt over and pitch the crew headlong into the sea. Contrast these conditions with those obtaining that Monday morning at 12.45 a.m., and it is impossible not to feel that, whether they had or had not drilled since coming on board, they did their duty in a way that argues the greatest efficiency. I cannot help feeling the deepest gratitude to the two sailors who stood at the ropes above and lowered us to the sea: I do not suppose they were saved.'

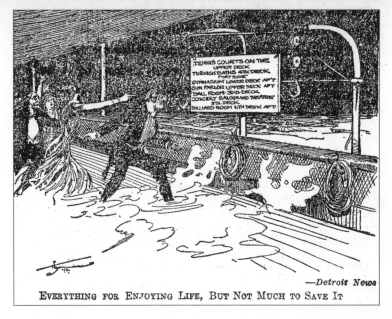

TENNIS COURTS ON THE
UPPER DECK
TURKISH BATHS 4TH DECK,
PORT SIDE
GYMNASIUM LOWER DECK AFT
SUN PARLOR UPPER DECK
BALL ROOM 3RD DECK
CONCERT SALOON AND THEATRE
5TH DECK
BILLIARD ROOM 6TH DECK AFT

—*Detroit News*

EVERYTHING FOR ENJOYING LIFE, BUT NOT MUCH TO SAVE IT

29. Cartoon from a 1912 newspaper about the *Titanic* disaster; the irony is obvious.

30. & 31. The lowering of the lifeboats. It was 75 feet from the boat deck to the sea, a distance that decreased as the night wore on and the *Titanic* sank lower and lower in the water.

32. Lawrence on the plight of passengers in the freezing Atlantic waters: 'The cries of the drowning floating across the quiet sea filled us with stupefaction: we longed to return and rescue at least some of the drowning, but we knew it was impossible. The boat was filled to standing-room, and to return would mean the swamping of us all, and so the captain-stoker told his crew to row away from the cries. We tried to sing to keep all from thinking of them; but there was no heart for singing in the boat at that time. The cries, which were loud and numerous at first, died away gradually one by one, but the night was clear, frosty and still. I think the last of them must have been heard nearly forty minutes after the *Titanic* sank. Lifebelts would keep the survivors afloat for hours; but the cold water was what stopped the cries.'

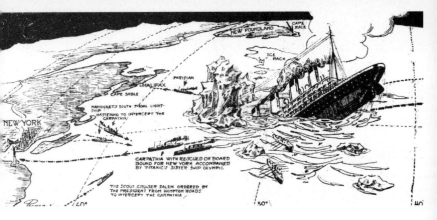

33. A contemporary newspaper depiction of the location of the sinking of the *Titanic* and positions of other ships in the area.

34. Contemporary illustration showing the *Titanic*'s two wireless operators working the Marconi set as water washes over the boat deck.

STRIKES STARBOARD BOW -12 ft AFT

11 45 P.M.

SETTLES BY HEAD - BOATS ORDERED OUT

12 05 A.M

SETTLES TO FORWARD STACK
BREAKS BETWEEN STACKS

1 40 A.M.

This page & opposite page: 35, 36, 37, 38, 39 & 40. Series of sketches executed on board *Carpathia* by Lewis Skidmore (a young art teacher), based on conversations with *Titanic* survivor Jack Thayer following the rescue. Jack Thayer was one of a number of survivors to describe the ship breaking in two as she sank. Lawrence Beesley refuted this assessment but seventy years later Thayer and others was proved right when the wreck was discovered resting on the seabed in two halves.

FORWARD END FLOATS,
THEN SINKS

1.50 A.M

STERN SECTION
PIVOTS AMIDSHIPS AND
SWINGS OVER SPOT WHERE FORWARD SECTION SANK

2.00 A.M

LAST POSITION
IN WHICH "TITANIC"
STAYED 5 MINUTES BEFORE
THE FINAL PLUNGE

J.R. Skidmore
S.S. "Carpathia" Apr 15th
1912.

41. *Titanic* survivors in one of the lifeboats approaching the *Carpathia*. Possibly lifeboat 6, as Quartermaster Hichens wore a blanket and was at the tiller.

42. Lifeboat 14 towing collapsible lifeboat D towards *Carpathia*.

43. *Titanic* survivors in collapsible lifeboat D, one of the last to be launched at *c.* 2.05 am.

44. *Titanic* survivors in a lifeboat.

Opposite: 45. Lawrence: 'The surface was like a lake of oil, heaving gently up and down with a quiet motion that rocked our boat dreamily to and fro. We did not need to keep her head to the swell: often I watched her lying broadside on to the tide, and with a boat loaded as we were, this would have been impossible with anything like a swell. So when one of the stokers said he had been to sea for twenty-six years and never yet seen such a calm night, we accepted it as true.'

Images on this page: 46, 47, 48 & 49. Four candidates photographed in the immediate aftermath of the sinking for 'iceberg that sank the *Titanic*'. These photographs were reproduced around the world in newspapers and books.

Images on this page: 50, 51 & 52. Views of two lifeboats alongside the *Carpathia*. One is clearly far from full, the other looks overloaded. Captain Rostron of the *Carpathia*: 'They started climbing aboard. Obviously they had got away in a hurry, for there were only twenty-five of them whereas the capacity of the boat was fully forty.' Lawrence's lifeboat reached *Carpathia* at about 4.30 a.m.

Above: 53. Photograph of the *Carpathia* with the recovered *Titanic* lifeboats aboard.

Right: 54. *Carpathia*'s deck strewn with lifeboats.

Below: 55. Group of survivors of the *Titanic* disaster aboard the *Carpathia* after being rescued. Howard Chapin, *Carpathia* passenger: 'Practically everyone was quiet and subdued, apparently stunned by the shock and the cold.'

56. Lawrence on the state of mind of survivors as they boarded *Carpathia*: 'The hysterical scenes that have been described are imaginative; true, one woman did fill the saloon with hysterical cries immediately after coming aboard, but she could not have known for a certainty that any of her friends were lost: probably the sense of relief after some hours of journeying about the sea was too much for her for a time.'

57. Harold Bride, surviving wireless operator of the *Titanic*, with feet bandaged, being carried up ramp of ship. He was washed off the deck of the *Titanic* just as it sank but managed to attach himself to the upturned hull of collapsible lifeboat B: 'There were men all around me – hundreds of them. The sea was dotted with them, all depending on their lifebelts.'

Above: 58. The Navatril children, Michel and Edmond, passengers on the *Titanic* who had been abducted by their father, here returned to their mother. Lawrence observed the two children playing in the covered corridor outside the library. They escaped the sinking ship in lifeboat D; their father perished. To board the ship, their father assumed the name Louis Hoffman and used their nicknames, Lolo and Mamon.

Above left: 59. American Colonel Archibald Gracie was one of the few passengers to have survived in the freezing waters before scrambling onto the upturned lifeboat B. he describes vividly how he went down with the ship: 'I was in a whirlpool of water, swirling round and round, as I still tried to cling to the railing as the ship plunged to the depths below. Down, down, I went.' Like Lawrence, he would go on to write his memoirs of how he survived the sinking.
Above right: 60. Another noted *Titanic* victim, first class passenger Archibald Butt, military aid to two US presidents. Lawrence states in his account that reports of Butt beating back a crowd rushing a lifeboat with a pistol were media exaggerations.

Above left: 61. Herbert Pitman, third officer of *Titanic* testifying before the US Senate investigation into the sinking. Lawrence incorrectly refers to him as the fouth officer.

Above right: 62. John Phillips, senior wireless operator on *Titanic* who perished.

Below: 63. Major Peuchen gets a mention in Lawrence's account. He is identified as [4] in this photograph of the US Senate investigation. [5] is Herbert Pitman and [6] is P. A. S. Franklin, White Star Line Vice President. When the New York office of the White Star Line was informed that *Titanic* was in trouble, he announced, 'We place absolute confidence in the *Titanic*. We believe the boat is unsinkable.' By the time Franklin spoke those words *Titanic* was at the bottom of the ocean.

64. Bruce Ismay, Managing Director of the White Star Line and fellow survivor of the sinking, being questioned by the Senate Investigating Committee.

65. The day after they had been picked up, Lawrence together with other survivors met in the saloon of *Carpathia* and established a committee to collect donations to aid survivors and crew in hardship. They also paid for the 'loving cup' presented here on 29 May 1912 by the 'unsinkable' Molly (Margaret) Brown to Captain Roston, for his service in the rescue of the *Titanic*.

Above: 66. Lawrence Beesley as a young man.

Below: 67. Lawrence and his children on the golf course. From left to right: Hugh, Laurien (Nicholas Wade's mother), Lawrence, Dinah, Lawrence's wife Muriel and Waveney (about to swing).

Top right: 68. Lawrence among his pupils at Dulwich College *c.* 1908.

down without an effort to save herself, without a murmur of protest against such a foul blow. For the sea could not rock her: the wind was not there to howl noisily round the decks, and make the ropes hum; from the first what must have impressed all as they watched was the sense of stillness about her and the slow, insensible way she sank lower and lower in the sea, like a stricken animal.

The mere bulk alone of the ship viewed from the sea below was an awe-inspiring sight. Imagine a ship nearly a sixth of a mile long, 75 feet high to the top decks, with four enormous funnels above the decks, and masts again high above the funnels; with her hundreds of portholes, all her saloons and other rooms brilliant with light, and all round her, little boats filled with those who until a few hours before had trod her decks and read in her libraries and listened to the music of her band in happy content; and who were now looking up in amazement at the enormous mass above them and rowing away from her because she was sinking.

I had often wanted to see her from some distance away, and only a few hours before, in conversation at lunch with a fellow passenger, had registered a vow to get a proper view of her lines and dimensions when we landed at New York: to stand some distance away to take in a full view of her beautiful proportions, which the narrow approach to the dock at Southampton made impossible. Little did I think that the opportunity was to be found so quickly and so dramatically. The background, too, was a different one from what I had planned for her: the black outline of her profile against the sky was bordered all round by stars studded in the sky, and all her funnels and masts were picked out in the same way: her bulk was seen where the stars were blotted out. And one other thing was different from expectation: the thing that ripped away from us instantly, as we saw it, all sense of the beauty of the night, the beauty of the ship's lines, and the beauty of her lights – and all these taken in themselves were intensely beautiful – that thing was the awful angle made by the level of the sea with the rows of porthole lights along her side in dotted lines, row above row. The sea level and the rows of lights should have been parallel – should never have met – and now they met at an angle inside the black hull of the ship. There was nothing else to indicate she was injured; nothing but this apparent violation of a simple geometrical law – that parallel lines should 'never meet even if produced ever so far both ways'; but it meant the *Titanic* had sunk by the head until the lowest portholes in the bows were under the sea, and the portholes in the stern were lifted above the normal height. We rowed away from her in the quietness of the night, hoping and praying with all our hearts that she would sink no more and the day would find her still in the same position as she was then. The crew, however, did not think so. It has been said frequently that the officers and crew felt assured that she would remain afloat even after they knew the extent of the damage. Some of them may have done so – and perhaps, from their scientific knowledge of her construction, with more reason at the time than those who said she would sink – but at any rate the stokers in our boat had no such illusion. One of them – I think he was the same man that cut us free from the pulley ropes – told us how he was at work in the stokehole, and in anticipation of going off duty in quarter of an hour – thus confirming the time of the collision as 11.45 – had near him a pan of soup keeping hot on some part of the machinery; suddenly the whole side of the compartment came in, and the water rushed him off his feet. Picking himself up, he sprang for the compartment doorway and was just through the aperture when the watertight door came down behind him, 'like a knife,' as he said; 'they work them from the bridge.' He had gone up on deck but was ordered down again at once and with others was told to draw the fires from under the boiler, which they did, and were then at liberty to come on deck again. It seems that this particular knot of stokers must have known almost as soon as anyone of the extent of injury. He added mournfully, 'I could do with that hot soup now' – and indeed he could: he was clad at the time of the collision, he said, in trousers and singlet, both very thin on account of the intense heat in the stokehole; and although he had added a short jacket later, his teeth were chattering with the cold. He found a place to lie down underneath the tiller on the little platform where our captain stood, and there he lay all night with a coat belonging to another stoker thrown over him and I think he must have been almost unconscious. A lady next to him, who was warmly clad with several coats, tried to insist on his having one of hers – a fur-lined one – thrown over him, but he absolutely refused while some of the women were insufficiently clad; and so the coat was given to an Irish girl with pretty auburn hair standing near, leaning against the gunwale – with an 'outside berth' and so more exposed to the cold air. This same lady was able to distribute more of her wraps to the passengers, a rug to one, a fur boa to another; and she has related with amusement that at the moment of climbing up the *Carpathia*'s side, those to whom these articles had been lent offered them all back to her; but as, like the rest of us, she was encumbered with a lifebelt, she had to say she would receive them back at the end of the climb, I had not seen my dressing gown since I dropped into the boat, but some time in the night a steerage passenger found it on the floor and put it on.

It is not easy at this time to call to mind who were in the boat, because in the night it was not possible to see more than a few feet away, and when dawn came we had eyes only for the rescue ship and the icebergs; but so far as my memory serves the list was as follows:

no first class passengers; three women, one baby, two men from the second cabin; and the other passengers steerage – mostly women; a total of about 35 passengers. The rest, about 25 (and possibly more), were crew and stokers. Near to me all night was a group of three Swedish girls, warmly clad, standing close together to keep warm, and very silent; indeed there was very little talking at any time.

One conversation took place that is, I think, worth repeating: one more proof that the world after all is a small place. The ten months' old baby which was handed down at the last moment was received by a lady next to me – the same who shared her wraps and coats. The mother had found a place in the middle and was too tightly packed to come through to the child, and so it slept contentedly for about an hour in a stranger's arms; it then began to cry and the temporary nurse said: 'Will you feel down and see if the baby's feet are out of the blanket! I don't know much about babies but I think their feet must be kept warm.' Wriggling down as well as I could, I found its toes exposed to the air and wrapped them well up, when it ceased crying at once: it was evidently a successful diagnosis! Having recognised the lady by her voice – it was much too dark to see faces – as one of my vis-à-vis at the purser's table, I said 'Surely you are Miss — ?' 'Yes,' she replied, 'and you must be Mr Beesley; how curious we should find ourselves in the same boat!' Remembering that she had joined the boat at Queenstown, I said, 'Do you know Clonmel? A letter from a great friend of mine who is staying there at — [giving the address] came aboard at Queenstown.' 'Yes, it is my home: and I was dining at — just before I came away.' It seemed that she knew my friend, too; and we agreed that of all places in the world to recognise mutual friends, a crowded lifeboat afloat in mid-ocean at 2 a.m. twelve hundred miles from our destination was one of the most unexpected.

And all the time, as we watched, the *Titanic* sank lower and lower by the head and the angle became wider and wider as the stern porthole lights lifted and the bow lights sank, and it was evident she was not to stay afloat much longer. The captain-stoker now told the oarsmen to row away as hard as they could. Two reasons seemed to make this a wise decision: one that as she sank she would create such a wave of suction that boats, if not sucked under by being too near, would be in danger of being swamped by the wave her sinking would create – and we all knew our boat was in no condition to ride big waves, crowded as it was and manned with untrained oarsmen. The second was that an explosion might result from the water getting to the boilers, and debris might fall within a wide radius. And yet, as it turned out, neither of these things happened.

At about 2.15 a.m. I think we were any distance from a mile to two miles away. It is difficult for a landsman to calculate distance at sea but we had been afloat an hour and a half, the boat was heavily loaded, the oarsmen unskilled, and our course erratic: following now one light and now another, sometimes a star and sometimes a light from a port lifeboat which had turned away from the *Titanic* in the opposite direction and lay almost on our horizon; and so we could not have gone very far away.

About this time, the water had crept up almost to her sidelight and the captain's bridge, and it seemed a question only of minutes before she sank. The oarsmen lay on their oars, and all in the lifeboat were motionless as we watched her in absolute silence – save some who would not look and buried their heads on each others' shoulders. The lights still shone with the same brilliance, but not so many of them: many were now below the surface. I have often wondered since whether they continued to light up the cabins when the portholes were under water; they may have done so.

And then, as we gazed awestruck, she tilted slowly up, revolving apparently about a centre of gravity just astern of amidships, until she attained a vertically upright position; and there she remained – motionless! As she swung up, her lights, which had shone without a flicker all night, went out suddenly, came on again for a single flash, then went out altogether. And as they did so, there came a noise which many people, wrongly I think, have described as an explosion; it has always seemed to me that it was nothing but the engines and machinery coming loose from their bolts and bearings, and falling through the compartments, smashing everything in their way. It was partly a roar, partly a groan, partly a rattle, and partly a smash, and it was not a sudden roar as an explosion would be: it went on successively for some seconds, possibly fifteen to twenty, as the heavy machinery dropped down to the bottom (now the bows) of the ship: I suppose it fell through the end and sank first, before the ship. But it was a noise no one had heard before, and no one wishes to hear again: it was stupefying, stupendous, as it came to us along the water. It was as if all the heavy things one could think of had been thrown downstairs from the top of a house, smashing each other and the stairs and everything in the way.

Several apparently authentic accounts have been given, in which definite stories of explosions have been related – in some cases even with wreckage blown up and the ship broken in two; but I think such accounts will not stand close analysis. In the first place the fires had been withdrawn and the steam allowed to escape some time before she sank, and the possibility of explosion from this cause seems very remote. Then, as just related, the noise was not sudden and definite, but prolonged – more like the roll and crash of thunder. The probability of the noise being caused by engines falling down will be seen by referring to illustration 4, where the engines are placed in compartments 3, 4, and 5. As the *Titanic* tilted up they would almost certainly fall loose from their bed and plunge down through the other compartments.

No phenomenon like that pictured in some American and English papers occurred – that of the ship breaking in two, and the two ends being raised above the surface. I saw these drawings in preparation on board the *Carpathia*, and said at the time that they bore no resemblance to what actually happened.

When the noise was over the *Titanic* was still upright like a column: we could see her now only as the stern and some 150 feet of her stood outlined against the star-specked sky, looming black in the darkness, and in this position she continued for some minutes – I think as much as five minutes, but it may have been less. Then, first sinking back a little at the stern, I thought, she slid slowly forwards through the water and dived slantingly down; the sea closed over her and we had seen the last of the beautiful ship on which we had embarked four days before at Southampton.

And in place of the ship on which all our interest had been concentrated for so long and towards which we looked most of the time because it was still the only object on the sea which was a fixed point to us – in place of the *Titanic*, we had the level sea now stretching in an unbroken expanse to the horizon: heaving gently just as before, with no indication on the surface that the waves had just closed over the most wonderful vessel ever built by man's hand; the stars looked down just the same and the air was just as bitterly cold.

There seemed a great sense of loneliness when we were left on the sea in a small boat without the *Titanic*: not that we were uncomfortable (except for the cold) nor in danger: we did not think we were either, but the *Titanic* was no longer there.

We waited head on for the wave which we thought might come – the wave we had heard so much of from the crew and which they said had been known to travel for miles – and it never came. But although the *Titanic* left us no such legacy of a wave as she went to the bottom, she left us something we would willingly forget forever, something which it is well not to let the imagination dwell on – the cries of many hundreds of our fellow passengers struggling in the ice-cold water.

I would willingly omit any further mention of this part of the disaster from this book, but for two reasons it is not possible – first, that as a matter of history it should be put on record; and secondly, that these cries were not only an appeal for help in the awful conditions of danger in which the drowning found themselves – an appeal that could never be answered – but an appeal to the whole world to make such conditions of danger and hopelessness impossible ever again; a cry that called to the heavens for the very injustice of its own existence; a cry that clamoured for its own destruction.

We were utterly surprised to hear this cry go up as the waves closed over the *Titanic*: we had heard no sound of any kind from her since we left her side; and, as mentioned before, we did not know how many boats she had or how many rafts. The crew may have known, but they probably did not, and if they did, they never told the passengers; we should not have been surprised to know all were safe on some lifesaving device.

So that unprepared as we were for such a thing, the cries of the drowning floating across the quiet sea filled us with stupefaction: we longed to return and rescue at least some of the drowning, but we knew it was impossible. The boat was filled to standing room, and to return would mean the swamping of us all, and so the captain-stoker told his crew to row away from the cries. We tried to sing to keep all from thinking of them; but there was no heart for singing in the boat at that time.

The cries, which were loud and numerous at first, died away gradually one by one, but the night was clear, frosty and still, the water smooth, and the sounds must have carried on its level surface free from any obstruction for miles, certainly much farther from the ship than we were situated. I think the last of them must have been heard nearly forty minutes after the *Titanic* sank. Lifebelts would keep the survivors afloat for hours; but the cold water was what stopped the cries.

There must have come to all those safe in the lifeboats, scattered round the drowning at various distances, a deep resolve that, if anything could be done by them in the future to prevent the repetition of such sounds, they would do it – at whatever cost of time or other things. And not only to them are those cries an imperative call, but to every man and woman who has known of them. It is not possible that ever again can such conditions exist; but it is a duty imperative on one and all to see that they do not. Think of it! A few more boats, a few more planks of wood nailed together in a particular way at a trifling cost, and all those men and women whom the world can so ill afford to lose would be with us today, there would be no mourning in thousands of homes which now are desolate, and these words need not have been written.

5

The Rescue

All accounts agree that the *Titanic* sank about 2.20 a.m.: a watch in our boat gave the time as 2.30 a.m. shortly afterwards. We were then in touch with three other boats: one was 15, on our starboard quarter, and the others I have always supposed were 9 and 11, but I do not know definitely. We never got into close touch with each other, but called occasionally across the darkness and saw them looming near and then drawing away again; we called to ask if any officer were aboard the other three, but did not find one. So in the absence of any plan of action, we rowed slowly forward – or what we thought was forward, for it was in the direction the *Titanic*'s bows were pointing before she sank. I see now that we must have been pointing north-west, for we presently saw the Northern Lights on the starboard, and again, when the *Carpathia* came up from the south, we saw her from behind us on the south-east, and turned our boat around to get to her. I imagine the boats must have spread themselves over the ocean fanwise as they escaped from the *Titanic*: those on the starboard and port sides forward being almost dead ahead of her and the stern boats being broadside from her; this explains why the port boats were so much longer in reaching the *Carpathia* – as late as 8.30 a.m. – while some of the starboard boats came up as early as 4.10 a.m. Some of the port boats had to row across the place where the *Titanic* sank to get to the *Carpathia*, through the debris of chairs and wreckage of all kinds.

None of the other three boats near us had a light – and we missed lights badly: we could not see each other in the darkness; we could not signal to ships which might be rushing up full speed from any quarter to the *Titanic*'s rescue; and now we had been through so much it would seem hard to have to encounter the additional danger of being in the line of a rescuing ship. We felt again for the lantern beneath our feet, along the sides, and I managed this time to get down to the locker below the tiller platform and open it in front by removing a board, to find nothing but the zinc airtank which renders the boat unsinkable when upset. I do not think there was a light in the boat. We felt also for food and water, and found none, and came to the conclusion that none had been put in; but here we were mistaken. I have a letter from Second Officer Lightoller in which he assures me that he and Fourth Officer Pitman examined every lifeboat from the *Titanic* as they lay on the *Carpathia*'s deck afterwards and found biscuits and water in each. Not that we wanted any food or water then: we thought of the time that might elapse before the *Olympic* picked us up in the afternoon.

Towards 3 a.m. we saw a faint glow in the sky ahead on the starboard quarter, the first gleams, we thought, of the coming dawn. We were not certain of the time and were eager perhaps to accept too readily any relief from darkness – only too glad to be able to look each other in the face and see who were our companions in good fortune; to be free from the hazard of lying in a steamer's track, invisible in the darkness. But we were doomed to disappointment: the soft light increased for a time, and died away a little; glowed again, and then remained stationary for some minutes! 'The Northern Lights'! It suddenly came to me, and so it was: presently the light arched fanwise across the northern sky, with faint streamers reaching towards the Polestar. I had seen them of about the same intensity in England some years ago and knew them again. A sigh of disappointment went through the boat as we realised that the day was not yet; but had we known it, something more comforting even than the day was in store for us. All night long we had watched the horizon with eager eyes for signs of a steamer's lights; we heard from the captain-stoker that the first appearance would be a single light on the horizon, the masthead light, followed shortly by a second one, lower down, on the deck; if these two remained in vertical alignment and the distance between them increased as the lights drew nearer, we might be certain it was a steamer. But what a night to see that first light on the horizon! We saw it many times as the earth revolved, and some stars rose on the clear horizon and others sank down to it: there were 'lights' on every quarter. Some we watched and followed until we saw the deception and grew wiser; some were lights from those of our boats that were fortunate enough to have lanterns, but these were generally easily detected, as they rose and fell in the near distance. Once they raised our hopes, only to sink them to zero again. Near what seemed to be the horizon on the port quarter we saw two lights close together, and thought this must be our double light; but as we gazed across the miles that separated us, the lights slowly drew apart and we realised that they were two boats' lanterns at different distances from us, in line, one behind the other. They were probably the forward port boats that had to return so many miles next morning across the *Titanic*'s graveyard.

But notwithstanding these hopes and disappointments, the absence of lights, food and water (as we thought), and the bitter cold, it would not be correct to say we were unhappy in those early morning hours: the cold that settled down on us like a garment that wraps close around was the only real discomfort, and that we could keep at bay by not thinking too much about it as well as by vigorous friction and gentle stamping on the floor (it made too much noise to stamp hard!). I never heard that anyone in boat 13 had any after effects from the cold – even the stoker who was so thinly clad came through without harm. After all, there were many things to be thankful for: so many that they made insignificant the temporary inconvenience of the cold, the crowded boat, the darkness and the hundred and one things that in the ordinary way we might regard as unpleasant. The quiet sea, the beautiful night (how different from two nights later when flashes of lightning and peals of thunder broke the sleep of many on board the *Carpathia*!), and above all the fact of being in a boat at all when so many of our fellow passengers and crew – whose cries no longer moaned across the water to us – were silent in the water. Gratitude was the dominant note in our feelings then. But grateful as we were, our gratitude was soon to be increased a hundred fold. About 3.30 a.m., as nearly as I can judge, some one in the bow called our attention to a faint faraway gleam in the south-east. We all turned quickly to look and there it was certainly: streaming up from behind the horizon like a distant flash of a warship's searchlight; then a faint boom like guns afar off, and the light died away again. The stoker who had lain all night under the tiller sat up suddenly as if from a dream, the overcoat hanging from his shoulders. I can see him now, staring out across the sea, to where the sound had come from, and hear him shout, 'That was a cannon!' But it was not: it was the *Carpathia*'s rocket, though we did not know it until later. But we did know now that something was not far away, racing up to our help and signalling to us a preliminary message to cheer our hearts until she arrived.

With every sense alert, eyes gazing intently at the horizon and ears open for the least sound, we waited in absolute silence in the quiet night. And then, creeping over the edge of the sea where the flash had been, we saw a single light, and presently a second below it, and in a few minutes they were well above the horizon and they remained in line! But we had been deceived before, and we waited a little longer before we allowed ourselves to say we were safe. The lights came up rapidly: so rapidly it seemed only a few minutes (though it must have been longer) between first seeing them and finding them well above the horizon and bearing down rapidly on us. We did not know what sort of a vessel was coming, but we knew she was coming quickly, and we searched for paper, rags – anything that would burn (we were quite prepared to burn our coats if necessary). A hasty paper torch was twisted out of letters found in someone's pocket, lighted, and held aloft by the stoker standing on the tiller platform. The little light shone in flickers on the faces of the occupants of the boat, ran in broken lines for a few yards along the black oily sea (where for the first time I saw the presence of that awful thing which had caused the whole terrible disaster – ice – in little chunks the size of one's fist, bobbing harmlessly up and down), and spluttered away to blackness again as the stoker threw the burning remnants of paper overboard. But had we known it, the danger of being run down was already over, one reason being that the *Carpathia* had already seen the lifeboat which all night long had shown a green light, the first indication the *Carpathia* had of our position. But the real reason is to be found in the *Carpathia*'s log: 'Went full speed ahead during the night; stopped at 4 a.m. with an iceberg dead ahead.' It was a good reason.

With our torch burnt and in darkness again we saw the headlights stop, and realised that the rescuer had hove to. A sigh of relief went up when we thought no hurried scramble had to be made to get out of her way, with a chance of just being missed by her, and having to meet the wash of her screws as she tore by us. We waited and she slowly swung round and revealed herself to us as a large steamer with all her portholes alight. I think the way those lights came slowly into view was one of the most wonderful things we shall ever see. It meant deliverance at once: that was the amazing thing to us all. We had thought of the afternoon as our time of rescue, and here only a few hours after the *Titanic* sank, before it was yet light, we were to be taken aboard. It seemed almost too good to be true, and I think everyone's eyes filled with tears, men's as well as women's, as they saw again the rows of lights one above the other shining kindly to them across the water, and 'Thank God!' was murmured in heartfelt tones round the boat. The boat swung round and the crew began their long row to the steamer; the captain called for a song and led off with 'Pull for the shore, boys.' The crew took it up quaveringly and the passengers joined in, but I think one verse was all they sang. It was too early yet, gratitude was too deep and sudden in its overwhelming intensity, for us to sing very steadily. Presently, finding the song had not gone very well, we tried a cheer, and that went better. It was more easy to relieve our feelings with a noise, and time and tune were not necessary ingredients in a cheer.

In the midst of our thankfulness for deliverance, one name was mentioned with the deepest feeling of gratitude: that of Marconi. I wish that he had been there to hear the chorus of gratitude that went out to him for the wonderful invention that spared us many hours, and perhaps many days, of wandering about the sea in hunger and storm and cold. Perhaps our gratitude was sufficiently intense and vivid to 'Marconi' some of it to him that night.

All around we saw boats making for the *Carpathia* and heard their shouts and cheers. Our crew rowed hard in friendly rivalry with other boats to be among the first home, but we must have been eighth or ninth at the side. We had a heavy load aboard, and had to row round a huge iceberg on the way.

And then, as if to make everything complete for our happiness, came the dawn. First a beautiful, quiet shimmer away in the east, then a soft golden glow that crept up stealthily from behind the skyline as if it were trying not to be noticed as it stole over the sea and spread itself quietly in every direction – so quietly, as if to make us believe it had been there all the time and we had not observed it. Then the sky turned faintly pink and in the distance the thinnest, fleeciest clouds stretched in thin bands across the horizon and close down to it, becoming every moment more and more pink. And next the stars died, slowly – save one which remained long after the others just above the horizon; and nearby, with the crescent turned to the north, and the lower horn just touching the horizon, the thinnest, palest of moons.

And with the dawn came a faint breeze from the west, the first breath of wind we had felt since the *Titanic* stopped her engines. Anticipating a few hours – as the day drew on to 8 a.m., the time the last boats came up – this breeze increased to a fresh wind which whipped up the sea, so that the last boat laden with people had an anxious time in the choppy waves before they reached the *Carpathia*. An officer remarked that one of the boats could not have stayed afloat another hour: the wind had held off just long enough.

The captain shouted along our boat to the crew, as they strained at the oars – two pulling and an extra one facing them and pushing to try to keep pace with the other boats – 'A new moon! Turn your money over, boys! That is, if you have any!' We laughed at him for the quaint superstition at such a time, and it was good to laugh again, but he showed his disbelief in another superstition when he added, 'Well, I shall never say again that 13 is an unlucky number. Boat 13 is the best friend we ever had.'

If there had been among us – and it is almost certain that there were, so fast does superstition cling – those who feared events connected with the number thirteen, I am certain they agreed with him, and never again will they attach any importance to such a foolish belief. Perhaps the belief itself will receive a shock when it is remembered that boat 13 of the *Titanic* brought away a full load from the sinking vessel, carried them in such comfort all night that they had not even a drop of water on them, and landed them safely at the *Carpathia*'s side, where they climbed aboard without a single mishap. It almost tempts one to be the thirteenth at table, or to choose a house numbered 13 fearless of any croaking about flying in the face of what is humorously called 'Providence'.

Looking towards the *Carpathia* in the faint light, we saw what seemed to be two large fully rigged sailing ships near the horizon, with all sails set, standing up near her, and we decided that they must be fishing vessels off the Banks of Newfoundland which had seen the *Carpathia* stop and were waiting to see if she wanted help of any kind. But in a few minutes more the light shone on them and they stood revealed as huge icebergs, peaked in a way that readily suggested a ship. When the sun rose higher, it turned them pink, and sinister as they looked towering like rugged white peaks of rock out of the sea, and terrible as was the disaster one of them had caused, there was an awful beauty about them which could not be overlooked. Later, when the sun came above the horizon, they sparkled and glittered in its rays; deadly white, like frozen snow rather than translucent ice.

As the dawn crept towards us there lay another almost directly in the line between our boat and the *Carpathia*, and a few minutes later, another on her port quarter, and more again on the southern and western horizons, as far as the eye could reach: all differing in shape and size and tones of colour according as the sun shone through them or was reflected directly or obliquely from them.

We drew near our rescuer and presently could discern the bands on her funnel, by which the crew could tell she was a Cunarder; and already some boats were at her side and passengers climbing up her ladders. We had to give the iceberg a wide berth and make a detour to the south: we knew it was sunk a long way below the surface with such things as projecting ledges – not that it was very likely there was one so near the surface as to endanger our small boat, but we were not inclined to take any risks for the sake of a few more minutes when safety lay so near.

Once clear of the berg, we could read the Cunarder's name – C A R P A T H I A – a name we are not likely ever to forget. We shall see her sometimes, perhaps, in the shipping lists – as I have done already once when she left Genoa on her return voyage – and the way her lights climbed up over the horizon in the darkness, the way she swung and showed her lighted portholes, and the moment when we read her name on her side will all come back in a flash; we shall live again the scene of rescue, and feel the same thrill of gratitude for all she brought us that night.

We rowed up to her about 4.30, and sheltering on the port side from the swell, held on by two ropes at the stern and bow. Women went up the side first, climbing rope ladders with a noose round their shoulders to help their ascent; men passengers scrambled next, and the crew last of all. The baby went up in a bag with the opening tied up: it had been quite well all the time, and never suffered any ill effects from its cold journey in the night. We set foot on deck with very thankful hearts, grateful beyond the possibility of adequate expression to feel a solid ship beneath us once more.

6

The Sinking of the *Titanic*, Seen From Her Deck

The two preceding chapters have been to a large extent the narrative of a single eyewitness and an account of the escape of one boat only from the *Titanic*'s side. It will be well now to return to the *Titanic* and reconstruct a more general and complete account from the experiences of many people in different parts of the ship. A considerable part of these experiences was related to the writer first hand by survivors, both on board the *Carpathia* and at other times, but some are derived from other sources which are probably as accurate as first-hand information. Other reports, which seemed at first sight to have been founded on the testimony of eyewitnesses, have been found on examination to have passed through several hands, and have therefore been rejected. The testimony even of eyewitnesses has in some cases been excluded when it seemed not to agree with direct evidence of a number of other witnesses or with what reasoned judgement considered probable in the circumstances. In this category are the reports of explosions before the

Titanic sank, the breaking of the ship in two parts, the suicide of officers. It would be well to notice here that the *Titanic* was in her correct course, the southerly one, and in the position which prudence dictates as a safe one under the ordinary conditions at that time of the year: to be strictly accurate she was sixteen miles south of the regular summer route which all companies follow from January to August.

Perhaps the real history of the disaster should commence with the afternoon of Sunday, when Marconigrams were received by the *Titanic* from the ships ahead of her, warning her of the existence of icebergs. In connection with this must be taken the marked fall of temperature observed by everyone in the afternoon and evening of this day as well as the very low temperature of the water. These have generally been taken to indicate that without any possibility of doubt we were near an iceberg region, and the severest condemnation has been poured on the heads of the officers and captain for not having regard to these climatic conditions; but here caution is necessary. There can be little doubt now that the low temperature observed can be traced to the icebergs and ice-field subsequently encountered, but experienced sailors are aware that it might have been observed without any icebergs being near. The cold Labrador current sweeps down by Newfoundland across the track of Atlantic liners, but does not necessarily carry icebergs with it; cold winds blow from Greenland and Labrador and not always from icebergs and icefields. So that falls in temperature of sea and air are not prima facie evidence of the close proximity of icebergs. On the other hand, a single iceberg separated by many miles from its fellows might sink a ship, but certainly would not cause a drop in temperature either of the air or water. Then, as the Labrador current meets the warm Gulf Stream flowing from the Gulf of Mexico across to Europe, they do not necessarily intermingle, nor do they always run side by side or one on top of the other, but often interlaced, like the fingers of two hands. As a ship sails across this region the thermometer will record within a few miles temperatures of 34°, 58°, 35°, 59°, and so on.

It is little wonder then that sailors become accustomed to place little reliance on temperature conditions as a means of estimating the probabilities of encountering ice in their track. An experienced sailor has told me that nothing is more difficult to diagnose than the presence of icebergs, and a strong confirmation of this is found in the official sailing directions issued by the Hydrographic Department of the British Admiralty. 'No reliance can be placed on any warning being conveyed to the mariner, by a fall in temperature, either of sea or air, of approaching ice. Some decrease in temperature has occasionally been recorded, but more often none has been observed.'

But notification by Marconigram of the exact location of icebergs is a vastly different matter. I remember with deep feeling the effect this information had on us when it first became generally known on board the *Carpathia*. Rumours of it went round on Wednesday morning, grew to definite statements in the afternoon, and were confirmed when one of the *Titanic* officers admitted the truth of it in reply to a direct question. I shall never forget the overwhelming sense of hopelessness that came over some of us as we obtained definite knowledge of the warning messages. It was not then the unavoidable accident we had hitherto supposed: the sudden plunging into a region crowded with icebergs which no seaman, however skilled a navigator he might be, could have avoided! The beautiful *Titanic* wounded too deeply to recover, the cries of the drowning still ringing in our ears and the thousands of homes that mourned all these calamities – none of all these things need ever have been!

It is no exaggeration to say that men who went through all the experiences of the collision and the rescue and the subsequent scenes on the quay at New York with hardly a tremor, were quite overcome by this knowledge and turned away, unable to speak; I for one, did so, and I know others who told me they were similarly affected.

I think we all came to modify our opinions on this matter, however, when we learnt more of the general conditions attending transatlantic steamship services. The discussion as to who was responsible for these warnings being disregarded had perhaps better be postponed to a later chapter. One of these warnings was handed to Mr Ismay by Captain Smith at 5 p.m. and returned at the latter's request at 7 p.m., that it might be posted for the information of officers; as a result of the messages they were instructed to keep a special lookout for ice. This, Second Officer Lightoller did until he was relieved at 10 p.m. by First Officer Murdock, to whom he handed on the instructions. During Mr Lightoller's watch, about 9 p.m., the captain had joined him on the bridge and discussed 'the time we should be getting up towards the vicinity of the ice, and how we should recognise it if we should see it, and refreshing our minds on the indications that ice gives when it is in the vicinity'. Apparently, too, the officers had discussed among themselves the proximity of ice and Mr Lightoller had remarked that they would be approaching the position where ice had been reported during his watch. The lookouts were cautioned similarly, but no ice was sighted until a few minutes before the collision, when the lookout man saw the iceberg and rang the bell three times, the usual signal from the crow's nest when anything is seen dead ahead.

By telephone he reported to the bridge the presence of an iceberg, but Mr Murdock had already ordered Quartermaster Hichens at the wheel to starboard the helm, and the vessel began to swing away from the berg. But it was far too late at the speed she was going to hope to steer the huge *Titanic*, over a sixth of a mile long, out of reach of danger. Even if the iceberg had been visible half a mile away it is doubtful whether some portion of her tremendous length would not have been touched, and it is in the highest degree unlikely that the lookout could have seen the berg half a mile away in the conditions that existed that night, even with glasses. The very smoothness of the water made the presence of ice a more difficult matter to detect. In ordinary conditions the dash of the waves against the foot of an iceberg surrounds it with a circle of white foam visible for some distance, long before the iceberg itself; but here was an oily sea sweeping smoothly round the deadly monster and causing no indication of its presence.

There is little doubt, moreover, that the crow's nest is not a good place from which to detect icebergs. It is proverbial that they adopt to a large extent the colour of their surroundings; and seen from above at a high angle, with the black, foam-free sea behind, the iceberg must have been almost invisible until the *Titanic* was close upon it. I was much struck by a remark of Sir Ernest Shackleton on his method of detecting icebergs – to place a lookout man as low down near the waterline as he could get him. Remembering how we had watched the *Titanic* with all her lights out, standing upright like 'an enormous black finger', as one observer stated, and had only seen her thus because she loomed black against the sky behind her, I saw at once how much better the sky was than the black sea to show up an iceberg's bulk.

And so in a few moments the *Titanic* had run obliquely on the berg, and with a shock that was astonishingly slight – so slight that many passengers never noticed it – the submerged portion of the berg had cut her open on the starboard side in the most vulnerable portion of her anatomy – the bilge. The most authentic accounts say that the wound began at about the location of the foremast and extended far back to the stern, the brunt of the blow being taken by the forward plates, which were either punctured through both bottoms directly by the blow, or through one skin only, and as this was torn away it ripped out some of the inner plates. The fact that she went down by the head shows that probably only the forward plates were doubly punctured, the stern ones being cut open through the outer skin only. After the collision, Murdock had at once reversed the engines and brought the ship to a standstill, but the iceberg had floated away astern. The shock, though little felt by the enormous mass of the ship, was sufficient to dislodge a large quantity of ice from the berg: the forecastle deck was found to be covered with pieces of ice.

Feeling the shock, Captain Smith rushed out of his cabin to the bridge, and in reply to his anxious enquiry was told by Murdock that ice had been struck and the emergency doors instantly closed. The officers roused by the collision went on deck: some to the bridge; others, while hearing nothing of the extent of the damage, saw no necessity for doing so. Captain Smith at once sent the carpenter below to sound the ship, and Fourth Officer Boxhall to the steerage to report damage. The latter found there a very dangerous condition of things and reported to Captain Smith, who then sent him to the mail room; and here again, it was easy to see, matters looked very serious. Mail bags were floating about and the water rising rapidly. All this was reported to the captain, who ordered the lifeboats to be got ready at once. Mr Boxhall went to the chartroom to work out the ship's position, which he then handed to the Marconi operators for transmission to any ship near enough to help in the work of rescue.

Reports of the damage done were by this time coming to the captain from many quarters, from the chief engineer, from the designer – Mr Andrews – and in a dramatic way from the sudden appearance on deck of a swarm of stokers who had rushed up from below as the water poured into the boiler rooms and coal bunkers: they were immediately ordered down below to duty again. Realising the urgent heed of help, he went personally to the Marconi room and gave orders to the operators to get into touch with all the ships they could and to tell them to come quickly. The assistant operator Bride had been asleep, and knew of the damage only when Phillips, in charge of the Marconi room, told him ice had been encountered. They started to send out the well-known 'CQD' message – which interpreted means: CQ 'all stations at tend,' and D, 'distress', the position of the vessel in latitude and longitude following. Later, they sent out 'SOS', an arbitrary message agreed upon as an international code-signal.

Soon after the vessel struck, Mr Ismay had learnt of the nature of the accident from the captain and chief engineer, and after dressing and going on deck had spoken to some of the officers not yet thoroughly acquainted with the grave injury done to the vessel. By this time all those in any way connected with the management and navigation must have known the importance of making use of all the ways of safety known to them – and that without any delay. That they thought at first that the *Titanic* would sink as soon as she did is doubtful; but probably as the reports came in they knew that her ultimate loss in a few hours was a likely contingency. On the other hand, there is evidence that some of the officers in charge of boats quite expected the embarkation was a precautionary measure and they would all return after daylight. Certainly the first information that ice had been struck conveyed to those in charge no sense of the gravity of the circumstances: one officer even retired to his cabin and another advised a steward to go back to his berth as there was no danger.

And so the order was sent round, 'All passengers on deck with lifebelts on'; and in obedience to this a crowd of hastily dressed or partially dressed people began to assemble on the decks belonging to their respective classes (except the steerage passengers who were allowed access to other decks), tying on lifebelts over their clothing. In some parts of the ship women were separated from the men and assembled together near the boats, in others men and women mingled freely together, husbands helping their own wives and families and then other women and children into the boats. The officers spread themselves about the decks, superintending the work of lowering and loading the boats, and in three cases were ordered by their superior officers to take charge of them. At this stage great difficulty was experienced in getting women to leave the ship, especially where the order was so rigorously enforced, 'Women and children only.' Women in many cases refused to leave their husbands, and were actually forcibly lifted up and dropped in the boats. They argued with the officers, demanding reasons, and in some cases even when induced to get in were disposed to think the whole thing a joke, or a precaution which it seemed to them rather foolish to take. In this they were encouraged by the men left behind, who, in the same condition of ignorance, said goodbye to their friends as they went down, adding that they would see them again at breakfast-time. To illustrate further how little danger was apprehended – when it was discovered on the first class deck that the forward lower deck was covered with small ice, snowballing matches were arranged for the following morning, and some passengers even went down to the deck and brought back small pieces of ice which were handed round.

Below decks too was additional evidence that no one thought of immediate danger. Two ladies walking along one of the corridors came across a group of people gathered round a door which they were trying vainly to open, and on the other side of which a man was demanding in loud terms to be let out. Either his door was locked and the key not to be found, or the collision had jammed the lock and prevented the key from turning. The ladies thought he must be afflicted in some way to make such a noise, but one of the men was assuring him that in no circumstances should he be left, and that his (the bystander's) son would be along soon and would smash down his door if it was not opened in the mean time. 'He has a stronger arm than I have,' he added. The son arrived presently and proceeded to make short work of the door: it was smashed in and the inmate released, to his great satisfaction and with many expressions of gratitude to his rescuer. But one of the head stewards who came up at this juncture was so incensed at the damage done to the property of his company, and so little aware of the infinitely greater damage done the ship, that he warned the man who had released the prisoner that he would be arrested on arrival in New York.

It must be borne in mind that no general warning had been issued to passengers: here and there were experienced travellers to whom collision with an iceberg was sufficient to cause them to make every preparation for leaving the ship, but the great majority were never enlightened as to the amount of damage done, or even as to what had happened. We knew in a vague way that we had collided with an iceberg, but there our knowledge ended, and most of us drew no deductions from that fact alone. Another factor that prevented some from taking to the boats was the drop to the water below and the journey into the unknown sea: certainly it looked a tremendous way down in the darkness, the sea and the night both seemed very cold and lonely; and here was the ship, so firm and well lighted and warm.

But perhaps what made so many people declare their decision to remain was their strong belief in the theory of the *Titanic*'s unsinkable construction. Again and again was it repeated, 'This ship cannot sink; it is only a question of waiting until another ship comes up and takes us off.' Husbands expected to follow their wives and join them either in

New York or by transfer in mid-ocean from steamer to steamer. Many passengers relate that they were told by officers that the ship was a lifeboat and could not go down; one lady affirms that the captain told her the *Titanic* could not sink for two or three days; no doubt this was immediately after the collision.

It is not any wonder, then, that many elected to remain, deliberately choosing the deck of the *Titanic* to a place in a lifeboat. And yet the boats had to go down, and so at first they went half full: this is the real explanation of why they were not as fully loaded as the later ones. It is important then to consider the question how far the captain was justified in withholding all the knowledge he had from every passenger. From one point of view he should have said to them, 'This ship will sink in a few hours: there are the boats, and only women and children can go to them.' But had he the authority to enforce such an order? There are such things as panics and rushes which get beyond the control of a handful of officers, even if armed, and where even the bravest of men get swept off their feet – mentally as well as physically.

On the other hand, if he decided to withhold all definite knowledge of danger from all passengers and at the same time persuade – and if it was not sufficient, compel – women and children to take to the boats, it might result in their all being saved. He could not foresee the tenacity of their faith in the boat: there is ample evidence that he left the bridge when the ship had come to rest and went among passengers urging them to get into the boat and rigorously excluding all but women and children. Some would not go. Officer Lowe testified that he shouted, 'Who's next for the boat?' and could get no replies. The boats even were sent away half-loaded – although the fear of their buckling in the middle was responsible as well for this – but the captain with the few boats at his disposal could hardly do more than persuade and advise in the terrible circumstances in which he was placed.

How appalling to think that with a few more boats – and the ship was provided with that particular kind of davit that would launch more boats – there would have been no decision of that kind to make! It could have been stated plainly: 'This ship will sink in a few hours: there is room in the boats for all passengers, beginning with women and children.'

Poor Captain Smith! I care not whether the responsibility for such speed in iceberg regions will rest on his shoulders or not: no man ever had to make such a choice as he had that night, and it seems difficult to see how he can be blamed for withholding from passengers such information as he had of the danger that was imminent.

When one reads in the press that lifeboats arrived at the *Carpathia* half full, it seems at first sight a dreadful thing that this should have been allowed to happen; but it is so easy to make these criticisms afterwards, so easy to say that Captain Smith should have told everyone of the condition of the vessel. He was faced with many conditions that night which such criticism overlooks. Let any fair-minded person consider some few of the problems presented to him – the ship was bound to sink in a few hours; there was lifeboat accommodation for all women and children and some men; there was no way of getting some women to go except by telling them the ship was doomed, a course he deemed it best not to take; and he knew the danger of boats buckling when loaded full. His solution of these problems was apparently the following: to send the boats down half full, with such women as would go, and to tell the boats to stand by to pick up more passengers passed down from the cargo ports. There is good evidence that this was part of the plan: I heard an officer give the order to four boats and a lady in number 4 boat on the port side tells me the sailors were so long looking for the port where the captain personally had told them to wait, that they were in danger of being sucked under by the vessel. How far any systematic attempt was made to stand by the ports, I do not know: I never saw one open or any boat standing near on the starboard side; but then, boats 9 to 15 went down full, and on reaching the sea rowed away at once. There is good evidence, then, that Captain Smith fully intended to load the boats full in this way. The failure to carry out the intention is one of the things the whole world regrets, but consider again the great size of the ship and the short time to make decisions, and the omission is more easily understood. The fact is that such a contingency as lowering away boats was not even considered beforehand, and there is much cause for gratitude that as many as seven hundred and five people were rescued. The whole question of a captain's duties seems to require revision. It was totally impossible for any one man to attempt to control the ship that night, and the weather conditions could not well have been more favourable for doing so. One of the reforms that seem inevitable is that one man shall be responsible for the boats, their manning, loading and lowering, leaving the captain free to be on the bridge to the last moment.

But to return for a time to the means taken to attract the notice of other ships. The wireless operators were now in touch with several ships, and calling to them to come quickly for the water was pouring in and the *Titanic* beginning to go down by the head. Bride testified that the first reply received was from a German boat, the *Frankfurt*, which was 'All right: stand by', but not giving her position. From comparison of the strength of signals received from the *Frankfurt* and from other boats, the operators estimated the *Frankfurt* was the nearest; but subsequent events proved that this was not so. She was, in fact, one hundred and forty miles away and arrived at 10.50 a.m. next morning, when the *Carpathia* had left with the rescued. The next reply was from the *Carpathia*, fifty-eight miles away on the outbound route to the Mediterranean, and it was a prompt and welcome one – 'Coming hard', followed by the position. Then followed the *Olympic*, and with her they talked for some time, but she was five hundred and sixty miles away on the southern route, too far to be of any immediate help. At the speed of 23 knots she would expect to be up about 1 p.m. next day, and this was about the time that those in boat 13 had calculated. We had always assumed in the boat that the stokers who gave this information had it from one of the officers before they left; but in the absence of any knowledge of the much nearer ship, the *Carpathia*, it is more probable that they knew in a general way where the sister ship, the *Olympic*, should be, and had made a rough calculation.

Other ships in touch by wireless were the *Mount Temple*, fifty miles; the *Birma*, one hundred miles; the *Parisian*, one hundred and fifty miles; the *Virginian*, one hundred and fifty miles; and the *Baltic*, three hundred miles. But closer than any of these – closer even than the *Carpathia* – were two ships: the *Californian*, less than twenty miles away, with the wireless operator off duty and unable to catch the 'CQD' signal which was now making the air for many miles around quiver in its appeal for help – immediate, urgent help – for the hundreds of people who stood on the *Titanic*'s deck.

The second vessel was a small steamer some few miles ahead on the port side, without any wireless apparatus, her name and destination still unknown; and yet the evidence for her presence that night seems too strong to be disregarded. Mr Boxhall states that he and Captain Smith saw her quite plainly some five miles away, and could distinguish the masthead lights and a red port light. They at once hailed her with rockets and Morse electric signals, to which Boxhall saw no reply, but Captain Smith and stewards affirmed they did. The second and third officers saw the signals sent and her lights, the latter from the lifeboat of which he was in charge. Seaman Hopkins testified that he was told by the captain to row for the light; and we in boat 13 certainly saw it in the same position and rowed towards it for some time. But notwithstanding all the efforts made to attract its attention, it drew slowly away and the lights sank below the horizon.

The pity of it! So near, and so many people waiting for the shelter its decks could have given so easily. It seems impossible to think that this ship ever replied to the signals: those who said so must have been mistaken. The United States Senate Committee in its report does not hesitate to say that this unknown steamer and the *Californian* are identical, and that the failure on the part of the latter to come to the help of the *Titanic* is culpable negligence. There is undoubted evidence that some of the crew on the *Californian* saw our rockets; but it seems impossible to believe that the captain and officers knew of our distress and deliberately ignored it. Judgement on the matter had better be suspended until further information is forthcoming. An engineer who has served in the transatlantic service tells me that it is a common practice for small boats to leave the fishing smacks to which they belong and row away for miles; sometimes even being lost and wandering about among icebergs, and even not being found again. In these circumstances, rockets are part of a fishing smack's equipment, and are sent up to indicate to the small boats how to return. Is it conceivable that the *Californian* thought our rockets were such signals, and therefore paid no attention to them?

Incidentally, this engineer did not hesitate to add that it is doubtful if a big liner would stop to help a small fishing boat sending off distress signals, or even would turn about to help one which she herself had cut down as it lay in her path without a light. He was strong in his affirmation that such things were commonly known to all officers in the transatlantic service.

With regard to the other vessels in wireless communication, the *Mount Temple* was the only one near enough from the point of distance to have arrived in time to be of help, but between her and the *Titanic* lay the enormous ice-floe, and icebergs were near her in addition.

The seven ships which caught the message started at once to her help but were all stopped on the way (except the *Birma*) by the *Carpathia's* wireless announcing the fate of the *Titanic* and the people aboard her. The message must have affected the captains of these ships very deeply: they would understand far better than the travelling public what it meant to lose such a beautiful ship on her first voyage.

The only thing now left to be done was to get the lifeboats away as quickly as possible, and to this task the other officers were in the meantime devoting all their endeavours. Mr Lightoller sent away boat after boat: in one he had put twenty-four women and children, in another thirty, in another thirty-five; and then, running short of seamen to man the boats he sent Major Peuchen, an expert yachtsman, in the next, to help with its navigation. By the time these had been filled, he had difficulty in finding women for the fifth and sixth boats for the reasons already stated. All this time the passengers remained – to use his own expression – 'as quiet as if in church'. To man and supervise the loading of six boats must have taken him nearly up to the time of the *Titanic's* sinking, taking an average of some twenty minutes to a boat. Still at work to the end, he remained on the ship till she sank and went down with her. His evidence before the United States Committee was as follows: 'Did you leave the ship?' 'No, sir.' 'Did the ship leave you?' 'Yes, sir.'

It was a piece of work well and cleanly done, and his escape from the ship, one of the most wonderful of all, seems almost a reward for his devotion to duty.

Captain Smith, Officers Wilde and Murdock were similarly engaged in other parts of the ship, urging women to get in the boats, in some cases directing junior officers to go down in some of them – Officers Pitman, Boxhall, and Lowe were sent in this way – in others placing members of the crew in charge. As the boats were lowered, orders were shouted to them where to make for: some were told to stand by and wait for further instructions, others to row for the light of the disappearing steamer.

It is a pitiful thing to recall the effects of sending down the first boats half full. In some cases men in the company of their wives had actually taken seats in the boats – young men, married only a few weeks and on their wedding trip – and had done so only because no more women could then be found; but the strict interpretation by the particular officer in charge there of the rule of 'Women and children only', compelled them to get out again. Some of these boats were lowered and reached the *Carpathia* with many vacant seats. The anguish of the young wives in such circumstances can only be imagined. In other parts of the ship, however, a different interpretation was placed on the rule, and men were allowed and even invited by officers to get in – not only to form part of the crew, but even as passengers. This, of course, in the first boats and when no more women could be found.

The varied understanding of this rule was a frequent subject of discussion on the *Carpathia* – in fact, the rule itself was debated with much heart-searching. There were not wanting many who doubted the justice of its rigid enforcement, who could not think it well that a husband should be separated from his wife and family, leaving them penniless, or a young bridegroom from his wife of a few short weeks, while ladies with few relatives, with no one dependent upon them, and few responsibilities of any kind, were saved. It was mostly these ladies who pressed this view, and even men seemed to think there was a good deal to be said for it. Perhaps there is, theoretically, but it would be impossible, I think, in practice. To quote Mr Lightoller again in his evidence before the United States Senate Committee – when asked if it was a rule of the sea that women and children be saved first, he replied, 'No, it is a rule of human nature.' That is no doubt the real reason for its existence.

But the selective process of circumstances brought about results that were very bitter to some. It was heartrending for ladies who had lost all they held dearest in the world to hear that in one boat was a stoker picked up out of the sea so drunk that he stood up and brandished his arms about, and had to be thrown down by ladies and sat upon to keep him quiet. If comparisons can be drawn, it did seem better that an educated, refined man should be saved than one who had flown to drink as his refuge in time of danger.

These discussions turned sometimes to the old enquiry – 'What is the purpose of all this? Why the disaster? Why this man saved and that man lost? Who has arranged that my husband should live a few short happy years in the world, and the happiest days in those years with me these last few weeks, and then be taken from me?' I heard no one attribute all this to a Divine Power who ordains and arranges the lives of men, and as part of a definite scheme sends such calamity and misery in order to purify, to teach, to spiritualise. I do not say there were not people who thought and said they saw Divine Wisdom in it all, so inscrutable that we in our ignorance saw it not; but I did not hear it expressed, and this book is intended to be no more than a partial chronicle of the many different experiences and convictions.

There were those, on the other hand, who did not fail to say emphatically that indifference to the rights and feelings of others, blindness to duty towards our fellow men and women, was in the last analysis the cause of most of the human misery in the world. And it should undoubtedly appeal more to our sense of justice to attribute these things to our own lack of consideration for others than to shift the responsibility on to a Power whom we first postulate as being All-wise and All-loving.

All the boats were lowered and sent away by about 2 a.m., and by this time the ship was very low in the water, the forecastle deck completely submerged, and the sea creeping steadily up to the bridge and probably only a few yards away.

No one on the ship can have had any doubt now as to her ultimate fate, and yet the fifteen hundred passengers and crew on board made no demonstration, and not a sound came from them as they stood quietly on the decks or went about their duties below. It seems incredible, and yet if it was a continuation of the same feeling that existed on deck before the boats left – and I have no doubt it was – the explanation is straightforward and reasonable in its simplicity. An attempt is made in the last chapter to show why the attitude of the crowd was so quietly courageous. There are accounts which picture excited crowds running about the deck in terror, fighting and struggling, but two of the most accurate observers, Colonel Gracie and Mr Lightoller, affirm that this was not so, that absolute order and quietness prevailed. The band still played to cheer the hearts of all near; the engineers and their crew – I have never heard anyone speak of a single engineer being seen on deck – still worked at the electric light engines, far away below, keeping them going until no human being could do so a second longer, right until the ship tilted on end and the engines broke loose and fell down. The light failed then only because the engines were no longer there to produce light, not because the men who worked them were not standing by them to do their duty. To be down in the bowels of the ship, far away from the deck where at any rate there was a chance of a dive and a swim and a possible rescue; to know that when the ship went – as they knew it must soon – there could be no possible hope of climbing up in time to reach the sea; to know all these things and yet to keep the engines going that the decks might be lighted to the last moment, required sublime courage.

But this courage is required of every engineer and it is not called by that name: it is called 'duty'. To stand by his engines to the last possible moment is his duty. There could be no better example of the supremest courage being but duty well done than to remember the engineers of the *Titanic* still at work as she heeled over and flung them with their engines down the length of the ship. The simple statement that the lights kept on to the last is really their epitaph, but Lowell's words would seem to apply to them with peculiar force:

> The longer on this earth we live
> And weigh the various qualities of men –
> The more we feel the high, stern-featured beauty
> Of plain devotedness to duty.
> Steadfast and still, nor paid with mortal praise,
> But finding amplest recompense
> For life's ungarlanded expense
> In work done squarely and unwasted days.

For some time before she sank, the *Titanic* had a considerable list to port, so much so that one boat at any rate swung so far away from the side that difficulty was experienced in getting passengers in. This list was increased towards the end, and Colonel Gracie relates that Mr Lightoller, who has a deep, powerful voice, ordered all passengers to the starboard side. This was close before the end. They crossed over, and as they did so a crowd of steerage passengers rushed up and filled the decks so full that there was barely room to move. Soon afterwards the great vessel swung slowly, stern in the air, the lights went out, and while some were flung into the water and others dived off, the great majority still clung to the rails, to the sides and roofs of deck-structures, lying prone on the deck. And in this position they were when, a few minutes later, the enormous vessel dived obliquely downwards. As she went, no doubt many still clung to the rails, but most would do their best to get away from her and jump as she slid forwards and downwards. Whatever they did, there can be little question that most of them would be taken down by suction, to come up again a few moments later and to fill the air with those heartrending cries which fell on the ears of those in the lifeboats with such amazement. Another survivor, on the other hand, relates that he had dived from the stern before she heeled over, and swam round under her enormous triple screws lifted by now high out of the water as she stood on end. Fascinated by the extraordinary sight, he watched them up above his head, but presently realising the necessity of getting away as quickly as possible, he started to swim from the ship, but as he did she dived forward, the screws passing near his head. His experience is that not only was no suction present, but even a wave was created which washed him away from the place where she had gone down.

Of all those fifteen hundred people, flung into the sea as the *Titanic* went down, innocent victims of thoughtlessness and apathy of those responsible for their safety, only a very few found their way to the *Carpathia*. It will serve no good purpose to dwell any longer on the scene of helpless men and women struggling in the water. The heart of everyone who has read of their helplessness has gone out to them in deepest love and sympathy; and the knowledge that their struggle in the water was in most cases short and not physically painful because of the low temperature – the evidence seems to show that few lost their lives by drowning – is some consolation.

If everyone sees to it that his sympathy with them is so practical as to force him to follow up the question of reforms personally, not leaving it to experts alone, then he will have at any rate done something to atone for the loss of so many valuable lives.

We had now better follow the adventures of those who were rescued from the final event in the disaster. Two accounts – those of Colonel Gracie and Mr Lightoller – agree very closely. The former went down clinging to a rail, the latter dived before the ship went right under, but was sucked down and held against one of the blowers. They were both carried down for what seemed a long distance, but Mr Lightoller was finally blown up again by a 'terrific gust' that came up the blower and forced him clear. Colonel Gracie came to the surface after holding his breath for what seemed an eternity, and they both swam about holding on to any wreckage they could find. Finally they saw an upturned collapsible boat and climbed on it in company with twenty other men, among them Bride, the Marconi operator. After remaining thus for some hours, with the sea washing them to the waist, they stood up as day broke, in two rows, back to back, balancing themselves as well as they could, and afraid to turn lest the boat should roll over. Finally a lifeboat saw them and took them off, an operation attended with the greatest difficulty, and they reached the *Carpathia* in the early dawn. Not many people have gone through such an experience as those men did, lying all night on an overturned, ill-balanced boat, and praying together, as they did all the time, for the day and a ship to take them off.

Some account must now be attempted of the journey of the fleet of boats to the *Carpathia*, but it must necessarily be very brief. Experiences differed considerably: some had no encounters at all with icebergs, no lack of men to row, discovered lights and food and water, were picked up after only a few hours' exposure, and suffered very little discomfort; others seemed to see icebergs round them all night long and to be always rowing round them; others had so few men aboard – in some cases only two or three – that ladies had to row and in one case to steer, found no lights, food or water, and were adrift many hours, in some cases nearly eight.

The first boat to be picked up by the *Carpathia* was one in charge of Mr Boxhall. There was only one other man rowing and ladies worked at the oars. A green light burning in this boat all night was the greatest comfort to the rest of us who had nothing to steer by: although it meant little in the way of safety in itself, it was a point to which we could look. The green light was the first intimation Captain Rostron had of our position, and he steered for it and picked up its passengers first.

Mr Pitman was sent by First Officer Murdock in charge of boat 5, with forty passengers and five of the crew. It would have held more, but no women could be found at the time it was lowered. Mr Pitman says that after leaving the ship he felt confident she would float and they would all return. A passenger in this boat relates that men could not be induced to embark when she went down, and made appointments for the next morning with him. Tied to boat 5 was boat 7, one of those that contained few people: a few were transferred from number 5, but it would have held many more.

Fifth Officer Lowe was in charge of boat 14, with fifty-five women and children, and some of the crew. So full was the boat that as she went down Mr Lowe had to fire his revolver along the ship's side to prevent any more climbing in and causing her to buckle. This boat, like boat 13, was difficult to release from the lowering tackle, and had to be cut away after reaching the sea. Mr Lowe took in charge four other boats, tied them together with lines, found some of them not full, and transferred all his passengers to these, distributing them in the darkness as well as he could. Then returning to the place where the *Titanic* had sunk, he picked up some of those swimming in the water and went back to the four boats. On the way to the *Carpathia* he encountered one of the collapsible boats, and took aboard all those in her, as she seemed to be sinking.

Boat 12 was one of the four tied together, and the seaman in charge testified that he tried to row to the drowning, but with forty women and children and only one other man to row, it was not possible to pull such a heavy boat to the scene of the wreck.

Boat 2 was a small ship's boat and had four or five passengers and seven of the crew.

Boat 4 was one of the last to leave on the port side, and by this time there was such a list that deck chairs had to bridge the gap between the boat and the deck. When lowered, it remained for some time still attached to the ropes, and as the *Titanic* was rapidly sinking it seemed she would be pulled under. The boat was full of women, who besought the sailors to leave the ship, but in obedience to orders from the captain to stand by the cargo port, they remained near; so near, in fact, that they heard china falling and smashing as the ship went down by the head, and were nearly hit by wreckage thrown overboard by some of the officers and crew and intended to serve as rafts. They got clear finally, and were only a short distance away when the ship sank, so that they were able to pull some men aboard as they came to the surface.

This boat had an unpleasant experience in the night with icebergs; many were seen and avoided with difficulty.

Quartermaster Hichens was in charge of boat 6, and in the absence of sailors Major Peuchen was sent to help to man her. They were told to make for the light of the steamer seen on the port side, and followed it until it disappeared. There were forty women and children here.

Boat 8 had only one seaman, and as Captain Smith had enforced the rule of 'Women and children only', ladies had to row. Later in the night, when little progress had been made, the seaman took an oar and put a lady in charge of the tiller. This boat again was in the midst of icebergs.

Of the four collapsible boats – although collapsible is not really the correct term, for only a small portion collapses, the canvas edge; 'surf boats' is really their name – one was launched at the last moment by being pushed over as the sea rose to the edge of the deck, and was never righted. This is the one twenty men climbed on. Another was caught up by Mr Lowe and the passengers transferred, with the exception of three men who had perished from the effects of immersion. The boat was allowed to drift away and was found more than a month later by the *Celtic* in just the same condition. It is interesting to note how long this boat had remained afloat after she was supposed to be no longer seaworthy. A curious coincidence arose from the fact that one of my brothers happened to be travelling on the *Celtic*, and looking over the side, saw adrift on the sea a boat belonging to the *Titanic* in which I had been wrecked.

The two other collapsible boats came to the *Carpathia* carrying full loads of passengers: in one, the forward starboard boat and one of the last to leave, was Mr Ismay. Here four Chinamen were concealed under the feet of the passengers. How they got there no one knew – or indeed how they happened to be on the *Titanic*, for by the immigration laws of the United States they are not allowed to enter her ports.

It must be said, in conclusion, that there is the greatest cause for gratitude that all the boats launched carried their passengers safely to the rescue ship. It would not be right to accept this fact without calling attention to it: it would be easy to enumerate many things which might have been present as elements of danger.

But at the same time, one question recurs constantly to thought, and seems to call instantly for some reply.

Was it not possible during the three and a half hours that elapsed between the collision and the foundering to construct some kind of raft, sufficiently substantial to keep some of the passengers afloat?

The captain certainly knew such a raft would be urgently needed: it would seem to have been possible to tear up the decks and lash the planks to tables, wardrobes, deckchairs, etc.

But the only men who could really undertake such work – the sailors – were far too few even to lower and man the boats: not one of them could be spared for making rafts.

Again, perhaps the very tools with which such work would be carried out were in those parts of the hold which were from the first flooded with water. Perhaps these are the answers to a question which must have been asked hundreds of times.

7

The *Carpathia*'s Return to New York

The journey of the *Carpathia* from the time she caught the 'CQD' from the *Titanic* at about 12.30 a.m. on Monday morning and turned swiftly about to her rescue, until she arrived at New York on the following Thursday at 8.30 p.m. was one that demanded of the captain, officers and crew of the vessel the most exact knowledge of navigation, the utmost vigilance in every department both before and after the rescue, and a capacity for organisation that must sometimes have been taxed to the breaking point.

The extent to which all these qualities were found present and the manner in which they were exercised stands to the everlasting credit of the Cunard Line and those of its servants who were in charge of the *Carpathia*. Captain Rostron's part in all this is a great one, and wrapped up though his action is in a modesty that is conspicuous in its nobility, it stands out even in his own account as a piece of work well and courageously done.

As soon as the *Titanic* called for help and gave her position, the *Carpathia* was turned and headed north: all hands were called on duty, a new watch of stokers was put on, and the highest speed of which she was capable was demanded of the engineers, with the result that the distance of fifty-eight miles between the two ships was covered in three and a half hours, a speed well beyond her normal capacity. The three doctors on board each took charge of a saloon, in readiness to render help to any who needed their services, the stewards and catering staff were hard at work preparing hot drinks and meals, and the purser's staff ready with blankets and berths for the shipwrecked passengers as soon as they got on board. On deck the sailors got ready lifeboats, swung them out on the davits, and stood by, prepared to lower away their crews if necessary; fixed rope ladders, cradle-chairs, nooses, and bags for the children at the hatches, to haul the rescued up the side. On the bridge was the captain with his officers, peering into the darkness eagerly to catch the first signs of the crippled *Titanic*, hoping, in spite of her last despairing message of 'Sinking by the head', to find her still afloat when her position was reached. A double watch of lookout men was set, for there were other things as well as the *Titanic* to look for that night, and soon they found them. As Captain Rostron said in his evidence, they saw icebergs on either side of them between 2.45 and 4 a.m., passing twenty large ones, one hundred to two hundred feet high, and many smaller ones, and 'frequently had to manoeuvre the ship to avoid them'. It was a time when every faculty was called upon for the highest use of which it was capable. With the knowledge before them that the enormous *Titanic*, the supposedly unsinkable ship, had struck ice and was sinking rapidly; with the lookout constantly calling to the bridge, as he must have done, 'Icebergs on the starboard', 'Icebergs on the port', it required courage and judgement beyond the ordinary to drive the ship ahead through that lane of icebergs and 'manoeuvre round them'. As he himself said, he 'took the risk of full speed in his desire to save life, and probably some people might blame him for taking such a risk'. But the Senate Committee assured him that they, at any rate, would not, and we of the lifeboats have certainly no desire to do so.

The ship was finally stopped at 4 a.m., with an iceberg reported dead ahead (the same no doubt we had to row around in boat 13 as we approached the *Carpathia*), and about the same time the first lifeboat was sighted. Again she had to be manoeuvred round the iceberg to pick up the boat, which was the one in charge of Mr Boxhall. From him the captain learned that the *Titanic* had gone down, and that he was too late to save anyone but those in lifeboats, which he could now see drawing up from every part of the horizon. Meanwhile, the passengers of the *Carpathia*, some of them aroused by the unusual vibration of the screw, some by sailors tramping overhead as they swung away the lifeboats and got ropes and lowering tackle ready, were beginning to come on deck just as day broke; and here an extraordinary sight met their eyes. As far as the eye could reach to the north and west lay an unbroken stretch of field ice, with icebergs still attached to the floe and rearing aloft their mass as a hill might suddenly rise from a level plain. Ahead and to the south and east huge floating monsters were showing up through the waning darkness, their number added to moment by moment as the dawn broke and flushed the horizon pink. It is remarkable how 'busy' all those icebergs made the sea look: to have gone to bed with nothing but sea and sky and to come on deck to find so many objects in sight made quite a change in the character of the sea: it looked quite crowded; and a lifeboat alongside and people clambering aboard, mostly women, in nightdresses and dressing gowns, in cloaks and shawls, in anything but ordinary clothes! Out ahead and on all sides little torches glittered faintly for a few moments and then guttered out – and shouts and cheers floated across the quiet sea. It would be difficult to imagine a more unexpected sight than this that lay before the *Carpathia*'s passengers as they lined the sides that morning in the early dawn.

No novelist would dare to picture such an array of beautiful climatic conditions – the rosy dawn, the morning star, the moon on the horizon, the sea stretching in level beauty to the skyline – and on this sea to place an icefield like the Arctic regions and icebergs in numbers everywhere – white and turning pink and deadly cold – and near them, rowing round the icebergs to avoid them, little boats coming suddenly out of mid-ocean, with passengers rescued from the most wonderful ship the world has known. No artist would have conceived such a picture: it would have seemed so highly dramatic as to border on the impossible, and would not have been attempted. Such a combination of events would pass the limit permitted the imagination of both author and artist.

The passengers crowded the rails and looked down at us as we rowed up in the early morning; stood quietly aside while the crew at the gangways below took us aboard, and watched us as if the ship had been in dock and we had rowed up to join her in a somewhat unusual way. Some of them have related that we were very quiet as we came aboard: it is quite true, we were; but so were they. There was very little excitement on either side: just the quiet demeanour of people who are in the presence of something too big as yet to lie within their mental grasp, and which they cannot yet discuss. And so they asked us politely to have hot coffee, which we did; and food, which we generally declined – we were not hungry – and they said very little at first about the lost *Titanic* and our adventures in the night.

Much that is exaggerated and false has been written about the mental condition of passengers as they came aboard: we have been described as being too dazed to understand what was happening, as being too overwhelmed to speak, and as looking before us with 'set, staring gaze', 'dazed with the shadow of the dread event'. That is, no doubt, what most people would expect in the circumstances, but I know it does not give a faithful record of how we did arrive: in fact it is simply not true. As remarked before, the one thing that matters in describing an event of this kind is the exact truth, as near as the fallible human mind can state it; and my own impression of our mental condition is that of supreme gratitude and relief at treading the firm decks of a ship again. I am aware that experiences differed considerably according to the boats occupied; that those who were uncertain of the fate of their relatives and friends had much to make them anxious and troubled; and that it is not possible to look into another person's consciousness and say what is written there; but dealing with mental conditions as far as they are delineated by facial and bodily expressions, I think joy, relief, gratitude were the dominant emotions written on the faces of those who climbed the rope ladders and were hauled up in cradles.

It must not be forgotten that no one in any one boat knew who were saved in other boats: few knew even how many boats there were and how many passengers could be saved. It was at the time probable that friends would follow them to the *Carpathia*, or be found on other steamers, or even on the pier at which we landed. The hysterical scenes that have been described are imaginative; true, one woman did fill the saloon with hysterical cries immediately after coming aboard, but she could not have known for a certainty that any of her friends were lost: probably the sense of relief after some hours of journeying about the sea was too much for her for a time.

One of the first things we did was to crowd round a steward with a bundle of telegraph forms. He was the bearer of the welcome news that passengers might send Marconigrams to their relatives free of charge, and soon he bore away the first sheaf of hastily scribbled messages to the operator; by the time the last boatload was aboard, the pile must have risen high in the Marconi cabin. We learned afterwards that many of these never reached their destination; and this is not a matter for surprise. There was only one operator – Cottam – on board, and although he was assisted to some extent later, when Bride from the *Titanic* had recovered from his injuries sufficiently to work the apparatus, he had so much to do that he fell asleep over this work on Tuesday night after three days' continuous duty without rest. But we did not know the messages were held back, and imagined our friends were aware of our safety; then, too, a roll call of the rescued was held in the *Carpathia*'s saloon on the Monday, and this was Marconied to land in advance of all messages. It seemed certain, then, that friends at home would have all anxiety removed, but there were mistakes in the official list first telegraphed. The experience of my own friends illustrates this: the Marconigram I wrote never got through to England; nor was my name ever mentioned in any list of the saved (even a week after landing in New York, I saw it in a black-edged 'final' list of the missing), and it seemed certain that I had never reached the *Carpathia*; so much so that, as I write, there are before me obituary notices from the English papers giving a short sketch of my life in England. After landing in New York and realising from the lists of the saved which a reporter showed me that my friends had no news since the *Titanic* sank on Monday morning until that night (Thursday 9 p.m.), I cabled to England at once (as I had but two shillings rescued from the *Titanic*, the White Star Line paid for the cables), but the messages were not delivered until 8.20 a.m. next morning. At 9 a.m. my friends read in the papers a short account of the disaster which I had supplied to the press, so that they knew of my safety and experiences in the wreck almost at the same time. I am grateful to remember that many of my friends in London refused to count me among the missing during the three days when I was so reported.

There is another side to this record of how the news came through, and a sad one, indeed. Again I wish it were not necessary to tell such things, but since they all bear on the equipment of the transatlantic lines – powerful Marconi apparatus, relays of operators, etc. – it is best they should be told. The name of an American gentleman – the same who sat near me in the library on Sunday afternoon and whom I identified later from a photograph – was consistently reported in the lists as saved and aboard the *Carpathia*: his son journeyed to New York to meet him, rejoicing at his deliverance, and never found him there. When I met his family some days later and was able to give them some details of his life aboard ship, it seemed almost cruel to tell them of the opposite experience that had befallen my friends at home.

Returning to the journey of the *Carpathia* – the last boatload of passengers was taken aboard at 8.30 a.m., the lifeboats were hauled on deck while the collapsibles were abandoned, and the *Carpathia* proceeded to steam round the scene of the wreck in the hope of picking up anyone floating on wreckage. Before doing so the captain arranged in the saloon a service over the spot where the *Titanic* sank, as nearly as could be calculated – a service, as he said, of respect to those who were lost and of gratitude for those who were saved.

She cruised round and round the scene, but found nothing to indicate there was any hope of picking up more passengers; and as the *Californian* had now arrived, followed shortly afterwards by the *Birma*, a Russian tramp steamer, Captain Rostron decided to leave any further search to them and to make all speed with the rescued to land. As we moved round, there was surprisingly little wreckage to be seen: wooden deckchairs and small pieces of other wood, but nothing of any size. But covering the sea in huge patches was a mass of reddish-yellow 'seaweed', as we called it for want of a name. It was said to be cork, but I never heard definitely its correct description.

The problem of where to land us had next to be decided. The *Carpathia* was bound for Gibraltar, and the captain might continue his journey there, landing us at the Azores on the way; but he would require more linen and provisions, the passengers were mostly women and children, ill-clad, dishevelled, and in need of many attentions he could not give them. Then, too, he would soon be out of the range of wireless communication, with the weak apparatus his ship had, and he soon decided against that course. Halifax was the nearest in point of distance, but this meant steaming north through the ice, and he thought his passengers did not want to see more ice. He headed back therefore to New York, which he had left the previous Thursday, working all afternoon along the edge of the icefield which stretched away north as far as the unaided eye could reach. I have wondered since if we could possibly have landed our passengers on this ice-floe from the lifeboats and gone back to pick up those swimming, had we known it was there; I should think it quite feasible to have done so. It was certainly an extraordinary sight to stand on deck and see the sea covered with solid ice, white and dazzling in the sun and dotted here and there with icebergs. We ran close up, only two or three hundred yards away, and steamed parallel to the floe, until it ended towards night and we saw to our infinite satisfaction the last of the icebergs and the field fading away astern. Many of the rescued have no wish ever to see an iceberg again. We learnt afterwards the field was nearly seventy miles long and twelve miles wide, and had lain between us and the *Birma* on her way to the rescue. Mr Boxhall testified that he had crossed the Grand Banks many times, but had never seen field ice before. The testimony of the captains and officers of other steamers in the neighbourhood is of the same kind: they had 'never seen so many icebergs this time of the year, or 'never seen such dangerous ice-floes and threatening bergs'. Undoubtedly the *Titanic* was faced that night with unusual and unexpected conditions of ice: the captain knew not the extent of these conditions, but he knew somewhat of their existence. Alas, that he heeded not their warning!

During the day, the bodies of eight of the crew were committed to the deep: four of them had been taken out of the boats dead and four died during the day. The engines were stopped and all passengers on deck bared their heads while a short service was read; when it was over the ship steamed on again to carry the living back to land.

The passengers on the *Carpathia* were by now hard at work finding clothing for the survivors: the barber's shop was raided for ties, collars, hairpins, combs, etc., of which it happened there was a large stock in hand; one good Samaritan went round the ship with a box of toothbrushes offering them indiscriminately to all. In some cases, clothing could not be found for the ladies and they spent the rest of the time on board in their dressing gowns and cloaks in which they came away from the *Titanic*. They even slept in them, for, in the absence of berths, women had to sleep on the floor of the saloons and in the library each night on straw *paillasses*, and here it was not possible to undress properly. The men were given the smoking room floor and a supply of blankets, but the room was small, and some elected to sleep out on deck. I found a pile of towels on the bathroom floor ready for next morning's baths, and made up a very comfortable bed on these. Later I was waked in the middle of the night by a man offering me a berth in his four-berth cabin: another occupant was unable to leave his berth for physical reasons, and so the cabin could not be given up to ladies.

On Tuesday the survivors met in the saloon and formed a committee among themselves to collect subscriptions for a general fund, out of which it was resolved by vote to provide as far as possible for the destitute among the steerage passengers, to present a loving cup to Captain Rostron and medals to the officers and crew of the *Carpathia*, and to divide any surplus among the crew of the *Titanic*. The work of this committee is not yet (1 June) at an end, but all the resolutions except the last one have been acted upon, and that is now receiving the attention of the committee. The presentations to the captain and crew were made the day the *Carpathia* returned to New York from her Mediterranean trip, and it is a pleasure to all the survivors to know that the United States Senate has recognised the service rendered to humanity by the *Carpathia* and has voted Captain Rostron a gold medal commemorative of the rescue. On the afternoon of Tuesday, I visited the steerage in company with a fellow passenger, to take down the names of all who were saved. We grouped them into nationalities – English, Irish, and Swedish mostly – and learnt from them their names and homes, the amount of money they possessed, and whether they had friends in America. The Irish girls almost universally had no money rescued from the wreck, and were going to friends in New York or places near, while the Swedish passengers, among whom were a considerable number of men, had saved the greater part of their money and in addition had railway tickets through to their destinations inland. The saving of their money marked a curious racial difference, for which I can offer no explanation: no doubt the Irish girls never had very much but they must have had the necessary amount fixed by the immigration laws. There were some pitiful cases of women with children and the husband lost; some with one or two children saved and the others lost; in one case, a whole family was missing, and only a friend left to tell of them. Among the Irish group was one girl of really remarkable beauty, black hair and deep violet eyes with long lashes, and perfectly shaped features, and quite young, not more than eighteen or twenty; I think she lost no relatives on the *Titanic*.

The following letter to the London *Times* is reproduced here to show something of what our feeling was on board the *Carpathia* towards the loss of the *Titanic*. It was written soon after we had the definite information on the Wednesday that ice warnings had been sent to the *Titanic*, and when we all felt that something must be done to awaken public opinion to safeguard ocean travel in the future. We were not aware, of course, how much the outside world knew, and it seemed well to do something to inform the English public of what had happened at as early an opportunity as possible. I have not had occasion to change any of the opinions expressed in this letter.

SIR

As one of few surviving Englishmen from the steamship *Titanic*, which sank in mid-Atlantic on Monday morning last, I am asking you to lay before your readers a few facts concerning the disaster, in the hope that something may be done in the near future to ensure the safety of that portion of the travelling public who use the Atlantic highway for business or pleasure.

I wish to dissociate myself entirely from any report that would seek to fix the responsibility on any person or persons or body of people, and by simply calling attention to matters of fact the authenticity of which is, I think, beyond question and can be established in any Court of Inquiry, to allow your readers to draw their own conclusions as to the responsibility for the collision.

First, that it was known to those in charge of the *Titanic* that we were in the iceberg region; that the atmospheric and temperature conditions suggested the near presence of icebergs; that a wireless message was received from a ship ahead of us warning us that they had been seen in the locality of which latitude and longitude were given.

Second, that at the time of the collision the *Titanic* was running at a high rate of speed.

Third, that the accommodation for saving passengers and crew was totally inadequate, being sufficient only for a total of about 950. This gave, with the highest possible complement of 3,400, a less than one in three chance of being saved in the case of accident.

Fourth, that the number landed in the *Carpathia*, approximately 700, is a high percentage of the possible 950, and bears excellent testimony to the courage, resource, and devotion to duty of the officers and crew of the vessel; many instances of their nobility and personal self-sacrifice are within our possession, and we know that they did all they could do with the means at their disposal.

Fifth, that the practice of running mail and passenger vessels through fog and iceberg regions at a high speed is a common one; they are timed to run almost as an express train is run, and they cannot, therefore, slow down more than a few knots in time of possible danger.

I have neither knowledge nor experience to say what remedies I consider should be applied; but, perhaps, the following suggestions may serve as a help:

First, that no vessel should be allowed to leave a British port without sufficient boat and other accommodation to allow each passenger and member of the crew a seat; and that at the time of booking this fact should be pointed out to a passenger, and the number of the seat in the particular boat allotted to him then.

Second, that as soon as is practicable after sailing each passenger should go through boat drill in company with the crew assigned to his boat.

Third, that each passenger boat engaged in the transatlantic service should be instructed to slow down to a few knots when in the iceberg region, and should be fitted with an efficient searchlight.

Yours faithfully,

LAWRENCE BEESLEY.

It seemed well, too, while on the *Carpathia* to prepare as accurate an account as possible of the disaster and to have this ready for the press, in order to calm public opinion and to forestall the incorrect and hysterical accounts which some American reporters are in the habit of preparing on occasions of this kind. The first impression is often the most permanent, and in a disaster of this magnitude, where exact and accurate information is so necessary, preparation of a report was essential. It was written in odd corners of the deck and saloon of the *Carpathia*, and fell, it seemed very happily, into the hands of the one reporter who could best deal with it, the Associated Press. I understand it was the first report that came through and had a good deal of the effect intended.

The *Carpathia* returned to New York in almost every kind of climatic conditions: icebergs, icefields and bitter cold to commence with; brilliant warm sun, thunder and lightning in the middle of one night (and so closely did the peal follow the flash that women in the saloon leaped up in alarm saying rockets were being sent up again); cold winds most of the time; fogs every morning and during a good part of one day, with the foghorn blowing constantly; rain; choppy sea with the spray blowing overboard and coming in through the saloon windows; we said we had almost everything but hot weather and stormy seas. So that when we were told that Nantucket Lightship had been sighted on Thursday morning from the bridge, a great sigh of relief went round to think New York and land would be reached before next morning.

There is no doubt that a good many felt the waiting period of those four days very trying: the ship crowded far beyond its limits of comfort, the want of necessities of clothing and toilet, and above all the anticipation of meeting with relatives on the pier, with, in many cases, the knowledge that other friends were left behind and would not return home again. A few looked forward to meeting on the pier their friends to whom they had said au revoir on the *Titanic*'s deck, brought there by a faster boat, they said, or at any rate to hear that they were following behind us in another boat: a very few, indeed, for the thought of the icy water and the many hours' immersion seemed to weigh against such a possibility; but we encouraged them to hope the *Californian* and the *Birma* had picked some up; stranger things have happened, and we had all been through strange experiences. But in the midst of this rather tense feeling, one fact stands out as remarkable – no one was ill. Captain Rostron testified that on Tuesday the doctor reported a clean bill of health, except for frostbites and shaken nerves. There were none of the illnesses supposed to follow from exposure for hours in the cold night – and, it must be remembered, a considerable number swam about for some time when the *Titanic* sank, and then either sat for hours in their wet things or lay flat on an upturned boat with the sea water washing partly over them until they were taken off in a lifeboat; no scenes of women weeping and brooding over their losses hour by hour until they were driven mad with grief – yet all this has been reported to the press by people on board the *Carpathia*. These women met their sorrow with the sublimest courage, came on deck and talked with their fellow men and women face to face, and in the midst of their loss did not forget to rejoice with those who had joined their friends on the *Carpathia*'s deck or come with them in a boat. There was no need for those ashore to call the *Carpathia* a 'death-ship', or to send coroners and coffins to the pier to meet her: her passengers were generally in good health and they did not pretend they were not.

Presently land came in sight, and very good it was to see it again: it was eight days since we left Southampton, but the time seemed to have 'stretched out to the crack of doom', and to have become eight weeks instead. So many dramatic incidents had been crowded into the last few days that the first four peaceful, uneventful days, marked by nothing that seared the memory, had faded almost out of recollection. It needed an effort to return to Southampton, Cherbourg and Queenstown, as though returning to some event of last year. I think we all realised that time may be measured more by events than by seconds and minutes: what the astronomer would call '2.20 a.m. 15 April 1912', the survivors called 'the sinking of the *Titanic*'; the 'hours' that followed were designated 'being adrift in an open sea', and '4.30 a.m.' was 'being rescued by the *Carpathia*'. The clock was a mental one, and the hours, minutes and seconds marked deeply on its face were emotions, strong and silent.

Surrounded by tugs of every kind, from which (as well as from every available building near the river) magnesium bombs were shot off by photographers, while reporters shouted for news of the disaster and photographs of passengers, the *Carpathia* drew slowly to her station at the Cunard pier, the gangways were pushed across, and we set foot at last on American soil, very thankful, grateful people.

The mental and physical condition of the rescued as they came ashore has, here again, been greatly exaggerated – one description says we were 'half-fainting, half-hysterical, bordering on hallucination, only now beginning to realise the horror'. It is unfortunate such pictures should be presented to the world. There were some painful scenes of meeting between relatives of those who were lost, but once again women showed their self-control and went through the ordeal in most cases with extraordinary calm. It is well to record that the same account added: 'A few, strangely enough, are calm and lucid'; if for 'few' we read 'a large majority', it will be much nearer the true description of the landing on the Cunard pier in New York. There seems to be no adequate reason why a report of such a scene should depict mainly the sorrow and grief, should seek for every detail to satisfy the horrible and the morbid in the human mind. The first questions the excited crowds of reporters asked as they crowded round were whether it was true that officers shot passengers, and then themselves; whether passengers shot each other; whether any scenes of horror had been noticed, and what they were.

It would have been well to have noticed the wonderful state of health of most of the rescued, their gratitude for their deliverance, the thousand and one things that gave cause for rejoicing. In the midst of so much description of the hysterical side of the scene, place should be found for the normal – and I venture to think the normal was the dominant feature in the landing that night. In the last chapter I shall try to record the persistence of the normal all through the disaster. Nothing has been a greater surprise than to find people that do not act in conditions of danger and grief as they would be generally supposed to act – and, I must add, as they are generally described as acting.

And so, with her work of rescue well done, the good ship *Carpathia* returned to New York. Everyone who came in her, everyone on the dock, and everyone who heard of her journey will agree with Captain Rostron when he says: 'I thank God that I was within wireless hailing distance, and that I got there in time to pick up the survivors of the wreck.'

8

The Lessons Taught by the *Titanic*'s Loss

One of the most pitiful things in the relations of human beings to each other – the action and reaction of events that is called concretely 'human life' – is that every now and then some of them should be called upon to lay down their lives from no sense of imperative, calculated duty such as inspires the soldier or the sailor, but suddenly, without any previous knowledge or warning of danger, without any opportunity of escape, and without any desire to risk such conditions of danger of their own free will. It is a blot on our civilisation that these things are necessary from time to time, to arouse those responsible for the safety of human life from the lethargic selfishness which has governed them. The *Titanic*'s two thousand odd passengers went aboard thinking they were on an absolutely safe ship, and all the time there were many people – designers, builders, experts, government officials – who knew there were insufficient boats on board, that the *Titanic* had no right to go fast in iceberg regions – who knew these things and took no steps and enacted no laws to prevent their happening. Not that they omitted to do these things deliberately, but were lulled into a state of selfish inaction from which it needed such a tragedy as this to arouse them. It was a cruel necessity which demanded that a few should die to arouse many millions to a sense of their own insecurity, to the fact that for years the possibility of such a disaster has been imminent. Passengers have known none of these things, and while no good end would have been served by relating to them needless tales of danger on the high seas, one thing is certain – that, had they known them, many would not have travelled in such conditions and thereby safeguards would soon have been forced on the builders, the companies, and the Government. But there were people who knew and did not fail to call attention to the dangers: in the House of Commons the matter has been frequently brought up privately, and an American naval officer, Captain E. K. Roden, in an article that has since been widely reproduced, called attention to the defects of this very ship, the *Titanic* – taking her as an example of all other liners – and pointed out that she was not unsinkable and had not proper boat accommodation.

The question, then, of responsibility for the loss of the *Titanic* must be considered: not from any idea that blame should be laid here or there and a scapegoat provided – that is a waste of time. But if a fixing of responsibility leads to quick and efficient remedy, then it should be done relentlessly: our simple duty to those whom the *Titanic* carried down with her demands no less. Dealing first with the precautions for the safety of the ship as apart from safety appliances, there can be no question, I suppose, that the direct responsibility for the loss of the *Titanic* and so many lives must be laid on her captain. He was responsible for setting the course, day by day and hour by hour, for the speed she was travelling; and he alone would have the power to decide whether or not speed must be slackened with icebergs ahead. No officer would have any right to interfere in the navigation, although they would no doubt be consulted. Nor would any official connected with the management of the line – Mr Ismay, for example – be allowed to direct the captain in these matters, and there is no evidence that he ever tried to do so. The very fact that the captain of a ship has such absolute authority increases his responsibility enormously. Even supposing the White Star Line and Mr Ismay had urged him before sailing to make a record – again an assumption – they cannot be held directly responsible for the collision: he was in charge of the lives of everyone on board and no one but he was supposed to estimate the risk of travelling at the speed he did, when ice was reported ahead of him. His action cannot be justified on the ground of prudent seamanship.

But the question of indirect responsibility raises at once many issues and, I think, removes from Captain Smith a good deal of personal responsibility for the loss of his ship. Some of these issues it will be well to consider.

In the first place, disabusing our minds again of the knowledge that the *Titanic* struck an iceberg and sank, let us estimate the probabilities of such a thing happening. An iceberg is small and occupies little room by comparison with the broad ocean on which it floats; and the chances of another small object like a ship colliding with it and being sunk are very small: the chances are, as a matter of fact, one in a million. This is not a figure of speech: that is the actual risk for total loss by collision with an iceberg as accepted by insurance companies. The one-in-a-million accident was what sunk the *Titanic*.

Even so, had Captain Smith been alone in taking that risk, he would have had to bear all the blame for the resulting disaster. But it seems he is not alone: the same risk has been taken over and over again by fast mail-passenger liners, in fog and in iceberg regions. Their captains have taken the long – very long – chance many times and won every time; he took it as he had done many times before, and lost. Of course, the chances that night of striking an iceberg were much greater than one in a million: they had been enormously increased by the extreme southerly position of icebergs and field ice and by the unusual number of the former. Thinking over the scene that met our eyes from the deck of the *Carpathia* after we boarded her – the great number of icebergs wherever the eye could reach – the chances of *not* hitting one in the darkness of the night seemed small. Indeed, the more one thinks about the *Carpathia* coming at full speed through all those icebergs in the darkness, the more inexplicable does it seem. True, the captain had an extra lookout watch and every sense of every man on the bridge alert to detect the least sign of danger, and again he was not going so fast as the *Titanic* and would have his ship under more control; but granted all that, he appears to have taken a great risk as he dogged and twisted round the awful 200-foot monsters in the dark night. Does it mean that the risk is not so great as we who have seen the abnormal and not the normal side of taking risks with icebergs might suppose? He had his own ship and passengers to consider, and he had no right to take too great a risk.

But Captain Smith could not know icebergs were there in such numbers: what warnings he had of them is not yet thoroughly established – there were probably three – but it is in the highest degree unlikely that he knew that any vessel had seen them in such quantities as we saw them Monday morning; in fact, it is unthinkable. He thought, no doubt, he was taking an ordinary risk, and it turned out to be an extraordinary one. To read some criticisms it would seem as if he deliberately ran his ship in defiance of all custom through a region infested with icebergs, and did a thing which no one has ever done before; that he outraged all precedent by not slowing down. But it is plain that he did not. Every captain who has run full speed through fog and iceberg regions is to blame for the disaster as much as he is:

they got through and he did not. Other liners can go faster than the *Titanic* could possibly do; had they struck ice they would have been injured even more deeply than she was, for it must not be forgotten that the force of impact varies as the *square* of the velocity – i.e., it is four times as much at sixteen knots as at eight knots, nine times as much at twenty-four, and so on. And with not much margin of time left for these fast boats, they must go full speed ahead nearly all the time. Remember how they advertise to 'Leave New York Wednesday, dine in London the following Monday', – and it is done regularly, much as an express train is run to time. Their officers, too, would have been less able to avoid a collision than Murdock of the *Titanic* was, for at the greater speed, they would be on the iceberg in shorter time. Many passengers can tell of crossing with fog a good deal of the way, sometimes almost all the way, and they have been only a few hours late at the end of the journey.

So that it is the custom that is at fault, not one particular captain. Custom is established largely by demand, and supply too is the answer to demand. What the public demanded the White Star Line supplied, and so both the public and the line are concerned with the question of indirect responsibility.

The public has demanded, more and more every year, greater speed as well as greater comfort, and by ceasing to patronise the low-speed boats has gradually forced the pace to what it is at present. Not that speed in itself is a dangerous thing – it is sometimes much safer to go quickly than slowly – but that, given the facilities for speed and the stimulus exerted by the constant public demand for it, occasions arise when the judgement of those in command of a ship becomes swayed – largely unconsciously, no doubt – in favour of taking risks which the smaller liners would never take. The demand on the skipper of a boat like the *Californian*, for example, which lay hove-to nineteen miles away with her engines stopped, is infinitesimal compared with that on Captain Smith. An old traveller told me on the *Carpathia* that he has often grumbled to the officers for what he called absurd precautions in lying-to and wasting his time, which he regarded as very valuable; but after hearing of the *Titanic*'s loss he recognised that he was to some extent responsible for the speed at which she had travelled, and would never be so again. He had been one of the travelling public who had constantly demanded to be taken to his journey's end in the shortest possible time, and had 'made a row' about it if he was likely to be late. There are some businessmen to whom the five or six days on board are exceedingly irksome and represent a waste of time; even an hour saved at the journey's end is a consideration to them. And if the demand is not always a conscious one, it is there as an unconscious factor always urging the highest speed of which the ship is capable. The man who demands fast travel unreasonably must undoubtedly take his share in the responsibility. He asks to be taken over at a speed which will land him in something over four days; he forgets perhaps that Columbus took ninety days in a forty-ton boat, and that only fifty years ago paddle steamers took six weeks, and all the time the demand is greater and the strain is more: the public demand speed and luxury; the lines supply it, until presently the safety limit is reached, the undue risk is taken – and the *Titanic* goes down. All of us who have cried for greater speed must take our share in the responsibility. The expression of such a desire and the discontent with so-called slow travel are the seed sown in the minds of men, to bear fruit presently in an insistence on greater speed. We may not have done so directly, but we may perhaps have talked about it and thought about it, and we know no action begins without thought.

The White Star Line has received very rough handling from some of the press, but the greater part of this criticism seems to be unwarranted and to arise from the desire to find a scapegoat. After all they had made better provision for the passengers the *Titanic* carried than any other line has done, for they had built what they believed to be a huge lifeboat, unsinkable in all ordinary conditions. Those who embarked in her were almost certainly in the safest ship (along with the *Olympic*) afloat: she was probably quite immune from the ordinary effects of wind, waves and collisions at sea, and needed to fear nothing but running on a rock or, what was worse, a floating iceberg; for the effects of collision were, so far as damage was concerned, the same as if it had been a rock, and the danger greater, for one is charted and the other is not. Then, too, while the theory of the unsinkable boat has been destroyed at the same time as the boat itself, we should not forget that it served a useful purpose on deck that night – it eliminated largely the possibility of panic, and those rushes for the boats which might have swamped some of them. I do not wish for a moment to suggest that such things would have happened, because the more information that comes to hand of the conduct of the people on board, the more wonderful seems the complete self-control of all, even when the last boats had gone and nothing but the rising waters met their eyes – only that the generally entertained theory rendered such things less probable. The theory, indeed, was really a safeguard, though built on a false premise.

There is no evidence that the White Star Line instructed the captain to push the boat or to make any records: the probabilities are that no such attempt would be made on the first trip. The general instructions to their commanders bear quite the other interpretation: it will be well to quote them in full as issued to the press during the sittings of the United States Senate Committee:

Instructions to Commanders

Commanders must distinctly understand that the issue of regulations does not in any way relieve them from responsibility for the safe and efficient navigation of their respective vessels, and they are also enjoined to remember that they must run no risks which might by any possibility result in accident to their ships. It is to be hoped that they will ever bear in mind that the safety of the lives and property entrusted to their care is the ruling principle that should govern them in the navigation of their vessels, and that no supposed gain in expedition or saving of time on the voyage is to be purchased at the risk of accident.

Commanders are reminded that the steamers are to a great extent uninsured, and that their own livelihood, as well as the company's success, depends upon immunity from accident; no precaution which ensures safe navigation is to be considered excessive.

Nothing could be plainer than these instructions, and had they been obeyed, the disaster would never have happened: they warn commanders against the only thing left as a menace to their unsinkable boat – the lack of 'precaution which ensures safe navigation'.

In addition, the White Star Line had complied to the full extent with the requirements of the British Government: their ship had been subjected to an inspection so rigid that, as one officer remarked in evidence, it became a nuisance. The Board of Trade employs the best experts, and knows the dangers that attend ocean travel and the precautions that should be taken by every commander. If these precautions are not taken, it will be necessary to legislate until they are. No motorist is allowed to career at full speed along a public highway in dangerous conditions, and it should be an offence for a captain to do the same on the high seas with a ship full of unsuspecting passengers. They have entrusted their lives to the government of their country – through its regulations – and they are entitled to the same protection in mid-Atlantic as they are in Oxford Street or Broadway. The open sea should no longer be regarded as a neutral zone where no country's police laws are operative.

Of course there are difficulties in the way of drafting international regulations: many governments would have to be consulted and many difficulties that seem insuperable overcome; but that is the purpose for which governments are employed, that is why experts and ministers of governments are appointed and paid – to overcome difficulties for the people who appoint them and who expect them, among other things, to protect their lives.

The American Government must share the same responsibility: it is useless to attempt to fix it on the British Board of Trade for the reason that the boats were built in England and inspected there by British officials. They carried American citizens largely, and entered American ports. It would have been the simplest matter for the United States Government to veto the entry of any ship which did not conform to its laws of regulating speed in conditions of fog and icebergs – had they provided such laws. The fact is that the American nation has practically no mercantile marine, and in time of a disaster such as this it forgets, perhaps, that it has exactly the same right – and therefore the same responsibility – as the British Government to inspect, and to legislate: the right that is easily enforced by refusal to allow entry. The regulation of speed in dangerous regions could well be undertaken by some fleet of international police patrol vessels, with power to stop if necessary any boat found guilty of reckless racing. The additional duty of warning ships of the exact locality of icebergs could be performed by these boats. It would not of course be possible or advisable to fix a 'speed limit', because the region of icebergs varies in position as the icebergs float south, varies in point of danger as they melt and disappear, and the whole question has to be left largely to the judgement of the captain on the spot; but it would be possible to make it an offence against the law to go beyond a certain speed in known conditions of danger.

So much for the question of regulating speed on the high seas. The secondary question of safety appliances is governed by the same principle – that, in the last analysis, it is not the captain, not the passenger, not the builders and owners, but the governments through their experts, who are to be held responsible for the provision of lifesaving devices. Morally, of course, the owners and builders are responsible, but at present moral responsibility is too weak an incentive in human affairs – that is the miserable part of the whole wretched business – to induce owners generally to make every possible provision for the lives of those in their charge; to place human safety so far above every other consideration that no plan shall be left unconsidered, no device left untested, by which passengers can escape from a sinking ship. But it is not correct to say, as has been said frequently, that it is greed and dividend-hunting that have characterised the policy of the steamship companies in their failure to provide safety appliances: these things in themselves are not expensive. They have vied with each other in making their lines attractive in point of speed, size and comfort, and they have been quite justified in doing so: such things are the product of ordinary competition between commercial houses.

Where they have all failed morally is to extend to their passengers the consideration that places their lives as of more interest to them than any other conceivable thing. They are not alone in this: thousands of other people have done the same thing and would do it today – in factories, in workshops, in mines, did not the government intervene and insist on safety precautions. The thing is a defect in human life of today

– thoughtlessness for the well-being of our fellow men; and we are all guilty of it in some degree. It is folly for the public to rise up now and condemn the steamship companies: their failing is the common failing of the immorality of indifference.

The remedy is the law, and it is the only remedy at present that will really accomplish anything. The British law on the subject dates from 1894, and requires only twenty boats for a ship the size of the *Titanic*: the owners and builders have obeyed this law and fulfilled their legal responsibility. Increase this responsibility and they will fulfil it again – and the matter is ended so far as appliances are concerned. It should perhaps be mentioned that in a period of ten years only nine passengers were lost on British ships: the law seemed to be sufficient in fact.

The position of the American Government, however, is worse than that of the British Government. Its regulations require more than double the boat accommodation which the British regulations do, and yet it has allowed hundreds of thousands of its subjects to enter its ports on boats that defied its own laws. Had their government not been guilty of the same indifference, passengers would not have been allowed aboard any British ship lacking in boat accommodation – the simple expedient again of refusing entry. The reply of the British Government to the Senate Committee, accusing the Board of Trade of 'insufficient requirements and lax inspection', might well be – 'Ye have a law: see to it yourselves!'

It will be well now to consider briefly the various appliances that have been suggested to ensure the safety of passengers and crew, and in doing so it may be remembered that the average man and woman has the same right as the expert to consider and discuss these things: they are not so technical as to prevent anyone of ordinary intelligence from understanding their construction. Using the term in its widest sense, we come first to:

Bulkheads & Watertight Compartments

It is impossible to attempt a discussion here of the exact constructional details of these parts of a ship; but in order to illustrate briefly what is the purpose of having bulkheads, we may take the *Titanic* as an example. She was divided into sixteen compartments by fifteen transverse steel walls called bulkheads. If a hole is made in the side of the ship in any one compartment, steel watertight doors seal off the only openings in that compartment and separate it as a damaged unit from the rest of the ship and the vessel is brought to land in safety. Ships have even put into the nearest port for inspection after collision, and finding only one compartment full of water and no other damage, have left again, for their home port without troubling to disembark passengers and effect repairs.

The design of the *Titanic*'s bulkheads calls for some attention. The *Scientific American*, in an excellent article on the comparative safety of the *Titanic*'s and other types of watertight compartments, draws attention to the following weaknesses in the former – from the point of view of possible collision with an iceberg. She had no longitudinal bulkheads, which would subdivide her into smaller compartments and prevent the water filling the whole of a large compartment. Probably, too, the length of a large compartment was in any case too great – fifty-three feet.

The *Mauretania*, on the other hand, in addition to transverse bulkheads, is fitted with longitudinal torpedo bulkheads, and the space between them and the side of the ship is utilised as a coal bunker. Then, too, in the *Mauretania* all bulkheads are carried up to the top deck, whereas in the case of the *Titanic* they reached in some parts only to the saloon deck and in others to a lower deck still – the weakness of this being that, when the water reached to the top of a bulkhead as the ship sank by the head, it flowed over and filled the next compartment. The British Admiralty, which subsidises the *Mauretania* and *Lusitania* as fast cruisers in time of war, insisted on this type of construction, and it is considered vastly better than that used in the *Titanic*. The writer of the article thinks it possible that these ships might not have sunk as the result of a similar collision. But the ideal ship from the point of bulkhead construction, he considers to have been the *Great Eastern*, constructed many years ago by the famous engineer Brunel. So thorough was her system of compartments divided and subdivided by many transverse and longitudinal bulkheads that when she tore a hole eighty feet long in her side by striking a rock, she reached port in safety. Unfortunately the weight and cost of this method was so great that his plan was subsequently abandoned.

But it would not be just to say that the construction of the *Titanic* was a serious mistake on the part of the White Star Line or her builders, on the ground that her bulkheads were not so well constructed as those of the *Lusitania* and *Mauretania*, which were built to fulfil British Admiralty regulations for time of war – an extraordinary risk which no builder of a passenger steamer – as such – would be expected to take into consideration when designing the vessel. It should be constantly borne in mind that the *Titanic* met extraordinary conditions on the night of the collision: she was probably the safest ship afloat in all ordinary conditions. Collision with an iceberg is not an ordinary risk; but this disaster will probably result in altering the whole construction of bulkheads and compartments to the *Great Eastern* type, in order to include the one-in-a-million risk of iceberg collision and loss.

Here comes in the question of increased cost of construction, and in addition the great loss of cargo-carrying space with decreased earning capacity, both of which will mean an increase in the passenger rates. This the travelling public will have to face and undoubtedly will be willing to face for the satisfaction of knowing that what was so confidently affirmed by passengers on the *Titanic*'s deck that night of the collision will then be really true – that 'we are on an unsinkable boat' – so far as human forethought can devise. After all, this *must* be the solution to the problem how best to ensure safety at sea. Other safety appliances are useful and necessary, but not useable in certain conditions of weather. The ship itself must always be the 'safety appliance' that is really trustworthy, and nothing must be left undone to ensure this.

Wireless Apparatus & Operators

The range of the apparatus might well be extended, but the principal defect is the lack of an operator for night duty on some ships. The awful fact that the *Californian* lay a few miles away, able to save every soul on board, and could not catch the message because the operator was asleep, seems too cruel to dwell upon. Even on the *Carpathia*, the operator was on the point of retiring when the message arrived, and we should have been much longer afloat – and some boats possibly swamped – had he not caught the message when he did. It has been suggested that officers should have a working knowledge of wireless telegraphy, and this is no doubt a wise provision. It would enable them to supervise the work of the operators more closely and from all the evidence, this seems a necessity. The exchange of vitally important messages between a sinking ship and those rushing to her rescue should be under the control of an experienced officer. To take but one example – Bride testified that after giving the *Birma* the 'CQD' message and the position (incidentally Signer Marconi has stated that this has been abandoned in favour of 'SOS') and getting a reply, they got into touch with the *Carpathia*, and while talking with her were interrupted by the *Birma* asking what was the matter. No doubt it was the duty of the *Birma* to come at once without asking any questions, but the reply from the *Titanic*, telling the *Birma*'s operator not to be a 'fool' by interrupting, seems to have been a needless waste of precious moments: to reply 'We are sinking' would have taken no longer, especially when in their own estimation of the strength of the signals they thought the *Birma* was the nearer ship. It is well to notice that some large liners have already a staff of three operators.

Submarine Signalling Apparatus

There are occasions when wireless apparatus is useless as a means of saving life at sea promptly.

One of its weaknesses is that when the ships' engines are stopped, messages can no longer be sent out, that is, with the system at present adopted. It will be remembered that the *Titanic*'s messages got gradually fainter and then ceased altogether as she came to rest with her engines shut down.

Again, in fogs – and most accidents occur in fogs – while wireless informs of the accident, it does not enable one ship to locate another closely enough to take off her passengers at once. There is as yet no method known by which wireless telegraphy will fix the direction of a message; and after a ship has been in fog for any considerable length of time it is more difficult to give the exact position to another vessel bringing help.

Nothing could illustrate these two points better than the story of how the *Baltic* found the *Republic* in the year 1909, in a dense fog off Nantucket Lightship, when the latter was drifting helplessly after collision with the *Florida*. The *Baltic* received a wireless message stating the *Republic*'s condition and the information that she was in touch with Nantucket through a submarine bell which she could hear ringing. The *Baltic* turned and went towards the position in the fog, picked up the submarine bell signal from Nantucket, and then began searching near this position for the *Republic*. It took her twelve hours to find the damaged ship, zigzagging across a circle within which she thought the *Republic* might lie. In a rough sea it is doubtful whether the *Republic* would have remained afloat long enough for the *Baltic* to find her and take off all her passengers.

Now on these two occasions when wireless telegraphy was found to be unreliable, the usefulness of the submarine bell at once becomes apparent. The *Baltic* could have gone unerringly to the *Republic* in the dense fog had the latter been fitted with a submarine emergency bell. It will perhaps be well to spend a little time describing the submarine signalling apparatus to see how this result could have been obtained: twelve anxious hours in a dense fog on a ship which was injured so badly that she subsequently foundered, is an experience which every appliance known to human invention should be enlisted to prevent.

Submarine signalling has never received that public notice which wireless telegraphy has, for the reason that it does not appeal so readily to the popular mind. That it is an absolute necessity to every ship carrying passengers – or carrying anything, for that matter – is beyond question. It is an additional safeguard that no ship can afford to be without.

There are many occasions when the atmosphere fails lamentably as a medium for carrying messages. When fog falls down, as it does sometimes in a moment, on the hundreds of ships coasting down the traffic ways round our shores – ways which are defined so easily in clear weather and with such difficulty in fogs – the hundreds of lighthouses and lightships which serve as warning beacons, and on which many millions of money have been spent, are for all practical purposes as useless to the navigator as if they had never been built: he is just as helpless as if he were back in the years before 1514, when Trinity House was granted a charter by Henry VIII 'for the relief ... of the shipping of this realm of England', and began a system of lights on the shores, of which the present chain of lighthouses and lightships is the outcome.

Nor is the foghorn much better: the presence of different layers of fog and air, and their varying densities, which cause both reflection and refraction of sound, prevent the air from being a reliable medium for carrying it. Now, submarine signalling has none of these defects, for the medium is water, subject to no such variable conditions as the air. Its density is practically non-variable, and sound travels through it at the rate of 4,400 feet per second, without deviation or reflection.

The apparatus consists of a bell designed to ring either pneumatically from a lightship, electrically from the shore (the bell itself being a tripod at the bottom of the sea), automatically from a floating bell-buoy, or by hand from a ship or boat. The sound travels from the bell in every direction, like waves in a pond, and falls, it may be, on the side of a ship. The receiving apparatus is fixed inside the skin of the ship and consists of a small iron tank, 16 inches square and 18 inches deep. The front of the tank facing the ship's iron skin is missing and the tank, being filled with water, is bolted to the framework and sealed firmly to the ship's side by rubber facing. In this way a portion of the ship's iron hull is washed by the sea on one side and water in the tank on the other. Vibrations from a bell ringing at a distance fall on the iron side, travel through, and strike on two microphones hanging in the tank. These microphones transmit the sound along wires to the chart room, where telephones convey the message to the officer on duty.

There are two of these tanks or 'receivers' fitted against the ship's side, one on the port and one on the starboard side, near the bows, and as far down below the water level as is possible. The direction of sounds coming to the microphones hanging in these tanks can be estimated by switching alternately to the port and starboard tanks. If the sound is of greater intensity on the port side, then the bell signalling is off the port bows; and similarly on the starboard side.

The ship is turned towards the sound until the same volume of sound is heard from both receivers, when the bell is known to be dead ahead. So accurate is this in practice that a trained operator can steer his ship in the densest fog directly to a lightship or any other point where a submarine bell is sending its warning beneath the sea. It must be repeated that the medium in which these signals are transmitted is a constant one, not subject to any of the limitations and variations imposed on the atmosphere and the ether as media for the transmission of light, blasts of a foghorn, and wireless vibrations. At present the chief use of submarine signalling is from the shore or a lightship to ships at sea, and not from ship to ship or from ship to the shore: in other words ships carry only receiving apparatus, and lighthouses and lightships use only signalling apparatus. Some of the lighthouses and lightships on our coasts already have these submarine bells in addition to their lights, and in bad weather the bells send out their messages to warn ships of their proximity to a danger point. This invention enables ships to pick up the sound of bell after bell on a coast and run along it in the densest fog almost as well as in daylight; passenger steamers coming into port do not have to wander about in the fog, groping their way blindly into harbour. By having a code of rings, and judging by the intensity of the sound, it is possible to tell almost exactly where a ship is in relation to the coast or to some lightship. The British Admiralty report in 1906 said: 'If the lightships round the coast were fitted with submarine bells, it would be possible for ships fitted with receiving apparatus to navigate in fog with almost as great certainty as in clear weather.' And the following remark of a captain engaged in coast service is instructive. He had been asked to cut down expenses by omitting the submarine signalling apparatus, but replied: 'I would rather take out the wireless. That only enables me to tell other people where I am. The submarine signal enables me to find out where I am myself.'

The range of the apparatus is not so wide as that of wireless telegraphy, varying from 10 to 15 miles for a large ship (although instances of 20 to 30 are on record), and from 3 to 8 miles for a small ship.

At present the receiving apparatus is fixed on only some 650 steamers of the merchant marine, these being mostly the first class passenger liners. There is no question that it should be installed, along with wireless apparatus, on every ship of over 1,000 tons gross tonnage. Equally important is the provision of signalling apparatus on board ships: it is obviously just as necessary to transmit a signal as to receive one; but at present the sending of signals from ships has not been perfected. The invention of signal-transmitting apparatus to be used while the ship is under way is as yet in the experimental stage; but while she is at rest a bell similar to those used by lighthouses can be sunk over her side and rung by hand with exactly the same effect. But liners are not provided with them (they cost only £60!). As mentioned before, with another £60 spent on the *Republic*'s equipment, the *Baltic* could have picked up her bell and steered direct to her – just as they both heard the bell of Nantucket Lightship. Again, if the *Titanic* had been provided with a bell and the *Californian* with receiving apparatus – neither of them was – the officer on the bridge could have heard the signals from the telephones near.

A smaller size for use in lifeboats is provided, and would be heard by receiving apparatus for approximately five miles. If we had hung one of these bells over the side of the lifeboats afloat that night we should have been free from the anxiety of being run down as we lay across the *Carpathia*'s path, without a light. Or if we had gone adrift in a dense fog and wandered miles apart from each other on the sea (as we inevitably should have done), the *Carpathia* could still have picked up each boat individually by means of the bell signal.

In those ships fitted with receiving apparatus, at least one officer is obliged to understand the working of the apparatus: a very wise precaution, and, as suggested above, one that should be taken with respect to wireless apparatus also.

It was a very great pleasure to me to see all this apparatus in manufacture and in use at one of the principal submarine signalling works in America and to hear some of the remarkable stories of its value in actual practice. I was struck by the aptness of the motto adopted by them – 'De profundis clamavi' – in relation to the *Titanic*'s end and the calls of our passengers from the sea when she sank. 'Out of the deep have I called unto Thee' is indeed a suitable motto for those who are doing all they can to prevent such calls arising from their fellow men and women 'out of the deep'.

Fixing of Steamship Routes

The 'lanes' along which the liners travel are fixed by agreement among the steamship companies in consultation with the Hydrographic departments of the different countries. These routes are arranged so that east-bound steamers are always a number of miles away from those going west, and thus the danger of collision between east- and west-bound vessels is entirely eliminated. The 'lanes' can be moved farther south if icebergs threaten, and north again when the danger is removed. Of course the farther south they are placed, the longer the journey to be made, and the longer the time spent on board, with consequent grumbling by some passengers. For example, the lanes since the disaster to the *Titanic* have been moved one hundred miles farther south, which means one hundred and eighty miles longer journey, taking eight hours.

The only real precaution against colliding with icebergs is to go south of the place where they are likely to be: there is no other way.

Lifeboats

The provision was of course woefully inadequate. The only humane plan is to have a numbered seat in a boat assigned to each passenger and member of the crew. It would seem well to have this number pointed out at the time of booking a berth, and to have a plan in each cabin showing where the boat is and how to get to it the most direct way – a most important consideration with a ship like the *Titanic* with over two miles of deck space. Boat drills of the passengers and crew of each boat should be held, under compulsion, as soon as possible after leaving port. I asked an officer as to the possibility of having such a drill immediately after the gangways are withdrawn and before the tugs are allowed to haul the ship out of dock, but he says the difficulties are almost insuperable at such a time. If so, the drill should be conducted in sections as soon as possible after sailing, and should be conducted in a thorough manner. Children in school are called upon suddenly to go through fire drill, and there is no reason why passengers on board ship should not be similarly trained. So much depends on order and readiness in time of danger. Undoubtedly, the whole subject of manning, provisioning, loading and lowering of lifeboats should be in the hands of an expert officer, who should have no other duties. The modern liner has become far too big to permit the captain to exercise control over the whole ship, and all vitally important subdivisions should be controlled by a separate authority. It seems a piece of bitter irony to remember that on the *Titanic* a special chef was engaged at a large salary – larger perhaps than that of any officer – and no boatmaster (or some such officer) was considered necessary. The general system again – not criminal neglect, as some hasty criticisms would say, but lack of consideration for our fellow man, the placing of luxurious attractions above that kindly forethought that allows no precaution to be neglected for even the humblest passenger. But it must not be overlooked that the provision of sufficient lifeboats on deck is not evidence they will all be launched easily or all the passengers taken off safely. It must be remembered that ideal conditions prevailed that night for launching boats from the decks of the *Titanic*: there was no list that prevented the boats getting away, they could be launched on both sides, and when they were lowered the sea was so calm that they pulled away without any of the smashing against the side that is possible in rough seas. Sometimes it would mean that only those boats on the side sheltered from a heavy sea could ever get away, and this would at once halve the boat accommodation. And when launched, there would be the danger of swamping in such a heavy sea. All things considered, lifeboats might be the poorest sort of safeguard in certain conditions.

Liferafts are said to be much inferior to lifeboats in a rough sea, and collapsible boats made of canvas and thin wood soon decay under exposure to weather and are danger-traps at a critical moment.

Some of the lifeboats should be provided with motors, to keep the boats together and to tow if necessary. The launching is an important matter: the *Titanic*'s davits worked excellently and no doubt were largely responsible for all the boats getting away safely: they were far superior to those on most liners.

Pontoons

After the sinking of the *Bourgogne,* when two Americans lost their lives, a prize of £4,000 was offered by their heirs for the best lifesaving device applicable to ships at sea. A board sat to consider the various appliances sent in by competitors, and finally awarded the prize to an Englishman, whose design provided for a flat structure the width of the ship, which could be floated off when required and would accommodate several hundred passengers. It has never been adopted by any steamship line. Other similar designs are known, by which the whole of the after deck can be pushed over from the stern by a ratchet arrangement, with air-tanks below to buoy it up: it seems to be a practical suggestion.

One point where the *Titanic* management failed lamentably was to provide a properly trained crew to each lifeboat. The rowing was in most cases execrable. There is no more reason why a steward should be able to row than a passenger – less so than some of the passengers who were lost; men of leisure accustomed to all kinds of sport (including rowing), and in addition probably more fit physically than a steward to row for hours on the open sea. And if a steward cannot row, he has no right to be at an oar; so that, under the unwritten rule that passengers take precedence of the crew when there is not sufficient accommodation for all (a situation that should never be allowed to arise again, for a member of the crew should have an equal opportunity with a passenger to save his life), the majority of stewards and cooks should have stayed behind and passengers have come instead: they could not have been of less use, and they might have been of more. It will be remembered that the proportion of crew saved to passengers was 210 to 495, a high proportion.

Another point arises out of these figures – deduct 21 members of the crew who were stewardesses, and 189 men of the crew are left as against the 495 passengers. Of these some got on the overturned collapsible boat after the *Titanic* sank, and a few were picked up by the lifeboats, but these were not many in all. Now with the 17 boats brought to the *Carpathia* and an average of six of the crew to man each boat – probably a higher average than was realised – we get a total of 102 who should have been saved as against 189 who actually were. There were, as is known, stokers and stewards in the boats who were not members of the lifeboats' crews. It may seem heartless to analyse figures in this way, and suggest that some of the crew who got to the *Carpathia* never should have done so; but, after all, passengers took their passage under certain rules – written and unwritten – and one is that in times of danger the servants of the company in whose boats they sail shall first of all see to the safety of the passengers before thinking of their own. There were only 126 men passengers saved as against 189 of the crew, and 661 men lost as against 686 of the crew, so that actually the crew had a greater percentage saved than the men passengers – 22 per cent against 16.

But steamship companies are faced with real difficulties in this matter. The crews are never the same for two voyages together: they sign on for the one trip, then perhaps take a berth on shore as waiters, stokers in hotel furnace rooms, etc. – to resume life on board any other ship that is handy when the desire comes to go to sea again. They can in no sense be regarded as part of a homogeneous crew, subject to regular discipline and educated to appreciate the morale of a particular liner, as a man of war's crew is.

Searchlights

These seem an absolute necessity, and the wonder is that they have not been fitted before to all ocean liners. Not only are they of use in lighting up the sea a long distance ahead, but as flashlight signals they permit of communication with other ships. As I write, through the window can be seen the flashes from river steamers plying up the Hudson in New York, each with its searchlight, examining the river, lighting up the bank for hundreds of yards ahead, and bringing every object within its reach into prominence. They are regularly used too in the Suez Canal.

I suppose there is no question that the collision would have been avoided had a searchlight been fitted to the *Titanic*'s masthead: the climatic conditions for its use must have been ideal that night. There are other things besides icebergs: derelicts are reported from time to time, and fishermen lie in the lanes without lights. They would not always be of practical use, however. They would be of no service in heavy rain, in fog, in snow, or in flying spray, and the effect is sometimes to dazzle the eyes of the lookout.

While writing of the lookout, much has been made of the omission to provide the lookout on the *Titanic* with glasses. The general opinion of officers seems to be that it is better not to provide them, but to rely on good eyesight and wide-awake men. After all, in a question of actual practice, the opinion of officers should be accepted as final, even if it seems to the landsman the better thing to provide glasses.

Cruising Lightships

One or two internationally owned and controlled lightships, fitted with every known device for signalling and communication, would rob those regions of most of their terrors. They could watch and chart the icebergs, report their exact position, the amount and direction of daily drift in the changing currents that are found there. To them, too, might be entrusted the duty of police patrol.

9

Some Impressions

No one can pass through an event like the wreck of the *Titanic* without recording mentally many impressions, deep and vivid, of what has been seen and felt. In so far as such impressions are of benefit to mankind they should not be allowed to pass unnoticed, and this chapter is an attempt to picture how people thought and felt from the time they first heard of the disaster to the landing in New York, when there was opportunity to judge of events somewhat from a distance. While it is to some extent a personal record, the mental impressions of other survivors have been compared and found to be in many cases closely in agreement. Naturally it is very imperfect, and pretends to be no more than a sketch of the way people act under the influence of strong emotions produced by imminent danger.

In the first place, the principal fact that stands out is the almost entire absence of any expressions of fear or alarm on the part of passengers, and the conformity to the normal on the part of almost everyone. I think it is no exaggeration to say that those who read of the disaster quietly at home, and pictured to themselves the scene as the *Titanic* was sinking, had more of the sense of horror than those who stood on the deck and watched her go down inch by inch. The fact is that the sense of fear came to the passengers very slowly – a result of the absence of any signs of danger and the peaceful night – and as it became evident gradually that there was serious damage to the ship, the fear that came with the knowledge was largely destroyed as it came. There was no sudden overwhelming sense of danger that passed through thought so quickly that it was difficult to catch up and grapple with it – no need for the warning to 'be not afraid of sudden fear', such as might have been present had we collided head-on with a crash and a shock that flung everyone out of his bunk to the floor. Everyone had time to give each condition of danger attention as it came along, and the result of their judgement was as if they had said: 'Well, here is this thing to be faced, and we must see it through as quietly as we can.' Quietness and self-control were undoubtedly the two qualities most expressed. There were times when danger loomed more nearly and there was temporarily some excitement – for example when the first rocket went up – but after the first realisation of what it meant, the crowd took hold of the situation and soon gained the same quiet control that was evident at first. As the sense of fear ebbed and flowed, it was so obviously a thing within one's own power to control, that, quite unconsciously realising the absolute necessity of keeping cool, every one for his own safety put away the thought of danger as far as was possible. Then, too, the curious sense of the whole thing being a dream was very prominent: that all were looking on at the scene from a nearby vantage point in a position of perfect safety, and that those who walked the decks or tied one another's lifebelts on were the actors in a scene of which we were but spectators: that the dream would end soon and we should wake up to find the scene had vanished. Many people have had a similar experience in times of danger, but it was very noticeable standing on the *Titanic*'s deck. I remember observing it particularly while tying on a lifebelt for a man on the deck. It is fortunate that it should be so: to be able to survey such a scene dispassionately is a wonderful aid in the destruction of the fears that go with it. One thing that helped considerably to establish this orderly condition of affairs was the quietness of the surroundings. It may seem weariness to refer again to this, but I am convinced it had much to do with keeping everyone calm. The ship was motionless; there was not a breath of wind; the sky was clear; the sea like a millpond – the general 'atmosphere' was peaceful, and all on board responded unconsciously to it. But what controlled the situation principally was the quality of obedience and respect for authority which is a dominant characteristic of the Teutonic race. Passengers did as they were told by the officers in charge: women went to the decks below, men remained where they were told and waited in silence for the next order, knowing instinctively that this was the only way to bring about the best result for all on board. The officers, in their turn, carried out the work assigned to them by their superior officers as quickly and orderly as circumstances permitted, the senior ones being in control of the manning, filling and lowering of the lifeboats, while the junior officers were lowered in individual boats to take command of the fleet adrift on the sea. Similarly, the engineers below, the band, the gymnasium instructor, were all performing their tasks as they came along: orderly, quietly, without question or stopping to consider what was their chance of safety. This correlation on the part of passengers, officers and crew was simply obedience to duty, and it was innate rather than the product of reasoned judgement.

I hope it will not seem to detract in any way from the heroism of those who faced the last plunge of the *Titanic* so courageously when all the boats had gone – if it does, it is the difficulty of expressing an idea in adequate words – to say that their quiet heroism was largely unconscious, temperamental, not a definite choice between two ways of acting. All that was visible on deck before the boats left tended to this conclusion and the testimony of those who went down with the ship and were afterwards rescued is of the same kind.

Certainly it seems to express much more general nobility of character in a race of people – consisting of different nationalities – to find heroism an unconscious quality of the race than to have it arising as an effort of will, to have to bring it out consciously.

It is unfortunate that some sections of the press should seek to chronicle mainly the individual acts of heroism: the collective behaviour of a crowd is of so much more importance to the world and so much more a test – if a test be wanted – of how a race of people behaves. The attempt to record the acts of individuals leads apparently to such false reports as that of Major Butt holding at bay with a revolver a crowd of passengers and shooting them down as they tried to rush the boats, or of Captain Smith shouting, 'Be British,' through a megaphone, and subsequently committing suicide along with First Officer Murdock. It is only a morbid sense of things that would describe such incidents as heroic. Everyone knows that Major Butt was a brave man, but his record of heroism would not be enhanced if he, a trained army officer, were compelled under orders from the captain to shoot down unarmed passengers. It might in other conditions have been necessary, but it would not be heroic. Similarly there could be nothing heroic in Captain Smith or Murdock putting an end to their lives. It is conceivable men might be so overwhelmed by the sense of disaster that they knew not how they were acting; but to be really heroic would have been to stop with the ship – as of course they did – with the hope of being picked up along with passengers and crew and returning to face an enquiry and to give evidence that would be of supreme value to the whole world for the prevention of similar disasters. It was not possible; but if heroism consists in doing the greatest good to the greatest number, it would have been heroic for both officers to *expect* to be saved. We do not know what they thought, but I, for one, like to imagine that they did so. Second Officer Lightoller worked steadily at the boats until the last possible moment, went down with the ship, was saved in what seemed a miraculous manner, and returned to give valuable evidence before the commissions of two countries.

The second thing that stands out prominently in the emotions produced by the disaster is that in moments of urgent need men and women turn for help to something entirely outside themselves. I remember reading some years ago a story of an atheist who was the guest at dinner of a regimental mess in India. The colonel listened to his remarks on atheism in silence, and invited him for a drive the following morning. He took his guest up a rough mountain road in a light carriage drawn by two ponies, and when some distance from the plain below, turned the carriage round and allowed the ponies to run away – as it seemed – downhill. In the terror of approaching disaster, the atheist was lifted out of his reasoned convictions and prayed aloud for help, when the colonel reined in his ponies, and with the remark that the whole drive had been planned with the intention of proving to his guest that there was a power outside his own reason, descended quietly to level ground.

The story may or may not be true, and in any case is not introduced as an attack on atheism, but it illustrates in a striking way the frailty of dependence on a man's own power and resource in imminent danger. To those men standing on the top deck with the boats all lowered, and still more so when the boats had all left, there came the realisation that human resources were exhausted and human avenues of escape closed. With it came the appeal to whatever consciousness each had of a Power that had created the universe. After all, some Power had made the brilliant stars above, countless millions of miles away, moving in definite order, formed on a definite plan and obeying a definite law: had made each one of the passengers with ability to think and act; with the best proof, after all, of being created – the knowledge of their own existence; and now, if at any time, was the time to appeal to that Power. When the boats had left and it was seen the ship was going down rapidly, men stood in groups on the deck engaged in prayer, and later, as some of them lay on the overturned collapsible boat, they repeated together over and over again the Lord's Prayer – irrespective of religious beliefs, some, perhaps, without religious beliefs, united in a common appeal for deliverance from their surroundings. And this was not because it was a habit, because they had learned this prayer 'at their mother's knee': men do not do such things through habit. It must have been because each one saw removed the thousand and one ways in which he had relied on human, material things to help him – including even dependence on the overturned boat with its bubble of air inside, which any moment a rising swell might remove as it tilted the boat too far sideways, and sink the boat below the surface – saw laid bare his utter dependence on something that had made him and given him power to think – whether he named it God or Divine Power or First Cause or Creator, or named it not at all but recognised it unconsciously – saw these things and expressed them in the form of words he was best acquainted with in common with his fellow men. He did so, not through a sense of duty to his particular religion, not because he had learned the words, but because he recognised that it was the most practical thing to do – the thing best fitted to help him. Men do practical things in times like that: they would not waste a moment on mere words if those words were not an expression of the most intensely real conviction of which they were capable. Again, like the feeling of heroism, this appeal is innate and intuitive, and it certainly has its foundation on a knowledge – largely concealed, no doubt – of immortality. I think this must be obvious: there could be no other explanation of such a general sinking of all the emotions of the human mind expressed in a thousand different ways by a thousand different people in favour of this single appeal.

The behaviour of people during the hours in the lifeboats, the landing on the *Carpathia*, the life there and the landing in New York, can all be summarised by saying that people did not act at all as they were expected to act – or rather as most people expected they would act, and in some cases have erroneously said they did act. Events were there to be faced, and not to crush people down. Situations arose which demanded courage, resource, and in the cases of those who had lost friends most dear to them, enormous self-control; but very wonderfully they responded. There was the same quiet demeanour and poise, the same inborn dominion over circumstances, the same conformity to a normal standard which characterised the crowd of passengers on the deck of the *Titanic* – and for the same reasons.

The first two or three days ashore were undoubtedly rather trying to some of the survivors. It seemed as if coming into the world again – the four days shut off from any news seemed a long time – and finding what a shock the disaster had produced, the flags half-mast, the staring headlines, the sense of gloom noticeable everywhere, made things worse than they had been on the *Carpathia*. The difference in 'atmosphere' was very marked, and people gave way to some extent under it and felt the reaction. Gratitude for their deliverance and a desire to 'make the best of things' must have helped soon, however, to restore them to normal conditions. It is not at all surprising that some survivors felt quieter on the *Carpathia* with its lack of news from the outside world, if the following extract from a leading New York evening paper was some of the material of which the 'atmosphere' on shore was composed:

Stunned by the terrific impact, the dazed passengers rushed from their staterooms into the main saloon amid the crash of splintering steel, rending of plates and shattering of girders, while the boom of falling pinnacles of ice upon the broken deck of the great vessel added to the horror ... In a wild ungovernable mob they poured out of the saloons to witness one of the most appalling scenes possible to conceive ... For a hundred feet the bow was a shapeless mass of bent, broken and splintered steel and iron.

And so on, horror piled on horror, and not a word of it true, or remotely approaching the truth.

This paper was selling in the streets of New York while the *Carpathia* was coming into dock, while relatives of those on board were at the docks to meet them and anxiously buying any paper that might contain news. No one on the *Carpathia* could have supplied such information; there was no one else in the world at that moment who knew any details of the *Titanic* disaster, and the only possible conclusion is that the whole thing was a deliberate fabrication to sell the paper.

This is a repetition of the same defect in human nature noticed in the provision of safety appliances on board ship – the lack of consideration for the other man. The remedy is the same – the law: it should be a criminal offence for anyone to disseminate deliberate falsehoods that cause fear and grief. The moral responsibility of the press is very great, and its duty of supplying the public with only clean, correct news is correspondingly heavy. If the general public is not yet prepared to go so far as to stop the publication of such news by refusing to buy those papers that publish it, then the law should be enlarged to include such cases. Libel is an offence, and this is very much worse than any libel could ever be.

It is only right to add that the majority of the careful only to report such news as had been o survivors or from *Carpathia* passengers. It wa and sometimes not true at all, but from the point of reporting what was heard, most of it was quite correct.

One more thing must be referred to – the prevalence of superstitious beliefs concerning the *Titanic*. I suppose no ship ever left port with so much miserable nonsense showered on her. In the first place, there is no doubt many people refused to sail on her because it was her maiden voyage, and this apparently is a common superstition: even the clerk of the White Star Office where I purchased my ticket admitted it was a reason that prevented people from sailing. A number of people have written to the press to say they had thought of sailing on her, or had decided to sail on her, but because of 'omens' cancelled the passage. Many referred to the sister ship, the *Olympic*, pointed to the 'ill luck' that they say has dogged her – her collision with the *Hawke*, and a second mishap necessitating repairs and a wait in harbour, where passengers deserted her; they prophesied even greater disaster for the *Titanic*, saying they would not dream of travelling on the boat. Even some aboard were very nervous, in an undefined way. One lady said she had never wished to take this boat, but her friends had insisted and bought her ticket and she had not had a happy moment since. A friend told me of the voyage of the *Olympic* from Southampton after the wait in harbour, and said there was a sense of gloom pervading the whole ship: the stewards and stewardesses even going so far as to say it was a *'death-ship'*. This crew, by the way, was largely transferred to the *Titanic*.

The incident with the *New York* at Southampton, the appearance of the stoker at Queenstown in the funnel, combine with all this to make a mass of nonsense in which apparently sensible people believe, or which at any rate they discuss. Correspondence is published with an official the White Star Line from someone imploring them not to name the new 'Gigantic', because it seems like 'tempting fate' when the *Titanic* has unk. It would seem almost as if we were back in the Middle Ages hes w burned because they kept black cats. There seems no more reason why a black stoker should be an ill omen for the *Titanic* than a black cat should be for an old woman.

The only reason for referring to these foolish details is that a surprisingly large number of people think there may be 'something in it'. The effect is this: that if a ship's company and a number of passengers get imbued with that undefined dread of the unknown – the relics no doubt of the savage's fear of what he does not understand – it has an unpleasant effect on the harmonious working of the ship: the officers and crew feel the depressing influence, and it may even spread so far as to prevent them being as alert and keen as they otherwise would; may even result in some duty not being as well done as usual. Just as the unconscious demand for speed and haste to get across the Atlantic may have tempted captains to take a risk they might otherwise not have done, so these gloomy forebodings may have more effect sometimes than we imagine. Only a little thing is required sometimes to weigh down the balance for and against a certain course of action.

At the end of this chapter of mental impressions it must be recorded that one impression remains constant with us all today – that of the deepest gratitude that we came safely through the wreck of the *Titanic*; and its corollary – that our legacy from the wreck, our debt to those who were lost with her, is to see, as far as in us lies, that such things are impossible ever again. Meanwhile we can say of them, as Shelley, himself the victim of a similar disaster, says of his friend Keats in 'Adonais':

Peace, peace! he is not dead, he doth not sleep,
He hath awakened from the dream of life …
He lives, he wakes –' T is Death is dead, not he;
Mourn not for Adonais.

List of Illustrations

Also available from Amberley Publishing

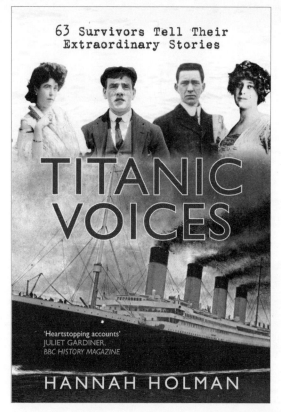

The sinking of the Titanic *in the words of the survivors*

'Heartstopping accounts' JULIET GARDINER, *BBC HISTORY MAGAZINE*
'A fascinating collection... an extraordinary, heart-wrenching read' *DISCOVER BRITAIN*
'Survivors' stories still have power to shock' *NAUTILUS INTERNATIONAL TELEGRAPH*

There were 712 survivors of the *Titanic* disaster and their horrific experience has captivated readers and movie goers for almost 100 years. But what was it actually like for a woman to say goodbye to her husband? For a mother to leave her teenage sons? For the unlucky many who found themselves in the freezing Atlantic waters? *Titanic Voices* is the most comprehensive collection of *Titanic* survivors' accounts ever published and includes many unpublished, and long forgotten accounts, unabridged, together with an authoritative editorial commentary. It is also the first book to include substantial accounts from women survivors - most of the previously well known accounts were written by men.

£14.99 Paperback
135 illustrations (11 colour)
512 pages
978-1-4456-1443-4

Available from all good bookshops or to order direct
Please call **01453-847-800**
www.amberleybooks.com

Titanic History from Amberley Publishing

TITANIC
W.B. Bartlett

'Enthralling' THE DAILY MAIL

'Quite the best and most level-headed telling of the whole story I have ever read' THE INDEPENDENT ON SUNDAY

| £20.00 | 978-1-84868-422-5 | 368 pages HB 72 illus, 14 col |
| £9.99 | 978-1-4456-0482-4 | 368 pages PB 72 illus, 14 col |

A GIRL ABOARD THE TITANIC
Eva Hart

The remarkable memoir of Eva Hart, a 7-year old passenger on the doomed Titanic.

£16.99   978-1-4456-0089-5   192 pages HB 65 illus

THE LOSS OF THE TITANIC
Lawrence Beesley

'The best first-hand account of a passenger's experiences... a first-rate piece of descriptive writing' THE GUARDIAN

£9.99   978-1-4456-1383-3   192 pages HB 67 illus

TITANIC VOICES
63 Survivors Tell Their Extraordinary Stories
Hannah Holman

'Heartstopping accounts' JULIET GARDINER, BBC HISTORY MAGAZINE

The sinking of the Titanic in the words of the survivors.

£14.99   978-1-4456-1443-4   512 pages HB 135 illus, 11 col

TITANIC
Filson Young

'If you only read one book about Titanic, read this one; if you've read every book published about the Titanic, read this one again'
NAUTILUS INTERNATIONAL TELEGRAPH

£9.99   978-1-4456-1278-2
160 pages HB 60 illus

THE TRUTH ABOUT THE TITANIC
Archibald Gracie

'Very vivid... the truth about the Titanic'
NEW YORK TIMES

The classic account by passenger Archibald Gracie who survived on top of an upturned lifeboat. With a new introduction and rare images.

£8.99   978-1-4456-0594-4
240 pages PB 76 illus

THE ILLUSTRATED SINKING OF THE TITANIC
L.T. Myers

America's first 'instant book' about the sinking of the Titanic.

£17.99   978-1-84868-053-1
192 pages PB 78 illus

WHY THE TITANIC SANK
W. B. Bartlett

Although the answer appears obvious, there is far more to the sinking of the Titanic than is popularly understood.

Feb 2012 £12.99 978-1-4456-0630-9
192 pages PB 50 illus

TITANIC
Campbell McCutcheon

The ideal introduction to the history and fate of the Titanic.

Feb 2012 £4.99   978-1-4456-0415-2
32 pages PB 78 illus, 30 col

TITANIC HERO
Arthur Rostron

'A gem... Arthur Rostron was actually there, and his account is about real people and the practicalities of helping them'
NAUTILUS INTERNATIONAL TELEGRAPH

£17.99   978-1-4456-0420-6
192 pages PB 39 illus

Available from all good bookshops or to order direct
Please call 01453-847-800 www.amberleybooks.com

"I've been looking forward to tonight all afternoon long."

"First you want me to pack and return to Chicago and then you tell me you've been wanting to go out with me. That's contradictory," Destiny said, but Wyatt saw the desire in her gaze.

"My feelings are contradictory," he said. "You're a complication in my quiet life." Her wide green eyes made him yearn to tell her to do whatever she wanted in Verity.

"A few complications in life sometimes makes it more interesting. You'll be able to handle this one, I'm sure."

"I can't wait to handle this complication," he said in a husky voice, his heart drumming as he looked at her full lips.

He knew she wasn't going to leave quietly. She would be a constant challenge to him…the most enticing challenge he'd ever had in his life.

* * *

A Texan in Her Bed
is part of the Lone Star Legends series from
USA TODAY bestselling author Sara Orwig

Reading Borough Council

3412601104872 8

A TEXAN IN HER BED

BY
SARA ORWIG

Paper from responsible sources. All papers used by Mills & Boon are natural, renewable and recyclable products and made from wood grown in sustainable forests. The logging and manufacturing processes conform to the legal environmental regulations of the country of origin.

Printed and bound in Spain
by Blackprint CPI, Barcelona

All rights reserved including the right of reproduction in whole or in part in any form. This edition is published by arrangement with Harlequin Books S.A.

This is a work of fiction. Names, characters, places, locations and incidents are purely fictional and bear no relationship to any real life individuals, living or dead, or to any actual places, business establishments, locations, events or incidents. Any resemblance is entirely coincidental.

This book is sold subject to the condition that it shall not, by way of trade or otherwise, be lent, resold, hired out or otherwise circulated without the prior consent of the publisher in any form of binding or cover other than that in which it is published and without a similar condition including this condition being imposed on the subsequent purchaser.

® and ™ are trademarks owned and used by the trademark owner and/or its licensee. Trademarks marked with ® are registered with the United Kingdom Patent Office and/or the Office for Harmonisation in the Internal Market and in other countries.

Published in Great Britain 2014
by Mills & Boon, an imprint of Harlequin (UK) Limited,
Eton House, 18-24 Paradise Road, Richmond, Surrey, TW9 1SR

© 2014 Sara Orwig

ISBN: 978-0-263-91477-1

51-0914

Harlequin (UK) Limited's policy is to use papers that are natural, renewable and r̶   ̶rests.
The l̶   ̶onmental
regul̶

Print̶
by B̶

**READING BOROUGH
LIBRARIES**

Askews & Holts	
AF	£5.49

Sara Orwig lives in Oklahoma. She has a patient husband who will take her on research trips anywhere, from big cities to old forts. She is an avid collector of Western history books. With a master's degree in English, Sara has written historical romance, mainstream fiction and contemporary romance. Books are beloved treasures that take Sara to magical worlds, and she loves both reading and writing them.

With many thanks to Stacy Boyd, Senior Editor.

One

What Sheriff Wyatt Milan liked most about his job was that he knew what to expect in his quiet town of Verity, Texas. But on this October afternoon when he turned his car around the corner onto Main Street he knew change was in the air.

A red limousine took up his parking space, plus some, right in front of city hall.

"What the hell?" he said quietly.

"Gosh almighty, there goes a quiet afternoon," Deputy Lambert whispered. "Will you look at that," he said louder.

Wyatt was looking. Directly in front of the small city hall building stood a prominent sign with large letters: No Parking—Reserved for the Sheriff of Verity, Texas.

He had expected the usual big empty space where he could park Verity's official black-and-red sheriff's car. Instead, the red stretch limousine took every inch of the allotted area.

He and his family had money, as did many families in

the town, but no one owned anything as flashy as an all-red limo. "That limo doesn't belong to anyone living in these parts," Wyatt said, more to himself than to his deputy, thinking something was about to shatter some of the peacefulness of his hometown.

"In my whole life, I've never seen a limo that big and that red," Val said with awe in his voice. "I'll go look for the driver."

"He may be inside."

"No one was scheduled to see you today, were they?"

"No," Wyatt said, halting beside the limo. "You write a ticket and stick it on the windshield. Come in when you're through. If the owner or the driver isn't here, we'll go look around town for him. The people who live here want a quiet, peaceful town. I want one, too. Thanks to my sister marrying a Calhoun, the old Milan-Calhoun feud has finally died down. I don't want something happening to bring trouble elsewhere in town."

"Amen to that. Why would anyone park a big limo in the sheriff's space?"

"Either he's lazy, starting trouble, unobservant or he's someone who thinks he can do whatever he wants. Who knows?"

Deputy Lambert stepped out and Wyatt drove around the corner and parked in the alley behind the building, in the small space allotted for two cars and a nearby Dumpster. His life had had enough upheavals—an emotional breakup years earlier with his fiancée and then coming home to his brother fighting with a Calhoun neighbor, keeping the century-old family feud explosive. When people wanted him to run for sheriff of Verity County, based in the town of Verity, he'd had to quiet fights between his brother Tony and Tony's neighbor Lindsay Calhoun. Everything was finally coming under control. He didn't want someone to come to town and destroy the peace he had worked hard to establish. He shook his head as he entered city hall. He hoped this was settled quickly and quietly and the red limo drove out of Verity the same way it'd come in.

Entering the Verity County sheriff's office through the back door, Wyatt walked down the long hall. His boot heels scraped the scuffed boards as he passed the large file room, a small break room and a meeting room with a small table and chairs. The hallway continued, dissecting the stone building. To the right were the mayor's office, the town records office and the utilities office. To the left were the sheriff's office and a two-cell jail. The center reception area was lined with vinyl-covered benches and in the middle was a desk where a clerk sat. Wyatt looked at Corporal Dwight Quinby whose wide eyes sent a silent message that something was up here at the office. Dwight's tangled light brown hair became more snarled as he ran his fingers through it.

"Sheriff, there's a woman in your office. When she said she wanted to see you, I told her to have a seat out here, that you'd be back soon, but she talked me into telling where your office is and letting her go back there. I don't even know how she did it. First thing I knew she smiled and was gone," he said, sounding dazed.

"Dwight, slow down," Wyatt drawled quietly. "Who is she? What's her name?"

"I didn't get her name. I don't know—one moment she was here and the next she was in your office. I don't know what happened."

"Tell Val when he comes in that I've found the limo passenger. Tell him to look around town for a uniformed driver and get that thing moved out of my parking place. Or call Argus and tell him to come tow that limo away from here."

"You might change your mind after you meet her," Dwight said.

Startled, Wyatt shook his head. "I don't think so. You call and get it towed," he said, curious now who was waiting in his office and why Dwight would say such a thing or look so dazed.

"Yes, sir," Dwight replied, glancing through the oval glass in the front door that offered a good view of the red limousine.

"Sheriff, you haven't ever met anyone like her," Dwight said, surprising Wyatt even more with such an uncustomary reaction.

With a long sigh, Wyatt headed for his office. Whatever the woman wanted, she'd have to move the limo before they did anything else. He hoped she wasn't moving to Verity. The town was filled with enough affluent people who thought they had special rights and privileges. It took tact and diplomacy to deal with them, including his own family sometimes.

In this case, he felt the owner of the limo lost all rights to tact and diplomacy when she had the limo parked in the sheriff's space.

Wyatt opened the door of his office and walked in. Instantly he forgot all about the limo.

His gaze focused on a long-legged redhead seated in a leather wingback chair that was turned slightly toward the door. Big green eyes immobilized him, a sensation that Wyatt was unaccustomed to. With an effort his gaze left hers, trailing over her while his breath left his body. Dimly, he wondered if another movie was going to be filmed in or near Verity and this was the star. A riot of curly auburn hair spilled over her shoulders, giving her a sensual, earthy look that heated his insides. Flawless, smooth skin heightened her allure. Her green dress emphasized the color of her eyes and clung to a figure that threatened to melt his thought processes. Lush curves turned the room temperature to the heat of a West Texas summer. He noted her tiny waist, but then his gaze traveled down where the dress ended at her crossed knees, down long shapely legs.

"Well, good morning to the illustrious sheriff of Verity County," she said, drawing out her words in a throaty voice that sounded like a suggestive invitation to sin instead of a greeting.

Without conscious thought of what he was doing, Wyatt walked toward her. He stopped in front of her. A faint hint of a smile gave a slight curve to her full, red lips and he couldn't keep from wondering what it would be like to kiss her.

"Good morning. It's Wyatt Milan," he said, waiting for her to respond and give him her name.

She smiled and his knees almost buckled. Her smile was dazzling and lit up her face as if she were the friendliest person in the state of Texas, and in that moment he understood why his clerk had been so dazzled.

When she held out her hand, he took it, his fingers closing around a dainty, warm hand that sent electricity streaking through him. A beautiful pearl-and-diamond band was on one of her fingers. He glanced at her other hand to see it was bare of rings.

"I'm Destiny Jones, Sheriff Milan. I'm from Chicago."

As if she had plunged a knife into his heart, Wyatt came out of his daze. He had never met the woman, but he knew the name and he knew about her. His wits began to work again and his breathing steadied, and he could almost view her without an intense physical reaction. As if his emotions were on a pendulum, his feelings about her swung in the opposite direction and he viewed her as pure trouble.

"Destiny Jones, as in Desirée Jones's sister," he said, recalling the headline-making, temperamental, stunningly beautiful movie star he had once had an affair with while she was on location in Verity. An affair that had ended badly. He remembered Desirée talking about her older sister who hosted a television show about unsolved mysteries and had written a bestselling book, *Unsolved Mysteries of the South*.

"Ah, you remember," she replied.

"I always remember a beautiful woman," he said, his gaze traveling leisurely over Destiny's features even as his guard came up. Both sisters were breathtaking, but they were both probably casual about their relationships. He had known that with Desirée and he guessed that now about Destiny.

"I've been waiting three years to meet the illustrious sheriff of Verity, Texas, and now I finally get to do so," she said with a smile that threatened to melt the polar ice caps. "You're a Milan, the family involved in a feud with the Calhouns."

"So you know about the feud," he said, suspecting trouble was coming his way within hours.

He turned a leather chair to face her and sat only a couple of feet away. "So you're in town for what purpose?" he asked bluntly, mildly amused that she had taken his parking place, made herself comfortable in his office and now with him. He saw no reason to waste time in polite chitchat. He was still idly curious, however, and he couldn't deny the thought of asking her to dinner crossed his mind.

"For one thing, I hope I can have an interview with you about the Lavita Wrenville house. I think it will be a wonderful subject for my *Unsolved Mysteries* television show."

Her words made him focus more rationally on her. He smiled only to be polite. The Wrenville house was where a Milan and a Calhoun had once fought over the same woman and both men, along with her father, had been shot to death. Century-old murders that could stir up the feud again.

"The Wrenville house," he said. "That place really isn't very interesting and there is nothing you can do at this time to solve the murders that happened in the house. That was over a century ago, old news with cold clues. At best, you might come back next year when the town of Verity has full rights to the property."

"That's interesting. I'd like to hear more about the town getting full rights. Even if I can't get a solution, I'd like to present the story about the house and family because it's unknown, unusual and I think it could be of interest to my audience."

"You might check Texas history because I think you'll find other unsolved mysteries that are far more fascinating in places far more appealing."

"That's interesting to know, too, Sheriff Milan," she said, giving him a sweet smile. "But I really want to do this one. And you should know I pursue what I want."

"And I imagine you're accustomed to getting what you want," he said, his gaze flicking over her. He guessed most men found it difficult to tell her no, especially with her devastating smile.

"That happens often," she said, leaning forward and shortening the gap between them. "I'm curious, Sheriff Milan," she said in a pleasant tone that probably ended most men's resistance, "why are you so set on discouraging me about the Wrenville house?"

"Verity is a quiet town with residents who like the status quo. As sheriff, I definitely like peace and quiet. If you'll look around, you won't find any tourist attractions. We do have a tiny museum, but it's not very interesting. Ditto our small library."

She smiled. "I assure you, I'm not planning to make this a tourist attraction. Maybe it's well you don't work for the Chamber of Commerce or the Tourist Center."

"We don't have a Tourist Center," he said quietly. "That should give you an idea."

From the moment he had discovered the red limo, this

woman had been surprising him, but her purpose for being here was an even bigger surprise—and an unpleasant one.

"I'm sorry you came all this way, Ms. Jones. You should have contacted me and I could have saved you the trouble. Lavita Wrenville was the last surviving Wrenville and she deeded the place to the town of Verity. According to the deed, we can't do anything to the grounds or house until next year, when it reverts totally to the town. I'm sheriff and I'm not opening that house."

"I am so sorry that you're unhappy about this, Sheriff Milan." Leaning back, she rummaged through a large purse. Gold bangles jingled on her arm and while her attention was on her purse, he looked her over from head to toe once again, his insides tightening as he envisioned her without the dress. As he gazed at her, she withdrew two envelopes and held them out to him. With a sinking feeling, he recognized the logo on one. "I wrote the governor of Texas, and I've written the mayor of Verity. I have letters from both stating clearly that I may look through the Wrenville house. Actually, I'm here as a guest of the state of Texas. You have such a nice governor. If you'd like to read the letters, here they are."

Wyatt held back a groan and resisted swearing. The last thing he wanted was someone stirring up the old family feud and drawing tourists who would want to walk through the Wrenville house. The dread that he experienced earlier—that his peaceful life and the public serenity of Verity were on the brink of destruction by one headstrong, sexy redhead—was coming true before his eyes.

A few moments later, after he'd read the letters, Wyatt made a mental note to talk to the mayor. Gyp Nash hadn't let him know one thing about Destiny Jones coming to Verity to see the Wrenville house. Gyp didn't like conflict, so that's probably why he had avoided telling Wyatt. But for the mayor to say how "thrilled" the townspeople would be that the Wrenville story would be the subject of one of her shows… Did Nash know this town at all?

He gave her back her letters. "Very nice," he said in clipped tones, trying to think what he could do to get rid of her.

"The Wrenville house is a big, dusty, empty house. There are all sorts of rumors and a legend about the property. People and kids have looked through it over the years until finally there's no interest in it. I want to keep it that way," he said. He felt a clash of wills with the charming, breathtaking bit of trouble that was sitting only a few feet from him. Along with the friction was a strong physical appeal that he didn't want, but couldn't shake.

"I suspect you've been through the house?"

"Oh, sure, when I was in high school. Kids used to be curious and there were all sorts of wild rumors, but they all died out. Ask people who have high school kids—there's no interest now. Jump back to my grandparents' generation and fights would break out over whether a Milan or a Calhoun shot first and killed the other as well as Lavita Wrenville's father that fatal night. In the three years that I've been sheriff we haven't had a fight break out over who fired the killing shots, nor have I had a trespassing call at the Wrenville place. It'll be better for the Calhouns and the Milans when the old house is gone. It serves as a reminder of the feud."

"Well, I'm curious and you're not discouraging me. It's a fascinating story of three unsolved murders and perhaps a hidden fortune. That's an intriguing mystery."

"Not really. There were three murders, but they took place in the late 1800s. That's so long ago no one cares now," he said, hoping he sounded convincing. "And as for the so-called fortune, Lavita Wrenville never married, was eccentric and may have saved some money and hidden it, but she was considered by most to be poverty stricken after she went through the money left to her by her father. All I've ever heard was that she lived in poverty and off other people's charity."

"Maybe you're too closely involved," Destiny said lightly, her constant smiles softening her persistent argument with him. "I find that it's still an interesting subject and I hope I can persuade you to give me an interview. I would be absolutely thrilled," she said in a throaty voice that made him think of hot kisses instead of a factual interview. "After all, you are a Milan and one of the men murdered in that house was a Milan—wasn't one of your ancestors rumored to have been murdered by a Calhoun?"

"Unfortunately, yes, that's my family's version, though the Calhouns say it was a Calhoun murdered by a Milan. But it was way before my time and I sure as hell didn't know him. There's not that much to talk about. Later in her life, Lavita Wrenville was considered a recluse and an eccentric old maid. End of information."

"Sheriff Milan, I hope it's not the end of information or our conversations. I imagine you know all sorts of things, maybe more than anyone else, about history here." She rewarded him with another dazzling smile that made him want to stop arguing with her. "I have been looking forward so much to meeting you."

He could see why Dwight didn't know how she had talked him into letting her wait in Wyatt's office. It was difficult to keep his mind on his subject with her hanging on his every word, smiling at him constantly and sounding as if she might be talking to the most brilliant man in Verity. That plus her looks probably caused her to get her way almost 100 percent of the time. Of their own will, his eyes glanced down at her long legs. Just looking at them sparked desire. He didn't want to give her an interview. He wanted to seduce her and then send her on her way.

"Maybe I can get you to change your mind about the interview," she said in a breathy voice.

"You can try," he replied with amusement.

"I think that will be a fun project."

He found himself excited by the challenge. Yes, it was going to be difficult to say no to Destiny Jones.

With an effort he looked up again. He gazed into the green eyes that held him captive. His every nerve sizzled, his pulse quickened and his breathing altered. He wanted to reach for her and close the last bit of distance between them even though he knew this whole conversation was to get what she wanted from him.

"Sheriff Milan," she drawled.

With an effort he sat straighter. "No interview," he gasped, struggling to get his voice back to normal while fighting the urge to lean the last few inches and kiss her.

She smiled. "I hope you'll change your mind. You're part of this town and one of families involved in the famous feud and you're sheriff—there would be a lot of interest."

"I lead a quiet life. I don't think I would be that interesting and the feud is fading, so I don't care to bring it back into the limelight."

She laughed, a sunny, contagious, merry sound that he could listen to all day. His mind groped for sanity and to get back to a factual, impersonal conversation. He felt as if he wanted to loosen his collar. Even more, he wanted to reach for her, to kiss that full mouth and feel her softness pressed against him. Lost in that mental picture, he struggled to remember what he had to discuss with her.

"Your limo is in my parking place and you have a ticket," he blurted in an effort to get back to business. His voice came out with a husky note and it was difficult to think about business or anything except giving in to her or kissing her. He didn't like that loss of control. He didn't give in to his urges anymore, not after getting his heart broken by Katherine. "We've called to have the limo towed," he said, beginning to gather his wits. "Where's your driver?"

"I told him I'd call him when I'm through talking to you. He's just looking at the town or getting coffee. He's not far."

"You need to get that limo moved now," Wyatt declared, barely aware of what he said to her, also barely noticing that she had no reaction to his announcement that her limo would be towed.

"Oh, he will as soon as I'm finished here. I can be persistent, Sheriff Milan, when I want something," she said. "I want to try to change your mind. You do change your mind sometimes, don't you?" She asked in such a friendly, good-natured tone, he had to laugh.

"Yes, I can change my mind," he replied, thinking she was the biggest challenge he had had in too long to remember. He couldn't recall ever being so totally distracted. "Are you staying in Verity tonight, or somewhere else?" he said, knowing her answer but hoping for a different one.

"My staff and I are staying in the Verity Hotel."

"A good place to stay. The Verity Hotel doesn't have any unsolved mysteries or even ancient legends, but it's an old hotel dating back to 1887. It burned in the early 1900s and was rebuilt. It has been remodeled several times including in 2002, as well as in the past three years when it was completely renovated. It's a nice place to stay."

As he talked, he continued to study her, struggling to drag his attention elsewhere. Her movie star, younger sister was breathtakingly beautiful, far more flirty, but Destiny was a combination of friendly charm and sensuality, a sexual appeal that set his pulse pounding. He suspected his reaction was generally the same as it was with every man she encountered.

"Did Mayor Nash tell you the history of Verity or the Wrenville house?"

"No," she said. "He merely welcomed me to town and seemed happy that I had an interest in using the Wrenville house for one of my subjects. I have an appointment with him later this week."

Wyatt wanted to say, *I'll bet you do.* Instead, different words came out of his mouth. "Since you don't know our history, let me take you to dinner tonight and I'll tell you about it." The words just popped out as if he had no control over what he said. For his own good he should get rid of this woman and avoid her as much as possible. Instead, he had invited her out. And dammit, he could not keep from hoping she would accept.

"How delightful," she said, smiling again. "Thank you. I would love to go to dinner with you and hear about your life, Verity and the Wrenville house. I can send my limo to pick you up."

Her words lifted the fog that had settled on his brain. Smiling, he shook his head. "Thanks. I'll come to the hotel and get you. Seven?"

"Fine," she said, standing and offering her hand.

He wrapped his fingers around hers, stepping closer to her at the same time. She didn't step back, but instead continued to smile as she looked up at him. He was within inches, his hand holding hers, sending streaks of fire from the simple physical contact. She had a lush body made for love, and tonight, he intended to take her to dinner and afterward, to seduce her. And he hoped she would be willing in an effort to get what she wanted from him.

"It's been interesting," he said in a husky voice.

"But you wish I'd go away," she said, softening her words with another one of her fabulous smiles.

"I didn't say that I didn't like you. You're big city—

we're small town," he said in a husky voice. "Charming, stunning and captivating."

"Thank you, Sheriff Milan. How nice you are."

"It's Wyatt. I have a feeling we'll see each other often while you're here," he said, wondering if she would be as enticing to kiss as he thought she might be.

"We'll see each other," she said, the breathless note returning to her voice. "I think hierarchy is on my side on this one. The governor of Texas trumps the sheriff of Verity. I came prepared. My sister has told me about you in great detail."

He merely smiled, recalling how angry her sister had been with him the last hour they had spent together. She had wanted him to go back to California with her and she was accustomed to getting her way. When he had refused, it did not go well. If she'd planned to stay, he'd have broken up with her, but since she was leaving Verity forever, he played the affair to its end, even though he had grown tired of her and her appeal had fizzled.

He suspected her older sister was just as stubborn. In spite of Destiny's smiles and polite charm, he continually felt their clash of wills.

He dropped her hand and headed to the door. As she walked beside him, he inhaled the scent of her mesmerizing perfume. He opened his office door and they walked out into the reception area where a group had gathered. Cameras flashed while people clamored noisily as they surged toward her.

Wyatt stepped in front of her, shielding her from the reporters that he easily recognized, two local, the others from the area and one from a Fort Worth station and one from Dallas. His deputy came forward to help, but Destiny stepped easily in front of Wyatt.

"I'll be happy to answer your questions," she said, smiling at the media.

"Not in here, please," Wyatt said in an authoritative tone that caused a hush. "Folks, take the interview across the street. We have to conduct business here, not a press conference. Jeff, Millie, Duncan—outside, please," Wyatt said, calling the names of the reporters that had the most influence. He knew nearly everyone in the crowd.

"We'll go across the street," Destiny said, smiling at the crowd and shaking someone's outstretched hand.

Wyatt watched a man and a woman emerge from the crowd. He didn't know them, but they flanked Destiny and he guessed they were two of her staff members.

"Dammit," he said quietly, thinking about Destiny putting the Wrenville house—and, as a result, the Milans, the Calhouns and their feud—on television for the world to view. He didn't think it would be any easier to keep her out of the Wrenville house than to get her out of his parking spot.

"I'm going to see Gyp," he said tersely to his deputy.

He shook his head. "The mayor left for the day. He said to tell you he would see you in the morning."

"Dammit," Wyatt repeated, turning to go back into his office, figuring Gyp had ducked out on him because he knew Wyatt would be unhappy. Wyatt shook his head as he swore again. Townspeople would not be thrilled when Destiny Jones fanned the flames of old animosities.

Abruptly, Wyatt headed out the back door of city hall, circling to Main Street in long strides, hoping the limo was gone and her impromptu press conference was over. As he turned the corner, he stopped short. Not only was the red limo still in his parking place, but her audience had grown. In addition, a TV truck was parked down the street, lights had been set up and he could see men with video cameras. Shaking his head, Wyatt stared at the circus going on across the street. The lady knew how to draw a crowd. He made a mental note to get a private room for their dinner.

Wyatt scanned the crowd that spilled into the street and lined the sidewalk. He recognized Dustin Redwing and Pete Lee, two men who worked for him. He saw the curly white hair of Horace Pringle, the president of Verity's largest bank. Ty Hemmings, the owner of the movie theater, was in the audience, along with several other shop owners. He spotted Farley White, his mechanic.

Wyatt knew nearly everyone in the gathering. He shook his head at the sight of Charlie Akin, the local eccentric who lived in a shack along the river in a neighboring county. Periodically, the river flooded, taking Charlie's shack. He moved downriver or upriver, staying in the general area and built another shack, taking his goats and chickens with him. Wyatt wondered how Charlie had gotten word that Destiny Jones was in Verity.

Deputy Lambert stood nearby, watching the crowd, and Wyatt was certain his deputy was there out of a sense of duty. Wyatt continued studying the crowd, recognizing face after face, being only slightly surprised that Destiny had drawn such a gathering because she would draw attention wherever she went.

He looked at her as she answered a question. A breeze tugged long tendrils of her deep auburn hair. She looked like a movie star standing there in the sunshine while people asked her questions. She glanced his way. Even though he knew it was ridiculous, he felt as if she had reached out and touched him. Her gaze held his while she finished her answer. Then she turned to look at someone asking her a question.

His cell phone rang and he pulled it out to see he had a text from his brother Nick. "Dammit," Wyatt said quietly, scanning Nick's text.

Watching Destiny Jones in Verity on TV. Why didn't you let us know? When can I meet her? How long will she be in Verity? The Wrenville murders?

As he read it he received another text, this one from his youngest brother, Tony, also wanting to know about Destiny. Wyatt shook his head and strode through the front door of city hall.

"Sheriff," Dwight said, shaking his head, "Argus is dealing with two wrecked cars on the highway and he can't tow the limo for several hours."

"Okay. Val is across the street. Do you know if he found the driver?"

"He did. The man said he would move the limo when his boss told him to move it."

Wyatt smiled and shook his head again. Was she doing this deliberately to get his attention? Beneath her smiles and charm was a strong will. He shook his head and went to his office to call Nick first on his private line.

"Nick, you have too many questions for a text. I didn't know she was coming. Yes, I've met her. I don't know about introducing you, but are you sure you want to meet her?"

"You've got to be kidding. Look at the crowd she's drawn. If you didn't know she was coming, then the town didn't know," Nick replied.

"I think that's right."

"She knows how to draw a crowd."

"All she has to do is walk down the street."

"Amen. You've got that right. Try to figure some way we can meet her. Tony's already sent me a text. How come you're not out there?"

"I've already met her, and my deputy is there."

"So you've talked to her."

"A little. I'll get you the introduction, and I'll call you about when and where."

"Thanks, Wyatt. She said she's staying at the Verity Hotel."

"So she told everyone, including the press, where she'll be. The lady does want attention. Don't tell me you're going to hang out in the lobby?"

Nick chuckled. "Hardly. No, I'll meet her, but not that way. Thanks for calling."

"I'll keep in touch."

Wyatt sent Tony a text. Three minutes later his phone rang.

"I'm watching Destiny Jones in Verity on TV."

"I'm sure you are. I've talked to Nick and I promise I'll introduce both of you sometime."

"Cool. Don't forget. Right now you're missing her interview."

"I'll live. Talk to you soon, Tony." Wyatt picked up an iPad from his desk and switched to the television cable to pick up her interview. He watched her deftly field questions, give answers that would bring laughter and generally captivate the audience. He gazed at her green eyes and auburn hair. It wouldn't matter if she had mumbled and had nothing to say. She was gorgeous and charming and her audience was enchanted.

Wyatt's jaw clamped shut a little more tightly as he listened to her talk about wanting to learn about Lavita Wrenville and how fascinating Verity's history was, including the Milan-Calhoun feud. Each minute he watched her his hopes sank lower because at dinner he had hoped to discourage her from using the unsolved murders at the Wrenville house for a show. There would be no way, now that she'd spoken about it to the media, that she'd pack up and go back to Chicago.

He thought about her parking the red limo in his space. That had not been a casual, thoughtless event. She wanted the town's attention and she had known exactly what she was doing then, just as she knew what she was doing now in talking to the crowd that was still growing. Shortly, he would have to go out there and break it up because they would be blocking traffic on Main if many more people came to watch her.

Even as he thought that and watched, she told the crowd farewell. A man stepped in front of her and a woman moved on one side of her. To Wyatt's surprise Val moved beside her on the other side as a second woman fell in behind them. They crossed the street, the man in the lead clearing the way while a smaller crowd flowed with her. When they reached the red limo, the man leading the way held the door. She turned to smile and wave at the crowd, thanking them, throwing them a kiss and then vanishing into the limo, followed by the two women, the tinted windows hiding the interior. In seconds the limo slowly eased from the curb and the crowd dispersed.

He switched off the iPad and stood, rubbing the back of his neck.

He had mixed feelings about dinner with her, but his desire to spend the evening with her outweighed his dislike of having to deal with her about the Wrenville murders and the old family feud. Seven o'clock couldn't come too soon.

Wyatt nodded. This might be a night to remember.

Two

Destiny and her staff entered the hotel and took the VIP elevator to the top floor where she had all four suites. In addition to hers, Virginia and Duke Boyden, her camera operator and her chauffeur, shared a suite, while Amy had her own suite next to Destiny's.

Destiny entered her suite, followed by Amy Osgood, her cousin and assistant. Destiny barely glanced at a huge bouquet of pink-and-white lilies on the oval glass table in front of the sofa. Amy paused beside a large round platter holding cheeses, crackers and fruit. A stack of china plates and cutlery was on a tray next to the hors d'oeuvres. Amy picked up a card. "Compliments of the Verity Hotel," she read.

"Take all that to your room. I really don't want any of it."

"Thanks, Destiny. I'll take some. I have a smaller version in my room and the Boydens have one, also."

"Y'all can share mine," Destiny said as she tossed aside

her large bag. She was remembering the moment in his office that Sheriff Wyatt Milan had entered. The most vivid, crystal-blue eyes she had ever seen had taken her breath away, holding her immobile, stopping her thoughts while they had stared at each other. She had seen pictures of him, but she wasn't prepared for the man in person. No wonder Desirée had fallen for him. She had never understood what had gotten into her little sister to go to some tiny town in Texas and fall head over heels in love with the sheriff.

She had learned soon enough that she had been wrong in her views of the small Texas town. Verity's residents had enormous wealth. She had been surprised when she had learned the sheriff himself was a billionaire rancher, a member of an old-time Texas family, a former professional football player and he held a law degree. But looking into his blue eyes today, feeling the force of his personality when he had simply entered the room, she realized why Desirée had been bowled over. The man was larger-than-life. One look and her opinions of Wyatt Milan had changed instantly.

Wavy brown hair above a face with rugged features, prominent cheekbones, a slight bump in his nose, maybe from a break, a stubborn jut to his chin. He wore a neat brown uniform with an unofficial hand-tooled leather belt around his narrow waist and boots on his feet. It wouldn't have mattered what he wore; just standing quietly he had a commanding presence.

She spun around in a circle with her arms outstretched. "Congratulate me, Amy. Sheriff Milan is taking me to dinner tonight. Just what I want, but coming sooner than I expected."

"Congratulations!" Amy said, glancing at her boss with a frown.

"Don't look so worried."

"You said he doesn't want you here or want you using Verity for a show," Amy said.

"Sheriff Milan will change his mind. You'll see. Besides, I have the letter from the governor of Texas and a letter from Mayor Nash."

"So when are you going to make it public that you have a tie to this town?" Amy asked.

"I told you—when I can get the most attention by doing so. Attention for the show. I'll make my announcement when I'm taping. Until then it's our little secret. Verity doesn't make the news, so it's never been picked up by the media that I have a connection here."

"Sheriff Milan already isn't happy with you. He'll really dislike learning your mother is in a branch of the Calhoun family from here."

Destiny smiled. "We'll see when the time comes. Until then—bury it."

"I will. It's a shame the sheriff doesn't want you here. I think the story of the murders should be interesting. People in the crowd today seemed to like you and want you here."

"Verity is a small town and they keep to themselves. No one has ever made an issue about the house or publicized it. It's just gone unnoticed. Lots of towns that have something like this capitalize on it and make it a tourist attraction or Halloween event and get attention, but not here. That makes it good for me to use in my book whether or not I find anything. I don't really expect to solve the old murders. It's been more than a hundred years since Lavita Wrenville's demise."

"You must have made an impression on Sheriff Milan since he asked you to dinner tonight."

"He invited me to dinner to try to talk me out of staying here and doing a show about the Wrenville house. He doesn't know that I've heard about the murders, the legend and the feud from Mimi," she said, using the name she had called her grandmother since she had learned to talk

"Your grandmother seems to know a lot about this town even though she never lived here."

"She lived in Dallas and had other Calhoun relatives here. She's the one who interested me in the story of Lavita Wrenville and the triple murders."

"It will shock people when you announce you're a Calhoun," Amy said and Destiny smiled. "It will add a little spice to the story of the Wrenville murders. I hope it doesn't rock the sheriff too badly."

Amy continued, "I heard a woman broke their engagement and Sheriff Milan hasn't had a serious affair since. That might explain his actions with your sister. He's about the only one who had an affair with her and didn't propose."

"So he's had a broken heart? Interesting," Destiny said, thinking about Wyatt. "I don't think Desirée knew that, but she's more interested in herself than the men she dates, so she doesn't really learn a lot about them. Wyatt keeps himself all buttoned up. He likes women—and vice versa, I'm sure. Desirée probably did what every other single female in this town has done—fallen in love with him. Have you ever seen such blue eyes?"

"I haven't met him yet. I think he stood across the street today when you talked to all the people."

"Yes, he did. Did any of you find out why our billionaire rancher is also sheriff of Verity? Mimi knew nothing about that."

"Actually, from what we've pieced together it's because of the Wrenville house."

Destiny stopped looking through her purse and raised her head. "How so?" She held up her hand. "Wait. I better get ready for tonight. He's picking me up at seven. Come tell me while I decide what to wear." She headed into the large bedroom. A huge bouquet of red anthurium and purple gladioli stood on a table. She glanced at the card. "Enjoy your stay. Verity Chamber of Commerce."

Amy went on to explain what they'd learned. "All we could find out is that next year the Wrenville house reverts totally to the town and the town officials can do what they want with the house and property. The people wanted someone for sheriff they could trust when that happens and by general consensus, Wyatt Milan is a trustworthy and honest man, so they talked him into running for office."

"And he's probably not happy with someone—me—coming in and poking around before he has control," Destiny added.

"Everyone seems to like him as sheriff."

"Especially the ladies, I imagine. According to Desirée, men like him, too." Destiny looked through her clothes. "About tonight, did you let some of the press know that I'm going out with Sheriff Milan?"

"Yes, I did."

"Good. I'm going to shower. And I'll make a call to Mimi and to Desirée."

"If you don't need anything else right now, I'll go unpack some more of my things."

"Thanks for doing mine earlier."

"Sure," Amy said over her shoulder as she left the suite.

Destiny showered, then pulled on undergarments and a robe and got her iPad to do FaceTime with her grandmother. She felt better if she could see the frail, aging woman. Destiny settled back to talk, waiting patiently because it took time for her grandmother to deal with FaceTime.

"Mimi, I've met Sheriff Milan," she said after inquiring about her grandmother's health and listening to her talk about her day.

"Did he take it well to discover you're a Calhoun? Desirée never told him she was," Mimi said. "Then again Desirée can barely remember her heritage and really doesn't care."

"I haven't told him yet either. I'm waiting for the perfect moment. He's taking me to dinner tonight."

"He's a Milan, Destiny. You can't trust a Milan."

"Mimi, I think I can trust this one. He got elected sheriff because everyone in Verity trusts him, even Calhouns. Besides, tonight is a business dinner. He wants to talk me out of putting Verity on my show."

"Pay no attention," her white-haired grandmother said, smiling. "He's a Milan and they're hardheaded and I still say he probably won't give you straight answers."

Destiny held back a laugh. Her grandmother never even lived in Verity and knew about the feud only from her parents and grandparents, yet she harbored strong feelings against the Milans. She was the one who had told Destiny of her Calhoun genealogy.

"I'll let you know how it went," Destiny said, moving to other subjects until finally, she told her grandmother she needed to go.

"Take care of yourself, Destiny. If the sheriff doesn't want you there, maybe you should reconsider. Please be careful."

"I'll be careful. I love you, Mimi," she said. "Call me anytime," she added, wishing she could do more to make her grandmother comfortable, knowing her arthritis bothered her and she didn't get enough sleep at night.

She thought about the tall, ruggedly appealing sheriff of Verity and her pulse quickened. This would be more interesting than she had anticipated. And more challenging. Most men she encountered were struck by her looks and eager to please her. Wyatt Milan was an exception, but she enjoyed a challenge.

Desirée had told Destiny if she wanted cooperation from the sheriff, she should flirt with him and resort to her female wiles to get what she wanted. He might be happy with some flirting, but Destiny didn't think it would change his opinion one bit. It certainly hadn't worked with her sister. He'd been one of the few men able to resist Desirée.

Desirée had gotten over Wyatt and he was all but forgotten within a month after she returned to California. She could forget men as easily as she fell in love with them. Now that Destiny knew Wyatt, she wondered why her sister had ever thought he would go with her back to California. She could, however, understand why Desirée had been attracted to him.

She crossed the room to look in the closet again to decide what she would wear, finally selecting a dress that she hoped would get Wyatt's attention.

At five before seven she critically studied her image in the full-length mirror, trying to decide if she had achieved the look she wanted. The straight black dress hugged her curves from her waist down, and the top of the dress had a one-shoulder neckline in hot pink that matched her high-heeled sandals. Her hair was pinned up, with curly strands falling free around her face. Gold earrings dangled from her ears and along with the gold bracelets complemented her gold necklace with three diamonds centered in it.

Satisfied with her appearance, she picked up a small black purse just as the phone rang and she answered to hear Wyatt's voice saying he was in the lobby.

Since she had told the media why she was in Verity, she expected to get attention all the time she was in town. When she stepped down into the lobby from the curving staircase from the mezzanine, she noticed two men with cameras aimed at her. In fact, every man in the lobby looked in her direction. Her pulse skipped a beat when she spotted Wyatt Milan. Dressed in a charcoal suit, black boots, a black wide-brimmed hat, he stood a few yards from the bottom step.

His gaze met hers, causing her heart to thud. Smiling at him, she walked down the stairs. She was aware of the cameras, but her gaze was on Wyatt, who looked back with the faintest hint of a smile.

At the bottom step he came forward. "Destiny," he said, the simple pronunciation of her name sounding different from anyone else she had heard say it. She tingled from her head to her toes. She'd never had a physical reaction to a man as intense as with Wyatt. She had never expected to be so attracted to him. His electronic pictures had not conveyed his appeal.

He gave her a full smile, laugh lines creasing the corners of his mouth, and she actually felt weak in the knees as he linked her arm with his.

A man holding a camera stepped close. "Evening, Wyatt. Ms. Jones, I'm Carl Stanley with the Verity paper. Is Sheriff Milan taking you to the Wrenville house now?"

"I didn't dress this way to go to the Wrenville house," she said, laughing along with Carl and the others around her. "That will come a little later," she answered, smiling at him.

"How did you hear about Verity and the Wrenville house? Was it from your sister when she visited?"

"I heard about it before that. Maybe Verity is more famous than people who live here realize," she said while the reporter took notes.

"Do you hope to solve the mystery of the three murders in Lavita's house?"

"That would be a fabulous result, but I don't expect to get answers to questions that people have been asking for over a century. We're just looking into the situation. Sometimes my show, *Unsolved Mysteries,* prompts people to come forward. We've had some solutions to puzzling cases since we started the series."

"Are you going to interview local people for your show?"

"Carl, in due time you'll see how the show unfolds. Thank you for your questions and your interest. Verity is one of the friendliest towns I've ever visited. We'll talk again," Destiny said, smiling as he raised his digital camera and got a close-up of her. Two more men moved closer and she smiled and posed while they took pictures.

Wyatt stepped forward. "Okay, guys, you have your pictures. We'll be going now. Ms. Jones will be around to answer questions later this week." He whisked her outside and into a black sports car. In long strides he circled the car and climbed inside to drive away.

"You handled that well," she said.

"I believe you're the one who handled it. You're news right now and they're interested, which you expected them to be, and I can't blame them. This is a quiet town."

She laughed softly. "Are they following us?"

"No, they won't follow us. Sorry if you're disappointed."

"Why are you so certain they won't follow?"

"They know me and they know I don't want them trailing after me. They want my cooperation too often to cross me."

"So what if someone does?" she persisted.

"We'll see. It hasn't ever happened."

"I don't think I'm the only one here who's accustomed to getting his way."

The corner of Wyatt's mouth lifted slightly, but he didn't glance her way or answer and they rode a few minutes in silence.

"Am I really the first outside person to show an interest in the Wrenville house?" Destiny asked. "That's what someone told me."

"As far as I know. I can't really speak for before my time." He checked his mirrors. "My deputy and I stayed out there once, just to see if anything happened or if vagrants were in there. Nothing happened and no one was staying there. The house is run-down, neglected. No one's lived in it since the 1800s. It was well built to begin with or it would be falling in by now, but when something is abandoned, it doesn't last."

"So the house is ignored by one and all."

"That sums it up. I think you'll have a difficult time filling half an hour about the house or the people who died in it."

"We'll see. I hope you'll consider a brief interview. Since you're a Milan, I think it would be of interest."

"Sorry, the answer's still the same. No interview. So far, no occasion has ever arisen in Verity that warrants an interview from me, other than just answering brief questions for the news. And that's the way I hope it remains. I wouldn't be that interesting, anyway."

"I differ on that topic. I'm not accustomed to getting turned down."

Wyatt gave her a quick glance. "I'm sure that's the truth. I imagine you're accustomed to getting what you want from men."

"Most of the time, I do. So far, you're proving to be an exception, but I hope I can change your mind."

He glanced over at her. "It all depends on what you want from me," he said, a husky note coming into his voice that gave her the satisfaction of knowing he had some kind of reaction to her.

"Wyatt," she said, "you haven't discouraged me. I still hope to get an interview from you. I know it would be interesting."

"You'd be surprised how dull I can get. Ask a local reporter. Their eyes glaze over sometimes, but it shortens interviews."

She laughed softly again. "I don't think you really do

that—at least I would guess it is rare. I'm still going for an interview of my own." She received another glance and this time his crystal-blue eyes darkened slightly and the look he gave her raised the temperature in the car.

"You go ahead and try," he said in a deep voice that made her heart race.

"So that doesn't scare you?" she asked.

"Hardly. It'll be interesting to see you bargain for an interview," he replied. He shook his head. "The evening has definitely taken a turn for the better."

"We'll see," she replied.

Leaning back in the seat, she gave thought to the situation. Wyatt wasn't reacting to her the way the majority of men did. She had grown up knowing that she was not the pretty daughter in her family. Desirée was breathtakingly beautiful and had been so all her life. Destiny had unruly red hair, was tall, but not stunning in her physical appearance, especially during her awkward teen years, but from an early age, she had learned to please and charm those around her to get what she wanted. With her relatives, she had poured out her love, being cooperative, obedient, helpful and turning on the sweetness when she needed to. During her later teens with boys her age, she had flirted, and it hadn't taken much to melt them into hopeful males eager to please her.

It shocked her that, so far, Wyatt had resisted her smiles and easy requests.

She studied his profile, the firm jaw, prominent cheekbones, a slight bump near the bridge of his nose. He was not what she had expected and she was having a reaction to him that surprised and disturbed her.

"Do you have other places in Texas that you'll visit?" he asked.

"Not at this time."

As she watched him drive, he gave her a quick glance. "So how is Desirée?" he asked.

"She's fine. She recently married."

"I saw that she did. I hope she's very happy."

"I'll tell her you said that."

"Does she know you're in Verity?"

"Yes, she does. From what I hear, you're still single, which surprises me."

"Now why would that surprise you?" he asked.

"You're handsome, in your early thirties, appealing, influential and well-known. I'm sure every female in this county knows you. If we consider just the single ladies, I'd guess the ones in this county plus the next three or four counties know you. Texas women are beautiful. The elements are right for you to fall in love and marry."

He smiled without taking his attention from the road. "You'd think, but it hasn't happened."

"So there's no one you had to explain to about taking me to dinner tonight?"

"No, there isn't. By the way, while you're here, two of my brothers want to meet you. They saw you on TV today, and one of them has read your last book."

"Well, I'm happy to discuss my book with anyone who is interested," she replied. "So my book is why they want to meet me?"

"Not altogether," Wyatt replied. "It's part of the reason. I imagine every man in Verity would like to meet you. And maybe every male over fifteen in the next four or five counties," he said.

"I take it your brothers are single."

"One is widowed and the other is my single, youngest brother, so you're right. Nick lost his pregnant wife. He's still hurting pretty badly. It's been a rough time for him and he's not dating anyone."

"I'm sorry to hear that," she said, startled about the loss in Wyatt's family. "I don't think Desirée knew that."

"There's no reason for her to keep up with Nick, and that hadn't happened when she was here."

Destiny gazed out the window, taken aback once again by seeing a more serious side to Wyatt. Now that she was getting to know him a little, she wanted to be more up-front with him and thought about the right moment to reveal her genealogy. "Well, I, for one, have been curious about you. There aren't many men who can upset my sister."

"I'm sorry if I did, but I don't think it was devastating since she was married within the year—I believe her first marriage. In the three years since we dated, isn't this marriage number two? I don't think she's been pining away over me."

"Perhaps not. It's too bad. Now that I've met you, I imagine you would have had a settling influence on her. A sheriff, rock solid, mid-America, a Texan. How the two of you got together in the first place, I can't imagine," she added. "You don't look the type to be knocked off your feet simply because she's a movie star."

"You have that much right," he said, smiling again. "Look again at your sister. She's one of the most beautiful women I've ever seen. You're one of the most stunning. And she flirts outrageously, which I'm sure you already know."

"Thank you. My sister is beautiful. She's been beautiful from the day she was born." After a moment of silence, Destiny turned to him. "You were rather laid-back today. Do you ever get upset, Sheriff?"

"Sure, when things get bad enough. Most of the time in Verity, there's nothing bad enough."

"So my reporting about the Wrenville house murders isn't bad enough to get you riled up?"

"Not so far," he said. "Maybe your quest is annoying, but not critical. We'll see as time goes by."

She saw that the buildings on Main Street had given way to houses. Heading east, they passed two blocks of wooden Victorian-style homes, some single story, some two or three stories with tall trees that had thick trunks in what looked like an old part of town.

"We have passed most of Verity's restaurants. Where are we going?"

"To the airport. We'll fly to Dallas to eat. You have no objection to that, do you?"

"Of course not," she said. "So you'll avoid the press for the rest of the night."

"I sure hope so," he replied, "and I hope that doesn't disappoint you."

"If it did, I don't think you'd turn around and go back," she said, amused. "So the sheriff of Verity has his own plane. Interesting."

"Actually, it's mutually owned by me and my siblings. We all have ranches and want to be able to come and go, so we bought two planes and hired pilots and the necessary employees. I have my own pilot's license, as do my brothers Nick and Tony. It's worked out great."

"Nice, if you can afford it." She looked out at the passing scenery. "I recall we came into town this way so we should be passing the Wrenville house. There it is," she said, looking at a wooden three-story home surrounded by a three-foot wrought-iron fence and a front gate hanging on one hinge. She noticed several of the windows had been broken out.

"Just an old, empty house that the town will own shortly," Wyatt said. "Nothing exciting there. And there can't be any clues in it about the three men who died there."

"You don't discourage me. It's more interesting than that." Destiny said, taking in the weeds and high grass that filled the yard while the two tall oaks by the house were overgrown with vines. "No, I'm excited, filled with curiosity. Sometimes it's surprising what my show stirs up. Maybe someone will come forth with information that has been passed down through the generations. A Milan and a Calhoun both in love with the same woman and both shot dead over her, along with her father—that's an interesting unsolved mystery. You have to admit it."

"Interesting to an outsider, I suppose, but we don't need the old feud stirred up. As generations pass it has weakened and with my generation, I think the feud is dying. I want it to die. We're a quiet little town. I don't want to see that disturbed needlessly."

"A quiet little town with a high percentage of millionaires," she said. She realized she had never known anyone as protective of his hometown and his family and she had to respect Wyatt for that.

"West Texas is good cattle and oil country, plus a few other businesses that have done well here," he replied.

In minutes he turned along a narrow asphalt road and shortly she saw two hangars and a control tower ahead. A jet was outside and she assumed it would be the plane they would take to Dallas.

Wyatt picked up his phone to talk to his pilot, letting him know they were almost there, and she tingled with anticipation, looking forward to an evening with Wyatt Milan. She wondered what he would think when he learned she was a Calhoun. He acted as if he thought the old feud should die, but she barely knew him. When it involved him personally, would he still think the feud should end? Mimi had painted such a dark picture of the Milans as dishonest, crafty and manipulative that Destiny had expected a man far different from the Milan she was getting to know tonight. None of those descriptions fit Wyatt. Far from it. Honest, straightforward, hoping for good—he embodied admirable qualities. She loved Mimi and they were close, but her grandmother was wrong about this Milan.

Her gaze lowered to his mouth. Strong, firm, his lips made her wonder if he would kiss her tonight. The chemistry between them was exciting. She felt it, and she was certain he did, too. Could she kiss him into agreeing to an interview?

Three

As they reached the plane, Wyatt stopped near a brown-haired man with touches of gray in his hair. He smiled at Destiny.

"Destiny, meet our pilot, Jason Whittaker. Jason, this is Ms. Jones from Chicago."

"It's Destiny," she said, offering her hand. "I'm happy to meet you and looking forward to the flight."

"Unsolved Mysteries," Jason said and Destiny's smile broadened. Wyatt watched her step forward and charm his pilot who could not take his gaze from her. Wyatt could understand. She'd stolen his breath when she had appeared at the top of the stairs at the hotel. The woman knew how to make a grand entrance. Every man in the hotel lobby had been watching her and Wyatt had heard an audible sigh from several who were standing near him when she appeared. She wasn't the delicate, perfect beauty her sister was. Instead, she was hot, sexual, lush, with a voluptuous body, a come-hither look and unruly red hair that

looked as if she had just left a romp in bed. How was he going to keep denying her an interview or discouraging her from the Wrenville house? She left him tongue-tied, on fire, unable to think clearly, torn between wanting to seduce her and hoping she would pack up and go. Never had a woman rocked him like this one.

"We have good weather," the pilot remarked, pulling Wyatt from his reverie.

"Let's get going," Wyatt said, taking her arm and boarding the plane. The moment he touched her, the casual contact electrified him. Her perfume deepened his awareness of her at his side. He motioned to a seat and as she sat near a window and buckled herself in, he sat facing her.

She looked out the window and the plane began to taxi away from the hangar. When they were airborne and headed southeast, she turned to Wyatt.

"So tell me the history of the Lavita Wrenville house."

"In the early days Verity was a hub for cattle ranchers. The Wrenville family was successful and built their big home. Lavita's father still had eastern interests and was partners with his brother in a large bank in Boston. At one time, according to legend or family history, the Wrenvilles were enormously wealthy—in a time and place where there were an unusually high number of wealthy families."

"The Milans and the Calhouns included, right?"

"Yes. According to local history, the Milans made a fortune with cattle and ranching. I guess that's where I get my love of ranching. So did the Calhouns. From the earliest days, I think the Calhouns and Milans clashed over land, cattle, water, running the town, all sorts of reasons, including the women they loved, so the feud started."

"I think I'm getting the short version of Milan and Wrenville history."

"You're getting the only version I have," he remarked.

"Sorry, I interrupted you. Go ahead."

"As local history goes, the Wrenvilles gradually amassed more money than anyone else in town. Hubert Wrenville had cattle, land, the big bank, the feed store, the biggest saloon."

"Was this Lavita's father?"

"Yes. Finally, there was only Lavita Wrenville who lived alone in the house. She was an eccentric old maid who did not want anyone to inherit or buy the house. Lavita deeded the property, house, stable, outbuildings and all personal property in those buildings to Verity with the stipulation that the property is not to be sold or changed until next year. At that time the Wrenville property and everything on it will revert totally to Verity to do with as it pleases. I imagine the town will sell the property if they can. That's what is in Lavita's official will and she was the last surviving Wrenville."

"Ah, I see. So what about information regarding the murders or a fortune she amassed and hid somewhere in the house?"

"I think that's just rumors, legend, wishful thinking of people way back and handed down through generations. There's nothing in the will about either one."

"Interesting," she said. "Maybe I'll do a show on Lavita Wrenville and the unsolved killings and then come back next year."

"You might consider just coming then. I don't think you'll find much of interest now. I've just told you everything about it. I don't think there's a fortune or a letter that revealed what happened."

"Suppose I search and find a fortune and a letter revealing what happened the night of the murders?"

"You wouldn't be the first to search. But there's nothing in her will about a fortune or a letter. That's legend."

"You really don't want me here, do you?" she asked, smiling slightly.

He leaned close, looking into her big green eyes that widened. "Oh, yes, I want you here. I have plans for tonight. From the moment I walked into my office and saw you, I've wanted you here," he said in a husky tone that was barely above a whisper.

She leaned in a fraction, so close they were almost touching, and he fought the urge to close the distance and kiss her. "Then we should have an interesting evening because I've been looking forward to tonight since we parted this afternoon," she whispered. Her words were slow, sultry, increasing the sexual tension between them. As they gazed at each other, again he was hot, tied in knots with desire, yet at the same time aware of the clash of wills between them.

She smiled and sat back. "This should be an interesting evening."

"I'll admit, you're not like other women I've known."

"That's a relief," she said and he gave her a faint smile.

"Tell me about the murders. All I know is that Lavita's father, a Milan and a Calhoun all were shot to death."

Wyatt settled back, inhaled deeply and tried to get his wits about him. "All I've ever heard is that Lavita had two men in love with her—unfortunately, a Milan and a Calhoun. The feud had been in existence through at least two generations by then, so it was going strong and the two men did not speak to each other. The night of the shootings, they both called on her at the same time and neither would leave. She was upset. The men were angry and according to the old story, they were going to fight and pistols were drawn. Her father heard the argument, appeared and mixed in the struggle. Terrified what would happen, Lavita ran to get their stable keeper. As she rushed back to the house, shots were fired. According to the story, all three men were armed and had fired at each other, killing each other."

"So far, that's what I've been told."

"Some stories say that, on her deathbed, Lavita admitted that one of the men was still alive and conscious when she returned to the house and told Lavita what happened before he died. At the time of the murders, she had stated they were all dead by the time she got back."

"Couldn't the stable keeper verify her story?"

Wyatt smiled. "Remember, this was the late 1800s and the story has been passed down by word of mouth since. According to the story, the stable keeper went to get his pistol and was far enough behind Lavita that all three men were dead when he arrived at the scene. The three men died that night, presumably shortly after the shooting. And Lavita never revealed anyone talked to her until she was on her deathbed. Until then, she claimed she didn't know what had happened after she ran out of the house to get help."

"If that's the true story about what happened, it makes one wonder what she was told and why she hid it from the world. Nowadays, withholding information would put her behind bars."

"Early-day justice may have been dispensed differently and hers was an influential family. If the legend is true, she may not have wanted the true story to come out because of the feud. The Calhouns and the Milans had a history of getting revenge."

"This story holds possibilities for an interesting chapter in my next book."

Wyatt wanted to groan. He had hoped to discourage her with the story, which he found vague and probably hearsay. "It all comes down to trying to find an old letter Lavita wrote that reveals the truth about that night."

Destiny shifted in her seat, drawing his attention to her dress. The unique design left one shoulder bare. The other shoulder was covered by a short sleeve that had four buttons running down a center seam in the sleeve, so if unbuttoned, the front half of her dress would no longer be attached to the back half above the waist. The thought consumed him, distracting him from his story. He had to figuratively shake himself to get back on track.

"The letter has been rumored to be in the house," he continued. "I've never heard a version that included the grounds as a possibility," he added.

"Think there will be a bidding war on the property?"

"I don't. You never know what might appeal to a developer, but that property is in the industrial part of Verity, small as that is. In my view, it's far out for a likely shopping area. The town grew in all other directions. The house overlooks the cemetery on one side. The river runs behind it. Nearby is the airport and to the front is the highway. Not the greatest location. No one wanted the house and it was left to crumble." He sat back and crossed his leg over the other at the knee.

"Now that you know about it—and there is little to tell you—I hope you'll rethink using it on your show. The killings were long, long ago and of little interest," he said, watching her closely.

"I simply think you're trying to get rid of me," she replied sweetly, her green eyes sparkling. "The deaths of the three men are an interesting puzzle, plus the feud between two of them, two families who have many descendants today, you included."

"I suppose only the ratings will indicate which of us is right. There are far more intriguing unsolved mysteries in Texas. Come by the office and you can look at a list. It would be nice for all the residents if you would move on down the road."

"You're serious, aren't you?"

"Yes. I have a quiet, peaceful, pleasant town. The biggest problems this past year have been getting the Dixons' cat out of their chimney and getting Doc Lamon's dock back after it collapsed in a storm and floated downriver."

"When I talked to the group that gathered today, they were curious, interested and very friendly."

"They were curious, interested and friendly because you're a stunning, sexy woman. They were curious about you, not the old Wrenville place."

"Thank you. But I didn't get the feeling from any of them that someone would prefer that I didn't put Lavita Wrenville's story on my show. Did it occur to you that you might be wrong?"

"I know my town pretty well. I don't think I'm wrong," he said, knowing their quiet clash grew stronger and neither changed the other's opinion. "Today was a bunch of men who wanted to see you and talk to you. Wait until the women are involved and you're in Chicago and the results of your visit are right here in Verity for the locals to deal with. They won't be so happy or so cooperative, especially if you stir up that Milan-Calhoun feud."

"Have you always been right?"

"No, but I'm right often enough that I trust my own judgment."

She laughed and in spite of their steady battle, her stubborn refusal to leave Verity, her flagrant disregard for law in Verity, he wanted to wrap her in his arms and make love to her.

"It doesn't bother you that you're going to upset a whole town?"

"Of course it would bother me if I thought that would happen." She gave him an assessing look out of the corner of her eye. "It must be wonderful to feel you're always right."

He stifled a laugh and a retort

"Come by the office and look at that list of other unsolved Texas murders," he said, eliciting a smile from her. It seemed they had once again agreed to disagree.

Needing a break from his tenacious but beautiful opponent, he picked up the phone to confer with Jason on the arrival time. When he got his answer, he should have simply turned to look out the window but his eyes lit on Destiny instead. "No wedding ring," he observed. "So you're single."

"Definitely. There's no special man in my life at the moment."

"I'm glad to hear that since I'm taking you out."

"This wouldn't count anyway. You're taking me out to tell me about Lavita Wrenville and the unsolved murders. This is a business evening."

He leaned close again, placing his hands on the arms of her seat to hem her in while they gazed into each other's eyes. "There is no way this evening will be a business trip. The closest we'll come is the conversation we just had, and now I've finished giving you the Wrenville history. I've been looking forward to tonight all afternoon long."

"You want me to pack and return to Chicago and then you tell me you've been wanting to go out with me. That's contradictory," she said.

"My feelings are contradictory. You're a complication in my quiet life," he said, gazing into her big, green eyes that threatened to make him tell her to do whatever she wanted in Verity.

"A few complications in life sometimes make it more interesting. You'll be able to handle this one, I'm sure."

"I can't wait," he said, his heart drumming. He knew she wasn't going to leave quietly and she would be a constant challenge to him. The most enticing challenge he had ever had in his life.

As Destiny walked to a waiting limo, Wyatt took her arm and in minutes they were headed into downtown Dallas. Wyatt sat across from her, looking totally relaxed, his booted foot resting on his other knee, his hand on the arm of the seat. In spite of all appearances of a relaxed man who cared nothing about the outcome of their discussion, she could feel an undercurrent between them. A clash of wills.

There were moments he flirted and set her heart racing. Other times, like now, he seemed remote. She couldn't gauge her effect on him and it disturbed her because she was accustomed to red-blooded thirtysomething males succumbing to her charms or trying to charm her. Especially when she had flirted with them.

"Do you own the red limo?" he asked.

"No, I leased it for this trip. We flew to Dallas and picked it up there."

"You always travel with this staff?"

She shook her head. "No. My assistant, Amy, works for me full-time since the success of my first book. Virginia Boyden, a camera operator—she's a field operator who works for the show and her husband, Duke Boyden, is my chauffeur, whom I've known forever. He worked for my mom, so he's like a relative. He drives for others, too. I hire him when I need him. I don't travel like this as much for the show as for background for my next book."

"Busy person, accustomed to getting what you want."

"I think that description fits you best. You're the oldest of your siblings, aren't you?" she asked.

"Yes, just the same as you are."

"So tell me about your life, Sheriff Milan. Why are you sheriff? You don't have to do that if you don't want to."

"My family has an old tradition. All the Milan males go into law—enforcing the law, practicing law, creating laws. For the most part in our family all Milan males get a law degree and practice law, which I did for three years, but, like my brother Tony, I'm a rancher at heart, so since I can afford to do what I want, ranching is what I've done most of the time. People in town wanted me to run for sheriff in the last election and I let them talk me into it."

"So I heard. According to gossip, people trust you and they think you're an honest man. When the Wrenville house reverts fully to the town of Verity and a fortune is found hidden away in the house, you're the man people will trust. That's a high recommendation about you."

"I was honored and it was something I could do to contribute to my town," he said.

She believed him. In spite of their clash, she was not only physically attracted to him, but she was also beginning to like him. She could see why people in town liked him.

"So what do all your brothers do?"

"Nick is a state representative. His background is the law firm of Milan, Thornridge and Appleton. Tony has a law degree, went to work for the firm for a year and then quit to be a rancher, his first love. We all love our ranches. My sister, Madison, is an artist and a newlywed."

"Madison Milan Calhoun—a very successful and very talented artist. I stopped in her gallery here. Am I allowed to write about this family tradition of male Milans going into law?"

"If you want."

"It'll add to my story about the Milans."

"Frankly, I hope you decide to not have any story about the Milans, the Calhouns or Verity," he said. "We're really a small, quiet town. Or we were until today."

She just smiled at him.

The limo parked in front of the entrance to the three-story, Tudor-style country club in Dallas. Soft music played and a fountain splashed as they walked inside. Destiny was conscious of being close at Wyatt's side, even more aware of him following her across the restaurant, her back tingling because she was certain his gaze was on her. After they entered a small private room, the waiter took orders for their drinks and left.

As soon as they were alone, she smiled across the linen-covered table at Wyatt. "A private room with music from the large dining room, flowers, candlelight—you've taken care of everything."

"Not quite everything yet," he said in a tone that was as disturbing as his touch. "Sorry if you hoped to give another interview to the local press."

She didn't ask what he hadn't taken care of, having a feeling it involved her. "No. This is much nicer. Now I can hear more about the history and people of Verity and the Milans," she said, but her thoughts were on Wyatt, curious about him. "So tell me about your family."

"We're an ordinary family. My dad is a judge and he lives here in Dallas with my mom. I told you earlier that I have two brothers and one sister who live close to me. That's my family. If I remember correctly about yours, your mom was an actress and your father was a scriptwriter and later a director and now both are deceased. You're a Californian and you grew up in L.A. You've never been married. You have a background in television and cohosted a California show about celebrities. Now you host your own successful show from Chicago, *Unsolved Mysteries,* which has done well. You're also a published author."

"You're correct so far. Good memory," she said.

He stood and came around to take her hand. "Care to dance? I saw couples dancing when we came in."

Smiling at him, she placed her hand in his, experiencing a tingle from the physical contact. When they reached the dance floor, she was happy the band played rock with an enthusiastic small crowd on the floor. He dropped her hand as they began to dance. She was surprised how well he danced, reminding herself not to underestimate him. She danced around him, aware of his blue eyes constantly on her, a dance that was exhilarating and fun, allowing her to release pent-up energy.

By the third song, he caught her hand and pulled her to the edge of the dance floor. "Let's go back and I'll shed this coat and we can see if our drinks are here."

She nodded as the crowd sang to a familiar song while they danced.

In their private room, Wyatt draped his jacket over a chair. They had a wine bottle chilling and tall glasses of ice water on the table. Wyatt drank half the glass before he asked, "Want to dance again?"

"I'd love to. I'm surprised it's not sentimental ballads. It sounds like a bar out there, not a country club dining room."

"It's just people having fun."

"So what do you call fun, Wyatt?"

"Dancing, laughter, friends," he said as they approached the dance floor. At the edge of the dance floor he leaned close to talk softly, his breath warm on her ear. "Sexy, hot kisses, flirting with a beautiful woman." Before she could answer him, he began to dance and she joined him, moving her body in time to the beat while she smiled at him.

He flirted and he responded to her, a reaction she often had from men, but she hadn't expected to be drawn to him. She was accustomed to men flirting with her, coming on to her, but she rarely felt an intense physical response to any of them. She never carried it further than flirting, unlike Desirée who had far too many affairs and who liked men indiscriminately, according to Destiny's thinking.

Destiny's gaze rested on Wyatt's mouth and she wondered what it'd be like to kiss him. But hadn't she heard that Wyatt had part of himself locked away and only one woman had ever really touched his heart? Rumor had it that his heart had been broken when his fiancée had returned his ring and he'd never had another serious relationship.

She barely knew Wyatt, but once or twice she had seen a shuttered look in his eyes and felt he had closed himself off emotionally. Physically, he made it obvious that he desired her, but nothing beyond that. Far from it, since she no doubt annoyed him with her purpose in coming to Verity.

She couldn't understand her reaction to him. She couldn't control her racing pulse or breathlessness or the tingles dancing over her insides. Wyatt was handsome but he wasn't her type. He was a laid-back, quiet, cowboy sheriff, a cowboy who loved his ranch, a man accustomed to running things and getting his way. How could she find him exciting?

The men she enjoyed in Chicago and in L.A. were more outgoing, enjoyed the theater, concerts, art exhibits. Some had been involved in television—men more like her. She and Wyatt were poles apart in backgrounds, personalities, ambitions, likes and dislikes. The only reason they were out tonight was because he wanted to talk her out of filming the Wrenville house and because he had promised to tell her the history about the killings in the house. This wasn't a regular date. Even though they flirted, laughed and danced, she could feel the constant clash of wills. And he was going to be even more annoyed with her soon, when she announced she was a Calhoun descendant. A faint chill made her shiver while she had a premonition of the bad moments to come. It would be one more clash between them, perhaps one bad enough to end any friendliness beginning to develop between them.

Throwing herself into the dance, she blocked out thoughts about the Calhouns and the Milans and just enjoyed being with an appealing, sexy man, the anticipation of finding some answers to old secrets of the town of Verity and, most of all, finding material for an intriguing show.

She had no intention of leaving Verity without doing what she had come to do. She was more interested now in the unsolved murders than she had been before.

As they danced, Wyatt's blue eyes were on her every move. Occasionally they brushed against each other. Would he kiss her good-night? The errant thought pulled her up short. When had she wondered that on a first date before? Probably not since she had been sixteen years old. But she was almost certain he would kiss her. He had seemed on the verge of it almost half a dozen times since he had walked into his office to meet her. And this wasn't a date, she reminded herself. The whole evening was meant to discourage her as far as the sheriff was concerned. So why, she asked herself, was he such good company?

When they finally returned to their table, Wyatt pulled on his jacket again.

"You don't need to wear your jacket. We're in a private room and I don't mind."

"I'm with a beautiful Chicago television personality who has her own show—I think I'll wear my jacket," he said.

"Thank you."

They both became silent when the waiter entered the room with their salads.

"I'm not talking you out of filming and investigating the Wrenville house, am I?" Wyatt asked as they began to eat. "Or of forgetting about the family feud?"

"Not at all. I'm not going to be in the Wrenville house forever—just briefly. It's a big house. You can come join us and watch if you want."

"No thanks. I'm not appearing on a TV show."

"We might make a deal—you give me an interview about being a Milan, about the Wrenville house and what you think you'll find there next year and you can name what you want in return."

"Cut Verity totally and I'll give you the interview," he countered.

"If I don't film the Wrenville house, then the interview will be useless," she replied.

"Your camera operator is with you to film or to take pictures of the house?"

"To take pictures. We're just in the earliest stages right now. I want to find out if there is enough material for a show and if it's interesting, things like that. This is preliminary to take back and present as a possible show."

"Isn't it unusual for the host to be doing all this investigation?" Wyatt asked.

"Yes, but I'm deeply involved with the show and I've come up with some other stories that were produced. Also, this is important information for my next book."

"Sounds as if the book is the major reason."

"It is an intriguing story if I can find enough information about it. There must be old newspapers on file about the murders. I have an appointment tomorrow with the head of the Library Board and I'm going to the Verity genealogy society office."

"What I've told you will be repeated in the paper. Beyond what I've said, I don't think there's much more about it."

"We'll see what I can find."

"Do I need to come out with you and check there is no vagrant living there now?"

Smiling, she shook her head. "No. My chauffeur will be with us. Duke is a retired police officer who is a chauffeur now."

"Ah, an ex-cop. That's the first good news since I saw your red limo in my parking place."

She laughed and leaned forward, placing her hand on his forearm, feeling the solid muscle through his sleeves. "The first good news? I'm disappointed. You rate that above meeting me, above this evening together, above dancing with me—"

He leaned over the table until his face was inches from hers and she felt as if she was drowning in his blue eyes. "You're out with me, dancing with me, because you want something from me. Not one second of this evening is because you want to be spending the evening with me."

His words were harsh, but the look in his eyes wasn't. His gaze conveyed desire and she couldn't move or catch her breath. Her heart pounded. If the table hadn't been between them, she would have expected him to kiss her right there and she wanted him to, which shocked her.

"That isn't exactly accurate," she said breathlessly. "You felt something when we met—deny that, Wyatt."

"Okay, so I did. You're a beautiful, sexy woman."

The words heated her and her desire intensified. "I wanted to go out with you tonight and I think you've enjoyed this evening, too," she whispered.

"I have, but I can't forget that you want something from me."

"That doesn't have one thing to do with having fun dancing with you," she said, still breathless. "We—"

She stopped and sat back as they heard a slight knock on the door right before it opened. Their waiter brought their dinners—prime rib for Wyatt and chicken breast for her.

While they ate, Wyatt told her about Texas legends he knew and she tried to charm him, realizing she was having a better time than she had had in a long time. After dinner they danced to more loud rock and it wasn't until over an hour later when the band played a ballad that Wyatt took her in his arms to slow dance.

Being in his arms heightened her awareness of him, made her think of kisses and wanting to be alone with him. She danced with him, aware of his height, his body against hers, his legs brushing hers.

"I think you've been scared to slow-dance with me. It's taken until almost midnight for us to have this first slow dance," she teased.

He looked down at her and she couldn't get her breath. "Fear isn't the emotion I've experienced with you," he said. His voice had lowered again, that warm, husky timbre that was as tangible as a caress. "Far from it. You know the effect you have. I want you in my arms, Destiny. I have all night."

Her heart began to thud and as they pressed lightly together while they danced, she wondered if he could feel her heartbeats.

"You want me, Wyatt, even though I don't think you like me."

"Like? You're spectacular, a gorgeous woman. I've enjoyed being with you tonight." A muscle worked in his jaw and his eyes were a vivid blue.

"Thank you, but I don't believe you're really dazzled. Maybe I've started something here that I shouldn't have," she whispered.

"You started it when you entered my office today," he said. "As they say, 'Be careful what you wish for.'"

"That applies to you, too."

He spun her around and dipped her low so she had to cling to him as she gazed into blue eyes that conveyed his desire. She forgot the other dancers, the band, everything except Wyatt. He made her want to close her eyes and raise her lips to his for a kiss. He swung her up and they stood on the dance floor for an instant while her heart drummed and she couldn't move. Then he began to dance again, dancing her to the sidelines.

"Ready to head home?" he asked in a voice that implied much more.

"Yes," she answered. He took her arm lightly to walk

back to their table, leaving the door open as they entered the small room and she retrieved her purse.

In the limo ride back to the airport, and in the plane, she couldn't take her eyes off him. Her whole body seemed to vibrate with the anticipation of what was to come when they touched down in Verity.

Finally, when they reached her hotel and he helped her out of the car, she turned to him. "Would you like to come up for a drink, Wyatt?" she asked.

"I'd like that," he replied, following her to her suite.

She could feel him watching her, and her back tingled as she walked ahead of him into the living area. "You've probably been in these suites before, haven't you?"

He nodded. "The old-fashioned furniture was selected to replicate the early-day furnishings of the hotel."

She watched while he dropped his suit jacket on a chair and loosened his tie to unbutton the collar button. His gaze held hers and there was no mistaking the desire she saw in his eyes.

"There's a fully stocked bar," she said. "What would you like to have?"

He closed the distance between them, standing in front of her, and she couldn't get her breath as she looked up at him. While her heart hammered, she anticipated his kiss.

"Finally," he said softly, sliding his arm around her waist and pulling her up tightly against him in a way he had not done while they had been dancing.

Her insides twisted and heated, her breasts tingling as his gaze lowered slowly and he looked down at her.

"I've been waiting all night for this." One by one he drew the pins out of her hair until finally her red locks spilled over her shoulders and fell in disarray around her face.

With both hands he combed his fingers through the curly locks, and the light tugs on her scalp were tantalizing. Desire was intense, a yearning she couldn't understand because she'd never felt it so strongly, and for Wyatt, of all people, someone who was blocking what she wanted. They were at odds, no matter how civil they both were. Unlike her grandmother she couldn't blame it on Wyatt being a Milan while she was a Calhoun. This wasn't because of a feud. It was because they were at cross-purposes. His goal was to keep the status quo of his quiet life and town while hers was to unravel the mysteries of the past that might undo Wyatt's peace at the same time.

She was afraid he would find a way to keep her out of the house or keep her from airing the show later. Yet at the moment, none of that mattered. All she knew now was that his arms were around her and she was caught and held in the compelling vivid blue of his thickly lashed eyes. She turned her face up slightly. Stubborn sheriff, a Milan—it no longer mattered. She wanted his kiss.

All the time he had freed her hair, he had gazed into her eyes, the depths of his conveying a promise of pleasure.

Wanting him with an intensity that had built through the evening, she tilted her head, closing her eyes to relish the feel of his hard body against hers, his arms holding her tightly. Finally his mouth covered hers. With her heart pounding, she wrapped her arms around his neck, clinging tightly, feeling her world shift and change. His kiss was possessive, as if he were taking her heart, claiming her as his own. She trembled with sudden hunger and need.

She savored being in his embrace and kissing him, feeling his rock-solid muscles pressed against her, his arms holding her tightly while his kisses made her want to be free of the barriers between them.

"Wyatt," she whispered, feeling the stubble of his beard against her lips, running her fingers in his thick hair at the back of his head.

"Wyatt," she repeated, pulling his head close again and

pressing her mouth against his, her tongue tangling with his. All evening Wyatt had teased, flirted, touched and danced and all her pent-up control had spilled out. Now desire became a white-hot flame that consumed her. It had been a long, long time since a man had made love to her.

She never felt Wyatt's fingers undoing the buttons on the sleeve and shoulder of her dress, but after the kiss, he leaned away a fraction and lowered the top part of her dress. Cool air brushed her shoulders, and her heart drummed as he looked at her and cupped her breasts, his thumbs playing lightly over the sensitive buds, making her gasp.

She had come to Verity for research, and had given little thought to meeting Wyatt. She had never expected to be swept off her feet this way. She hadn't expected to feel this dizzying need for his kisses and caresses, or the hungry longing that she hadn't experienced before. Her reaction to him, both physical and emotional, shocked her each time they had touched, but now in his arms with him kissing her senseless, kisses that claimed possession, that threatened to capture her heart, her need for him consumed her. She gasped for breath, raising her head slightly to look at him, and the impact of the need in his expression made her knees go weak and heightened what she felt. Her fingers went to his shirt and she opened the buttons until she pushed his shirt away.

She ran her fingers over his rock-hard, sculpted chest. Locks of dark hair had fallen on his forehead and his mouth was red from their kisses. She closed her eyes as desire rocked her while he caressed her breasts lightly.

"You're beautiful," he whispered, burying his face against her softness, his tongue stroking her.

With a moan of pleasure, she ran her fingers through his thick, coarse hair. Sliding her hand down over his broad shoulder, she felt the solid muscles. As he suckled her breast, she gasped.

He raised his head and looked down at her with hooded eyes. Drawing her to him, he leaned over her, kissing her possessively until she was on fire and all reason had fled.

She clung to him, dimly aware this was what she had wanted, yet feeling she was the one headed for heartbreak and Wyatt was the one taking her heart. She didn't want to feel this desperate need for him and for his loving. She didn't want to lose her control.

"Wyatt, wait," she said, leaning away and gasping for breath at the same time as she wanted to pull him back and remove the last barriers of clothing between them. "We just met—"

"I don't think that matters," he whispered. "You want this. You made that clear with our first kiss." He drew her into his embrace again. His gaze devoured her, his hands stroked her and he pushed her dress over her hips, letting it fall around her ankles.

She moaned. Lost in a haze of desire, she couldn't think straight. A part of her knew this was where the evening was headed as she flirted with him, but was lovemaking what she had really intended? She couldn't answer that question, as his kiss demolished all thought and she could do nothing but yield to the passion he incited in her.

She showered her own kisses on him, trailing them down across his chest, running her fingers over his hard muscles. He groaned and pulled her up to kiss her.

With clothing soon tossed aside, Wyatt picked her up and carried her to bed.

His hands drifted over her in light, feathery caresses that built her need to a fever pitch. Finally, one thought broke through.

"Wyatt, I don't have protection."

His eyes narrowed a fraction before he left to get a

packet from his wallet. When he returned, she caressed his thighs, wanting him more than she would have ever dreamed possible. How could she want this man who was so totally different from everything in her life? How could she feel this way about him when she had just met him hours earlier? She ached to pull him close, to make love and hold him. She knew he had no idea how rare, how shocking her reaction to him was.

He came down to kiss her, sliding his arm beneath her to hold her to him, and as he entered her slowly, he paused. It had been a long time since she had made love and she suspected he had been startled, but the hesitation was fleeting and gone as she tightened her arms to hold him.

With a cry she arched to meet him, and when she had taken him fully she moved with him, in perfect synchronization, as if they had known each other's bodies for years.

She sensed that he struggled for control, felt the sweat beading on his shoulders and brow. Yet he continued kissing her, pumping and filling her, and he drove her to the brink.

"Wyatt," she cried his name, torn from her in a pounding need for his loving as her long legs tightened around him. She held him against her heart, moving with him, dazed and spinning into ecstasy.

Release burst with a fury, a blinding surge of fulfillment and rapture that spilled over her. With one last thrust he groaned and climaxed, taking her with him to another heart-stopping release. She gasped for breath as she clung to him, lost in sensation.

As their pulse returned to normal, his weight came down on her and she ran her fingers over him and hugged him against her heart. Lost in euphoria, she would have to sort out her thoughts and feelings later.

Wyatt rolled on his side, taking her with him while they clung to each other. She was conscious of one emotion. Shock. She was shocked by how desperately she had wanted him, how strongly she felt for him. Right now she didn't ever want to leave his arms.

"You're a sexy, beautiful woman, Destiny," he whispered, kissing her temple, then trailing tender little kisses to her mouth. "I think we might have been headed to this moment since we met," he said.

Smiling at him, she raised slightly to place her mouth on his, her tongue stroking his, stirring his arousal.

He pulled her down to kiss her hungrily, hard and passionately, as if they hadn't just made love. In minutes, he rolled over her, moving between her legs.

Her heartbeat raced as the fire he'd sparked in her ignited into flame. She wanted him more than ever and more than she would have thought possible. She felt bereft when he moved from her to get protection and then rejoiced when he drew her into his embrace once again.

All logic and thought had stopped and she moved blindly, yielding to desire, not weighing consequences.

Pulling her to sit astride him, he entered her. They moved in unison, a heart-pounding rhythm that sent her into a dizzying spiral of need. His hands roamed over her, storming her senses until she cried out in ecstasy along with him.

She fell across him, holding him, while he wrapped an arm around her waist and kissed her.

He looked at her, brushing locks of curly hair away from her face. "You're an enigma."

"You could tell I haven't made love in a long, long time. There haven't been many men in my whole life that I've been deeply involved with," she said, wondering whether that scared him or not. "News you may find difficult to believe. I know I convey a different image."

"That you do. You surprise me again. You've been a steady stream of surprises," he said, running his fingers lightly over her lower lip. She brushed a kiss on his hand and he smiled at her.

"You're casting your own spell, Destiny."

"You're incredibly sexy, but even so, I'm not going to agree to pack and go home because you want me to."

"I don't recall asking or giving you any conditions before we made love," he said, toying with her hair as he talked.

He turned on his side and held her close so she lay facing him. "You're stunning."

She felt a blush heat her cheeks. "On one level we can communicate and we're compatible, thank goodness. For a while our differences became minimized. When you see that I'm not going to cause the town harm, maybe we can get along."

"I'd say we're getting along rather well," he said, toying with her bare breasts and stirring her yearnings again.

"Yes, we are, Wyatt," she whispered. She raked her fingers slowly through his hair, watching the short, dark brown strands spring back. "I want you to stay here in my arms tonight. It's already more than half past two."

"Shortly, I will get up, shower and dress to go home. I don't care to have it all over town tomorrow that we were together here all night."

She smiled and traced circles on his bare chest and ripped abdomen. "You're embarrassed for people to know you're with me?"

"Of course not. I'm a private person and like to keep what I do private if possible. I suspect you don't understand that and you don't feel that way. You're a public figure and it's good for your career to have the world want to know about you." He shrugged. "To each his own."

She laughed. "I'm accustomed to attention and I'm not sure with my bright auburn hair I could keep people from noticing me even if I wanted to."

"Beautiful hair. I like your hair," he said, playing with the long strands and letting them curl around his fingers. They looked into each other's eyes and once again she felt that sizzling current of electricity arc in the air between them to send sparks flying.

Breaking the circuit, he stood up and grabbed his suit pants. "I'll shower and dress and go."

"So we're not going to see each other again?" she asked, pulling the sheet to her chin and placing her hands behind her head. The sheet followed the curves of her body.

He leaned down, sliding an arm beneath her and kissing her. His mouth was hard, possessive, his tongue stroking hers slowly.

Moaning softly she wrapped her arms around his neck to return his kiss. He raised his head a fraction. "We'll see each other again and we'll make love again. This hot attraction hasn't cooled yet for either one of us. I can feel your pulse and it's racing as much as mine is," he said in a husky voice.

Releasing her, he walked away, gathering the rest of his clothes and then leaving the room without looking back.

She got up to pick up her things and go to the shower in her adjoining bathroom, still tingling and wanting Wyatt's kisses, his touch and his body in bed next to hers for the rest of the night. How had it never occurred to her how much she wanted him, or that she would respond to him the way she had? It was a surprise development and one she didn't want or like. They were very different people with a feud and an old house between them. The Wrenville project and the feud could become bigger problems in their lives, something Wyatt had already made clear he didn't want to happen. Even so, she couldn't stop wanting him. Her desires and responses were not going away and she wouldn't be able to ignore them. Was she in any danger of falling in love with him?

She dismissed the thought as ridiculous. She had never been deeply, truly in love in her whole life. The sheriff of Verity, Texas, was certainly not going to capture her heart. Even though he was a billionaire, successful and sexy beyond any other man she had ever known, he was a rancher, a cowboy, a sheriff and a West Texan, as remote from her world as the moon from earth.

She was astounded that she had liked making love and being out with him. She paused to think about the past evening. She'd had the best time ever, made love with the sexiest man ever. It had been a night she would never forget, even though she wanted to. She didn't want this heart-pounding, breathtaking reaction. This rancher was not the man to fit into her life and she needed to get over this intense response to him.

She half expected making love would shoo away the pesky attraction, but it hadn't. At least, not yet. She wanted to get him back into the proper perspective—that of an ordinary man, like all others in town. Then, when she left Verity, she'd simply forget Wyatt.

She showered, dressed in jeans and a sweatshirt, and followed the aroma of freshly brewed coffee into the kitchen.

He was seated at the kitchen table, sipping a cup of coffee. When she entered, he came to his feet, his gaze drifting over her. Tall, lanky, moving with a lazy ease that hid the strength he had, he set her heart pounding despite her resolve. "I thought I'd have a little fortification before I head home," he said. "Can I pour you a cup?"

"I'll get it, thank you. Sit again and I'll join you." She poured a cup and carried it to the table. He stood waiting, holding out her chair, and as she walked up, they gazed at each other. Once again, she was held by his blue eyes that conveyed so much heat, it was difficult to catch her breath.

Without looking at it, he took her coffee and set it down

with one hand. He slipped his other hand across her nape and drew her close to kiss her. All her intentions to view him the way she did other men dissolved and vanished.

While she returned his kiss, his arms banded her waist. Shoving the chair away, he drew her fully against him and it was as if they hadn't made love only a short time earlier.

When he finally released her, both of them were breathing hard. "I'm not staying the rest of the night," he said, more as if to remind himself than to inform her.

She sat at the table, her coffee in front of her.

"You've been a surprise in nearly every way," she said, looking intently at him.

"I have to say that you have, too. You're not at all like your sister."

"No, we're not alike, but we've always been close. Mom was sick from the time Desirée was little until we lost her when Desirée was seventeen, so in some ways I guess I've been a mother to her all her life. Our mom was a model, then later she was involved in advertising and always busy. I took care of Desirée." She couldn't count the times she'd been there for her sister, willingly, patiently. "I'm the one who gives the impression of liking men, but that's really Desirée. I've been intimate with very few—I can count them on one hand easily. My sister? She could count them on one hand in high school. She collects men like some women collect jewelry. I've talked to her about her lifestyle, but she's headstrong and there are parts of her life I can't influence."

"At least you tried. A sister can't do anything else. I'd hate to try to change my sister."

"Ah, being stubborn runs in the family," she said lightly and he chuckled.

"Takes two to have 'stubborn.'" Finishing his coffee, he set the cup in the saucer, carried it to the sink to rinse and placed it in the dishwasher. "I'll go now, Destiny."

She followed him to the door of her suite, her gaze running from his thick, dark brown hair, down across broad shoulders to his narrow waistline and then down his long legs. He carried his jacket and tie on his arm.

"Thanks for telling me about the Wrenvilles," she said. "And thanks for the dinner. The evening has been great, Wyatt."

"It has," he replied. His voice had lowered and his eyes darkened, making her draw a deep breath. "Go out again with me tonight."

"I can't, but thank you. I have a dinner date. Your mayor and his wife have invited me to their house. I couldn't refuse after such a nice letter."

"Maybe I'll see you later today," Wyatt said. They gazed at each other and she wanted him to kiss her again.

Instead of leaving, he stood there and her heart began to drum. She placed a hand lightly on his forearm. "Wyatt," she whispered, wanting his kiss, wanting him to stay.

"See you later," he said as he turned and left.

As soon as the elevator doors closed behind him, she stepped inside and locked her door. She wanted to see him again, go out with him again, even though they were at cross-purposes. With their lifestyles and careers, there was no future in any relationship between them. She had a busy life in Chicago, family in L.A. and this Wrenville project, plus her Calhoun heritage. All things Wyatt wanted no part of and would not be compatible with him. Plus, he had never opened himself up to her. She had already been warned that Wyatt kept part of himself shut away, so she didn't want to get into a relationship that would be any risk to her own heart. And Wyatt would be a heartbreaker.

What would happen when he learned she was a Calhoun? Destiny wondered whether he would even speak to her. No matter what he'd said, that old feud had not died yet or Wyatt wouldn't be so disturbed by it.

Destiny planned to be gone in a few days. It shouldn't take long to draw some conclusions about the murders. She wanted to check out old papers. Talk to locals. She wanted to find the oldest generation, talk to some of them and get their account of the story. She would be gone and soon Wyatt Milan would be forgotten.

She went back to her bedroom, eyeing the empty bed, the covers awry, seeing Wyatt there with the sheet across his middle, his lean, muscled body sexy, irresistible to her. She might not feel as if she was in danger of falling in love with him, but he was the sexiest man she'd ever met and one of only two she had really been attracted to. But what she felt for Wyatt was more intense. Maybe it was because she was older now. But at twenty-nine she still couldn't fully understand her own reactions.

She planned to make her announcement this afternoon about her Calhoun heritage. Would that end the relationship with Wyatt? A pang chilled her. Or should she keep her heritage secret? Instantly, she shook her head even though she was alone. If she did a show on the Wrenville house, some way her bloodline and her Calhoun ancestors would come out. This was the time to get the most drama out of revealing her ties to Verity and the feud before someone else broke the news. She just hoped it didn't make a world of difference to Wyatt.

She changed to cotton pajamas—not what she would have worn with Wyatt, yet what she found comfortable. As she slid into bed she could feel Wyatt's presence there, smell his scent. She thought about the evening, still surprised at how she had reacted to him and the effect he had on her. Had the evening meant anything to him?

She didn't really know him well enough to discern what he felt. So many times men she had dated and never been intimate with had claimed to be in love with her. She'd never reciprocated those emotions. In fact, she had never really been in love. Yet she had known clearly how the men felt, and when they wanted to be intimate, some of the men had proposed. It was different with Wyatt. They'd been physically intimate and yet he remained a mystery, as closed off and as much a stranger in some ways as he was when he had first walked into his office to meet her. She couldn't fathom her own feelings because she was in new territory with Wyatt. Her dealings with him in one day were light-years from those with any other man she had ever known.

One refreshing thing with Wyatt—he wasn't impressed by her fame, her television show, any of that. He seemed to be truly interested in *her* and honest with her. She didn't need to turn on the charm with him because she felt she had his full attention all the time she was with him. And he had some rare qualities that she liked—easygoing, loyal to his family and evidently close with his siblings, straightforward with her, obviously the town trusted him. He was a leader, a take-charge person, which she liked even though in her own situation, she would have been better off if he had given in to whatever she wanted.

How had she gotten so involved with him almost instantly? Her actions went against all her beliefs and all the advice she'd given to her sister over the years. One thing she knew—Wyatt was going to be difficult to forget. What was worse, he might be difficult to deal with in the coming days. She hoped he would not interfere enough to wreck her intention to have the Wrenville unsolved murders on her show. She had her own plans regarding the Milans and the Calhouns and Wyatt was not going to like what she intended to do. He wasn't going to like it at all.

Four

To his dismay, Wyatt could not shake Destiny out of his thoughts. He had slept only a few hours and then stirred, wanting her beside him. He had yearned to seduce her from the first moment he saw her and though she didn't disappoint him, she had shocked him.

Destiny conveyed hot sex. Everything about her appeared wanton, steamy and earthy, from her riot of red hair down to her long, shapely legs. Yet she'd told him she had been intimate with only a few men, and no one in the past several years.

Her sister, however, looked virginal with her Dresden Doll beauty, yet Desirée was the one who liked men and went from one relationship to another.

Yes, Destiny had surprised him. He wondered if she had ever been in love and decided to ask her the next time he had a chance.

He thought of Katherine, the woman he had thought was the love of his life. Tall, blonde, blue-eyed, she was the most beautiful woman he had known and he had loved her with his whole heart, opening himself in every way, planning a lifetime with her, expecting them to be wrapped in their love that he thought she felt as deeply as he.

It still hurt to think about the pain of their breakup. He should have seen it coming when she began to find excuses for not seeing him, but, as the saying went, love was blind. When she finally had broken it off, it had been crushing. Eventually he had gotten over Katherine, but since then he tried to keep that emotional part of his life shut away and out of his thoughts. He didn't want to risk his heart again, make himself vulnerable, get hurt like that again. He thought of his brother Nick who suffered deeply from losing his wife. Like Nick, Wyatt had no intention of giving his heart again—at least not for a long time. Hot, satisfying sex was fulfilling, but falling in love was too big a risk.

There was no risk to his heart with Destiny. She was desirable and sexy, and they'd enjoyed each other in bed, but they each could walk away without emotional damage. Their lives were vastly different and they were each accustomed to getting what they wanted so there was no danger of falling in love.

If he couldn't talk her out of it, Destiny would check out the Wrenville place and story, pack and go out of his life, and neither one of them would look back.

In the meantime, sex with her had been fantastic. Last night had been all he had hoped and then some. She was the sexiest woman he had ever known. Just thinking about her made him hot. He wished he could have stayed the rest of the night and made love again this morning but if he had been seen leaving her suite early this morning that would have stirred a firestorm of gossip and questions, including from his own family. He didn't need that drama in his life.

Then why couldn't he stop thinking about her? Destiny was a walking, talking, gorgeous threat to his peace of mind. In spite of all logic, he wanted her with him in his bed, in his arms right now.

He needed to back off. She was too unpredictable; he couldn't figure her out, which was unusual. Most people never surprised him. He didn't want Destiny falling in love with him. Her sister had been enough worry when she wanted him to go back to California with her.

He had to laugh at himself. Destiny fall in love with him? She was very much her own person, highly at odds with him over the Wrenville murders and her show. He couldn't imagine her in his life all the time. From the moment she rode into town in her big red limo, she had done nothing except stir people up. He had found a tranquil life on his ranch and in Verity and after the pain from his breakup with Katherine, he wanted peace and quiet. He guessed Destiny hadn't had peace and quiet in her life since she was five years old. She thrived on attention.

There was no way either of them would fall in love with the other. Destiny may have already moved on and shoved last night out of her mind.

Remembering the night, he paused, standing still, lost in memories. He didn't know how long he stood there, but he finally realized time had passed and he was still lost in thoughts of Destiny. He had to get to the office and he was going to be late if he didn't get moving.

Swearing under his breath, Wyatt hurried to get down a fast breakfast of cereal and leave for work.

He wanted to keep up with what Destiny would do at the Wrenville house. Writing the governor had been a smart move on her part because Wyatt couldn't overrule the governor. If it had just been the mayor, Wyatt could have seen to it that she wasn't legally allowed on the property. He'd finally gotten in touch with the governor's office to confirm Destiny's letter. She had the right to look at the old house, search it, take pictures and there was nothing he could do.

She also was free to search for a letter and a fortune or anything else she might find, but the property still belonged officially to Verity and so would anything she found.

How he wished he could legally keep her off the property, but that wasn't going to happen. She had outmaneuvered him with the governor's permission and he had to give her grudging admiration for it.

At the office he entered to find Dwight filing papers. Dwight ran his fingers through his tangled hair. "Morning. We've been getting calls. I sent them to the mayor's office. People want to know if Destiny is going to film the Wrenville house today. They want to know if she'll talk to reporters again today. The hotel called and said their lobby is filled with people waiting to get her autograph."

"Oh, hell," Wyatt said. "She'll be gone soon. Just keep telling them we don't know what she's doing or when she's doing it."

"That's what I've been saying. Mabel Lake called and wanted to know since you took Destiny out last night if you're dating. I told her that was a business evening."

"Thanks for that one and it was a business evening," he said, thinking it partially had been. "As much as any man who takes her out is going to spend a purely business evening. With her, that isn't possible."

"I don't imagine so," Dwight said wistfully. "Do you think she'll come here today?"

"I don't know what that woman is doing," Wyatt said, causing Dwight's eyes to widen. "I don't have any control over her. She has a letter from the governor of Texas giving her a big welcome and an invitation to put the Wrenville murders on her show. There's nothing I can do about it."

"Mercy. How did she get a letter from the governor?"

"She wrote him, Dwight," Wyatt replied, thinking most men would do whatever Destiny asked. Her show was popular and he imagined the governor had watched her show and knew what she looked like.

The phone rang and Dwight answered, his face wreathed in a smile until he glanced at Wyatt and his smile vanished.

"I'm fine," he said. "He's right here and headed toward his office, Ms. Jones. I'll transfer your call."

Wyatt hurried to his office and picked up his phone. "Good morning," he drawled in a deep voice.

"Morning, Wyatt," she said in a honeyed tone that made him think of last night and wish he was with her.

"I wanted to let you know we're going to the Wrenville house to look it over for the show."

"You're sure this will be a show?"

"No, not at all yet. I'll have to get everything ready and present it. I thought perhaps you'd like to drive out and see what we're doing, maybe show me where the men were murdered."

Wyatt wanted to refuse to do anything to promote the Wrenville house. On the other hand, he wanted to see Destiny. "I'll drive out later today," he said as if the words came without thought.

"Good. I have a few questions for you. We'll see you later, Wyatt. I should run now," she said. "Bye."

She was gone. Longing struck him. He wanted to see her, hold her and kiss her. He glanced at his calendar and saw calls and meetings listed. He phoned Dwight and asked him to move the 1:00 p.m. meeting. As he stared at the paperwork on his desk, he realized Destiny was already disrupting his life, just as he had feared. How much worse would it get?

It was one o'clock before he told Dwight he was leaving. After a short drive out of the east side of town, he turned into the Wrenville house. The long drive from the highway to the house was overgrown with weeds that were tamped down from recent activity. He pulled up in the drive that circled in front of the house and stopped.

He hadn't been at the place in years, had only driven by on the highway. The house was in worse shape than he had remembered. Paint was gone, the boards gray and weathered. One step had fallen in leading up to the porch, but it had been partially repaired and he suspected it was the work of the mayor getting ready for her visit. He intended to catch Gyp and talk to him about not informing him about Destiny's visit.

Windows were broken and shutters hung awry if they still hung at all. Some lay on the porch.

Chains hung where a porch swing had once been, he assumed. Moving carefully, stairs creaking beneath his weight, he climbed the stairs to the porch and watched his step, avoiding holes as he crossed to knock on the door.

It opened instantly and he faced her chauffeur, a broad-shouldered man who probably outweighed him by forty pounds, all of it pure muscle. Shorter than Wyatt by half a foot, the man stood relaxed, yet Wyatt felt he was being studied carefully.

"Hi. I'm Sheriff Wyatt Milan," Wyatt said, extending his hand.

"Duke Boyden," the chauffeur said, giving Wyatt a firm handshake.

"Former police officer, Destiny said."

"Yes, sir. I moved to Chicago when Destiny went because my wife is with the television show."

"I came to see what's going on and if Destiny is still going ahead with plans to use this place for a show."

"She's looking around. I think she has some questions for you. Come in."

As he stepped back, Wyatt entered a wide hallway that

ran through the house. He glanced around to see the house had been cleaned. Cobwebs and dust had disappeared. While the place looked abandoned, run-down and dilapidated, it was no longer filled with leaves, debris and dust.

"Wyatt," Destiny said, her throaty voice making him think about the previous night. She came into the hall from one of the rooms and a pretty brown-haired woman followed her. "I see you met Duke. Meet Amy Osgood, my cousin. She's my assistant. Amy, this is Sheriff Wyatt Milan."

"It's just Wyatt. Glad to meet you," he said, shaking her hand, finding it difficult to shift his gaze from Destiny, whose clinging red sweater held his attention. Her tight designer jeans were snug on her tiny waist, flaring over her hips. He remembered trailing his hands over those curves last night, and desire bombarded him once again. He met her gaze, unable to look away, feeling she was thinking about the same thing.

"This place looks clean," he said after a stretch of silence. "I'm surprised."

"Thank Mayor Nash. He had a cleaning crew come. I told him if there are bloodstains, to leave them alone. I don't want evidence of the shootings cleaned away. According to one of your librarians, after the murders, the front room was closed and never used again," Destiny said.

"I wouldn't be surprised because Lavita lived here alone. She had servants and some probably lived in the house, but they wouldn't have used the formal parlor. So you've talked to Philomena Latham. She's very knowledgeable about the town and the library."

Destiny nodded. "She was interesting. I talked to her before I came to town."

Wyatt wondered how many people had known she was coming to town before he did. He tried to focus on what she was telling him.

"Too bad the furniture is gone." She glanced over her shoulder. "We're looking the house over now. We just got here about an hour ago. We started upstairs and have worked our way down to this floor."

"So you haven't seen much of this floor."

"Nothing. There are a lot of stains on these old floors so I can't go by the stains," she said, her voice a notch lower. "We've just barely covered this floor and Amy and Duke are trying to map out the place, but it's difficult and each floor is different."

"You're right. I know from staying here years ago that the house has big rooms and tiny rooms. There's a large attic and a big basement. There's a storm cellar in the back that shares a wall with the basement, but there is no way to go back and forth from the basement."

As Wyatt walked at her side, he reached around her to open doors, and he caught the scent of her perfume, a heady, heavy, sensual scent that made him wish they were alone. He followed her into a kitchen with a high ceiling and cabinets with doors missing, glass broken in some of the doors. When they entered, a slender blonde turned to face him.

"Virginia, meet Sheriff Wyatt Milan. Wyatt, this is Virginia Boyden, who is fantastic with a camera."

"Hi, Virginia," Wyatt said, shaking her small hand.

"Glad to meet you, Sheriff," she said and looked at Destiny. "I'll go to the front room—that's the important room."

As Virginia left the room, Destiny looked around. "This must be a kitchen, but it doesn't resemble one."

"Think how old this house is. The kitchen was supposed to be the latest thing when it was built with piped-in water," Wyatt replied.

"I'm glad I didn't live in that era."

As she looked around, Wyatt looked at her. He could hear the others talking in the front part of the house, their voices sounding hollow in the empty spaces. He was alone with Destiny and he was tempted to step close and kiss her, but someone could return at any time.

She turned her head, her red hair swinging across her shoulders. "Wyatt—" Whatever she had been about to say was lost as he stepped forward.

"I've thought about you all day long," he said. He held her chin lightly with his fingers. "I've remembered every moment of our night together."

"Wyatt, we're not alone. I have three people with me."

"Kisses seem more urgent and more important to me than this old house," he said, giving her another long, intense look before turning away.

He heard her take a deep breath. "Come on, Sheriff, let's look at the front parlor. The others are already in there."

Wyatt took her arm. The minute he touched her, everything faded except memories of the night with her. He wanted to be with her tonight, wanted to get her to his house where they could stay undisturbed and he wouldn't have to leave in the middle of the night. He inhaled deeply, smelling her perfume that triggered more memories. He didn't want this intense reaction to her. Destiny was an increasing disruption in his quiet life. Even as he thought that, he couldn't stop looking at her and wanting to be with her through the night. He wanted, needed to kiss her.

As if she knew what he was thinking, she glanced up at him. His insides tightened and he could feel the current between them as his gaze lowered to the enticing V of her red sweater. "I like your sweater," he said, running his finger along the neckline, down to the V, feeling her softness and aching to hold her.

She stepped away. "Wyatt—" she said, her voice breathless. She stepped past him and he caught up to walk down the hall to a large room. Some windows were broken and some boarded up, casting shadows on a stone fireplace at one end of the room.

"We could have a basketball game in this room," Duke said from behind him and Wyatt turned slightly while he glanced at the high ceilings.

"You're right. This is probably the formal parlor and as far as I know, it's where the shootings took place."

Duke strolled slowly around, looking at holes in the walls.

Wyatt glanced at the ancient and aging floor that had many stains. "Some of these are the bloodstains. I've never known exactly which ones because it's never been important to know."

Destiny stopped and looked at a large brown stain on the worn wooden floor. "I have an appointment with Philomena again later this afternoon."

"She may be helpful," he said, sorry he had not been particularly helpful about town history, but he didn't care to encourage Destiny. "What time is your appointment?"

"Not until four o'clock today," she replied. She looked around the floor again. "Amy, you stand where one bloodstain is. Duke, you stand where one is and I'm at what has to be one."

As they moved into place, she looked at Virginia. "Virginia, take pictures of us and then when we move away, get the stains in the floor so I'll have some pictures of possibly where the men stood the fatal night."

Wyatt watched her, he couldn't help thinking about her and wanting to be alone with her. He wanted to make love more than he had before last night.

Surprising him, Destiny said, "I think we might as well get back to town and let me get the information about the killings because that's what will be important. If there isn't much story or mystery here, then none of this matters. We'll pack and go and forget this project." She looked at Wyatt. "You still have a chance of getting your way. I'll know after I talk more to people in town about what they know and see how much information we can get about the night of the murders and about Lavita Wrenville."

She glanced at her staff. "Let's go back to the hotel to regroup. I have some appointments." She walked to Wyatt to loop her arm in his. "Unless you can tell me more about that night or steer me to someone else I should talk to in town, I'll have to tell you goodbye."

"Not goodbye." They stepped into the hall and he took her arm to draw her with him into the next room, which was a dining room. Wyatt closed the door quietly.

"Wyatt, what are you doing?"

"Giving us some privacy," he said in a husky tone as he returned.

Her voice was shaky when she replied, "I'll call you later tonight."

Wyatt glanced at the closed door and then back at her. "I want you, Destiny. I want to make love to you again and I will. And you want me, too, don't you?"

She hesitated a moment. "You know the answer to your question," she whispered, gazing back at him intently. "But now I should join the others." She brushed past him to leave the room.

Did she feel the same as he did—wanting more than anything to have another night together? Or was she having regrets? She didn't act like a woman with regrets.

When Wyatt caught up with her and her crew, everyone started to gather the equipment that was piled near the door. Duke took some equipment from Virginia's hand and shook his head at Amy. "You ladies go ahead to the car. I'll bring these things."

"I can get the rest," Wyatt said easily. "We'll get it all."

As he gathered camera equipment, tablets, laptops and notebooks, Duke worked beside him. At the front door

Duke paused, turning to face Wyatt. "My boss leaves a general impression with most men she meets," Duke said casually, looking around the room and then letting his gaze rest on Wyatt. "It usually isn't correct. Contrary to what she conveys and how she appears, there have been few men in her life."

Wyatt was startled that Duke would relay such personal information to a total stranger. He focused more closely on the man, whose brown eyes were intent on Wyatt.

"I just don't want to see her hurt," Duke said. "She's not Desirée who was mad as hell because she's accustomed to getting her way. Desirée's a kid with unreasonable expectations, immature and spoiled. Success and fame came when she was too young to handle it. Destiny tries to protect her, but of course, she can't and now Destiny is in Chicago, far away from her sister. Destiny is entirely different. I don't want to see her get hurt."

Wyatt's eyes narrowed and he tilted his head to one side. "Did you just threaten me?"

"Not at all," Duke said, smiling at Wyatt, a cold smile that Wyatt considered unfriendly. "I would never, ever threaten a sheriff. No, I'm just talking and giving you some information about Destiny so you understand the woman you're dealing with a little better. Men get the wrong impression about Destiny because of her looks, the way she dresses and she comes on friendly and smiling, usually turning on the charm. It's a front to get what she wants, to get attention. It's only a surface thing. Like I said, I just don't want her hurt."

"Don't worry where I'm concerned. I barely know her."

"When we travel, I try to look out for my wife and also Amy and Destiny. Destiny seems interested in you."

"I'd just as soon she would give this up and go on to something else. There are far more interesting unsolved mysteries in Texas. There's no need to stir up old animosities," Wyatt said. "See you, Duke." He stepped outside and deposited everything he carried behind the man's car. When he noticed Destiny waiting at his car, he walked over to her.

"Thanks for carrying out stuff," she said. "Call me."

"I'll keep in touch," he said.

"Bye, Wyatt. Thanks for coming out." She left him standing there, watching her for a moment, remembering the night and wanting her with him again.

Wyatt drove to his house in Verity that he had built when he got elected sheriff so he wouldn't have to commute daily from his ranch. In an exclusive gated community, his home was on five acres, set back with trees hiding it from the winding street. He drove around to enter in the back and as he got a cold beer, he heard his phone beep with a text from Nick and one from Tony. Both still wanted to know when they could meet Destiny.

He shook his head and thought about her. He wanted to see her again himself. He wanted to be alone with her and have a complete night with her. Or longer. Even knowing that she was nothing but trouble in the long run. He walked down the hall to the room that he used for an office. Looking at the calendar, he tried to figure when he could ask her to his place for a cookout and invite his brothers. Madison had just married Jake Calhoun and Wyatt didn't know whether they were even back yet from their honeymoon. He didn't think either one of them would have a shred of interest in meeting Destiny. He left messages for all of them and then stood staring into space, lost in thought about Destiny. He had no idea how soon she would go back to Chicago.

From the first moment in his office, she had stormed his senses and he had wanted to get to know her. He had wanted to seduce her and when he did, she had been far more than he had expected. She had left him wanting her more than ever and unable to get her out of his thoughts.

Wyatt drove back to his office, stopping to talk to people on the way and going to his desk to look at his calendar and think about when he could have her out for dinner.

He mulled over his talk with Duke—Duke who had been so protective of the women, checking out Wyatt, threatening him. In spite of his denial, it had been a threat and Duke looked like the type who meant what he said. Wyatt recalled clearly facing Duke, receiving the warning.

"My boss leaves a general impression with most men she meets.... Contrary to what she conveys and how she appears, there have been few men in her life.... I just don't want her hurt."

So now he might have to worry about Duke. How much more was Destiny going to complicate and change his life? What would she do next?

Five

Wednesday morning Duke drove Destiny down Main Street, parking behind the sheriff's car in front of city hall. He held the door for Destiny who stepped out and strolled in to ask Dwight to tell Wyatt that she would like to see him.

In seconds he appeared and her heart beat faster at the sight of him. In his freshly pressed plain brown sheriff's uniform, he took her breath away. She knew movie stars, celebrities, politicians and none of those men had the dazzling effect that Wyatt did. What was the chemistry between them and how long would it last? Wyatt was not the person she wanted to feel steaming attraction to at all. She still couldn't believe how attracted she was to him and how after making love with him, she only wanted more.

The moment she looked into Wyatt's eyes she remembered their night together. His gaze swept over her, a quick glance, yet it sped her already racing heartbeat.

"Hi," he said. "Come into my office."

"Good morning," she said breathlessly, smiling at him and walking past him.

Shedding her jacket, she sat in a leather chair opposite his. This time his gaze traveled slowly over her. "You should have stopped traffic out on Main Street in those jeans and that sweater," he said and she smiled, smoothing the low-cut V neckline of her purple sweater.

"No, I was hidden away inside the red limo and all was quiet as usual."

"You had to get out and walk into my office. You look great. They should hire you to model jeans."

"Thank you, but I'm not the model type. Skinny? I think not. That's nice of you to say. And you can look all you want." She felt his gaze trailing over her as if it was his fingers. She wanted so badly to step into his arms and kiss him.

Wyatt redirected her attention with his question. "Now that you've seen the Wrenville house, what's the verdict?"

"I'm still interested. Whether the producer will be— that's another matter. I'm interested in it for my next book. I still have people to talk to here before I move on. I'll go back to Chicago from here and then I'm going to a little town in east Texas to look into another possibility for a show. Care to join me? We could think of ways to pass the hours," she asked, smiling at him.

"I'm tempted," he replied, his voice getting a slightly husky note. "For now, how about coming to dinner Friday night at my place? I'll admit there's a particular reason for this invitation—it's my brothers wanting to meet you. They are hounding me with texts."

"I'd be delighted." She tilted her head and perused him. "Why do I think your brothers are very different from you?"

"That's not unusual. You and your sister are different," he said.

"Friday night is fine with me," she said, glancing at her watch. "I'll look forward to meeting your family."

"Good. They've wanted to meet you since you arrived."

"Tomorrow I'm going to Dallas to talk to a librarian there because they have some articles in their archives. I have some other appointments and then I'll be back late tomorrow night, so I'll be here Friday."

"Good. That will make my family happy."

"I better go now. Actually, I came here because I'm supposed to meet Ernie Grant from the Verity Chamber of Commerce. He's giving me a tour and the history of Verity. I told him I would come to his office."

"His office is in the other side of this building. I'll show you. You have a good time," he said, standing when she did. With mere inches between them she lost her breath again as she gazed into his blue eyes.

"That is the prettiest purple sweater I've ever seen," he said, slipping his fingers beneath the neckline at her collarbone and then sliding his hand down the V. His feathery touch drifted down and she tingled, wanting his hands on her, remembering his caresses.

"Wyatt," she whispered.

He closed the sliver of space between them, sliding his arm around her waist and drawing her to him while he kissed her. She wrapped her arms around his neck and kissed him in return. Her heart raced as she inhaled the scent of his tangy aftershave, felt the hardness of his body pressed against her, tasted him, reacted to his kisses. She wanted another night with him, hours of loving.

Finally, she stepped away. "Wyatt, what you do to me is a sin," she whispered.

"No, it's not. What I want to do to you is a sin. And I will again, Destiny."

"I'm going to be late," she said, gazing up at him. She stepped away, straightening her clothing.

Wyatt held the door for her and as they entered the reception area, he pointed to a hallway.

"Take that hallway and you'll see his office or you can go out and enter through the other front door."

"I'm going to say something to Duke who's in the limo, so I'll just go the front way." She smiled at Corporal Quinby. "Thanks, Dwight. You have a real nice day," she said and he smiled in return.

"Bye, Ms. Jones," Dwight said, jumping to his feet and going to hold the front door for her, something Wyatt could not recall seeing Dwight do for anyone under seventy years of age.

"Dwight, it's Destiny. Call me Destiny," she said, pausing to look into his eyes. As he grinned, his face turned red.

"Yes, ma'am," he said. "Yes, Destiny."

As the door closed behind her, he turned and looked at Wyatt. "A man could get paralyzed looking at her," he said, blinking and pushing his glasses back up on the bridge of his nose.

"I hope not," Wyatt said, looking at the door and thinking about Destiny.

"What's funny—my wife wants to meet her because she loves her book."

"Get your wife down here and introduce them. Destiny loves people." With a sigh Wyatt went back to his office to call Nick and see about dinner. He would give Jake and Madison a call in case they were back and wanted to come meet Destiny.

When he couldn't get any of the three of them, he left word on their answering machines and then sat back to send each sibling a text, but his mind was on Destiny. Her perfume still lingered and he recalled running his fingers beneath the edge of the neckline of her sweater, feeling her warm, soft skin and curves that made him hot.

Dinner at his place—and then when the brothers left, he would have her there to himself. He made a mental note to tell her he would pick her up. He didn't want Duke bringing her to his place in the limo and then hanging out until after dinner to take her home. No, Wyatt wanted her all to himself after the family left.

He wondered what she and Ernie were seeing and what Ernie was telling her. He suspected a historic tour of Verity had new sights to see. The tour probably would keep Ernie busy for the next two hours.

His phone rang and caller ID indicated Jake Calhoun.

"So you're back," he said.

"Yes, we are." It was Madison who answered.

"You sound happy."

"I am, Wyatt. Happier than I've ever been." She paused to take a breath. "So I hear you've met Destiny Jones. We weren't here when she came to town, but she said she met you."

"Oh, yes. You've talked to Destiny?"

"Yes. That's why I'm calling. She called me this morning and asked me for an interview this afternoon at two o'clock. She's heard about the Milan-Calhoun feud and she wants to talk about it."

Wyatt shook his head. "Damn. I told her no interview with me. She hasn't said a word to me about any Milan-Calhoun interview with you today and I just saw her. She didn't tell me she would ask other members of my family." His hand tightened on the phone. He had known she would stir up trouble over the feud. He'd been right about that from the start.

"Well, I'm sorry, but evidently, you're not going to get interviewed by Ms. Jones," Madison said and he could hear the laughter in her voice, which added to his annoyance.

"I don't want to be interviewed, dammit. I've turned her down on an interview. I don't want her to stir up that old feud. With your marriage to Jake, things are smoothing over a bit between the families. We don't need a stranger to sail into town and fan the flames of old angers and bad feelings."

"Maybe she'll just talk about how the feud is over and how happy a Milan can be married to a Calhoun." Madison's smile was audible.

"She didn't come to Texas to get background for a show of sweetness and light."

"She'll interview Jake and me, and I think she is calling one of his siblings and maybe another one of mine. Obviously, it's not you. I thought I'd give you a heads-up."

"Thank you for that," Wyatt said. "Any chance of getting you to back out of it?"

"I don't think so. Why should I? It's an old story that everyone around here knows, so what's the harm?"

"I just figure it may stir up hard feelings."

"I won't do that and neither will Jake. Especially since we just got married," she said, the tone of her voice softening. He was happy for her and didn't want to intrude on that happiness or spoil even a fraction of it.

"Sure. When and where is this interview—at Jake's ranch or yours?"

"Neither. I've moved into Jake's home on his ranch, but the interview is in Verity. It's in the Verity Hotel lobby," she replied. "You can come observe if you'd like."

He wanted to groan. "I should have known. Thank you for the heads-up. When she came to town she drew a crowd and had an impromptu press conference that got reporters here from as far away as Dallas. They must have been coming to Verity anyway or got a chopper here. Get ready for a lot of attention. Have you seen her yet?"

"No. She said I can't miss her—she has red curly hair. So do a lot of other people, but I'll find her."

"Madison, you couldn't miss her if you were blind. You'll smell her perfume, hear her jewelry clinking, hear her laughter. No one else in Texas looks like her."

"Am I talking to Wyatt Milan?"

"Very funny."

"Well, now I'm interested in meeting her. Really interested. I've never heard you give that much description of a woman."

"As sheriff I've learned to be more observant," he remarked, knowing his sister was teasing him. "I'll be there with my deputy. Do your best to convey that the feud is over."

"I will. All she has to do is look at me with Jake."

"I'm sure that's the truth. Now, on another subject—how about you and Jake come for dinner Friday night at my place? Nick and Tony want to meet Destiny, although now they'll get to if they come watch this interview, but they want to get to talk to her."

"Friday night is fine with me. I'll check with Jake and let you know."

"Good. See you this afternoon."

He ended the call and swore quietly, getting up and going to the lobby where Dwight was at his desk, typing on his computer.

"If you want to let your wife know, Destiny Jones is going to interview members of my family at the Verity Hotel this afternoon at two o'clock. That will draw another crowd."

"She's a busy woman. She'll put Verity on the map."

"Yeah, well, I'm not sure Verity wants to be on the map." Wyatt rubbed his neck. "She's interviewing my family about the feud."

"Oh, my. Which one? Nick?"

"No, Madison and Jake Calhoun. Who knows who else, but she sure as hell didn't ask me to give her an okay to do this." Wyatt thought his deputy looked as if he tried to hide a laugh.

"I'm sure she didn't. You would have killed the interview."

"Yes, I would have." He left and heard his cell phone ring.

When he answered, it was his brother Tony. "I know you've already talked to Madison. I thought I'd tell you two things. One, thanks for the dinner invitation and I'll be there Friday night."

"Great. You'll have a chance to talk to her at length. Now, what else?"

"She called me and I have an interview with her this afternoon at the Verity Hotel about the feud."

"Would it do me any good to ask you to try to avoid stirring up trouble? That feud is beginning to die a natural death. Don't bring it back to life."

"I'll try not to, Wyatt, but I know she's also interviewing Lindsay Calhoun, so don't expect too much."

"Oh, dammit, Tony. You and Lindsay fight constantly. The two of you will fan the flames of this old feud until it's blazing away again."

"I'll try to soften my answers, but she better lay off antagonizing me."

"If she antagonizes you, try to save up telling her off until you're away from a microphone and far away from Destiny."

"I'll keep that in mind."

"Tony, don't make things worse," Wyatt said.

"Okay, okay. Are you going to be there?"

"Wouldn't miss it for the world."

"See you then," Tony said right before he hung up. Once again Wyatt swore quietly. He walked back to the lobby.

"I called my wife. She's coming for the interview."

"Yeah, and everyone else in town, including all the Milans and the Calhouns. I don't want it to turn into a circus. Destiny doesn't have a calming effect on people. If I can just keep my family calm, hopefully, Jake or one of the Calhouns will keep a cool head. It damn well won't be Lindsay or Tony." Wyatt shook his head and left, walking across the street in long strides as he headed to the Verity Hotel.

Without stopping at the desk, Wyatt went to Destiny's suite and knocked.

In minutes she opened the door and her eyes widened when she faced him. "Come in, I think." She stepped back as he entered.

"I thought it was Amy or Duke or Virginia at the door. I didn't even look out," Destiny said.

"Maybe you should be more careful."

"Come in," she said, leading the way into the living area. His blue eyes were as dark as a stormy sky and she could feel his disapproval when she opened the door. "Have a seat, Wyatt," she said, sitting on a corner of the sofa and folding one leg beneath her. The look of fury had lessened and now he had a faint smile playing at the corners of his mouth. Puzzled at the change in him, she wondered why he was here. He sat near the center of the sofa, not far from her. Her gaze dropped to his mouth while memories of his kisses made her conscious of how close he sat.

"So this is the way you sit around the house when you're just hanging out?" he asked.

She looked down at her designer clothes. She wore lounging slacks and a silk top in bold black-and-white stripes and high-heeled black sandals.

"Sometimes," she said. "When I travel I see others

whom I don't know or don't know well. Sometimes it pays to be dressed decently. Like right now."

"I don't know about 'decently.' What you do for that outfit—I'd describe it in a different way."

"I know you didn't come here to check out what I'm wearing."

"I sure as hell didn't," Wyatt said. "Did you know you're getting ready to do something that will hurt my family and maybe a lot of people?"

"Wyatt, you and I have different views of the world. I'm not trying to hurt your family or anyone else. The feud is interesting and I'm not going to rekindle it with my questions. Your sister married a Calhoun. If anything this should show the town and the state that feuds can be resolved—time passes and they die. Now, what's wrong with that?"

"If you were just interviewing Madison and Jake, I would not be as concerned. You're interviewing Tony and Lindsay who despise each other and fight on a weekly basis in every way they can."

"Is that right? Just because those two can't get along, it isn't going to start the feud up again. Besides, it obviously has never completely died. It's just news and interesting. If I don't write about it, sooner or later someone else will."

"I'd rather take that chance and maybe it would be way later and not even matter so much when there are Milan-Calhoun descendants who have blood from both families."

"You're worrying for nothing. Sheriff Milan, take the afternoon off, go fishing, enjoy life and you won't know the difference tomorrow."

"So you're going ahead with the interview?"

"That's what I came to Verity to do, and you're not giving me a valid reason to cancel it, so yes, I'm going to interview your sister, who is very nice and friendly. She didn't seem worried about having an interview."

"She is just back from her short honeymoon. She isn't going to worry about anything right now. The whole world is a rosy place and she is deliriously happy."

"How nice. Well, that should come across in the interview. Relax, Wyatt. I'm not going to stir up a generations-old feud."

He turned away, not answering her, and she sat in silence studying his profile, wishing he wasn't angry with her. But he was being ridiculous about an ancient family feud. Through the years, it seemed to have turned more into a legend, and while her grandmother didn't have kind words for the Milans, she really hadn't ever been involved with one.

Finally, he stood. "All right, Destiny. I'll be back at two o'clock just to make sure everything stays quiet and peaceful."

As she stood, she faced him. "I really think you'd be happier if you would go fishing, play golf, ride a horse or whatever it is that you enjoy doing."

His expression changed, one corner of his mouth lifting slightly as he stepped closer. "You know what I enjoy doing most?" he asked in a husky voice that warmed her insides and changed their conversation.

"You know what I meant, Wyatt. Something fun you like."

"I'm talking about the most fun possible and what I like most." The deep tone of his voice seemed to caress her as his hands would have. She tingled and lost her train of thought for a moment.

"I'll be happy to have you in the audience," she whispered finally. "As a matter of fact, would you like me to ask you to say a few words from your perspective about the family feud?"

He stepped closer to her, making her heart race. She tried to keep from looking at his mouth and thinking about kisses. "You ask me anything about the family feud and you'll regret bringing it up. I'll be so damn dull, I'll kill your interview."

Her smile broadened. "I do believe I've pierced our sheriff's laid-back armor, that 'nothing ever really disturbs me' attitude."

"Watch out, Destiny," he said in a low voice.

"Now you're giving me a challenge. You think you can dull my interview? It might be worth it just to try to break through that impenetrable cool attitude you carry off in the face of all kinds of turmoil."

"If you want to break through my laid-back attitude, there's a far easier way to do so," he said.

Her smile faded. He stood as close as he could without touching her. His eyes were no longer dark blue with anger, but had transformed to crystal blue with a heavy-lidded gaze that held blatant desire. His attention shifted lower to her mouth and her lips parted. Without thought, she leaned toward him a fraction, pressing against him, and his arm circled her waist. He pulled her up against him and leaned down to kiss her, his mouth hard and demanding, his kiss passionate. His other hand tangled in her hair, sending pins and the ribbon flying, causing locks to fall over her shoulders.

He leaned over her and she held him tightly, clinging to him while she moaned, wanting him desperately. His hand slid over her, caressing her, freeing buttons, and he shoved the top open to cup her breast in his hand. Her small cry of pleasure seemed to come from far away. She held Wyatt, sliding one hand over his muscled shoulders and chest, kissing him wantonly, desiring him with all her being. How could he do this to her so effortlessly?

"Wyatt, the bedroom," she whispered.

Never breaking contact with her lips, he picked her up. She didn't open her eyes, but was lost in his kisses. She felt him carrying her, not caring what was happening as long as she was in his arms and he was kissing her.

As he stood her on her feet, his hands caressed her breasts. "You're so beautiful. All I can think about is you," he whispered and leaned down to kiss her breast while his hand slipped beneath the silk pants and he stroked her between her thighs.

She gasped and held his shoulders while writhing with need. With an urgency that made her hands tremble she peeled away his brown shirt and trailed kisses over his chest as she undid his belt and then his uniform slacks, pushing them off his narrow hips.

After he picked her up to place her on the bed, he turned away to get protection.

"Wyatt, come to me," she whispered, running her hands over his muscled thighs.

"I wanted you, Destiny." He lowered himself between her legs and entered her, filling her in one smooth motion, moving slowly while she thrashed beneath him.

Wanting him with her whole being, she scaled the peak quickly, bursting with release, enveloped in ecstasy. He pumped faster, until seconds later she felt him shudder. His arms wrapped around her, pressing her close while they still moved together, even after they were sated.

"Wyatt, if only I could just hold this moment forever," she whispered more to herself than to him. He showered light kisses on her cheek and temple and rolled on his side, keeping her close so they faced each other.

"Ah, Destiny. You're fantastic," he whispered, combing curly strands of red hair away from her face. "Beautiful."

"You did this, Wyatt, to make me late for my interview," she said lightly.

His hand stilled and for an instant she wondered if that was exactly what he had done.

"I made love to you because you came to the door in

clothes that clung to you like a second skin and your big, green eyes held desire while your kisses were an invitation. Tell me you didn't want to make love."

She looked into the bluest eyes she had ever seen. "You know I wanted to," she whispered. "So did you." Like an intruder, reality broke through her thoughts. "Wyatt, I can't stay here in bed. A crew will be arriving shortly to set up so I can record the interview."

"This interview will be televised, won't it?"

"Not today. Not live. It will be taped and whether it's aired will depend on other things, my stay in Verity, my story about Verity. The interview may go into archives and never be heard of again, so cheer up. Few may ever even know about it, but I have to get ready and get downstairs, so you, Sheriff Milan, are going to have to dress and go."

He kissed her long and passionately and then released her. "I'll go, but you won't forget our time together, our making love." He stepped out of bed. "I'll get dressed in your guest bathroom." He picked up his things as she gathered hers and headed for her shower.

When she came out, Wyatt had gone.

At ten minutes before two o'clock, Wyatt entered the hotel lobby. Destiny was nowhere in sight, nor was there anyone else present who would be involved in the interview, which made him wonder if she had followed his urging and canceled it.

He was beginning to feel better and pleased with her when he spotted a sign on a pedestal as he approached the elevators. The sign directed anyone interested in the Milan-Calhoun interview to go to the second-floor central ballroom.

He headed for the stairs and on the second floor when he passed through open double doors into the large ball-

room, Wyatt spotted Destiny instantly as she stood looking at a sheaf of papers in her hands.

Potted plants had been moved to a corner, five chairs
were set up in the front of the room, lit by TV lights and
framed by cameras whose wires snaked across the polished
hotel floor. Briefly he wondered where she got the camera crew, when all she'd brought to Verity was Virginia
Boyden. His pulse quickened and he wanted to go talk to
her, but he knew she was working now and her thoughts
would be on the interview.

Looking sophisticated, Destiny had her hair looped and
pinned on the top and back of her head, yet he couldn't
keep from remembering all that red hair spilled over her
bare shoulders and breasts less than a couple of hours earlier. She was in a blue dress that clung to her figure and
had a V neckline—another dress that would turn heads.
Watching her, he felt a mixture of emotions—annoyance
that she would do the interview and desire to be with her
the rest of the day and night, which he knew was impossible. He had wanted peace and quiet—something that
had settled over Verity since he took office and he trea-
sured it in the town and in his own life. Now his world
was churning and he could feel trouble boiling beneath
the surface, ready to bubble up at any time with Destiny's
troublemaking.

People were beginning to gather and some had even
brought their own chairs. There was a buzz of conversation among the people, who looked as if they were at a
party with eagerness and expectation in their expressions.
When Wyatt spotted his sister and new brother-in-law, he
went over to greet them.

He walked up to Madison, giving her a hug. "Welcome
home, Mrs. Calhoun."

Hugging him in return, Madison laughed. "That makes
me feel as if I should look around for Jake's mother."

"Hi, Jake. You've been able to put up with her for a while now," Wyatt said, shaking hands with his new brother-in-law.

"I don't view her quite the same way as her brothers do," he remarked, hugging her against him and keeping his arm around her. Madison smiled and stuck her tongue out at Wyatt.

"So there, brother, dear," she said sweetly. "We go on first and I will tell about the legend and how it's faded to almost nothing."

"Definitely nothing," Jake said. "I'm friends with all of you and in love with one of the Milans. No feud there." Jake smiled at Madison who smiled up at him. In that instance they were wrapped in their own world, their happiness obvious. Looking at them, Wyatt thought of Katherine and the marriage he had hoped and expected to have, and probably the children they would have had by now. He closed his mind on those memories. His eyes lit on Destiny and his ache vanished, replaced by memories of their lovemaking a couple of hours earlier, holding Destiny in his arms as he kissed her, her softness and warmth.

Sometime later he realized Madison was talking. "...then at some point, she will interview Lindsay and Tony. That's what you should worry about, not when I talk about marrying Jake," she said, smiling at her new husband, who brushed a light kiss on her cheek. "See— no feud between us. It's dead forever. I love the Calhouns, particularly one of them."

Wyatt had to laugh. "I think I'll go say hi to Tony. You two need your own island. Don't start smooching on television."

"I'll try to remember," she said, without taking her gaze from Jake.

Wyatt smiled and walked away, strolling up to Tony, who looked just what he was—a Texas rancher. He wore a blue Western shirt, his wide-brimmed black hat, jeans and boots. His belt was wider than Wyatt's and the silver belt buckle larger. Wyatt shook hands with his brother.

"Please don't get people really stirred up," he told Tony. "There are a lot of people around with Calhoun blood even if their name isn't Calhoun."

"I know. I won't. I'll be civil if the little witch will button her lips."

"Please don't call her 'the little witch.' I want to avoid stirring up old feelings or making this feud any worse than it currently is. You and Lindsay Calhoun fan the flames constantly and keep this feud alive more than any other Milans or Calhouns."

"Maybe so, but there's damn good reason. She is a pestiferous— There isn't a word to describe her except *witch*."

Wyatt groaned. "Try to avoid it for the next three hours. I want peace and quiet in here and no fistfights."

"Okay, for you, I will. And because I have a dinner invitation to your house this week to meet Destiny Jones. She is one good-looking woman," Tony said, his face taking on a dazed expression as he sought out the lady in question. Wyatt, too, turned to look at her again.

"That is as true as Texas," Wyatt said, forgetting his brother and thinking about Destiny. He had plans for Friday night that went beyond the dinner he was hosting for his brothers. For him, it was a means to an end. He couldn't wait to be alone with her again.

"Here comes Nick," Tony said. He greeted his brother when Nick joined him and shook hands with Wyatt.

"I have to go," Tony said. "Destiny is motioning me over. I'm most happy to do whatever she wants. See you guys."

Wyatt turned to Nick. "Well, you and I are just spectators to this unless something's changed during the past hour," he said.

"That suits me fine. I'm impressed with her ability to deal with a crowd and her ability to draw a crowd. I can't tell you how much I'd like to hire her for my PR person. She would be fantastic in that position."

She's fantastic in all sorts of positions, Wyatt thought. He sighed, wishing this would be over quickly and he could have some time alone with her again.

He scanned the room, noticing that the number of people had risen considerably since his arrival.

Nick slapped him on the back. "Relax, Sheriff. There hasn't been an actual fight between a Milan and a Calhoun since—"

"Not since a month ago when Lindsay dumped a truckload of manure on one of Tony's ranch roads."

Nick grinned. "Those two are your troublemakers. He did something to provoke her, you can bet on that."

Knowing Nick was right, Wyatt strolled away, greeting the new arrivals and making his presence known. He was certain Nick was right—fights would not break out—but it was a crowd and there were a few strong feelings, although he suspected Destiny could keep a crowd under control with the greatest of ease.

One half of the ballroom was already filled and Wyatt kept moving. He knew it would be like this. The audience had grown steadily and now that it was nearing time to start, more and more people had come. He saw people who worked for Lindsay and some who worked for Tony.

Finally, Destiny took her seat in a chair facing the audience. A small table was beside her and it held some papers, a pitcher of ice water and paper cups. Madison and Jake sat nearby, angled to one side, yet where they could see both the audience and Destiny.

Wyatt looked at his sister, who was wearing a navy suit and matching blouse and heels, a far more tailored look than she usually had. He swore she almost had a glow about her; the faint smile and starry-eyed look she gave Jake as he sat close beside her conveyed her bliss, which made Wyatt happy for her. Jake was a good guy and Wyatt was glad they were finally married. He hoped the past was really behind them.

Rising, Destiny opened the program. "Folks, thanks for your interest today. I'm Destiny Jones. I have a show originating in Chicago, which I hope all of you watch, called *Unsolved Mysteries*." She smiled while the onlookers applauded, led by Jake, who was facing everyone. "Thank you to all who enjoy the show. Some of the mysteries we attempt to solve on the show date back to another century and that's what has brought me to the unique town of Verity, Texas."

She waited for more applause from the crowd.

"I'm interested in three unsolved murders from years ago. Two of the men killed one spring night several generations ago were Mortimer Milan and Reuben Calhoun.

"As I understand the history here, almost since the first few days they settled in this area, the Milans and the Calhouns have been feuding, blaming each other for all sorts of trouble. For a lot of years, members of each family would not speak to members of the other family.

"Today, that feud may be dying out because now we have a Milan and a Calhoun who have married and so the families are brought together and hereafter will be related."

As the audience applauded, Jake took Madison's hand and smiled at her.

When they quieted, Destiny continued, "Folks, I'm guessing everyone in the room knows both of these people—Mr. and Mrs. Jake Calhoun." There was more enthusiastic applause.

"I'm sure all of you from Verity already know Mrs. Jake Calhoun is Madison Milan, so now these two famous families are joined."

Destiny took her seat and as she continued talking about Verity and Texas legends, Wyatt stepped back and watched the crowd. Everyone seemed interested, sat quietly and attentively and he relaxed a bit. To his relief, he knew the majority of the people who were present.

Destiny gave a lively talk and then asked Jake to tell about the feud as he knew it from the Calhoun point of view.

Looking relaxed, dressed in a navy shirt, jeans and boots, Jake took Madison's hand again, smiling at her, and Wyatt had another surge of relief that Jake was on camera because he was levelheaded and obviously in love with a Milan.

"I've heard the legend as far back as my memory goes. It's two early-day families—both with big families that included aunts, uncles, grandparents, mothers, fathers and brothers who settled here. According to all the stories, there were several things that contributed to trouble between the Calhouns and the Milans. The land they staked out and claimed for each ranch shared the same border. Calhouns and Milans were neighbors with the same creeks running across both ranches so water became an issue between them. They didn't have fences at first, so they fought over cattle. There weren't as many women out on the frontier, so the men fought over their women. There were other problems, too—Milans claimed that a Calhoun bet and lost part of the Calhoun land to the Milans in a card game. The battle continued through the years as this area settled and became more civilized. Gradually, some Milans began to speak to some Calhouns and some Calhouns began to speak to some Milans. And now," he said, pausing to smile at Madison, "one Calhoun has married a Milan and there is no feud as far as the two of us are concerned. I hope the old feud is over forever."

The audience clapped, but Jake noticed neither Tony nor Lindsay clapped.

Destiny quieted the crowd. "Madison, we haven't heard from you. Is that about the way you've always been told about the legend?"

"Yes, it is," she said, smiling at Jake. "Just about the same. Both families did things to the other one and from what I've always been told, the biggest fights have involved water and, I have to admit, women. The Milan-Calhoun feud is definitely over as far as we're concerned. I hope both our families are at peace with each other from now on."

Destiny smiled at the audience as they applauded Madison's statement.

"So maybe the end of the feud has come," Destiny said, smiling at the audience. She stood, moving freely with a lapel mike. "As all of you can see there are Milans and Calhouns in the audience this afternoon and everyone is peaceful, so it looks as if Jake and Madison are right and the feud is over and another Texas legend goes into the local history books."

The audience again applauded.

"Do any of the Milans or Calhouns want to come forward and add anything?"

Wyatt held his breath and glanced at Tony to see him standing at the edge of the crowd, his arms folded. He looked relaxed, mildly interested and not on the verge of moving. Wyatt was about to let out his breath when a hand went up and he wanted to groan out loud.

"Ah, someone has her hand in the air and we met right before I started taping," Destiny said. "It's Lindsay Calhoun, right?"

"That's right," Lindsay said. Wyatt had moments when he had to admire Lindsay because she was a competent rancher and had the respect of most all the ranchers in the area. She was another woman who didn't scare easily. He just wished both Lindsay and Tony would be more tolerant and cooperative and try to work out their disputes.

At the moment he wanted to grit his teeth and he braced for what was coming next.

"Come up here, Lindsay, and join your brother if you have something to add."

Jake stood, but he didn't applaud when the audience did. Even though he had a faint smile, he looked about as solemn as Wyatt felt.

Wyatt noticed that Madison made no attempt to hug her new sister-in-law or greet her in any way except with a smile.

With her blond hair in a long braid, and dressed in a long-sleeve green Western shirt and jeans, Lindsay took the empty chair Destiny motioned her to, as well as the handheld mike she offered.

"So, Lindsay, do you agree with your brother that the feud is over?" Destiny asked, once she was again seated.

"It definitely is for Jake and Madison, which is nice," she said, smiling at Jake and then turning to face the crowd. "I'm not so sure it is for all Calhouns and Milans," she stated. Someone in the audience whistled, while another man said, "Tell 'em, Lindsay."

Lindsay laughed. "Not all Calhouns and Milans get along like my brother and his new wife, so I don't think anyone can say the feud is over."

"Can you give me a modern-day example?" Destiny asked. "Why would any Calhoun be annoyed with any Milan, or vice versa?"

"Well, some of us are still ranchers and some of us still have neighboring ranches and that can set up a situation to be as volatile as it was a century ago. If someone lets their cattle overgraze a field, or diverts a creek, or dumps manure over a fence," she added, her voice getting a harsher tone, "then tempers flare." There was a smattering of applause and Lindsay smiled at the audience. "See, my feelings are shared."

"From my perspective," Jake said, "some Calhouns and some Milans are a little touchier than others. Time is against this feud and it's fading. I think Lindsay will have to agree that in our lifetime it's changed and not taken as seriously by as many family members as it used to be."

There was more applause for Jake, who smiled at the audience and then at his sister.

"I agree," Lindsay offered. "I'm just saying it isn't over as long as one family does something to someone from the other family. And that continues to happen. The day that stops between all Calhouns and Milans, then I'll agree the feud is over."

"There are cousins, aunts, uncles, members of both families, the Milans and the Calhouns, who have moved away from Verity," Destiny said. "For them this feud no longer exists, so would all of you agree that it's limited to Verity and family members who have ranches in this vicinity?"

Jake and Madison replied yes, but Lindsay shook her head. "No, I can't agree," she said. "There are Milans and Calhouns who live in Dallas and other Texas cities and I know they don't speak if they meet members of the other family."

"Are you and your neighbor on speaking terms?" Destiny asked.

"Only when we have to be or when either of us can't resist sounding off. Otherwise, we don't speak."

"So the feud is still alive. Do you think the feud goes beyond just local Milans and Calhouns?"

"I think it does," Lindsay replied.

"I guess I'll test out your theory, Lindsay," Destiny said. "I haven't been in Verity long, but I've been welcomed by all I've met, Milans and Calhouns, and I hope that doesn't change, but I can add my own background to this discussion."

Suddenly Wyatt's attention focused on Destiny and he forgot the crowd. Her gaze met his, but with the bright lights, he doubted whether she could really see him.

"I was born in Houston, Texas," she said and paused while there was applause from some of the onlookers. "My family on my mother's side was Calhouns."

Six

Shocked again by Destiny, Wyatt frowned. Why hadn't she told him? Stunned, annoyed. One after the other, the emotions battered Wyatt as he watched her. There was applause and Destiny walked closer to the crowd gathered to watch her while she still gazed at Wyatt.

She had rocked his world from the first moment he had spotted the red limo. So far, this was the biggest jolt of all and his annoyance transformed to a simmering anger. She was a paradox to him—physically intimate with him, yet holding back this vital information about herself until she decided to tell the whole town. Why hadn't she told him that she was a Calhoun, especially since she knew he'd been upset about her interviews because of the feud?

Instantly, he guessed she had waited for the biggest impact by announcing it during this interview. From the first second he should have realized she waited for the biggest public relations impact.

His anger eased only slightly because she still could

have told him and let him know that she would announce it this afternoon.

He folded his arms and stared at her while he absorbed the news that he had been in bed with a Calhoun. Again, he recalled the first moment he had seen the red limo in his parking spot and her in his office. He had known she would cause trouble in his peaceful town and his quiet life. She had proven him right over and over and this was a crowning touch—except he suspected the worst was still to come.

He watched Destiny in the front of the ballroom, calm and professional as she continued. "I was never caught up in the feud because my mother wasn't. I knew nothing about it until we moved to California when I was a teen and I was told by my grandmother, who has strong feelings about being a Calhoun," she said. "My heritage gives me a personal interest in the feud now."

She smiled at Lindsay. "I'm looking forward to meeting more of my Calhoun relatives."

"Jake and I'll be happy to introduce you," Lindsay said, smiling in return.

Destiny stepped forward, closer to her audience. "Since we've heard from Lindsay Calhoun, I think in all fairness, we should give her neighbor a chance to speak because he's in our audience—if he's willing to come forward. Tony Milan?" She looked at the audience.

Wyatt groaned. For a moment he hoped Tony had left, but then he saw his brother walking up to the front of the room, turning to the audience and saying, "I'll guarantee you, I'm speaking to this Calhoun. I have no quarrel with her," he said as he took Destiny's hand. "Welcome to Verity."

Wyatt noticed that everyone applauded except Lindsay. Jake said something to his sister and she shook her head.

"Thank you," Destiny said. "Sit and join us. Do you have anything to add to what Lindsay has told us?"

"She's covered it all," he said, still smiling as he pulled his chair a few inches away from Lindsay and sat.

Wyatt felt it was too soon to yield to the relief he was beginning to feel. He was proud of Tony for keeping the situation light and upbeat and placing Destiny in a position that might make her want to cooperate. Tony and Lindsay had not looked at each other. If he just kept his cool, the interview would move on.

"As big as these ranches are, I wouldn't think you would ever get in each other's way," Destiny said and Tony simply shrugged and smiled while Lindsay gazed solemnly at Destiny.

"Texas isn't big enough to avoid this clash," Lindsay said quietly, but some in the audience heard and laughed.

"You don't have anything to add to this?" Destiny asked Tony.

"I'm sitting between my new Calhoun brother-in-law and the beautiful Calhoun star and host of the television show, *Unsolved Mysteries,* so no, I'm not causing a ripple with Calhouns today," Tony said with a big grin and got a round of applause that Wyatt joined.

Destiny laughed. "I might move back to Texas," she said to the audience and smiled at Tony. The audience responded with hearty cheers.

"Move to Verity," someone yelled and she waved. Destiny smiled, looking at the audience. Wyatt had drifted slowly until he was standing near a cameraman. As she talked, Destiny looked directly into Wyatt's eyes.

"Since I've been here, I've met Milans and Calhouns and I like them all, so I see no reason for a feud to continue. I wish you happiness and an end to the feud," she said to Jake and Madison.

She turned to the audience. "So that's the history and

the story of a Texas feud from generations ago until the present day. Thank you, Lindsay, Madison, Jake and Tony. Thank all of you for stopping to join us and your gracious hospitality to me and my staff."

While the lights dimmed and the taping broke up. Destiny turned to talk to her guests while people from the audience began to line up to talk to her.

Wyatt let out his breath and moved to the edge of the crowd, stepping back, waiting to make sure everyone left without a problem. He walked to Tony. "Thank you and I'm proud you could resist coming back at her."

"I wanted to, but I figured the entire family would be relieved if I didn't and Madison is so happy right now—I don't want to do one thing to toss a damper on her joy."

"So maybe my little brother is growing up. That's good, Tony, because I know Lindsay is no saint."

"Don't get me started, Wyatt."

"I wouldn't think of it. I'm glad you can come to dinner Friday night."

"I'd like that." He glanced around the room. "Lindsay's talking to Destiny. I'll get out while everything is smooth. I don't care to join in any conversation that Lindsay is part of. If I do, Destiny might see the bad side of the feud come to life."

"See you Friday night and thanks again for averting more trouble." He watched his younger brother turn and leave the ballroom and he was proud of Tony. The room was emptying fast. Wyatt started to join Destiny, but Nick stepped in front of him.

"It went better than I expected," Nick said. "Still wish I could hire her."

Wyatt smiled. "Won't happen. Even for money, I don't think she would give up the limelight. She's a natural for the work she does."

"Yes, she is. I have to run now or I'm going to be late for an appointment, but I'll see you Friday night."

"Great."

"I was proud of Tony."

"He is growing up, Nick. He held it in and I know it took an effort."

"Amen. He surprised me because those two have strong feelings between them. See you," Nick said over his shoulder as he headed toward the door and was gone.

Wyatt moved on, hanging back until Lindsay turned to leave. He looked into her blue eyes. A Calhoun without brown eyes, he thought.

"Hi, Lindsay," he said.

"Wyatt," she answered coolly and he was surprised she even bothered to acknowledge him because most of the time she didn't. She hurried past him and out of sight.

He waited while Destiny finished talking to the camera crew and to Amy. She strolled over to Wyatt.

"Destiny Calhoun, that was a surprise," he said. "I suppose you waited for the most dramatic moment to break that news around here. Why didn't you tell me earlier?"

"It surely wouldn't have made a difference, would it?"

"Not at all," he answered. "It would have been nicer not to get it cold like I did. Maybe this way I felt shut out of your life even more than I am."

Something flickered in the depths of her eyes. "That does surprise me. What we have is a lusty, physical attraction with no future to it. I never thought about either of us getting closer otherwise. You keep part of yourself locked away all the time."

"I suppose I do," he said quietly. "Maybe today for a brief time I got closer and in the euphoria from that feeling, your announcement emphasized that I had made a mistake."

"Other than physically, I don't think we were one degree closer today," she said solemnly. "You just didn't like being surprised. You haven't shared your past with me or lost one bit of that wall you keep around yourself. I didn't think you'd care when I let you know my heritage, and I got a little drama out of announcing it when I did."

"You got your interview and it went better than I expected," he said, wanting to drop the discussion of deepening their relationship. That wasn't going to happen.

"Your brother is a charmer and it's a stretch to imagine him fighting with anyone, much less someone as pretty as Lindsay Calhoun," Destiny said.

"Tony has his moments. So where did you get all the camera crew?"

"An affiliate in Dallas." She checked her watch. "Shortly, I have an appointment to talk to one of your local historians—Gilda who works in the Verity Historical Museum."

"Gilda can tell you the history of this place. She'll be more informative than the little museum. She knows more about Verity and the people here than anyone else in town." He shifted his weight while he gazed into Destiny's expressive green eyes that relayed desire.

"Well, I was hoping we could go back to your room and finish what we started," he said, wanting to touch her, but resisting because of the people moving around them.

"I thought we did finish what we started."

"Hardly. I'll show you next time I get the opportunity." He resisted the urge to do so now, though he did lean a little closer to her. "I'm glad you did the interview because that's what caused me to go to the hotel to talk to you."

"I don't see any chance to really be with you until Friday night."

"I'll pick you up Friday night. That way I'll get to talk to you because once we get to my house, my brothers are going to take all your time."

She smiled at him. "Fine. I see Amy headed my way. I'd better get back to work."

"Okay, see you Friday," he said, leaving the ballroom and feeling Destiny watching him walk out.

Wyatt left for the office, but he didn't feel like dealing with business. He was thinking about his reactions to Destiny. Besides the fantastic sex, he enjoyed being with her and the more he got to know her, the more he wanted to have her with him. She was lively, bringing an enthusiasm for life into any situation she was in. Charm came naturally to her and she charmed everyone around her. She was usually positive, upbeat, filled with life, an extrovert who loved the people she met, interacted easily with them. Destiny was so many things he wasn't, but he liked that about her.

She would only be here a short time and then gone out of his life. He wanted Destiny here longer. The time would come when he'd be ready to tell her goodbye because since his breakup he never got deeply involved, but not this soon. It startled him to realize that he had stronger feelings for Destiny than for anyone since Katherine.

It surprised him even more to realize that he hadn't even thought about Katherine very much in the past two days. After all these years since law school, he usually couldn't get Katherine out of his thoughts—until now. The constant excitement with Destiny would drive everything else out of any man's thoughts. The pain of his breakup was fading more than ever. He was still certain he would never love again the way he had loved Katherine—consequently, he hoped he was never hurt again the way he had been with her—but Destiny was making a difference in his life and he enjoyed her flamboyant style and bubbling enthusiasm, which continually amazed him.

At the door, he glanced over his shoulder and met Destiny's gaze. He left, wondering what her next surprise would be.

* * *

After her last meeting of the day Destiny returned to her suite, tired but pleased with the information she got from the local historian. Changing out of her business clothes, she looked around her bedroom and her thoughts continually drifted to Wyatt and what they had done there earlier that afternoon. She thought about their lovemaking, being in his arms. In his quiet, determined way, he was the most exciting man she had ever known—something she had never expected to feel about him.

Would he ever come to Chicago to see her once she left Verity?

She felt a wishful stab of longing because she knew he wouldn't. Once she left Verity, they would be out of each other's lives forever—if they were ever in each other's lives at all except for the wild, lusty moments of hot sex. That was not enough substance to build a relationship on, she knew, so they would fade into oblivion. She had no illusions about their relationship. It was purely physical, nothing more. At least that had been the way she had viewed it until the past hour when Wyatt had told her he had felt shut out when she didn't tell him she was a Calhoun before the public announcement.

Wyatt's confession had shocked her. It was an indication that he felt something beyond a physical relationship. She knew that his heart was locked away, but maybe there was a crack in that rock wall around his heart. Maybe Wyatt was more vulnerable to deep feelings than he wanted to admit.

There had been a few moments when she had caught a shuttered look in Wyatt's eyes after making love. She felt he had shut his mind to even thinking about their relationship, but his remarks this afternoon indicated otherwise—and made her stop and question how deep her feelings ran for Wyatt.

Destiny shook her head. Wyatt was far more than she

had expected and she responded to him beyond her wildest imaginings. She liked being with him and had to admit he was a calming influence in her life. No matter how much they liked being together, she didn't expect to see him again when she left Verity—unless she returned for the show. She had never been in love in her life and Wyatt wasn't the man to give her heart to because it would be a hopeless love. He may have relented slightly, but he still guarded his heart.

Was she warning herself about him...or was she worrying after the fact? Was she already falling in love?

Was she going home in love with him?

But how could that be? He was not her style at all. She had dated famous men, movie actors, newsmen, dynamic people who moved on the national scene. Wyatt's world was one little town and one sparsely populated county in West Texas, and a ranch filled with cattle. True, he had flown her to Dallas for dinner in a private room, but overall he still led a quiet life. He was controlled, and low-key. He did have a streak of arrogance, expecting to get his way and what he wanted out of life. She had to laugh, though, because she might have a streak of that also. But still, Wyatt Calhoun was the most exciting man she had ever known.

"Sheesh," she said aloud, wondering how he had captured her interest. She couldn't really be in love. When she got back to Chicago, she expected to forget Wyatt fairly fast. At the same time, she liked the way he listened to her, giving her his full attention. She felt he liked her for who she truly was, not a television personality. She felt she could trust him and she understood why the townspeople wanted him for sheriff, because he was honest and trustworthy.

For now, though, she wanted to be in his arms and she wanted his kisses.

The interviews today had been interesting and she had eased off asking Lindsay Calhoun questions that she would have asked if she hadn't known how unhappy Wyatt was with the interview. Lindsay was a spitfire and Destiny knew she could have gotten some good quotes and sound bites out of her. Her nemesis, Tony, on the other hand, was a charmer. So different from his laid-back, laconic older brother.

In some ways, being in Verity County was like stepping back in time. The people here had old-fashioned habits and values, and they'd been incredibly friendly and courteous to her. Just like Wyatt, there was nothing in Verity that she thought would have been her taste but, to her surprise, the quiet little town held an appeal for her. She liked everyone she met and they had welcomed her, again in a sincere way that she felt had nothing to do with her show or her book. The town was refreshing with a relaxed atmosphere and, each day, she could see more of why Wyatt wanted to keep the peace and quiet. In hectic lives, the serenity was a welcome relief. No wonder he liked calling it home.

Shortly, she'd return to her home, Chicago. She'd leave Verity, and Wyatt, behind and return to her life. For some reason, that didn't seem to have the same appeal anymore.

Friday night Wyatt called her from the lobby promptly at seven.

"I'll be up to get you unless you want another grand entrance," he told her. "There is a Verity reporter and one from Lubbock and one from Fort Worth hanging out in the lobby. Word has gotten around that you're a Calhoun, so now they all have a new slant to a story about you. I think I know the answer, but I'll ask, do I come up to get you and we take the private exit?" he asked, sounding amused.

"Of course not. I'll make the grand entrance in the lobby and talk to the reporters. The publicity will be good. I'll get rid of them quickly because I've done this before, although it is easier to escape in the limo, I think. Are you parked at the front?"

"Yes, I am," he said. "Don't worry. When you want to escape, I'll see to it that we escape."

"I have no doubts. I'll bet you think I crave attention as much as Desirée."

"I think you thrive on it," he said and she laughed.

"I like reporters, politicians, even lawyers," she answered.

"Well, now, that's a good thing because you'll be knee-deep in lawyers tonight. And you'll get all their attention, I promise you, especially since you've announced your Calhoun blood."

Her nerves jangled. "Is that going to be a problem for your family?"

"They've already accepted Jake and they can't wait to get to know you, including Tony. I'll guarantee you that being a Calhoun doesn't deter Tony. Your looks overcome your heritage."

She laughed. "I can't wait. I'm coming now. I don't think you'll have any trouble spotting me."

"Oh, I don't think so either. I know I'm going to be dazzled. See you, hon," he said and was gone.

"Hon." She suspected he had thrown that in casually without thought, but it had sent a tingle through her. If only he had meant the emotion it implied, but she knew better.

She picked up her purse, locked up and left, excitement mounting over another evening with Wyatt.

Once again she took the elevator to the second level, stepped off and walked around a corner toward the stairs. The moment the lobby came into view, she saw Wyatt. Tall, dressed in a charcoal suit with a charcoal-and-black tie, a broad-brimmed hat on his head, he stood near the foot of the stairs. His gaze caught hers and she was barely aware in her peripheral vision of reporters and others converging awaiting her.

She couldn't tear her gaze from Wyatt. Tonight she was going to his house to meet part of his family. Tonight the ties between them would grow stronger. She would be in his arms later, sharing kisses, making—

Stop! She practically screamed the command at herself. She had to tear her thoughts from contemplation of what was to come and concentrate on now.

As she started down the steps, photographers and amateurs took her picture. She had long ago learned to descend a staircase while smiling at her audience waiting below.

"Have you talked to your Calhoun relatives who live here, Destiny?" one man called out.

A barrage of questions followed, and she couldn't understand any of them. She paused about five steps from the floor and held up her hand. Instantly, the crowd became silent. She glanced quickly around the lobby once again and saw a few women waiting to see her, holding copies of her book, which gave her a thrill.

Wyatt waited patiently while she answered questions, signed books and finally told the small crowd farewell.

He took her arm and in seconds they were in his car and driving away from the hotel.

"No one follows you," she said with amusement, looking over her shoulder.

"I'm the sheriff. They know me and they have sense enough to know I don't want to be followed. They want my cooperation when something happens, so they cooperate with me. You gave them your time and I waited. Now they're showing some manners and good sense and leaving us alone. This is a town filled with intelligent, kind people."

"You like Verity."

"Of course I do. This is home and these are my friends and relatives."

"They're nice. And Verity has the sexiest sheriff this side of the Atlantic Ocean."

One corner of his mouth curled in a faint smile. "Just wait until tonight and maybe you'll think the whole U.S.A.," he said.

Laughing, she ran her hand over his knee. "When I planned to come to Verity, I never, ever expected to see more of you than just a few moments when I arrived."

"You knew your sister and I saw each other."

"Desirée and I do not attract the same men. Or rather, go out with the same men."

"I can imagine in a way, but most any man would want to go out with either one of you. Looks run in the family."

"Thank you. My mother was the real beauty until her health failed. When I was little, I thought she was the most gorgeous woman in the world."

"That's nice for a little girl to think about her mother."

"She was beautiful. Desirée is, too. Since the day she was born people would stop to look at her. She's the one who looks like our mother. I resemble our grandmother on Mom's side."

"Desirée is one of the most beautiful women I've ever known."

"That's what most men say."

"You're not jealous either," he said, and she shook her head.

"Never. That would be like being jealous of my child. I practically raised her. Besides, I don't have any difficulty attracting men—at least since I reached sixteen. I was the awkward kid until then, too plump, too tall, a mess of unruly curly red hair that I didn't know how to deal with. Desirée was the pretty one."

She turned slightly in the bucket seat to face Wyatt,

comfortable with him, comfortable with talking about her past. "Like I said, our mother was beautiful—at least she was in pictures when she was in her twenties. She never was well after Desirée was born, so I had to help and my grandmother was around a lot. Also, my aunt. She had a son who was my age and like a brother to me." She shrugged. "We fought so much and maybe that's where I lost some of my fear of things, but I also learned a bit about dealing with boys."

"Do you still have your grandmother with you?"

"She's in L.A. and her health is failing. I try to talk to her daily. I love her deeply and we've always been close. She's the one who told me about my Calhoun heritage."

"Do you still see your cousin or your aunt?"

"Sure. They're in L.A., so I don't see them as much as I did when I lived there. He's a director and he's part of the reason Desirée is in the movies."

"You have an interesting family."

"I think you should tell me about your family since we're about to spend the evening with them," she said, studying Wyatt and thinking about later tonight when they would be alone. The thought of making love again started a fizzy current of excitement and anticipation bubbling in her. She wanted to be alone with him again. At the same time, it was one more tie that bound her heart. Wyatt had gotten to her in a way few men had, though she suspected he would forget her within a month after her leaving and he would never feel a pang when she went.

She didn't like to think about telling him goodbye. How could she get even this deeply involved with him in such a short time? She didn't believe in love at first sight—something her sister firmly believed and said had happened with almost every new eligible male she met.

Destiny's gaze roamed over Wyatt's profile and she

wondered what he thought and felt. All she knew was that he desired her and it was lusty, hot sex, nothing deeper.

Despite their connection and easy conversation, she felt she had never touched Wyatt emotionally and the realization that she wanted to disturbed her.

"Was Katherine your only real love?" she asked.

He drove silently for so long, she thought maybe he hadn't heard her. Then, finally, he answered. "I met her when I was finishing law school. I was so in love with her and we got engaged. She wasn't as much in love with me, apparently, and then someone else came along. He was older, successful, a U.S. senator, and the first thing I knew, we were no longer engaged and she was out of my life forever. That's the one time I've been truly and deeply in love."

"Are you over her?"

"In a way. In another way, I don't ever want to go through that kind of pain again so I'm careful about relationships. To that extent, maybe I'm not over her."

"You have your parents, your siblings—you're not accustomed to loss."

"I've lost grandparents I loved and it hurts. I guess I was deeply in love with Katherine, actually blindly in love with her or I would have seen what was happening. What about you? Ever been deeply in love?"

"No. I had a wild crush in college for a while, but then it sort of faded away for both of us. No big hurt when we parted. We just mutually agreed our feelings for each other were over. I'd like to love a man with all my heart—but that hasn't happened yet."

"Maybe you're fortunate. Love can hurt," he said in a matter-of-fact tone.

"At least you can talk about loving your ex-fiancée. That's a good sign."

"It's getting to be a long time since law school. Time helps."

"I'll bet you've left some broken hearts in Verity and probably anywhere else you've lived."

He smiled. "Don't know much about that. I haven't been close enough to a woman to break her heart."

"So now you've given me warning to avoid falling in love with you."

He smiled again. "I don't think there's the slightest danger of that happening. You and I are both too strong-willed to fall in love, plus too much at cross-purposes over your reasons for being in Verity. We have busy lives that are poles apart in what we do and where we live. Nope—we're both safe from even the slightest heartbreak. But I'll miss you and the best sex I ever had."

She laughed. "I better not fall in love with you. Sheesh! With that description, you would never return my love. You didn't add that you won't really risk your heart again. Part of you is closed to the world."

"You've got it right."

"Wyatt, sometimes in affairs of the heart, we can't always control what we feel. I know that you intend to control everything in your life, but it doesn't always work that way."

"It will where my heart is concerned," he said in a flat voice and a chill slithered around her heart because she had never heard so much determination in one brief sentence that had been spoken quietly.

"Thank heavens I'm not head over heels in love with you, then." She said it flippantly, but couldn't quell the disturbed feeling in her stomach. "Does Katherine live in Verity or Dallas or in D.C. with the senator?"

"No. He's no longer a senator and they live in Cleveland, his hometown, where he's head of a company that is headquartered there. I wish them well. If she showed up tomorrow, divorced and wanting to go out together, I don't feel like I'd be interested. I imagine we've grown apart over time and I wouldn't trust her again. We were kids, in law school. Life is different now and we're both different. Last I heard she had two kids."

"If you're truly over her, I wouldn't think your heart would still be locked away."

"I just don't want that kind of pain." He glanced quickly at her and then back at the road. "Trust me, I'm over her. Tonight I'll be with a sexy, gorgeous redhead so I'll be blind where other women are concerned. I definitely can't wait for the rest of the evening after my family leaves."

She reached over to place her fingers lightly on his thigh and saw his chest expand as he inhaled deeply.

"Who will be at your house?"

"You've met most of them now. Nick will be there. He's the state representative and his life is politics. He's the one who lost his pregnant wife in a car wreck."

"That's really tough. It hurt terribly when we lost Dad, Mom and my grandfather."

"Sorry. Nick hides his hurt, but he keeps busy and out in the public. I think part of that is to avoid going home and being by himself."

"I can understand. When Mom died, it tore up my grandparents and it was so hard on Desirée. We'd already lost Dad. I tried to be the rock for all of them, which actually helped me sometimes. You get through it because you have no choice. I'm sorry for Nick, though. That's a dreadful loss."

"They have a bad loss in the Calhoun family, too, if you get to meet all of Lindsay's siblings. Mike Calhoun's wife died from cancer. He has a little two-year-old, Scotty. You may not meet Mike. He lives on a ranch and stays home with Scotty. He isn't over his loss and he doesn't socialize much. Mike's quiet and a loner. At least Nick gets out and mingles with people all the time and that helps."

"It does help. That's what I've always done." She could see that Wyatt was affected by Mike's loss, even though he was a Calhoun. She tried to lighten the mood by asking, "Who else will be there tonight?"

"Tony—you know him." Wyatt smiled as he talked about his brother. "He's definitely his own person and has his own ideas."

"He's delightful. You, Nick, Tony," she said. "Where does Madison fit in?"

"I'm the oldest, then Madison, Nick and Tony's the baby. Madison and Jake were high school sweethearts and our parents didn't want them to marry. Dad got wind that they were planning to elope and he stopped it. Actually, he was underhanded about it, but he thought Jake might be headstrong—which he probably would have been. They didn't know what Dad had done until this year. They're happy now and old enough to know they want to be together." He cast her a glance. "While you're here, are you going to try to meet more Calhouns?"

"Yes, if I get the chance. I liked Lindsay and Jake. They were both cooperative and friendly."

"Jake usually is. Lindsay may offer to introduce you around to the rest of her family."

They passed two metal posts with barbed-wire fences stretching away on either side. They drove long enough on a graveled road that she turned to him.

"Where is your house? How big is this ranch?"

"It's big and I'm far away from the highway. The ranch is different from my house in town. This is where I'd rather be. There is nowhere on earth as great."

"That's a true Texan. Ah, finally," she said as they topped a rise and she saw lights. It was still dusk and she could see the sprawling house and buildings beyond it.

She was amazed by the number of buildings and the size of his house and outbuildings. Judging from the smile on Wyatt's face, he felt at home here, and she was seeing yet another side to Wyatt.

Cars and pickups were parked along the wide drive at the back of the house. He parked and came around the car and as she watched him, she forgot all about dinner with his family. Tall, broad-shouldered, purposeful in his stride, Wyatt took all her attention and she wanted to be in his arms. Again, she wondered how he had captured her interest so quickly and thoroughly.

The wraparound porch was welcoming with flowers in pots and flowers still blooming in beds that flanked the porch. Tall, wooden rocking chairs were scattered on the porch along with a hammock, small tables, a couple of padded chaise lounges. The place looked inviting and comfortable.

Inside, lights blazed and her curiosity rose about Wyatt's family. They entered through a wide hallway with boots lined against the wall, a hat stand that held half a dozen wide-brimmed Western hats. Wyatt held her arm lightly while tempting smells of cooking beef and barbecue assailed her. She could see part of the kitchen through an open door and two cooks in uniforms with aprons bustled back and forth.

Going through another door with Wyatt, she entered a wider hall that ran the length of the house. Two-story-high, beamed ceilings added to the spaciousness in the big hallway that was lined with oil paintings of Western scenes.

The house revealed more of the billionaire side of Wyatt with luxurious furniture, a thick hall runner on the polished hardwood floor, crystal chandeliers and, visible through the back of the house, a fountain and a pool.

"You have a beautiful home," she said.

He gave her a crooked grin. "Thanks. It's comfortable. You've only seen the back and the hall. Sometime later we'll take a tour. I want you to see my bedroom."

"I can't wait," she said, her mouth going dry. She knew his reason for wanting her there, and while she agreed, she thought she'd learn a lot about this handsome cowboy from his private quarters. His smile had vanished and the look in his eyes held a promise of hot kisses later in the night.

"Right now you get to know my family better. They have bugged me about getting together with you since they discovered you were in Verity."

"Here I am." She had enjoyed meeting them at the hotel and now she wanted to get to know them better.

"Follow the noise and we'll find them, probably out on the patio because it's a nice evening."

Wyatt turned to pass through a large living area with a giant-screen television, a wet bar, clusters of brown leather chairs, leather sofas and tables. A huge stone fireplace filled one corner of the room. They stepped outside onto a long patio that ran the length of the back of the house. Beds of blooming flowers filled the yard.

"This is so pretty," she said, gesturing around the yard.

"Thanks. I love it out here where it's quiet. Something you probably can't understand."

"You're accustomed to that life. I need people around me and things going on. It's what I'm accustomed to, just as this has always been your life."

As they joined the others, Destiny was greeted by Madison and Jake who glowed with happiness. Jake smiled at her. "I'm happy to have this chance to get to know another Calhoun better. How distantly are we related?" he asked.

"My great-great-great-grandfather was Eldridge Calhoun. It's my mother's side of the family. Her mother was a Calhoun and her grandfather was a Calhoun. I have a family tree at home."

"I'm not familiar with Eldridge Calhoun. I'll have to look him up. So the feud has never mattered in your family?"

"No," she replied, "at least not for my mom. Now, Mimi,

my grandmother, is different. She's more into the feud. She's warned me about the Milans," she replied, smiling and Jake grinned, slipping his arm around Madison's waist.

"Someone should have warned me she was going to steal my heart," he said lightly.

"My grandmother really hasn't ever known any Milans. We moved to California when I was young and we don't know a lot of family members who live around here. My mother lost touch completely and she died rather young."

"Sorry," Jake said. "We'll have to have you out so you can meet my family and at least know this branch of the Calhouns. You already know Lindsay, so there's just Mike, his little boy, Scotty, and my other brother Josh that you haven't met. Our parents live in California now."

"I'd love to meet the other Calhouns."

She turned as Nick greeted her with an infectious smile. "I enjoyed your interview and was delighted that all was harmonious between the Milans and the Calhouns," Nick said.

Destiny nodded her thanks. "I think it was entertaining and interesting. While Lindsay said the feud was still alive, she was quite pleasant."

Nick grinned. "I think Lindsay and Tony were on their best behavior for their families' benefit."

"I'll second that one," Jake said. "I suspect she was being nice to her newlywed brother and sister-in-law."

"I was happy with the interview and the audience we had," Destiny said.

"Have you seen the Wrenville house yet?" Jake asked her.

"Oh, yes. We plan to go back again while we're here. We might look around a bit for any hidden letter or fortune. That would be quite a discovery," she said, smiling, glancing at Wyatt, who looked amused.

"Don't get your hopes too high," he cautioned. "A lot of kids have searched that house."

"I'm surprised it's not more than kids," she said.

"According to rumors and gossip," Jake stated, "Lavita Wrenville was an eccentric old maid who lived on a pittance left by her father. People are divided on opinions about Lavita Wrenville, but the majority think she started the rumors of saving her money and living a miserly existence shut up in that old house. Most people think she died penniless just as she had lived in poverty. From the time she was young until she died an old woman, there was no money coming in, only what her father left for her."

Wyatt added to the story. "According to the old-time bankers, Lavita drew the money out of the bank and kept it at the house, so no one really knows, but with it going out and no more coming in, I don't expect we'll ever find a fortune there."

"Stories abound, although they're beginning to die out because we're far enough removed from Lavita's generation that there's little interest," Nick stated.

"I find all of it rather fascinating," Destiny said. "I saw her portrait that hangs in the historical museum along with her mother's and father's portraits. It was painted when she was a young woman and she looked pretty in the painting."

"I think it's a good thing no one painted her picture in later life," Madison remarked. "From all we've heard, she didn't take care of herself or her home."

"I still think it's an intriguing story," Destiny said. She caught Wyatt looking at her intently and she let her eyes lock with his. Whatever he thought, there was no way to tell by looking at him. His expression didn't change, yet in gazing at him, she felt that flash of attraction that made her forget Lavita and everyone around her for a few seconds as she felt shut away with Wyatt.

Someone was talking and she realized they might be saying something to her. She tried to shift her attention from Wyatt, feeling a faint flush because she had lost the entire train of conversation.

She heard greetings and laughter and turned to see Tony Milan enter the room and stop to talk to one of servers who approached to take their drink orders. Tony looked like the epitome of a Texas cowboy in jeans, boots and a red Western shirt. She was certain he had hung his hat when he entered the house. She seemed to remember Wyatt once saying that Tony was a rodeo rider, and she could easily see him in that venue.

"You can always tell when Tony arrives because his enthusiasm spills over. He doesn't make a quiet, unobtrusive entrance," Wyatt remarked, greeting his brother as Tony joined them.

"Hi, Destiny," he said and she smiled at him.

"I'm glad to see you again. Thanks for adding a nice touch to the interview."

"Wouldn't have missed it for the world," he said, grinning. "Good luck in making a story out of that old Wrenville place. That all happened a long time ago."

"If it isn't interesting, it won't be a show. Right now, I'm just looking into it."

She was delighted to find out he was a fan of her show, and knowledgeable about the mysteries they'd covered. While she liked talking about them, she turned the tables on Tony. "So I hear you're the rodeo performer."

Tony grinned. "I love the challenge. It beats politics." He elbowed Nick beside him. "I keep trying to talk my brother into taking up bronc riding but he won't bite. Now, Wyatt's deal is calf roping." Tony's blue eyes twinkled as he spoke and with his good-natured ribbing of his brothers, he looked ready for fun and interested in everyone.

Nick laughed. "I can't find riding a bucking bronc quite in the same league as dealing with the laws of the land and making decisions that may help our quality of life. I like the challenges of politics, too, but I will admit they're a far cry from trying to stick on the back of a contrary horse."

"Ask Madison about her barrel racing," Tony suggested to Destiny.

Madison laughed. "That was short-lived," she said. "Too hard on the legs and my art became a lot more important. Tony is definitely our family's rodeo performer."

"To each his own," he said, smiling at Destiny. Standing close to him, she could see flecks of green in his blue eyes. Handsome and charismatic, he would be fun to have on her show if she could think of a way to work him into the program, assuming there was one.

Over drinks Destiny listened to the Milans and Jake talk about Verity and telling funny stories about the locals, and she realized Wyatt had a warm, close-knit family with compatible siblings.

She sat beside Nick, who didn't have the exuberance of his younger brother, but had his own friendly manner.

"Destiny, tell me what politicians you've had on your show or worked with in California."

"There have been quite a few." She named several. "They were cooperative, easy to work with."

"That's because they were probably looking for votes," Nick said, smiling at her. "Goes with the job."

"You didn't get interviewed for the show. How do you feel about the feud?"

"It doesn't exist for me," he answered easily. "I don't have a quarrel with any of the Calhouns. Not until one runs against me for public office," he added, drawing a smile from Destiny.

She looked at the three brothers. "All of you are so different, but then I'm different from my sister. Wyatt is the quiet one, I see."

Nick agreed. "Wyatt is our rock. Our dad was a busy lawyer and later a judge. By high school if we had problems to take to Dad, we'd take them to Wyatt instead. He's levelheaded, smart, able to work through problems. He would have been a hell of a trial lawyer, but he's a cowboy at heart. He loves his ranch and he has the resources to do what he wants. Wyatt likes a simple life. He has an island where he spends time occasionally in the cold of January or February, but otherwise, he's on his ranch if he can be."

"True," Wyatt said as he clapped his brother on the back. "Can't think of any place I'd rather be."

Destiny turned to Wyatt, looking into his blue eyes and shutting out the others. For a moment she could only think about being alone with him later in the evening.

Through a delicious barbecue dinner with platters of ribs and afterward, she enjoyed the Milans and Jake and was surprised when Tony stood to go. Glancing at her watch, she saw it was almost midnight.

Madison and Jake stood next, saying they hadn't realized the time, and Nick followed.

It was another thirty minutes before each one finished telling her goodbye and they all went out the door. She stood on the porch with Wyatt as they left.

"So now do I get my purse to go?"

"Don't even think about it. I'm just waiting until they get underway."

"What a nice family you have," she said. "You're fortunate, Wyatt."

"I know I am. They're a great family. We enjoy each other and that's good. It's good we all live here, too. I expect Nick to be in D.C. at some point, but he'll always come home. Jake is gone a lot in his energy business, so Madison will be gone with him."

"I love her art. She's very talented."

"Yes, she is."

"So you and Tony are the ones who'll be here all the time."

"Probably. There they go," he said as the last car pulled away. He draped his arm across her shoulders. "We're alone. The cook has gone to his quarters, and his staff has left for the day."

They entered the house and Wyatt locked up, switching on the alarm. She watched as he moved around.

He took her hand. "Come let me give you a tour—we'll start with my bedroom."

"I can't wait," she said breathlessly. "It was a delightful evening."

"I enjoyed it, but I was ready for them to go home about two hours ago so we could be alone."

She smiled at him as they held hands and climbed the winding stairs to the second floor.

"You looked gorgeous tonight, but that's nothing new," he said.

"It's new to hear you tell me and I love to hear that from you. I want to dazzle you, Wyatt, to break through that armor you keep around yourself. You only give so much and no more."

"I've told you why and I didn't think there was anything lacking in our relationship. Is this a complaint?"

She smiled at him and ran her fingers across his chest as they walked down a wide hall together. "I think not. Absolutely no complaints over being with you. I just want to dazzle you is all."

"Believe me, I'm dazzled. I can barely get my breath. Here's my room," he said, switching on lights as they entered a large living area with a rolltop desk, bookshelves, a big-screen television and other electronic equipment, leather sofa and chairs, another huge rock fireplace, and a built-in fish tank with exotic fish.

"This is marvelous, Wyatt," she said, turning to face him.

"You're marvelous and I'm spellbound," he said in a

husky voice as he slid his arm around her waist. "I've waited way too long for this," he said before he silenced her reply with a kiss.

Her heart thudded and she wrapped her arms around his neck, holding him tightly, wanting him more than she would have guessed possible. She, too, felt as if it had been days she had waited for this moment. She wanted to be in his arms, making love, holding him close the rest of the night. She didn't want to think about how different they were, or the way he'd closed off his heart. She didn't want to think about parting with him or Wyatt going out of her life. The realization startled her momentarily.

Was she falling in love with him?

Seven

She felt caught in a dizzying spiral as desire for Wyatt consumed her. She wanted him with her whole being and felt she couldn't get enough if they loved for hours.

She kissed him passionately, pouring out her feelings, wanting to break through that barrier he kept around his heart. Each time they loved, it was hot, sexy, but there was always a part of him that he kept to himself, a shuttered look in his eyes. As slight as it was, she could feel it as they loved and she wanted him to lose that with her, to let go and pour himself completely into loving, to stop being afraid to give of himself completely.

Clothes were a barrier and soon tossed aside. She caressed him, determined to drive him as wild as he drove her.

Later, as Wyatt kissed her, he picked her up to carry her to his bed. He trailed kisses along her throat and over her breasts, his mouth following his hands as he caressed her, over her waist, her hips, her legs, taking his time as if he cherished her. Then he reversed the trail of kisses from her feet to her neck. No man had ever done this, kissed her like this, as if every part of her was special and deserving of attention. And she reveled in it.

But the warmth he elicited was nothing compared to the fire he ignited in her when he placed her legs on his shoulders and used his hands and tongue to stir a tempest in her. She enjoyed the sensations, allowed herself to bask in them, until she hovered near release. She didn't want to find that ecstasy alone; she wanted Wyatt with her. She lowered her legs and pulled him into the V they created, a special space just for him.

When he finally entered her, she held him tightly, her long legs wrapped around him, moving with him and trying to make their loving last as long as possible.

Her head thrashed, her long red hair spilling over her shoulders in wild disarray.

Sweat beaded on Wyatt's forehead and on his broad shoulders as he tried to keep control, to love her. She felt wound tighter and tighter until she crashed into release, her hips rocking with him as his control vanished and he pumped furiously.

Pleasure poured over her and she felt him shudder with his climax. She held him as close as possible and in that moment, she felt in love for the first time in her life.

Her eyes flew open. As if he sensed something, Wyatt slowed and turned his head to kiss her. She held him tightly, kissing him, even as she felt a sense of panic because she was in love with him and it was something that couldn't be and she never intended to have happen.

In his arms she'd found rapture, satisfaction and now an added factor. Love that couldn't be stopped or avoided because it had already happened. She was in love with a tall, Texas cowboy, a rancher, a man whose heart was locked away and a man as different from her as a city sidewalk from a country lane. "I love you." She mouthed the words, but didn't even whisper them.

She loved him. She trusted him. She wanted to be with him. He brought calmness to her life she didn't have. With Wyatt, as nowhere in her busy life, she wasn't always the one in charge. In her job, hers was often the final call, and in her life, it seemed as if she'd been taking care of her family forever, her mother, her grandmother and her sister. Wyatt made her feel that the decisions didn't all have to be hers, that everything wasn't resting on her shoulders alone.

She didn't want to tell him goodbye and return to Chicago and go on with her life without ever seeing Wyatt again.

How had she let this happen?

"You're fantastic," Wyatt whispered, kissing her lightly again as his weight came down more on her. She held him tightly still, absorbing the moment, putting off separation from him. For right now, she loved him and she held him against her heart and this was a good moment. But he didn't feel what she did. Wyatt's heart was locked away and there hadn't been a change in him. For Wyatt, theirs was a lusty relationship. For her, the relationship had changed and grown deeper.

She stroked his back. "Wyatt, this is so good," she whispered. "So very good."

He rolled over, keeping her close in his embrace and then he looked into her eyes. She gazed back, wondering how much he could see of what she felt.

He kissed her gently, carefully and then looked at her again, smoothing her damp curls away from her face. "This is all I could think about. I want you in my arms, in my bed all night long and tomorrow. You don't have to go back to town, do you?"

"I don't have appointments."

"Good. I don't want to let you go."

In due time she knew he would let her go. This was not something Wyatt wanted permanently. She'd been so sure she wouldn't fall in love with him. She had never really been in love before, but she could recognize it when it happened. She loved this tall cowboy and there was no undoing what was done.

"You're fantastic, Destiny. I just can't let you go. I want to hold you close all night, love again as often as we can. You're the sexiest woman on this earth."

"Ah, Wyatt, this is good. We should be together. You don't have to let me go. We've got the rest of the night, part of tomorrow."

"Tomorrow might not be quite enough," he said.

"You'll still have to go into town tomorrow, won't you?"

"No. That's why I have deputies. Without you there, everything will be quiet and peaceful," he said, smiling at her.

She looked up at him and laughed. "I haven't upset your life or the town that much. Don't tell me you don't ever have crime or anything going on in Verity?"

"Oh, sure. Fred Baines parked by the fire hydrant last week and within the hour the J.B. Grill caught on fire. The fire truck couldn't get up to the hydrant at first until we got the car moved. The next day I had to get the Wilcoxes' cat out of their chimney and the dead bird he carried in there."

She smiled. "I still don't think I'm the biggest problem that Verity has for the sheriff."

"You're definitely the most delightful problem," he said, nuzzling her neck and making her laugh again. She stroked his smooth back, relishing touching him, feeling the solid muscles beneath her palm.

"This is good," he whispered.

"I agree. It's perfect."

"What do you plan to do after this show? Few shows run forever."

"I have ideas for more books I want to write, and some other avenues I'd like to explore. I want to get back to California. If Desirée stays happily married, that's a responsibility I won't have, but I still try to help my grandmother. Chicago is far away from my family and I'm tied down by the show. What about you? Do you plan to retire as sheriff after the Wrenville house is taken care of and go back to being a rancher for the rest of your life? Will you be a hermit on your ranch—living out your life all alone because of something someone did years ago? You seem too full of life for that."

"I'll probably marry someday. Maybe a marriage of convenience even—"

She laughed. "Wyatt, if you marry, for her, it will not be a marriage of convenience."

He grinned and propped his head on his hand to look down at her. "I should keep you around to give my ego a boost."

"I don't think your ego needs the slightest boost. You have enough self-confidence—enough to slip over into arrogance."

"Arrogance? Me? I don't think I've been accused of that before."

"Then you've been around people who did not speak out as much as I do."

"That's accurate," he said and she laughed with him. He pulled her close, hugging her tightly as he stretched beside her. He felt hard, warm and solid and she felt another pang at the thought of telling him goodbye.

How had she fallen in love with him? She should have guarded her own heart. They hadn't known each other long but she suspected she might be in love with him for a long time to come. She shivered as she thought of how cold her life would be without him in it.

He pulled away slightly to look intently at her. "Are

you cold?" he asked, grabbing a sheet to pull over them. "Maybe I need to warm you again—or we can sit in a steamy tub or have a hot shower. What's your preference?"

"With you, how could I care which it is. You pick something. This is good right now."

He pulled her close. "So we stay right here in each other's arms." After a few moments of silence, he shifted so he could see her face. "Do you plan to marry? Have a family?"

"I've raised one child and feel as if I've had a family, so it's not so urgent, but I do want a family. A family is the best part of life. Later, maybe. I really have never found the right man."

"You would disillusion a universe of men if you made that announcement public."

"I know better than to do that," she said.

"My brother Nick is green with envy over your public relations skills. He would like to hire you, but he knows he can't."

She laughed. "He never gave an indication of that. After meeting your brother, though, I don't think he needs any help with PR. He's handsome, likable and with the tragedy in his life, he'll be sympathetic to some. He's a smart man and evidently, he's had successful political campaigns already and made all sorts of contacts here and in Washington."

"You've described Nick perfectly."

"Now, Tony… I would love to have your youngest brother on my show. Actually, each of you would be interesting. In fact, if I could get the three of you to appear—"

"Forget it, lady. No way will the sheriff of Verity, Texas, appear on *Unsolved Mysteries*."

She laughed. "I'll wager I can get Tony and Nick to appear if I ever do a show about Verity."

"I won't take that wager. Nick would love the publicity and Tony would love flirting with you."

"Maybe Lindsay Calhoun is taking the wrong approach with Tony. I can't imagine fighting with him."

"There's not a guy on this earth who would fight with you. But Lindsay can be tough. You haven't met any of the older generation of Calhouns and Milans—that's where the feud is still alive. Lindsay's mother won't speak to any of the Milans. The Judge talks to us, but he doesn't like us. My folks don't like the Calhouns. Go back and find any grandparents—that feud is still going."

"Now you tell me."

Destiny rolled Wyatt onto his back and lay on top of him, placing her hands on the bed on either side of him to raise herself slightly. Watching him, in a slow move, she rubbed her breasts lightly against his chest. His expression changed and his blue eyes darkened, desire burning in their depths.

He wound his hand in her thick hair and tugged lightly, drawing her down to kiss her. In seconds she pulled back enough to straddle him, running her fingers lightly over him and playing with him. He was aroused, ready to make love, and he placed his hands on her narrow waist and turned her over so he was above her.

"I want you now," he whispered and kissed away any answer she had.

Later Saturday morning, Destiny sent a text to Amy telling her to take a few days off and tell Duke and Virginia to do the same. Destiny wrote that she would see them Monday.

From that moment on, she tried to shut the future, even the next week, out of her thoughts. She lived for the present moment, enjoying Wyatt's company and his ranch, until late in the evening after they had made love and she was in his arms as they lay on their sides talking.

"Wyatt," she said, "you're not still in love with Katherine, are you? You're just afraid to risk loving again."

He stared at her for a few silent moments. "I suppose you're right. I don't really want Katherine in my life anymore. I just never want to go through that kind of loss."

"Life doesn't come with guarantees. Sometimes it's worth the risk."

He looked amused and one corner of his mouth lifted. "Is this a proposal?"

"Don't be silly." She cocked her head and looked intently at him. "I'm not ready to say goodbye." She ran her fingers in his thick hair. "I'm here, Wyatt. You better guard that frozen, locked-away heart of yours well. I may want to unlock it more than I want to find the secrets of the Wrenville house."

His eyes narrowed a fraction and then his expression changed when he gave her another faint smile. He ran his fingers lightly over her bare shoulder. "You just want what you can't have, Destiny. You rise to a challenge. If I'd propose to you, you'd say no and I'd probably have a difficult time getting to see you."

"You think? Well, you haven't, so hang on. As the man said, 'You ain't seen nothin' yet,'" she drawled in a breathy, sultry voice. She leaned closer, tracing the curve of his ear with the tip of her tongue, then the corner of his mouth and then his lower lip. "Maybe it is the challenge I love. We'll see," she whispered.

With a groan Wyatt enveloped her and he kissed her possessively, a hard, deep kiss that ended all talk.

Hours later, she lay stretched against him, held in his arms while he slept for the first time since they had been together. She shifted, turning on her side to look at him, placing her hand lightly on his chest. His arms tightened around her, but in a short time, he relaxed and soon his breathing was deep and even again.

She had found the thing he feared most—being hurt again. She knew that with his attitude toward love there was no permanent future for them, yet she loved him and she didn't want to pack, tell him goodbye and return to Chicago to never see him again. This was the first time love had come into her life. She was surprised, shaken and uncertain how to deal with it.

She settled against him, staring into the room that had only one soft lamp glowing. How could she have fallen in love with him?

Sunday night she was in his arms, sitting between his legs in a king-size bathtub of hot, sudsy water. "These have been decadent, wonderful days and nights, Wyatt. We've loved, danced, loved, eaten, showered and loved some more. Hasn't been much sleeping going on."

He chuckled. "We can catch up later on sleep. This is much better. A chance you might call and cancel going back tomorrow?"

"No way. We'd be the talk of the town."

"Might at that. I suspect we might already be. You've disappeared with me for the weekend and your staff is on a break. No one has missed us much—to put that correctly, no one has missed me. I hope they think I'm showing you the sights."

"Best sights ever," she said, caressing his thigh.

"I'm the one who has had the best sights," he said as he cupped her breasts in his warm, wet hands.

"It's been good, but I should go back to town tomorrow morning. You know I should have gone back tonight."

"I know no such thing. I want you here with me as long as possible."

"You're making me rethink Monday. Maybe we should let the town gossip. I'll bet they haven't had anything to gossip about you since my sister was here."

"Not even then. Everyone was so taken with the movie

as well as Desirée that they had a lot of things to talk about. Let's get out of this tub and you can text Amy and tell her you'll be back Thursday before you change your mind."

"So now it's Thursday you want. Wyatt, that's almost a whole week."

"There'll be gossip either way, so make it Thursday. We're already the number-one gossip topic in Verity."

"You'll get tired of me," she replied.

"Let me dispel that idea right now," he said, lifting her cascade of auburn hair to kiss her nape.

It was two in the morning on Thursday when he took her to her suite at the Verity Hotel and it was four in the morning before Wyatt left to drive to his Verity home and get an hour's sleep before work.

He got to the office before anyone else arrived. A little before seven Val arrived and minutes later Dwight entered.

"It's been a calm, quiet week," Val said.

"People have been getting to know the Boydens and Ms. Osgood, who is as nice as Destiny," Dwight said. "We had her out to dinner Sunday night because my wife got to know her when she talked to her at length about Destiny's first book," Dwight stated.

"The Boydens drove to Dallas. They got some tips on places to eat, things to see," Val added.

Wyatt didn't want to think about Destiny's staff and how their job here would soon be done. All too soon now she would leave for Chicago. He wasn't ready to tell her goodbye. He wanted her to stay a lot longer. "I'll go see what's on my desk," Wyatt said, turning to leave.

"Duke Boyden said they will go out to the Wrenville house today and spend the day. He didn't say, but I think they're going to look for the legendary letter that Lavita is supposed to have written," Dwight said.

"I wish them lots of luck," Wyatt remarked dryly. "I

don't think any such letter exists. I can't imagine that Lavita Wrenville had a fortune to hide or any big secret she actually intended to pass along. Kids have hunted through that house in years past over and over and never found anything."

"Are you going to try to stop her from looking?" Val asked.

"No. Let them look. It won't hurt, as long as they don't disturb the structure of the house. When it reverts to Verity next year, we'll go through it carefully first and tear it down, but that's different."

Wyatt headed to his office, leaving the door open as he sat behind his desk. There was no way he could stop her search, but at least she was bringing an air of excitement and fun to everyone so far. He might as well resign himself to acceptance. She'd won this round.

He received a text and pulled out his phone to read it.

Miss you. Going to W. house later if you want to join us. Will look around for the letter.

See you this pm. Plan on dinner with me, he replied. He wanted to see her and he missed her when he got to his house from the hotel in the early hours. For certain he wanted her in his arms when he went to bed tonight.

If he could, he would go to the hotel now and make love to her this morning, but he didn't think she would cooperate and he knew he had work to do. Nothing earthshaking though, but he would really stir gossip if he took more days off. He smiled, thinking she had set his world spinning a different direction. Nothing had been the same since he had spotted the red limo in his parking spot. It had been a red flag warning of change in his quiet life.

He thought about her going back to Chicago. Even though they hadn't talked about it, he knew it would be soon. He was going to miss her. That realization still shocked him. He never missed the women who went out of his life—at least, not since Katherine.

He thought about Destiny's warning that she wasn't ready to say goodbye. He was certain that simply was because if he had proposed or begged her to stay longer, he thought she would pack and go, turn down his proposal and be on her way without a qualm. She was accustomed to getting her way and having things under control in her life and that was what the warning to him had been about. They weren't in love.

The moment he declared that to himself, he frowned. What did he feel for her? He didn't want her to go back yet. Later, it would be okay, but right now she was a fantastic lover and he wanted her with him in his bed for a lot more nights before they said goodbye. He liked the long talks they had, the fun, the silly moments, just being with her and looking at her, holding her soft warmth close in his arms. She was one person he could talk freely to about whatever he wanted. She always seemed interested and was a good listener, even more so than Katherine had been. He wanted to keep her in his life a lot longer.

It was a good thing he hadn't fallen in love with her. She wouldn't return the emotion and she would be gone in a flash. He couldn't imagine Destiny settling on a ranch in obscurity. She was meant for the life she had—out in public, in the limelight, playing to an audience. He wasn't in love, but he wanted to be with her right now, tonight, and he didn't want her to go back to Chicago anytime in the near future.

His phone rang and he saw it was Dwight.

"Wyatt, Duke Boyden is here. He wants to see you."

"Send him back," Wyatt said, hanging up and standing to walk to the door. As soon as Duke came in sight, Wyatt smiled. Dressed in his black chauffeur's uniform that pulled across his thick shoulders, Duke approached him with a swing of his shoulders in a take-charge walk that was masculine and proclaimed control. In seconds, Wyatt offered his hand to receive a tight grip.

"Come in. Have a seat."

"Sure," Duke said, following Wyatt into his office and closing the door.

Figuring Destiny had sent Duke to ask him something about the Wrenville house, Wyatt sat in the other wing-back chair facing Duke.

"Sheriff, I don't want you to take offense, but I thought we should talk."

Startled, Wyatt focused more intently on Duke. "Sure. Go ahead."

"Virginia and I have known Amy and Destiny a long, long time. They're both like sisters to me."

Forgetting the Wrenville place, Wyatt waited in silence.

"I just want to try to avoid seeing Destiny get hurt."

Wyatt had to bite back a laugh. The moment was too ridiculous for him to get angry. "How's that?"

"It's just that she's never been interested, really interested in any of the men she meets. I think she might be in you. She doesn't usually get very involved with any of them. I don't want to see her unhappy."

"I think you made this clear before. And I think you're being influenced by Desirée."

"No, not at all. Desirée wants nearly every man she meets and she's on an emotional roller coaster over them."

"I still feel that there might be a threat in this conversation."

"Oh, no, not at all," Duke said blandly. "I'm just looking out for Destiny."

"She's a grown woman."

"I know, but she's still vulnerable. People are in matters of the heart."

"I think I can put your mind at ease. There is no matter of the heart here."

"Actually, she just spent a week with you. Destiny doesn't do things like that."

They stared at each other and Wyatt knew he had just been threatened and that Duke felt Destiny was in love, which was not the situation. They were deeply involved in hot sex, nothing more.

"Do you always talk to the men who take her out?"

Duke stared at him for a few seconds before shaking his head. "This is a first. There's never been a need before and I've known her and chauffeured her since her mother was alive."

Wyatt was silent. Now he was puzzled and his curiosity had deepened.

Duke stood so Wyatt came to his feet. "I've got to get back. She wouldn't be happy if she knew I was here, because she feels she can take care of herself. She's a caring woman. She's taken care of her parents, her sister, her grandparents, Amy. Destiny is a caring person and I don't want her hurt."

"She won't be unless it's because she doesn't find anything at the Wrenville house," Wyatt said and Duke gave him a hard look.

"Maybe we'll see you out there. Don't come to the door. I know my way out," Duke said and left, leaving the door open behind him.

Wyatt shook his head. The man was part bodyguard, part pit bull and all protector. Problem was Duke had threatened him and there was a law against threatening an officer of the law, but Wyatt wouldn't pursue it and Duke knew that he wouldn't.

According to Duke, that was the first time he'd ever talked to a man about his relationship with Destiny and he had known her for years—maybe since she was a teen.

That meant Duke thought she was more serious now than ever in her past. Did he think she was in love?

That thought shook him slightly, but Wyatt felt Duke was wrong about how serious his relationship was with Destiny.

Wyatt went back to his desk, trying to go through the mail. After thirty minutes, he shoved aside the stack of letters. He had read three, but his thoughts kept jumping back to Destiny. Twice he had reached for the phone to call her.

Wyatt slammed shut his desk drawer, got up and took his hat off the rack to jam it on his head. He walked down the hall in long strides.

When Dwight looked up, Wyatt nodded. "I'm going to the Wrenville house to see what Destiny and her staff are doing."

"Sure," Dwight said, his eyes getting wider. "She's going to be disappointed. No one thinks there is anything in that house. Not a fortune—not even a little money and no letter revealing which man shot the other."

"I agree, but she doesn't live here, so she has high hopes."

"Too bad. At least it's a pretty day."

"Sure is. I'll be back later." Clamping his jaw closed, Wyatt left the building and headed for his car. He made a U-turn and headed east for the Wrenville house. His pulse quickened and all he could think about was being with Destiny in a short time.

How disappointed would she be when she didn't find anything at the house? He figured she had been through things like this before and she would simply pack and go back to Chicago and move on to her next project. Each time he thought about her going home, the idea of life without her disturbed him more than it had before.

Eight

Destiny and Amy took the front half of the house while the Boydens took the back half to search for any hidden objects. Her pulse jumped and excitement sizzled through her bloodstream like an electrical current. But it wasn't the anticipation of finding a fortune or solving the mystery of this house that had her so excited. It was Wyatt. Tonight she would be going out with him again, and she could hardly wait. He was the talk of the town now, but it was his town and his decision to see her. He knew what he wanted to do.

She stood in the spacious front bedroom. Sunlight spilled through the wide windows that would have allowed breezes to cool the room in warm weather. She ran her hands over the walls, while Amy followed, tapping lightly with a small hammer to see if she could discover any hollow places. At one point, Destiny stood in the center of the room, studying it slowly and carefully, looking for anything out of the ordinary. She heard the car first and then

Amy glanced out the window. "It's the sheriff's car," she said, which Destiny had already guessed.

"He'll find us up here. We don't have to go down to the door," Destiny said, continuing to look around.

"You're going out with him tonight?"

"Yes, I am. He's taking me to dinner."

"We'll tell him goodbye soon."

"I know." Her gaze swept the room. "I hope I'm coming back to film this place. I would really like to find something."

"Me, too. Otherwise, it's an intriguing puzzle, but I don't know if it would be enough for a show."

"If Lavita Wrenville was old and sick and wrote the letter and hid what money she had left toward the end of her life, I think it would be in this bedroom, which I assume would have been hers if she had lived here alone."

"That makes sense. Or she could have stayed in the room she grew up in and hidden something there."

"We'll search the entire house, but I just want to go over this room extra carefully."

"Anybody home?"

"We're upstairs, Wyatt," Destiny replied and in seconds she heard his boots and the creaking boards as he climbed the stairs.

"How's the search?" he asked, stopping in the doorway and pushing his brown hat back on his head. She gazed at him, wanting to cross the room and kiss him, wanting his arms around her and knowing neither would happen because they weren't alone.

"I'm sure you won't be surprised—we haven't found anything."

He greeted Amy then asked, "Where are Duke and Virginia?"

"They're taking the back side of the house while we're going through the front," Destiny answered.

Wyatt looked around. "In less than a year, we'll officially search this place in a thorough hunt that will include tearing out walls and floorboards inside the house. You can come back and film then."

"Thanks for that offer," she replied. "I'll keep it in mind. In the meantime, we plan to continue this search. Have you ever heard which bedroom Lavita had?"

"No. I don't know any details other than what I've already told you."

She continued to move slowly around the room, tapping the walls, aware of Wyatt standing with his arms folded, watching the proceedings. After a while he left the room and she heard him go downstairs and outside.

Finally she had to admit they had come up empty. "Amy, I give up here. Let's move on."

"I agree. I don't think anything is hidden here."

As she passed the window, she saw Wyatt standing by his car while he talked on his phone.

As they searched another room, he returned, apparently just ending his conversation. "I'll be back at the office in a little while, once one of my deputies relieves me out here."

"You're waiting to see if we find something," Destiny said when he ended the call. "You don't have to worry. I'll tell you if we do."

He nodded. "I know, but the town has a vested interest and no doubt someone will ask if we checked to see if you found anything. I'm sure people know you're looking."

She laughed. "You want to make sure we don't find the treasure and take it back to Chicago."

"I don't really think there's much danger of that happening, but I'm going to have to answer questions."

"As long as you're just standing there, you ought to help search," Destiny teased, looking at him and feeling that flare of desire that she always did with Wyatt.

"Our turn will come and until then, I'm happy just to watch."

Destiny concentrated on looking, but she couldn't forget Wyatt behind her, standing nearby.

When they were finished with the upstairs, she and Amy moved to the attic next and Wyatt followed. The attic hadn't been cleaned for her arrival and was filled with cobwebs and dust. Most of it had been floored, which should make their search easier and she didn't have to worry about one of them falling.

When Duke and Virginia came up, Duke set up powerful flashlights that lit up a good portion of the attic.

"We can start here and work our way around," he said. "Why don't we all four search up here and get through and out of this dust?"

Destiny agreed.

Wyatt sat on a pile of boards that had been left years earlier. "In the winter there are probably rats and mice that take shelter in here, but it's still too warm for them to come in yet."

"I don't want to think about that," Destiny said. She assigned areas to each person and she took a far corner. She ran her hands lightly along some of the boards, but some had splinters sticking out and she avoided them. In the corner, she got down on her knees and crawled into a narrow space where the light was dimmer. Looking beside a long rafter that ran to the floor, she saw short boards had been clumsily nailed in the corner beside the rafter.

"Find something interesting in those old boards?" Wyatt asked. She glanced around to just see the lower part of his legs. He leaned down to look at her. "Is there something down here?"

"I don't know. Someone has nailed some boards back here. It's a sloppy job. Get a hammer from Duke and let me see if I can take this apart."

In seconds Wyatt was back and bent down again with a hammer in hand. "If you'll come out of there, I'll do whatever you want."

"You can't fold up enough to get in this corner. Let me have the hammer."

He handed it to her and she worked, trying to pry out nails, letting them fall on the attic flooring. Finally a board hung by one nail and she peered behind it.

"Wyatt, can I have a flashlight?"

When he handed her a flashlight, she aimed it at the space she had revealed. "Here's a box," she said, working to get the last nail out of the board.

"Don't tell me you've found something after all these years."

"This isn't a fun place to be. My knees are beginning to hurt." The board snapped away in her hands. She laid it on the floor and held out the flashlight. "Hold this, please."

Wyatt hunkered down and peered into the dark corner, trying to shine the light on the space she had found. "I'll be damned. You have found something."

She tugged on a metal box that filled the space. Wyatt reached past her to grasp it with one hand so they both could try to work it free. Finally, together, they got it out.

"Can you take the box, Wyatt? It's heavy. I have to get out of here and stand up."

He held a dust-covered metal box and stepped back, reaching down to help her up when she crawled out. As she did, everyone gathered around.

"I need to go back. There are some jars that were behind the box," she said.

"I can get down there to get them," Duke said.

Destiny shook her head. "I think you're too big."

"We'll see," he said. "All of you will have to get back."

Destiny picked up the box to set it on the pile of boards. She sat beside it while Amy and Virginia gathered around.

Wyatt got down to help Duke, who had scooted into the corner space. In moments he handed two sealed glass jars to Wyatt and a leather bag with a drawstring drawn tight and knotted at the top.

"Let's get all this out and take it downstairs to look at it," Wyatt said.

"That's fine," Destiny agreed, looking at everyone who worked for her. "I've had enough of this dust."

They climbed down, all brushing off dust. Wyatt combed a cobweb from her hair with his fingers while she brushed herself off.

"It's just the five of us," Destiny said, looking one by one at the group as they assembled in the front room. "I agreed and promised the governor that if we find any money, it's to go to the town of Verity."

They all looked at the glass jars Wyatt carried that held silver and gold coins. Duke carried the box and the leather bag.

"I think this is all money. It's heavy," Duke said.

"The jars hold silver dollars and coins that we can see. The box is heavy as if it's filled with money. Let's open the box and the leather bag and see what we have," Destiny said.

"The money is here," she said, touching one of the jars in which they could see the silver and gold coins. "The letter will be with this. I'm just sure."

Destiny looked down at the items they'd found, feeling a familiar thrill cascade over her body. She reached out to hug Amy and next Virginia and then Duke. "Thank you so much for taking on this job," she told them. "It's exciting to make these discoveries. We've done it before and now here again, and each time is the most thrilling ever. Let's look and see what we've found."

They all sat on the floor beside the box as she tried to open it. Wyatt reached out to help and the lid finally came off, revealing a piece of folded leather on the top. Destiny carefully removed it and beneath were silver and gold dollars. "There are coins," she said, "which go to the town. Let's see what this is."

Destiny unfolded the piece of leather with great care. Inside was a yellowed, wrinkled, folded sheet of paper. She held her breath as she scanned the opening words. She had found what she was looking for. She looked up to meet Wyatt's steady gaze and she wondered what he was thinking. Was he happy or disappointed? She couldn't tell.

"This stays between us for now," she said. "Listen..." She read it aloud.

"'I must finally reveal the truth of the deaths in this house. I am the last one alive who was involved that terrible night. The year had been the happiest of my life. Two men, Mr. Reuben Calhoun and Mr. Mortimer Milan, had asked Papa for my hand in marriage. To my deepest sorrow, Papa had someone else in mind for my future husband, Mr. Jerome Grayson. I fear I much preferred either Mr. Calhoun or Mr. Milan. My preference would have been Mr. Reuben Calhoun, but I had little choice where Papa was concerned.

"Mr. Calhoun and Mr. Milan both came to call on the same Saturday night. Their talk became heated and I feared they approached a fight. Papa heard them and joined them, telling them to each leave our house and land and not to return.

"The three men became more agitated and then pistols were drawn. I felt faint, but wanted to get help to stop what I feared was about to happen. I ran for our stable keeper, Leon Haymes, who had to get his pistol and then came behind me. When I was almost to the porch steps, I heard three shots.

"I dreaded what I would find and it was as terrible as I expected. Mr. Calhoun was not conscious and bleeding profusely. Mr. Milan was barely alive, but he drew my head close to whisper to me. Papa was no longer alive, but before he died, according to Mr. Milan, Papa had announced he did not want me to marry either of them. Mr. Milan told me that Papa fired at Mr. Calhoun and then turned his pistol and fired at Mr. Milan. Mr. Calhoun was not dead and he fired at Papa. Mr. Calhoun killed Papa with his shot. Mr. Milan died in my arms and by this time Leon was with Mr. Calhoun, who was never conscious and who died last. I could not go through talking about this to townspeople or officials. I did not want to bring shame to Papa or the Calhoun or Milan families, so I said they all died without revealing what happened. This is a true account of that night as told to me by Mr. Milan. Lavita Wrenville, October 12, 1891.'"

Destiny looked around. "Lavita's father shot the Calhoun and the Milan. I think we have a show."

Wyatt smiled at her as she looked at him and she still wondered what he really thought.

"This doesn't have to be made public yet," Destiny stated, staring at Wyatt.

"If the money goes into the bank, several people will know. I can talk to Horace Pringle and he'll take care of the matter and it won't make the news."

"I want to keep the letter and the governor gave me permission to use it for the show if I return it intact to Verity. I'll give you a copy."

"Why don't you take the copy and put the original in the bank until it's time for the show?" Wyatt asked.

"I'll think that over and talk to people at the station and see what they want. We might as well go back to town and regroup." She pointed to the leather bag, which was on the floor in front of Duke.

"Duke, let's see what's in the bag. Open it and we'll find out."

Excitement made her tense with anticipation. Money and a letter. She would have a great show and this would go into her book.

Duke untied the drawstring, opened the bag and reached in to withdraw another handful of coins and bills. "More money."

Virginia and Amy clapped with enthusiasm.

"I think this calls for a celebration," Wyatt said. "I'm not part of your group, but why don't all of you come to my house tonight? I'll have dinner and you can celebrate your discovery. You've found what a lot of people for a lot of years have searched for."

Destiny looked at the others. "I think it would be fun to take Wyatt up on his offer and to celebrate a little. How about it?"

"That's great," Amy replied.

Duke smiled, glancing at Virginia, who nodded. "We think that will be fun," Virginia replied.

"It's time for a celebration," Duke added.

"It's up to the four of you," Wyatt said, "and I know you want this kept quiet until you decide how to break the news to the best advantage for your show, but I'd like to invite my family, who knows how to keep secrets, and also my deputies and Dwight. They're all accustomed to keeping silent about what they know is official. It would make a party, but inviting others will be up to you."

"If we're doing that," Destiny said, "what about the bank president?"

"Good idea," Wyatt said, smiling at her. "That's a lot of people, but I can vouch for each one of them keeping this find out of the news."

"Actually, it keeps growing. Jake, your brother-in-law is a Calhoun. I'm a Calhoun," Destiny said. "Would the other Calhouns in Jake's family keep quiet about it?"

Wyatt thought about Jake. "I think they would. I'll ask

Jake because he'll know. Okay, party it is. I'll send a text to my cook to give him as much time as possible and I'll give you my address to put in your GPS."

Destiny wanted to celebrate and she wanted to be with Wyatt. Excitement rocked her. "Wyatt, it would be fun to read the letter tonight when we're all gathered together."

He smiled. "It will be your party. Do what you want. I'll call Horace before we head back to town," Wyatt said. "He'll take care of depositing the money so the least number of people know about it."

"I'll put the money in your car," Duke said, carrying the box and leather bag and taking keys from Wyatt, who was on his phone. Virginia and Amy followed Duke with the two jars.

Destiny waited as Wyatt continued to make calls, finally putting away his phone. "We're set. Jake is calling his family. Everyone understands that this is to be kept quiet. Once I get back to the office I should let the governor know," he said to Destiny, "since you contacted him about searching the house."

She nodded. "I'll get in touch with him, too."

"Horace Pringle will meet us at the back door of the bank and take care of the money. He'll also make a copy of the letter. I'll head back to town now. Destiny, do you want to go with me since I have the money?" Wyatt asked.

"Yes."

Duke reentered just then. "We're loaded up. The money and the letter are in your car, Sheriff."

Wyatt thanked him. "Duke, I've sent my address to your cell and you can put it in your GPS. I'll notify the gatekeeper you're all coming." He looked at Destiny. "Ready to go?"

They all left, locking the door, which seemed ridiculous to Destiny since windows were broken and the house stood vacant. Excitement hummed like a steady current and she was ready for a party and a celebration. Best of all, Wyatt had seemed to accept her finding the letter and the money and was helping them celebrate, so maybe she hadn't upset his life or his town too badly. It occurred to her, it might be her own life that received the upset if she couldn't get over her love for Wyatt.

Each minute with him just convinced her more that she had fallen in love with him, and this party and his quiet acceptance of her achievement was adding to her growing love for him.

As they drove away from the house, Wyatt took her hand. "Congratulations, you did it."

"Thank you. I'm so excited. I know this isn't what you wanted to have happen, but it's great as possible material for a show and it definitely will be material for my book."

"The news will be big until it's replaced by something else. Verity will go right along," he said.

"You've certainly mellowed about it."

"I can't fight you. You had the governor's permission. Besides, you've brought excitement and fun to Verity—and, I'll have to admit, maybe into my quiet life."

She laughed and squeezed his hand. "I could say the same back to you."

Flashing her a quick grin, he turned his attention back to the road. "You found the letter and the money, which I didn't think existed. I'll tell you what I really want. Let me pick you up tonight so you can stay at my place and I'll take you home tomorrow."

"Or take me home tonight and come in for a long nightcap," she said, placing her hand on his knee. "I'm excited, Wyatt."

"I am, too, just for a different reason."

She stroked his thigh lightly. "Not altogether a different reason," she said in a breathy voice, letting her fingers trail up the inside of his thigh.

"Maybe you should wait on that. I'd hate to explain why I drove off into a ditch in the official sheriff's car."

She laughed softly. "I'll take a rain check. It's nice of you to have us all for a party. It's short notice for your cook."

"Lawrence will rise to the occasion. He always does, and he can get additional people to help him tonight. He has a list."

Wyatt scanned his mirrors and then shot her a glance. "I'll pick you up at half past six so we will definitely be there when everyone else arrives. At the hotel, you can make another of your grand appearances. Or go out the side door and avoid the reporters. By the way, since this is short notice, I said it would be casual tonight."

"That's fine. I can do casual. Maybe you're right this time about avoiding reporters."

As they drove back to town, Destiny thought of the party that was to come, and then her time alone with Wyatt. Two or three more nights with him and then she would say goodbye. Would it really be goodbye? The realization put a damper on her excitement over her discovery. She shook away the dread of something she didn't know for certain and caressed his thigh, feeling his warmth through the thick cotton of his uniform.

"Do you really think that many people will keep this quiet?" she asked him.

"Yes, I do. I know my family can and Jake said his would. My deputies and Dwight will and Horace Pringle definitely will. I don't think there will be any problem."

"I'm amazed, but okay. I'd like to read the letter again tonight so all present can hear. They're all involved in small ways and not so small."

"Go ahead."

"It won't be the end of the world if word gets out," she reasoned. "By the time it's passed around, news of the find will be all garbled anyway. Next year's coming quick, so if the show is produced, it'll be timely."

It was another hour before they finished at the bank and Wyatt accompanied her to the door of her hotel suite. "I have the copy of the letter with me and I'll bring it tonight," she told him. "If we do the show, I'll want the original back just for the show."

"You found it. When this is all settled, it's probably yours, although I'm sure the Verity Historical Museum would appreciate a copy."

"They can have the real thing then." She opened her door. "I'd invite you in, but I am covered in dust."

"I can help you shower."

Laughing, she shook her head. "This time I need to scrub."

"I'll pick you up at six-thirty. Sure you don't want another grand exit when I pick you up?"

"No, I'll slip out the side."

"Then I'll come up and get you. See you then." He pulled her inside quickly, taking her into his arms and leaning over to kiss her.

"Now you'll be covered in dust," she said when he released her.

"It was worth it," he said and left.

She closed her door and put the copy of the letter on a table in her entryway. Excitement still danced in her, but part of it was because she was going out with Wyatt tonight and they would either both stay at his place or both stay in her suite.

How was she going to tell him goodbye?

She didn't want to think about that moment. The evening was ahead of her and she had no intention of adding a sour note.

She hurried to get ready.

At six-thirty she heard the light tap on her door and

opened it to face Wyatt, whose appreciative gaze went from her head to her feet in a look that made her toes curl. Her insides heated as she gazed at him. In a dark blue shirt, black slacks, black boots and a black wide-brimmed hat, he made her want to forgo the party and be alone with him for the entire evening.

"You're gorgeous, Destiny," he said in a hoarse voice, his gaze going over her red silk blouse and matching slacks with matching high heels again.

"Thank you. I'm ready," she said.

"I'm ready for you," he whispered. "What I'd like to do is carry you off to bed."

"I'd like that, too, but we can't. Too many people are waiting and the party is at your house so you have to go."

"Aw, gee whiz," he joked and she smiled.

He took her hand and they went to his car, which was parked by the side door.

"Now I get to see your Verity house," she said.

"I like it, though I like the ranch better. You may view it as the end of the world and almost totally isolated."

"If it's yours, Wyatt, I'll love it."

A little while later she was impressed when he pulled into an exclusive community. He waved at the gatekeeper as they drove through the open black iron gates and wound up a long drive to an impressive house with lights blazing.

Before she could get out, Wyatt stopped her. "It's our last night together, Destiny. I want to send everyone home early."

A sharp pain tore at her heart. *Last night together...* What did that mean to Wyatt? Did he really care or had this all been pure sex and nothing the slightest bit deeper? She had not penetrated that armor around his heart and now their affair was over. Did he care in the least?

Nine

Wyatt took her arm as they went up the steps to a wide porch with two-story Ionic columns. He opened the door and Destiny stood in a large circular entryway with an enormous crystal chandelier hanging over a round, ornate table. "Very pretty, Wyatt."

"I'll show you where you can put your purse," he said, taking her arm and walking into a wide hall to go through the first door to his right.

They entered a formal living area with a fireplace, silk-damask-covered chairs and heavy, ornate furniture that was not at all what she had envisioned would be in Wyatt's home. He closed the door and wrapped her in his arms to kiss her.

When she finally leaned away, she gazed up at him. "I think the others will be here soon."

"C'mon. You can leave your purse in here if you want. We'll gather on the patio because it's a nice night or inside in the great room."

She walked along the wide hall that opened into a large room with glass along one wall, giving a view of the pool, gardens with blooming flowers, fountains and a patio with an outdoor living area and kitchen.

"You have a beautiful home."

"Thank you. Ah, here are our first guests," he said, greeting Jake and Madison.

As people began to arrive, waiters passed drinks. Destiny was warmly greeted by Lindsay Calhoun, who introduced Destiny to her brothers, Josh and Mike.

"None of you look alike, especially Lindsay with her blond hair," Destiny said, looking at Mike's curly black hair and Josh with straight brown hair.

Josh laughed. "She's the odd one, our blondie. She doesn't even have our brown eyes either," he said. "We can't wait to hear the letter and find out who shot who."

"I'm guessing a Milan shot a Calhoun," Mike said, smiling at her. "I can't guess who shot Mr. Wrenville."

Destiny smiled. "It's interesting and I'm so excited over our discovery."

"Wyatt said you crawled back in a corner of the attic and found it. He's probably miffed because he's looked for it before," Josh said.

"We'll read it as soon as all the guests are here."

Josh was unrelenting. "All the Calhouns figure a Milan did the shooting and all the Milans probably think a Calhoun did the shooting. We figure whoever it was, he shot Lavita's father because he wouldn't give his approval for the wedding."

Destiny kept her smile. "I'm not going to spoil your surprise by telling you."

Jake and Madison joined them. "That letter better be read soon or there will be betting on who fired the fatal shots," Jake said.

Destiny couldn't help but laugh, though there was one

thing that she, too, was wondering about. "Lavita had two men who wanted to marry her. After the shooting, she never married. Why? She was one of the wealthiest young women in the town—probably in the county or in the West even. Did no one else ever want to marry her or did she grieve all her life for a lost love?"

"I suppose we do have an interesting town," Madison remarked.

Wyatt stepped up beside Destiny. "Let me have one guess what the topic of this conversation is," he said and the others laughed.

"Probably the same as every other group at this party," Mike said, shaking hands with Wyatt. "Thanks for having this tonight and inviting all of us. You had short notice."

"Lawrence is always ready to cook. I'm glad everyone could come. Josh, I'm glad you were in town. We caught our hotel mogul in a rare moment of coming home."

"Thanks, Wyatt," Josh said, shaking hands with him. "This sounds like an interesting night. I'm glad to be here."

"I guess by now Lindsay has made introductions all the way around." Destiny nodded and Wyatt continued. "Destiny, my deputy Val just arrived and I think we're all here, so this is the big moment." He looked at Destiny. "Are you ready?"

"Of course," she said, smiling at him. As she looked into his blue eyes, she was caught in a look of such longing that, momentarily, she forgot the others and the reason they were here. Her heartbeat quickened. In that moment she would have traded everything—her show, her books, her discovery—to have Wyatt's love. Startled, she tried to focus on where she was and what was happening.

"Folks—" Wyatt said in a voice that carried, but wasn't loud. Destiny wasn't surprised though when everyone became silent. "If all of you will find a seat, our Chicago celebrity, Destiny Jones, will read Lavita Wrenville's letter. I think everyone here now has met Destiny, so I don't think she needs an introduction, but we can all welcome her—Destiny Jones."

Wyatt stepped back and smiled at her and Destiny took a folded copy of the letter from her pocket.

"I'm delighted to be here and either meet you or get to know you better. You've welcomed me and my staff and made us feel at home in Verity. Today was exciting and I know you want to hear this letter and learn what happened that fateful night at the Wrenville house, especially all the Milans and the Calhouns."

She unfolded the letter and read it. The only other sound as she read was the splashing of the fountains in the gardens and the pool. When she finished, she looked up. "There you have the truth of what happened."

There was applause and conversation started again. "So a Milan didn't shoot a Calhoun and a Calhoun didn't shoot a Milan. Old man Wrenville did them both in," Josh said, shaking his head.

"I don't know the family named, the man that Lavita's father wanted her to marry," Mike added.

Josh and Mike looked at each other and then at Wyatt and all shook their heads. "No Graysons around here. Probably some older man Mr. Wrenville did business with and Lavita didn't want to marry him," Mike said.

"So you'll do a television show about this?" Josh asked her.

"I have to take all this back to my producer. But it looks a lot more likely now that we've found the letter and have a story to tell," Destiny answered. As she talked, she looked at Wyatt and for a second almost lost her train of thought. She wondered whether he would go back to the hotel with her or she would stay here with him tonight.

After a few moments, she moved on, going from cluster to cluster of guests to talk to each one. It amused her to see that Wyatt and Nick were doing the same.

Dinner was buffet style and tables had been set up on the patio that was large enough to easily hold them.

It was almost eleven before guests began to say goodnight.

As Destiny's staff was leaving, Amy stopped beside her. "Duke is taking us back to the hotel. I'm assuming Wyatt will bring you?"

"Yes, he will. I'll see you tomorrow. We can fly out of here then." As she said the words she had a hollow feeling. Flying home—away from Wyatt. How much would it hurt to tell him goodbye?

She suspected the real hurt was going to come when she was in Chicago and not seeing him again.

She told Duke and Virginia she would see them in the morning.

Finally she faced Wyatt and they were the only two in the hallway as the last of the Milans left.

"What about Lawrence and his help?"

"They left hours ago and when you read the letter I told Lawrence to keep them all in the kitchen, so they never heard the letter and don't know anything about it except Lawrence. I told him we found the letter and he'd hear about it later."

"Then you should tell him, too."

"I really don't think Lawrence cares." He took her in his arms. "What I care about is now and you. We have this house to ourselves and we are wasting time."

"I'm leaving for Chicago tomorrow, so I'll have to get back to the hotel in the morning."

"Cancel the flight and I'll fly all of you home a day later or two days later or whatever you want."

Her heart jumped because his offer meant he wanted her to stay longer. What was the depth of his feelings for her? Was there a crack in that barrier around his heart? "You don't mind?"

"Wouldn't have asked if I didn't want to."

"All right. Let me send a text to Amy and she can break the news."

"Make it a short text," he said, shedding his shirt.

She drew a deep breath. "How do you expect me to concentrate on a text while you're stripping in front of me?" she asked, dropping her phone on a table and walking over to wrap her arms around him and stand on tiptoe to kiss him.

She didn't know how long they kissed when he stopped her. "You send a text so they won't be looking for you in the morning and then we'll continue."

She tried to avoid looking at him as she sent the text and got an immediate "Okay" in return. "Now, that's done. I have other things to do," she said and began to unfasten his belt.

He drew her into his embrace and kissed her, and all her worries over parting temporarily vanished.

They made love all through Friday and into Saturday morning. Sunshine streamed in the window and Destiny sat up. "Wyatt, they're ready to go back to Chicago. I've stayed an extra day and I told them we would go back today."

"You mean it, don't you?"

"Yes," she said, hurting because they were going to part now and he was going to let her walk out of his life and he wouldn't look back.

She wrapped her arms around him and kissed him furiously, wanting to consume him, love him until he couldn't get along without her, just as she couldn't get along without him.

They made love again, so it was an hour later when she

once again sat up and told him she needed to get back to the
hotel. Stepping out of bed, she headed to a shower. When
she emerged, she was dressed in her red slacks and shirt.

"Now I have to go back to the hotel."

"Come eat breakfast and then we'll go."

She nibbled a few bites of toast and drank a small glass
of orange juice, but that was all she could get down.

They were quiet as he drove her to the hotel. At her door
when she faced him they looked into each other's eyes.
She could hardly believe the hurt she felt. It threatened to
crush her heart. She wanted Wyatt to want her in his life.
She didn't know how they would mesh their very different
lives, but she would find a way if only Wyatt loved her as
much as she loved him.

He stepped inside, closing the door behind him as he
kissed her.

Finally she stopped him. "I have to go, Wyatt. They're
just waiting for me to go home."

"All right. I'll talk to Duke and get someone to turn in
the limo after you go to the Verity airport. They'll take
you to my plane." He gave her one last lingering kiss. "I
may see you soon, Destiny. I'll call you," he said.

Hurting, she nodded because she didn't think he would
call or that she would see him—unless she returned to
Verity on business.

He turned and was gone, the suite door closing behind
him. She hurt all over and she trembled, feeling chilled.
She had to pull herself together because she didn't want
the others to see her this upset. It would be obvious it was
over Wyatt.

She rinsed her face in cold water, then she changed
and tossed her clothes into her bag so she would not keep
them waiting.

Two hours later, she sat quietly in Wyatt's luxurious

private jet as they gained altitude and Texas disappeared below. What was Wyatt doing? Did he hurt at all or did he even care?

Wyatt tried to work and couldn't concentrate. He gave up and told Dwight he needed to go to his ranch and would see him Monday.

As he sped along the highway, a plane went overhead. He looked up, knowing it was a commercial jet and not his plane flying Destiny home to Chicago. Even though their parting had been inevitable from the first, it hurt. He missed her and wanted her with him tonight and the rest of the week.

He would get over her. He always did, but he couldn't recall ever missing someone this badly. Was it purely the sex that had wrapped around him and ensnared him? At some point, he knew, that ardor would cool, although at the present moment, he couldn't imagine it cooling even one degree. Common sense said it would and then how would he feel about her?

He missed her, her laughter, her smiles, her surprises, her flirting, the constant excitement she stirred. Without her, the whole town of Verity seemed empty and devoid of life.

He'd give himself a few days and then he would probably be back to normal with his life back in a regular routine that did not include a fantastic, sexy, sensual redhead who had stirred his life into a tempest.

He could hear Duke threatening him, warning him to not hurt her and then admitting he had never talked to another man about that before. Why had Duke confronted him—even more seriously, threatened him? And Duke had known exactly what he was doing.

Wyatt shook his head. He couldn't answer his own questions and Duke remained a puzzle, but he had a feeling if

Destiny went back to Chicago missing him, he might be in a big heap of trouble when Duke returned to Verity if she came back for the show. That might be one more bit of trouble she had stirred into his life.

Wyatt hit the steering wheel with the palm of his hand. He missed her and wanted her. How long was it going to take to get over her? How long before she would be out of his thoughts?

He wanted her back in Verity. His life was going to be quiet and dull for the next few days. He didn't even know if he could get her television show out at the ranch.

"Destiny," he said, remembering driving with her beside him, her hand on his thigh, her flirting and teasing and sexy remarks.

Another plane went overhead and he gave it a dark look. She was flying away from him, back to her busy, fulfilling life, and she would forget Verity and its sheriff, their time together, everything here.

His spirits sank lower. He hadn't talked to her about seeing her again and that had been his fault. He pulled out his phone, looked at it and dropped it on the seat beside him. She was flying and wouldn't take the call.

"Dammit. Destiny." Why hadn't he made arrangements to fly up and see her?

Wyatt drove to the ranch, but unlike other times he didn't find the usual peace and quiet. He missed Destiny as much at the ranch as he had in Verity. He changed clothes, took a pickup and went to see if he could find some work to do and take his mind off Destiny.

By nightfall, he missed her beyond anything he had guessed possible. He hadn't felt this way since Katherine. The realization shocked him. Had he fallen in love without even knowing it?

He yanked out his phone to call Destiny. The moment he heard her voice, he felt better and worse at the same time. He wanted her in his arms, but he was glad to talk to her.

"Hi. I thought I'd see if you got in and if everything is okay."

"Yes. Thanks for the flight home. It was easy and a good flight. I'm just starting to unpack. I've been on the phone with my producer for the past hour. I think I have a show. Sorry, Wyatt, if you're still upset about Verity being on a television show."

"I've adjusted," he said. Then, as if the thought hit him from out of nowhere, he said, "I don't know where you live—a house, an apartment? Destiny, there's a lot I don't know about you."

She laughed. "We didn't spend a whole lot of time talking if you'll remember our moments together."

Oh, he did. Every hot one of them. "I miss you," he blurted, wondering about himself.

Her voice softened. "I miss you, Wyatt."

Silence stretched between them. "Let me know about the show."

"I will."

"Do you think I can get it at the ranch?"

"Wyatt, I don't have any idea what you can or cannot get on your television at your ranch," she said. "Are you okay?"

"I'm fine," he said, feeling anything but fine. "Do you see Duke, Amy and Virginia every day?"

"Heavens, no. Just Amy. I see a lot of Virginia, not so much of Duke."

"He's very protective of you."

"He is of all three of us when we travel with him. He's a great bodyguard, not that I've had any real trouble."

Wyatt settled back, listening to her talk, wanting her in his arms and finding talking to her was better than not talking to her, but he wanted her with him more than anything else.

When she finally said she had to go, it was two hours later. "Bye, Destiny. I miss you," he said again.

She broke the connection and he placed his phone on a table and sat back, lost in thought about her. He felt a huge empty void without her. How could he miss her this much? It would pass, he told himself again. Give it a week and he wouldn't feel this way at all.

He sat immobile, missing her, hurting, wishing he had made arrangements to see her, telling himself it was better to just break it off with her because he wasn't the marrying type. He was quiet and laid-back while Destiny was a whirlwind who wouldn't be happy settled on a ranch. He couldn't be in love. It was only lust, and she hadn't been in his life long enough for him to be all torn up over her going.

The next day he threw himself into work on the ranch, doing all the jobs that required physical labor, trying to keep his mind off Destiny, trying to keep busy and failing constantly. In the quiet of the ranch, or even with guys working around him some of the time, he couldn't stop thinking of Destiny.

By evening, he called her. When she didn't answer, his spirits sank lower. Was she out with someone else now? Even if she didn't have a serious or intimate relationship with anyone, he didn't want to think about her going out with someone else.

Monday he was back at the office in Verity. Everything in town reminded him of Destiny and being with her the past week. He was as miserable in Verity as he was on the ranch. She probably had moved on and was forgetting him by now, picking up the threads of her Chicago life and going on with living.

Thursday night he called her, as he'd done every night, and at the sound of her voice, he clutched the phone tightly. They just talked, more than they ever had. It was a two-hour phone call and before they hung up, she said she missed him and he told her he missed her, which seemed inadequate.

He ended the call and it hit him. He was in love with her. It was hopeless, something he had intended to avoid, but he loved her. He couldn't miss her this much, miss her constantly, and not be in love. She had filled his life in too many ways and now he wanted her back. Should he fly to Chicago and see her? She wouldn't want to come back to Texas.

He wondered if she really missed him as much. She said she did before ending their call, but how much did she mean it?

He knew how badly he missed her. He couldn't think at work and he had done some sloppy jobs at the ranch that he had had to do over.

He knew what he had to do.

He drove to Dallas and spent the next two days looking at wedding rings. Finally, wanting to impress her, he bought a ten-carat diamond ring with more diamonds and emeralds on the band. Now, if he could get a date to see her, he would fly to Chicago.

He was determined to see her and he was going to fly to Chicago. He had fallen in love with her without even knowing it, while trying to guard against doing any such thing.

When he was back home, he sat looking at the engagement ring he had bought and he felt ridiculous. He didn't know what she felt and he didn't want to tell her on the phone for the first time that he loved her.

He closed the box and put the ring in a bottom drawer while he sat staring into space, something he seemed to be doing a lot of since she had gone home. She had swept into his life, stolen his heart, left him in tangled knots and then left.

He picked up his phone to call and talk again.

Sunday night Destiny worked late. She had every night since she had returned from Texas. As she sat on her bed and reviewed a script for the newest show, she couldn't keep her mind on the words in front of her. It kept wandering to Wyatt. She wondered whether he ever watched her show or if he had even tried. He hadn't seemed to know whether he could get it at the ranch, so she imagined he had forgotten all about it. With each passing day, she missed him more. He called her each night, so he must miss her some, but he hadn't suggested that she come back to Texas and he hadn't said he was coming to Chicago.

She punched the pillows behind her, then checked her cell phone next to her on the blanket. She was waiting for his nightly call. Wyatt kept his heart sealed away, avoiding love. Was he going to let life pass him by because he didn't want to risk another hurt? Was she going to love him to no avail, just because he wouldn't risk loving again?

When the phone rang, she yanked it up, glad to hear from him yet almost angry with him. She wanted more from him than these long nightly conversations that didn't tell her anything about his feelings. She settled back to talk, wondering where they were going and how long things would go on this way, which was not typical of Wyatt, who was a decisive person.

After two hours he told her goodbye and ended the call. She sat staring at her phone. "Wyatt, why don't you come see me? I love you, Wyatt," she whispered.

She looked into her open closet, her gaze resting on her suitcase. Maybe if he wouldn't come to Chicago, she would go to Texas. She stared at the suitcase, wondering about Wyatt's feelings. Why hadn't he come to see her or asked her to come back? Two-hour calls every night had to mean something. But what? How deeply did his feelings run?

Of all men for her to fall in love with—it was one she couldn't figure out.

Ten

Wyatt sat at his desk at the ranch trying to go over his bookkeeping, the figures he needed to give his accountant, but he couldn't concentrate. His cell phone beeped and he saw it was his foreman. "Brant?"

"Wyatt, there's a bright red limo that's turned up the road to the house. Want me to stop and see who it is and what they want?"

Startled, Wyatt stood and his heart started to pound. "No. I know who it is, I think. I'll go watch for them. Thanks." His heart raced. Jamming the phone into his pocket, he went outside on the east side of the house that gave a good view of the road. He saw a plume of dust in the distance and then a red speck that soon became a long red limo.

"What the hell?" he mumbled. He didn't take his eyes off the limo as it finally neared the house. As he started down the steps the limo swept past him along the drive to the front of the house.

"Dammit," Wyatt swore, striding back through the house to the front door. Through the windows he saw the red limo turn and head back toward the highway and he ran for the door to yank it open.

Wyatt stopped in his tracks. Destiny stood beside a suitcase and a carry-on. Her purse hanging on her shoulder, dressed in tight-fitting jeans and her favorite red sweater, she stood facing him as the red limo disappeared down the ranch road.

He realized he was standing there and staring at her. He dashed down the steps, taking them three at a time, and ran to her.

"What are you doing here?" he said, looking into her wide, green eyes. He didn't give her a chance to answer. He swept her into his arms and kissed her, holding her tightly against him, wondering if this was a dream and he would wake up.

Her arms wrapped around his neck as he picked her up, still kissing her, and he carried her into the house and kicked the door closed behind him. He headed to the nearest downstairs guest bedroom, stepping inside and shoving the door closed.

Over an hour later, he rolled over, taking her with him. He looked down at her. "Hi," he said.

"Hi, yourself," she answered, gazing up at him wide-eyed and solemn.

"This was a surprise."

"I suppose it is," she said, trailing her fingers over his chest.

"Want to tell me what's going on? What are you doing here?"

"We've had a lot of long phone calls, but nothing much else. I've missed you, Wyatt," she said, sounding uncertain and cautious.

His heart began to drum. "Darlin', I've missed you so much, it's been hell. Destiny, I shouldn't have let you go home like that, but I didn't know my own feelings. You made me fall in love with you. I wasn't going to do that, but I did. I did, I have. I love you," he declared.

"Wyatt! I love you. I don't know what happened to either one of us. You're a cowboy, a Texas rancher and you always will be. You're quiet and you want a quiet life. I'm none of that."

"Hardly," he said, grinning. "You wrecked any peace and quiet in my life. You're the center of attention everywhere you go. Neither of us is going to change either. Another Calhoun to take hold of a Milan and change him completely."

"I don't think there is a shred of a feud between this Calhoun and Milan," she said, kissing his throat and looking up at him mischievously.

"Wyatt, I've loved you almost since the first night we went out," she said and he let out his breath, drawing her to him and kissing her hard and long, wanting to let her know every way possible that he loved her.

Suddenly he stopped. "Stay right here. Don't go anywhere," he said as he got up and left.

"Where would I go like this?" Destiny asked an empty room. She scooted up, pulling a sheet beneath her arms and wondering where he had gone. His words echoed again and again—he loved her.

He came back to slip beneath the sheet with her. "Destiny Jones, will you marry me?" he asked.

Her heart pounded with joy as she threw her arms around him. "Yes, oh, yes."

He kissed her and in minutes he leaned away and fumbled in the bed to hand her a box. "I got this for you."

Her eyes widened. "Wyatt, I'm surprised. Since I went

back to Chicago, we haven't even been dating—" She opened the box and gasped. "Oh, Wyatt, it's beautiful." She threw her arms around him to kiss him again. "I love you," she said after a long kiss.

"I love you, Destiny. I should have told you before you went back to Chicago, but I didn't know my own feelings."

"I thought you didn't care. When did you decide that you're in love?"

"I care. I love you with all my heart, but I didn't realize it until you were gone. Destiny, it's been hell without you. Hon, we've got so many problems."

She laughed and looked at him, throwing her arms around him again to kiss him. Finally, she leaned back. "Now, tell me about all the problems we have…after you put that ring on my finger."

She held out the ring and he took it to slip it on her finger. "A perfect fit," she said. "It's the most beautiful ring I've ever seen. Diamonds and emeralds. Perfect." She looked up at him. "So what are the problems?"

"You won't want to live on the ranch. You have a television show in Chicago. I do want to live on the ranch. I work in Verity."

She giggled. "We'll work it all out. You'll see. You have your own airplane. We don't have to be together every minute. Shows don't last forever and I have other things in my life I want to do. I might have a book career. There are jobs in Dallas and—" She stopped, realizing she was babbling. She took a breath and smiled at him. "Or I just might retire and have our babies. You do want babies, don't you?"

"Yes, as a matter of fact, I do now that you're going to be their mother. Little girls just like you so we always have excitement in our lives. I've spent the first half of my life resting up for what's coming." His smile lit up those amazing blue eyes.

"Wyatt, we can work through any problem as long as you love me and I love you and we're together a lot of the time."

He wrapped his arms tighter around her. "Well, so much for problems."

"Did you know I have a suitcase out in front of your house?"

"It won't go anywhere. I'll get it when I put on clothes, which isn't going to happen for a little while longer."

"Why not?"

"I'm going to make love to my fiancée."

How she loved the sound of that. She leaned in to kiss him before a thought struck her. "Wyatt, I need to tell Mimi and Desirée. Mimi is going to have to start liking Milans. She warned me you might be sneaky."

"I'll forgive her. And I want to tell all my family, too. I want you to meet my mom and dad."

"A judge. He may not approve of me."

"He's a man. He'll approve of you and if I love you, my mom will love you."

"Even when they find out I'm a Calhoun?"

"They managed with Madison. They will with me. Let's have this wedding soon."

"As soon as possible. Wyatt, I missed you so much. I didn't have any idea what you felt."

"From here on, you will always know. I'll tell you every morning and every night and all the times in between that I can. I love you, Destiny. I just didn't know it and didn't know how much."

She wiggled her fingers, looking at her ring. "Mrs. Wyatt Milan. That sounds beautiful." She wrapped her arms around him to kiss him. "A wonderful, joyous and exciting November wedding," she said, just before her mouth covered his.

* * * * *

Dax's gaze drifted lower and focused on Elise's mouth.

Because he was thinking about kissing her. She could read it all over his expression.

Emergency. This wasn't a date. She'd led him on somehow. They didn't like each other, and worse, he shied away from everything she desired—love, marriage, soul mates. She was supposed to be matching him with one of her clients.

First and foremost, she'd given him permission to ruin her business if he didn't find the love of his life. And she was compromising the entire thing.

Had she lost her mind?

Despite knowing he thought happily ever after was a myth, despite knowing he faked interest in her as a method of distraction, despite knowing he stood to lose five hundred thousand dollars and pretended to misunderstand her questions or refused to answer them strictly to prevent it—despite all that, she wanted him to kiss her.

Dax Wakefield was better at seducing a woman than she'd credited.

* * *

Matched to Her Rival
is part of the Happily Ever After, Inc. trilogy:
Their business is makeovers and matchmaking,
but love doesn't always go according to plan!

MATCHED TO
HER RIVAL

BY
KAT CANTRELL

All rights reserved including the right of reproduction in whole or in part in any form. This edition is published by arrangement with Harlequin Books S.A.

This is a work of fiction. Names, characters, places, locations and incidents are purely fictional and bear no relationship to any real life individuals, living or dead, or to any actual places, business establishments, locations, events or incidents. Any resemblance is entirely coincidental.

This book is sold subject to the condition that it shall not, by way of trade or otherwise, be lent, resold, hired out or otherwise circulated without the prior consent of the publisher in any form of binding or cover other than that in which it is published and without a similar condition including this condition being imposed on the subsequent purchaser.

® and ™ are trademarks owned and used by the trademark owner and/or its licensee. Trademarks marked with ® are registered with the United Kingdom Patent Office and/or the Office for Harmonisation in the Internal Market and in other countries.

Published in Great Britain 2014
by Mills & Boon, an imprint of Harlequin (UK) Limited,
Eton House, 18-24 Paradise Road, Richmond, Surrey, TW9 1SR

© 2014 Katrina Williams

ISBN: 978-0-263-91477-1

51-0914

Harlequin (UK) Limited's policy is to use papers that are natural, renewable and recyclable products and made from wood grown in sustainable forests. The logging and manufacturing processes conform to the legal environmental regulations of the country of origin.

Printed and bound in Spain
by Blackprint CPI, Barcelona

Kat Cantrell read her first Mills & Boon® novel in third grade and has been scribbling in notebooks since she learned to spell. What else would she write but romance? She majored in literature, officially with the intent to teach, but somehow ended up buried in middle management in corporate America, until she became a stay-at-home mom and full-time writer.

Kat, her husband and their two boys live in north Texas. When she's not writing about characters on the journey to happily-ever-after, she can be found at a soccer game, watching the TV show *Friends* or listening to '80s music.

Kat was the 2011 Harlequin So You Think You Can Write winner and a 2012 RWA Golden Heart finalist for best unpublished series contemporary manuscript.

To Jill Marsal, agent extraordinaire, because you stuck with me through all the revisions of this book and together, we made it great. And because this one was your favorite of the three.

One

In the media business—and in life—presentation trumped everything else, and Dax Wakefield never underestimated the value of putting on a good show.

Careful attention to every detail was the reason his far-flung media empire had succeeded beyond his wildest dreams. So why was KDLS, the former jewel of his crown, turning in such dismal ratings?

Dax stopped at the receptionist's desk in the lobby of the news station he'd come to fix. "Hey, Rebecca. How's Brian's math grade this semester?"

The receptionist's smile widened as she fluffed her hair and threw her shoulders back to make sure he noticed her impressive figure.

He noticed. A man who enjoyed the female form as much as Dax always noticed.

"Good morning, Mr. Wakefield," Rebecca chirped. "He made a C on his last report card. Such an improvement. It's been like six months since I mentioned his grades. How on earth did you remember?"

Because Dax made it a point to keep at least one personal detail about all his employees front and center when speaking to them. The mark of success wasn't simply who had the most money, but who had the best-run business, and no one could do it all by themselves. If people liked working for you, they stuck around, and turned themselves inside out to perform.

Usually. Dax had a few questions for Robert Smith, the station manager, about the latest ratings. Someone was tripping up somewhere.

Dax tapped his temple and grinned. "My mama encourages me to use this bad boy for good instead of evil. Is Robert around?"

The receptionist nodded and buzzed the lock on the security door. "They're taping a segment. I'm sure he's hovering near the set."

"Say hi to Brian for me," Dax called as he sailed through the frosted glass door and into the greatest show on earth—the morning news.

Cameramen and gaffers mixed it up, harried producers with electronic tablets stepped over thick cables on their way to the sound booth, and in the middle of it all sat KDLS's star anchor, Monica McCreary. She was conversing on camera with a petite dark-haired woman who had great legs, despite being on the shorter side. She'd done a lot with what she had and he appreciated the effort.

Dax paused at the edge of the organized chaos and crossed his arms, locking gazes with the station manager. With a nod, Robert scurried across the ocean of people and equipment to join him.

"Saw the ratings, huh?" Robert murmured.

That was a quality Dax fully appreciated in his employees—the ability to read his mind.

Low ratings irritated him because there was no excuse. Sensationalism was key, and if nothing newsworthy happened, it was their job to create something worth watching, and ensure that something had Wakefield Media stamped on it.

"Yep." Dax left it at that, for now. He had all day and the crew was in the middle of taping. "What's this segment?"

"Dallas business owners. We feature one a week. Local interest stuff."

Great Legs owned her own business? Interesting. Smart women equaled a huge turn-on.

"What's she do? Cupcakes?"

Even from this distance, the woman exuded energy—a perky little cheerleader type who never met a curlicue or excess of decoration she didn't like. He could see her dolloping frosting on a cupcake and charging an exorbitant price for it.

Dax could go for a cupcake. Literally and figuratively. Maybe even at the same time.

"Nah. She runs a dating service." Robert nodded at the pair of women under the spotlight. "EA International. Caters to exclusive clients."

The back of Dax's neck heated instantly and all thoughts of cupcakes went out the window.

"I'm familiar with the company."

Through narrowed eyes, Dax zeroed in on the Dallas business owner who had cost him his oldest friend. Someone who called herself a matchmaker should be withered and stooped, with gray hair. It was such an antiquated notion. And it should be against the law.

The anchor laughed at something the matchmaker said and leaned forward. "So you're Dallas's answer to a fairy godmother?"

"I like to think of myself as one. Who doesn't need a bit of magic in their lives?" Her sleek dark hair swung freely as she talked with her hands, expression animated.

"You recently matched the Delamerian prince with his fiancée, right?" Monica winked. "Women everywhere are cursing that, I'm sure."

"I can't take credit." The matchmaker smiled and it transformed her entire demeanor. "Prince Alain—Finn—

and Juliet had a previous relationship. I just helped them realize it wasn't over."

Dax couldn't stop watching her.

As much as he hated to admit it, the matchmaker lit up the set. KDLS's star news anchor was more of a minor celestial body compared to the matchmaker's sun.

And Dax was never one to underestimate star power.

Or the element of surprise.

He strode onto the set and dismissed the anchor with a jerk of his head. "I'll take over from here, Monica. Thanks."

Despite the unusual request, Monica smiled and vacated her chair without comment. No one else so much as blinked. No one who worked for him, anyway.

As he parked in Monica's still-warm chair, the petite dynamo opposite him nearly bowled him over when she blurted out, "What's going on? Who are you?"

A man who recognized a golden opportunity for improved ratings.

"Dax Wakefield. I own the station," he said smoothly. "And this interview has officially started over. It's Elise, right?"

Her confusion leveled out and she crossed her spectacular legs, easing back in the chair carefully. "Yes, but you can call me Ms. Arundel."

Ah, so she recognized his name. Let the fun begin.

He chuckled darkly. "How about if I call you Ms. Hocus-Pocus instead? Isn't that your gig, pulling fast ones on unsuspecting clients? You bibbidi-bobbidi-boo women into relationships with wealthy men."

This interview had also officially become the best way to dish up a side of revenge—served cold. If this ratings gold mine led to discrediting EA International, so much the better. Someone had to save the world from this matchmaker's mercenary female clients.

"That's not what I do." Elise's gaze cut from his face

to his torso and her expression did not melt into the typical sensuous smile that said she'd be happy to further discuss whatever he wanted to talk about over drinks. Unlike most women.

It whetted his appetite to get sparks on the screen another way.

"Enlighten us then," he allowed magnanimously with a wave of his hand.

"I match soul mates." Elise, pardon-me-Ms.-Arundel, cleared her throat and recrossed her legs as if she couldn't find a comfortable pose. "Some people need more help than others. Successful men seldom have time or the patience to sort through potential love interests. I do it for them. At the same time, a man with means needs a certain kind of mate, one not easily found. I widen the potential pool by polishing a few of my female clients into diamonds worthy of the highest social circles."

"Oh, come now. You're training these women to be gold diggers."

That was certainly what she'd done with Daniella White, whose last name was now Reynolds because she'd managed to snare Dax's college friend Leo. Who then promptly screwed Dax over in favor of his wife. A fifteen-year friendship down the drain. Over a woman.

Elise's smile hardened. "You're suggesting women need a class on how to marry a man for his money? I doubt anyone with that goal needs help honing her strategy. I'm in the business of making women's lives better by introducing them to their soul mates."

"Why not pay for them to go to college and let them find their own dates?" Dax countered swiftly.

The onlookers shifted and murmured but neither Dax nor Elise so much as glanced away from their staring contest. An indefinable crackle sliced through the air between them. It was going to be beautiful on camera.

"There are scholarship opportunities out there already. I'm filling another niche, helping people connect. I'm good at what I do. You of all people should know that."

Oh, she had not just gone there. Nearly nose to nose now, he smiled, the best method to keep 'em guessing. "Why would I know that? Because you single-handedly ruined both a business venture and a long-standing friendship when you introduced Leo to his gold digger?"

So, apparently that wound was still raw.

College roommates who'd seen the world through the same lens, he and Leo believed wholeheartedly in the power of success and brotherhood. Females were to be appreciated until they outlived their usefulness. Until Daniella, who somehow got Leo to fall in love with her and then she'd brainwashed his oldest friend into losing his ruthless business edge.

Not that he believed Daniella was 100 percent at fault. She'd been the instigator but Leo had pulled the plug on the deal with Dax. Both he and Leo had suffered a seven-figure loss. Then Leo ended their friendship for no reason.

The pain of his friend's betrayal still had the power to punch quite a hole through his stomach. That was why it never paid to trust people. Anyone you let in eventually stomped all over you.

"No!" She huffed a sigh of frustration and shut her eyes for a beat, clearly trying to come up with a snappy response. Good luck with that. There wasn't one.

But she tried anyway. "Because I single-handedly helped two people find each other and fall in love. Something real and lasting happened before your eyes and you had a front-row seat. Leo and Dannie are remarkably compatible and share values. That's what my computer does. Matches people according to who they are."

"The magic you alluded to earlier," Dax commented with raised eyebrows. "Right? It's all smoke and mirrors, though. You tell these people they're compatible and they fall for it. The power of suggestion. Quite brilliant, actually."

And he meant it. If anyone knew the benefit of smoke and mirrors, he did. It kept everyone distracted from what was really going on behind the curtain, where the mess was.

A red stain spilled across Elise's cheeks, but she didn't back down. "You're a cynical man, Dax Wakefield. Just because you don't believe in happily ever after doesn't mean it can't happen."

"True." He conceded the point with a nod. "And false. I readily admit to being cynical but happily ever after is a myth. Long-term relationships consist of two people who've agreed to put up with each other. No ridiculous lies about loving each other forever required."

"That's…" Apparently she couldn't come up with a word to describe it. So he helped her out.

"Reality?"

His mother had proven it by walking out on his father when Dax was seven. His father had never recovered from the hope she'd eventually come back. Poor sap.

"Sad," she corrected with a brittle smile. "You must be so lonely."

He blinked. "That's one I've never been called before. I could have five different dates lined up for tonight in about thirty seconds."

"Oh, you're in worse shape than I thought." With another slide of her legs that Dax couldn't quite ignore, she leaned toward him. "You need to meet the love of your life. Immediately. I can help you."

His own bark of laughter startled him. Because it wasn't funny. "Which part wasn't clear? The part where I said you were a phony or the part where I don't believe in love?"

"It was all very clear," she said quietly. "You're trying to prove my business, my life's work, is a sham. You can't, because I can find the darkest of hearts a match. Even yours. You want to prove something? Put your name in my computer."

Double ouch. He'd been bamboozled. And he'd never seen it coming.

Against all odds, he dredged up a healthy amount of respect for Elise Arundel.

Hell. He actually kind of liked her style.

Elise wiped her clammy hands on her skirt and prayed the pompous Mr. Wakefield didn't notice. This was not the scripted, safe interview she'd been promised or she never would have agreed to sit on this stage under all these burning hot lights, with what felt like a million pairs of eyes boring a hole through her.

Thinking on her feet was not her strong suit.

Neither was dealing with wealthy, spoiled, too-handsome, arrogant playboys who despised everything she believed in.

And she'd just invited him to test her skills. Had she accidentally inhaled paint thinner?

It hardly mattered. He'd never take her up on it. Guys like Dax didn't darken the door of a matchmaker. Shallow, unemotional relationships were a snap to find, especially for someone who clearly had a lot of practice enticing women into bed. And was likely an ace at keeping them there.

Dax stroked his jaw absently and contemplated her. "Are you offering to find me a match?"

"Not just a match," she corrected immediately and tore her gaze from the thumb running under his chiseled cheekbone. "True love. My gig is happily ever after."

Yes. It was, and she hadn't failed one single couple yet. She wasn't about to start today.

Matching hearts fulfilled her in so many ways. It almost made up for not finding her own match. But hope sprang eternal. If her mother's five marriages and dozens of affairs hadn't squeezed optimism and a belief in the power of love out of her, Dax Wakefield couldn't kill them either.

"So tell me about your own happily ever after. Is Mr. Arundel your one true love?"

"I'm single," she admitted readily. It was a common question from clients who wanted her credentials and the standard answer came easily now. "But it's not a commentary on my services. You don't decide against using a travel agent just because she hasn't been to the resort you're booking, right?"

"Right. But I would wonder why she became a travel agent if she doesn't ever get on a plane."

The crowd snickered and the muscles in her legs tensed. *Oh, spotlight how do I hate thee? Let me count the ways...*

She'd be happy to get on a plane if the right man came along. But clients were always right for someone else, not her, and well...she wasn't the best at walking up to interesting men in public and introducing herself. Friday nights with a chick flick always seemed safer than battling the doubts that she wasn't quite good enough, successful enough, or thin enough for dating.

She'd only agreed to this interview to promote her business. It was a necessary evil, and nothing other than EA International's success could entice her into making such a public spectacle.

"I always fly first class myself, Mr. Wakefield," she responded and if only her voice hadn't squeaked, the delivery would have been perfect. "As soon as you're ready to board, see me and I'll put you on the right plane in the right seat to the right destination.

"What do I have to do?" he asked. "Fill out a profile online?"

Was he actually considering it? She swallowed and the

really bad feeling she'd tamped down earlier roared back into her chest.

Talk him out of it.

It was a stupid idea in the first place. But how else could she have responded? He was disparaging not only her profession but a company with her name on it.

"Online profiles don't work," she said. "In order to find your soul mate, I have to know *you*. Personally."

Dax's eyelids drifted lower and he flashed a slumberous smile that absolutely should not have sent a zing through her stomach. "That sounds intriguing. Just how personal does this get, Ms. Arundel?"

Was he *flirting?* Well, she wasn't. This was cold, hard business. "Very. I ask a series of intensive questions. By the time I'm finished, I'll know you better than your own mother."

Something dark skittered through Dax's eyes but he covered it swiftly. "Tall order. But I don't kiss and tell, especially not to my mama. If I do this, what happens if I don't find true love? You'll be exposed as a fraud. Are you sure you're up for that?"

"I'm not worried," she lied. "The only thing I ask is that you take this seriously. No cheating. If you commit to the process and don't find true love, do your best to spread word far and wide that I'm not as good as I say I am."

But she *was* that good. She'd written the matching algorithm herself, pouring countless hours into the code until it was bulletproof. People often perplexed her, but a program either worked or it didn't, and she never gave up until she fixed the bug. Numbers were her refuge, her place of peace.

A well-written line of code didn't care how many chocolate bars she ate. Or how easily chocolate settled on her hips.

"That's quite a deal." His gaze narrowed. "But it's too easy. There's no way I can lose."

Because he believed she was pulling a fast one on her clients and that he'd never fall for it. "You're right. You don't lose either way. If you don't find love, you get to tear my business apart in whatever way makes sense to you. If you do find love, well…" She shrugged. "You'll be happy. And you'll owe me."

One brow quirked up and she refused to find it charming.

"Love isn't its own reward?"

He was toying with her. And he wasn't going to get away with it. "I run a business, Mr. Wakefield. Surely you can appreciate that I have expenses. Smoke and mirrors aren't free."

His rich laugh hit her crossways. Yeah, he had a nice laugh. It was the only nice anything he had that she'd admit to noticing. Dannie had certainly hit the mark when she described Dax Wakefield to Elise as "yummy with an extra helping of cocky and a side of reptile."

"Careful, Ms. Arundel. You don't want to give away all your secrets on the morning news."

He shook his head, and his carefully coiffed hair bounced back into place. A guy as well put-together as Dax Wakefield hadn't even needed an hour with a makeup artist to be camera-ready. It was so unfair.

"I'm not giving anything away. Especially not my matchmaking abilities." Elise sat back in her chair. The farther away she was from Pretty Boy, the better. "So if you find true love, you'll agree to advertise my business. As a satisfied client."

His eyebrows shot up and the evidence of surprise gave her a little thrill that she wasn't at all ashamed to wallow in.

If this had been about anything other than EA International, the company she'd breathed life into for seven years, she'd have been at a loss for words, stumbling around looking for the exit.

But attacking her business made it personal. And for what? Because his friend had broken the guy code? Dax needed someone to blame for Leo's falling in love with Dannie, obviously, not that he'd admit it. Elise made a convenient scapegoat.

"You want me to advertise your services?" Incredulity laced his deep voice.

"If you find love, sure. I should get something out of this experiment, too. A satisfied client is the best reference." A satisfied client who'd previously denounced her skill set in public was worth more than a million dollars in advertising. "I'll even waive my fee if you do."

"Now you've got me curious. What's the going rate for true love these days?"

"Five hundred thousand dollars," she said flatly.

"That's outrageous." But he looked impressed nonetheless. About time she got his attention.

"I have dozens of clients who disagree. I guarantee my fees, too. If you don't find your soul mate, I refund your money. Well, not yours," she conceded with a nod. "You get to put me out of business."

That's when she realized her mistake. You could only find a soul mate for someone who had a soul. Dax Wakefield had obviously sold his a long time ago. This was never going to work. Her code would probably chew him up and spit him out.

She had to get off this stage before all these eyes and lights and camera lenses baked her like a pie.

Rubbing his hands together with something resembling glee, he winked. "A proposition I can't lose. I'm so on board with that, I'll even do you one better than a simple reference. Five hundred K buys a fifteen-second spot during the Super Bowl. If you pull a rabbit out of your hat and match me with my true love, I'll sing your praises right before halftime in a commercial starring *moi*."

"You will not." She let her gaze travel over his smooth, too-handsome face, searching for a clue to his real intentions.

Nothing but sincerity radiated back. "I will. Except I won't have to. You'll need a lot more than smoke and mirrors to win."

Win. As though this was a race.

"Why, because even if you fall in love, you'll pretend you haven't?"

A lethal edge sharpened his expression. "I gave you my word, Ms. Arundel. I might be a cynic, but I'm not a liar."

She'd offended him. His edges smoothed out so quickly, she would have thought she'd imagined it. But she knew what she'd seen. Dax Wakefield would not allow himself to win any other way than fair and square. And that decided it.

This…contest between them was about *her* as much as it was about EA International. As much about Dax's views on love and relationships versus hers. If she matched him with his soul mate—not if, *when*—she'd prove once and for all that it didn't matter what she looked like on the outside. Matching people who wanted to fall in love was easy. Finding a match for a self-professed cynic would be a stellar achievement worthy of everyone's praise.

Her brain was her best asset and she'd demonstrate it publicly. The short fat girl inside who wanted her mother to love her regardless of Elise's weight and height would finally be vanquished.

"Then it's a deal." Without hesitation, she slid her hand into his and shook on it.

Something bold and electric passed between them, but she refused to even glance at their joined fingers. Unfortunately, whatever it was that felt dangerous and the slightest bit thrilling came from deep inside her and needed only Dax's dark gaze to intensify it.

Oh, goodness. What had she just agreed to?

Two

The uncut footage was exceptional. Elise Arundel glowed on camera, just as Dax thought she would. The woman was stunning, animated. A real live wire. He peered at the monitor over the producer's shoulder and earned a withering glare from the man trying to do his job.

"Fine," Dax conceded with a nod to the producer. "Finish editing it and air the interview. It's solid."

Dallas's answer to a fairy godmother was going to wave her magic wand and give KDLS the highest ratings the news show had seen in two weeks. Maybe even in this whole fiscal year.

It was totally worth having to go through the motions of whatever ridiculous process Ms. Arundel cooked up. The failure to find him a soul mate would be so humiliating, Dax might not even go through with denouncing her company afterward.

But that all depended on how miserable Elise deliberately tried to make him. He had no doubt she'd give it her best shot.

Within fifteen minutes, the producer had the interview clip queued and ready. The station crew watched it unfold on the monitors. As Dax hammered the matchmaker, she held her own. The camera even captured the one instance she'd caught him off balance.

Okay, so it had happened twice, but no one other than

Dax would notice—he was nothing if not a master at ensuring that everyone saw him precisely as he meant for them to.

Elise Arundel was something else, he'd give her that.

Shame those great legs were attached to such a misguided romantic, whom he should hate a lot more than he actually did. She'd refused to take any crap and the one-up she'd laid on him with the satisfied client bit…well, she'd done exactly what he'd have done in her shoes.

It had been kind of awesome. Or it would have been if he'd escaped without agreeing to put his name in her computer.

Dax spent the rest of the day immersed in meetings with the station crew, hammering each department as easily as he had Elise. They had some preliminary numbers by lunch on the fairy godmother interview—and they were very good indeed—but one stellar day of ratings would not begin to make up for the last quarter.

As Dax slid into the driver's seat of his Audi, his phone beeped and he thumbed up the text message.

Jenna: You could have dates lined up with five different women? Since you're about to meet the love of your life…which is apparently not me…let's make it four. I never want to see you again.

Dax cursed. How bad was it that he'd forgotten Jenna would most assuredly watch the program? Maybe the worse crime was the fact that he'd forgotten entirely about the redhead he'd been dating for four—no, five—weeks. Or was it closer to six?

He cursed again. That relationship had stretched past its expiration date, but he'd been reluctant to give it up. Obviously Jenna had read more into it than she should have. They'd been having fun and he'd told her that was the extent of it. Regardless, she deserved better than to find out she had more of an investment than Dax from a TV program.

He was officially the worst sort of dog and should be shot.

Next time, he'd be clearer up front—Dax Wakefield subscribed to the Pleasure Principle. He liked his women fun, sexy and above all, unattached. Anything deeper than that was work, which he had enough of. Women should be about decadent indulgence. If it didn't feel good, why do it?

He drove home to the loft he'd bought in Deep Ellum before it was trendy and mentally scrolled through his contacts for just such a woman. Not one name jumped out. Probably every woman he'd ever spoken to had seen the clip. Didn't seem as if there were much point in getting shot down a few more times tonight.

But jeez, spending the night alone sucked.

Stomach growling, Dax dumped his messenger bag at the door and strode to the stainless-steel-and-black-granite kitchen to survey the contents of his cupboard.

While pasta boiled, he amused himself by recalling Elise's diabolical smile as she suggested Dax put his name in her computer. Sweet dreams were made of dark-haired, petite women.

He wasn't looking forward to being grilled about his favorite color and where he went to college so Ms. Arundel could pull a random woman's name out of her computer. But he was, oddly enough, looking forward to sparring with her some more.

The next morning, Dax opted to drive to his office downtown. He usually walked, both to get in the exercise and to avoid dealing with Dallas traffic, but Elise had scheduled their first session at the mutually agreed-upon time of 10:00 a.m.

By nine forty-seven, he'd participated in three conference calls, signed a contract for the purchase of a regional newspaper, read and replied to an in-box full of emails, and drunk two cups of coffee. Dax lived for Wakefield Media.

And now he'd have to sacrifice some of his day to the Fairy Godmother. Because he said he would.

Dax's mother was a coldhearted, untrustworthy woman, but in leaving, had taught him the importance of living up to your word. That was why he rarely promised anything.

EA International resided in a tasteful two-story office building in Uptown. The clean, low-key logo on the door spoke of elegance and sophistication, exactly the right tone to strike when your clients were high-powered executives and entrepreneurs.

The receptionist took his name. Dax proceeded to wait until finally she showed him to a room with two leather chairs and a low table strewn with picture books, one sporting a blue-and-gold fish on the cover and another, a waterfall.

Boring. Did Ms. Arundel hope to lull her clients into a semi-stupor while she let them cool their heels? Looked as though he was about to find out.

Elise clacked into the room, high heels against the hardwood floor announcing her presence. He glanced up slowly, taking in her heels, those well-built legs, her form-fitting scarlet skirt and jacket. Normally he liked taller women, but couldn't remember why just then. He kept going, thoroughly enjoying the trip to her face, which he'd forgotten was so arresting.

Her energy swept across him and prickled his skin, unnerving him for a moment. "You're late."

Her composed expression didn't waver. "You were late first."

Not that late. Ten minutes. Maybe. Regardless, she'd made him wait in this pseudo dentist's office on purpose. Score one for the matchmaker. "Trying to teach me a lesson?"

"I assumed you weren't going to show and took a call.

I am running a business here." She settled into the second chair and her knee grazed his.

She didn't even seem to notice. His knee tingled but she simply crossed her legs and bounced one siren-red pump casually.

Just as casually, Dax tossed the fish book back on the table. "Busy day. The show does not go on without a lot of hands-on from yours truly."

But that didn't really excuse his tardiness. They were both business owners and he'd disrespected her. Unintentionally, but point taken.

"You committed to this. The profile session takes several hours. Put up or shut up."

Hours? He nearly groaned. How could it possibly take that long to find out he liked football, hated the Dallas Cowboys, drank beer but only dark and imported, and preferred the beach to the mountains?

Dax drew out his phone. "Give me your cell phone number." One of her eyebrows lowered and it was so cute, he laughed. "I'm not going to prank call you. If this is going to take hours, we'll have to split up the sessions. Then I can text you if I'm going to be late to the next one."

"Really?"

He shrugged, not certain why the derision in her tone raised his hackles. "Most women think it's considerate to let them know if you're held up. My apologies for assuming you fell into the category of females who appreciate a considerate man."

"Apology accepted. Now you know I'm in the category of woman who thinks texting is a cop-out. Try an actual phone call sometime." She smiled, baring her teeth, which softened the message not at all. "Better yet, just be punctual. Period."

She'd *accepted* his quasi-apology, as if he'd meant to really convey regret instead of sarcasm.

"Personal questions and punctuality?" He *tsk*ed to cover what he suspected might be another laugh trying to get out. When was the last time he'd been taken to task so expertly? Like never. "You drive a hard bargain, Ms. Arundel."

And she'd managed to evade giving out her digits. Slick. Not that he really wanted to call her. But still. It was kind of an amusing turnabout to be refused an attractive woman's phone number.

"You can call me Elise."

"Really?" It was petty repetition of her earlier succinct response. But in his shock, he'd let it slip.

"We're going to be working together. I'd like it if you were more comfortable with me. Hopefully it'll help you be more honest when answering the profile questions."

What was it about her and the truth? Did he look that much like a guy who skated the edge between black and white? "I told you I'm not a liar, whether I call you Elise, Ms. Arundel or sweetheart."

The hardness in her gaze melted, turning her irises a gooey shade of chocolate, and she sighed. "My turn to apologize. I can tell you don't want to be here and I'm a little touchy about it."

It was a rare woman who saw something other than what he meant for her to, and he did not want Elise to know anything about him, let alone against his will. Time for a little damage control.

"My turn to be confused. I do want to be here or I wouldn't have agreed to our deal. Why would you think otherwise?"

She evaluated his expression for a moment and tucked the straight fall of dark hair behind her ear, revealing a pale column of neck he had an unexplainable urge to explore. See if he could melt those hard eyes a little more. Unadulterated need coiled in his belly.

Down, boy.

Elise hated him. He didn't like her or anything she stood for. He was here to be matched with a woman who would be the next in a long line of ex-girlfriends and then declare EA International fraudulent. Because there was no way he'd lose this wager.

"Usually when someone is late, it's psychological," she said with a small tilt of her head, as if she'd found a puzzle to solve but couldn't quite get the right angle to view it.

"Are you trying to analyze me?"

She scowled. "It's not bargain-basement analysis. I have a degree in psychology."

"Yeah? Me, too."

They stared at each other for a moment, long enough for the intense spike in his abdomen to kick-start his perverse gene.

What was it about a smart woman that never failed to intrigue the hell out of him?

She broke eye contact and scribbled furiously in her notebook, color in her cheeks heightened.

She'd been affected by the heat, too.

He wanted to know more about Elise Arundel without divulging anything about himself that wasn't surface-level inanity.

"The information about my major was a freebie," he said. "Anything else personal you want to know is going to cost you."

If they were talking about Elise—and didn't every woman on the planet prefer to talk about herself?—Dax wouldn't inadvertently reveal privileged information. That curtain was closed, and no one got to see backstage.

Elise was almost afraid to ask. "Cost me what?"

When Dax's smoke-colored eyes zeroed in on her, she was positive she should be both afraid *and* sorry. His irises weren't the black smoke of an angry forest fire, but the wispy gray of a late November hearth fire that had just begun to blaze. The kind of fire that promised many delicious, warm things to come. And could easily burn down the entire block if left unchecked.

"It'll cost you a response in kind. Whatever you ask me, you have to answer, too."

"That's not how this works. I'm not trying to match myself."

Though she'd been in the system for seven years.

She'd entered her profile first, building the code around the questions and answers. On the off chance a match came through, well, there was nothing wrong with finding her soul mate with her own process, was there?

"Come on. Be a sport. It'll help me be more comfortable with baring my soul to you."

She shook her head hard enough to flip the ends of her hair into her mouth. "The questions are not all that soul-baring."

Scrambling wasn't her forte any more than thinking on her feet, because that was a total misrepresentation. The questions were designed to strip away surface-level BS and find the real person underneath. If that wasn't soul-baring, she didn't know what was. How else could the algorithm find a perfect match? The devil was in the details, and she had a feeling Dax's details could upstage Satan himself.

"Let's find out," he said easily. "What's the first one?"

"Name," she croaked.

"Daxton Ryan Wakefield. Daxton is my grandmother's maiden name. Ryan is my father's name." He shuddered in mock terror. "I feel exposed sharing my history with a virtual stranger. Help a guy out. Your turn."

This was so not a good idea. But he'd threatened her business, her livelihood. To prove her skills, his profile had to be right. Otherwise, he might be matched with an almost–soul mate or worse, someone completely incompatible. Dax wasn't a typical paying client, and she couldn't treat him like one. What was the harm in throwing him one bone? It wasn't as if she had to answer all of the questions, just enough to get him talking.

"Shannon Elise Arundel."

How in the world had that slipped out? She hadn't told anyone that her real first name was Shannon in years. Her shudder of terror wasn't faked.

Shannon, put down that cake. Shannon, have you weighed yourself today? Shannon, you might be vertically challenged but you don't have to be horizontally challenged too.

The words were always delivered with the disapproving frown her mother saved for occasions of great disappointment. Frowning caused wrinkles and Brenna Burke hated wrinkles more than photographers.

Dax circled his finger in a get-on-with-the-rest motion. "No comment about how your father was Irish and wanted to make sure you had a bit of the old country in your name?"

"Nope. My name is very boring."

Her mother was the Irish one, with milky skin and glowing red hair that graced magazine covers and runways for twenty years. Brenna Burke, one of the world's original supermodels, had given birth to a short Black Irish daughter prone to gaining weight by simply looking at cookies. It was a sin of the highest order in Brenna's mind that Elise had a brain instead of beauty.

Dax quirked his mouth in feigned disappointment. "That's okay. We can't all have interesting stories attached to our names. Where did you grow up?"

"This is not a date." The eye roll happened involuntarily, but the exasperation in her voice was deliberate. "I'm asking the questions."

"It's kind of like a date," he mused brightly as if the

thought fascinated him. "Getting to know each other. Awkward silences. Both of us dressed just a little bit more carefully than normal."

She glanced down at her BCBG suit, which she'd snipped the tags from that morning. Because red made her feel strong and fierce, and a session with Dax called for both. So what? "This is how I dress every day."

Now she felt self-conscious. Did the suit and five-inch stilettos seem as though she was trying too hard?

"Then I'm really looking forward to seeing what you look like tomorrow." He waggled his brows.

"Let's move on," she said before Dax drove her insane. "This is not a date, nor is it kind of like a date, and I'm getting to know you, not the other way around. So I can find you a match."

"Too bad. A date is the best place to see me in action." When she snorted, he inclined his head with a mischievous smile. "That's not what I meant, but since you started it, my favorite part of dates is anticipating the first kiss. What's yours?"

She lifted her gaze from his parted lips and blinked at the rising heat in his expression. The man had no shame. Flirting with his matchmaker, whose business he was also trying to destroy.

"Jedi mind tricks only work on the weak-minded. Tell me more about what you like about dating. It's a great place to start."

He grinned and winked. "Deflection only works on those who graduated at the bottom of their class. But I'll let it pass this time. I like long walks on the beach, hot tubs and dinner for two on the terrace."

Clearly this was slated to be the battle of who had the better psychology degree. Fine. *You want to play, let's play.*

"Why don't you try again, but this time without the *Love*

Connection sound bite? I didn't ask what you liked to *do* on dates. I asked what you like about *dating*."

"I like sex," he said flatly. "In order to get that, dating is a tiresome requirement. Is that what you're looking for?"

"Not really. Plus it's not true." His irises flashed from hearth-fire smoke to forest-fire smoke instantly and she backpedaled. "I don't mean you're lying. Get a grip. I mean, you don't have to date someone to have sex. Lots of women would gladly line up for a roll in the sheets with a successful, sophisticated man."

Who had a face too beautiful to be real, the physique of an elite athlete and eyelashes her mother would kill for. Not that she'd noticed.

"Would you?"

"I don't do one-night stands."

She frowned. When was the last time she'd even been on a date? Oh, yeah, six months ago—Kory, with a *K*. She should have known that one wouldn't work out the instant he'd introduced himself as such.

"There you go. A woman who would isn't worth my time."

Her head snapped back. Was that a compliment? More flirting? The truth?

"So you aren't just looking for sex. You want to put some effort into a relationship. Have drinks, spend some time together. And you want to know things about the women you date, their history, their likes and dislikes. Why?"

He contemplated her as he sat back in his chair, thumb to his jaw, a habit she'd noticed he fell into when she made the wheels in his convoluted head turn. Good.

"You're much more talented than I imagined," he allowed with a jerk of his chin. "I'm so impressed, I'm going to tell you why. It's so I can buy her something she'd genuinely appreciate and give it to her on our next date."

So the woman in question would sleep with him, no

doubt. And it probably never failed. "Another example of a considerate man?"

"Sure. Women like to be treated well. I like women. Ergo, it's no chore to do my best to make them happy."

There had to be something wrong with that, but she couldn't find the fault to save her life. Plus, the glow from his compliment still burned brightly. "If only all men subscribed to that theory. What do you find attractive in a woman?"

"Brains," he said instantly and she didn't even bother to write that down.

"You can't tell if a woman has brains from across the room," she responded drily. "If you walk into a bar, who catches your eye?"

"I don't meet women in bars, and last time I walked into one, I got four stitches right here." He tapped his left eyebrow, which was bisected by a faint line, and his chagrined smile was so infectious, she couldn't help but laugh.

"Okay, you win that round. But I have to note something. Redhead, blonde? Voluptuous, athletic?"

"Would you believe it if I said I have no preference? Or at least that used to be true." He swept her with a sizzling once-over that curled her toes involuntarily. "I might be reconsidering."

"The more you try to unsettle me, the less it works," she advised him and cursed the catch in her throat that told him her actual state far better than her words. This was ridiculous and getting them nowhere. "You promised to take this seriously and all I know about you so far is that distraction and verbal sleight of hand are your standard operating procedure. What are you hiding?"

The flicker of astonishment darting through his expression vanished when a knock sounded on the door. Dang it. She'd hardly begun to dig into the good stuff.

Elise's assistant, Angie, stuck her head in and said, "Your next appointment is here."

Both she and Dax shot startled glances at their watches. When he hadn't shown, she'd scheduled another appointment. How had the minutes vanished so quickly?

He stood immediately. "I'm late for a meeting."

What did it say that they'd both lost track of the hour? She nodded. "Tomorrow, then. Same time, same bat channel?"

He grinned. "You've got yourself a date, Ms. Arundel."

Three

Dax whistled a nameless tune as he pulled open the door to EA International. Deliberately late, and not at all sorry.

Today, he was in charge, and Elise would not get the drop on him again. He'd give her enough information to make it seem that he was going along willingly, simultaneously dragging out their interaction a little longer. Long enough to figure out what about Elise got under his skin, anyway. Then he was done here.

"Morning, Angie." Dax smiled at the receptionist and handed her the vase of stargazer lilies he'd brought. "For you. Is Ms. Arundel's calendar free?"

Angie moistened her lips and smiled in return. "Cleared, just as you requested yesterday. Thanks for the flowers. They're beautiful."

"I'll show myself to Ms. Arundel's office." He winked. "Don't tell her I'm coming. It's a surprise."

When Dax blew through the door of Elise's office, the location of which he'd noted yesterday on his way out, the look on her face was more wary disbelief than surprise.

"Look what the cat dragged in," was all she said and ignored him in favor of typing on her laptop. The clacking was too rhythmic to produce actual comprehensible sentences.

Faking it. For him. Warmed his heart.

"I'm taking you to lunch," he informed her. "Get your handbag and shut that thing down."

That earned her attention. She pierced him with that laser-sharp gaze he suspected had the power to drill right through his skull and read his mind like a book. "Are you this egotistical with all women? I'm shocked you ever get a second date."

"Yet I do. Have lunch with me and you'll find out why." He quirked a brow at her and pulled out the big guns. "Unless you're afraid."

She didn't scowl, didn't immediately negate the statement. Instead, she smiled and clicked the laptop closed. "Can't stand being under the spotlight, can you? If you don't like the setting I use to walk through the profile questions, just tell me."

A spontaneous and unexpected laugh shot from his mouth. Why was it such a surprise that she was on to him?

He held up both hands. "I surrender. You're right. That little room with the fish book is like being in therapy. Restaurants are more relaxed."

Elise opened a desk drawer and withdrew a brown leather bag. "Since my schedule is mysteriously clear, lunch it is. On one condition." She cocked her head, sending her dark hair swinging against her chin. "Don't evade, change the subject or try to outsmart me. Answer the questions so we can be done."

"Aww. You're not enjoying this?" He was. It was the most fun he'd had with a woman he wasn't dating in his life.

"You're quite honestly the most difficult, disturbing, contrary client I've ever dealt with." She swept passed him in a cloud of unidentifiable perfume that hit him in the solar plexus, and then she shot back over her shoulder, "Which means you're paying. But I'm driving."

He grinned and followed her to the parking lot, then slid

into the passenger seat of the sleek Corvette she motioned to. He would have opened her door, but she beat him to it.

New car smell wrapped around him. "Nice ride. I pegged you for more of a Toyota girl."

She shrugged. "Even fairy godmothers like to arrive at the ball in style."

"I'm not threatened by a woman driving, by the way." He crossed his arms so he didn't accidentally brush shoulders with Elise. The seats were really close together. Perfect for lovers. Not so good for business associates. "Just in case you were worried."

Elise selected an out-of-the-way bistro-type place without asking him and told the hostess they'd prefer to sit outside, also without his input. The wrought iron chairs and tables on the terrace added French charm and the wine list was passable, so he didn't mind. But two could play that game, so he ordered a bottle of Chianti and nodded to the waiter to pour Elise a glass whether she wanted one or not.

"To loosen you up?" she asked pertly and picked up her glass to sniff the bloodred wine with appreciation.

"Nah. To loosen you up." He dinged their rims together and watched her drink. Elise liked red wine. He filed that tidbit away. "I didn't actually agree to your condition, you know."

"I noticed. I'm banking on the fact that you're a busy man and can't continually take time away from work to finish something you don't want to be doing in the first place. So don't disappoint me. What's the difference between love, romance and sex?"

Dax choked on the wine he'd just swallowed and spent his time recovering. "Give a guy a warning before you lay that kind of question on him."

"Warning. Question imminent. Warning. Question imminent," she intoned in such a perfect robot voice, he sputtered over a second sip, laughing this time.

For an uptight matchmaker, she had an offbeat sense of humor. He liked it. More than he should. It was starting to affect his focus and the more Elise charmed him, the less he remembered why it was important to punish her for Leo's defection.

"Let's see," he said brusquely. "Fiction, Sade and yes, please."

"Excuse me?"

"The answer to your question. Love equals fiction, Sade is romantic music and critical to set the mood, and I would assume 'yes, please' is self-explanatory in relation to sex."

"That's not precisely what I was looking for."

"Then tell me what you would say. So I have an example to go by."

"You never give up, do you?"

"Took you long enough to figure that out. So?" he prompted with raised eyebrows.

She sighed. "They're intertwined so closely you can't remove one without destroying the value of the other two."

"That's a loaded statement. Tell me more before I proceed to tear it apart." He propped his chin on his hand and ignored the halibut a waiter placed in front of him, which he scarcely recalled ordering.

Her lips mushed together in apparent indecision. Or frustration. Hard to tell with her.

"You can have sex without being in love or putting on romantic music. But it's so much better with both. Without love and romance, sex is meaningless and empty."

As she warmed to the topic, her expression softened and that, plus the provocative subject matter, plus the warm breeze playing with her hair, plus...whatever it was about her that drew him all swirled together and spread like a sip of very old, very rare cognac in his chest. "Go on."

"On the flip side, you can certainly make a romantic gesture toward someone you're in love with and not end up in bed. But the fact that you've been intimate magnifies it. Makes it more romantic. See what I mean?"

"Philosophy." He nodded sagely and wondered if the thing going on inside might be a heart attack. "I see. You want to understand how I feel about the three, not give you examples. Rookie mistake. Won't happen again."

"Ha. You did it on purpose so you could probe me."

That was so close to the truth, the back of his neck heated. Next his ears would turn red and no woman got to have that strong of an effect on him. "Yeah, well, guess what? I like the spotlight. When you accused me of that earlier, it was nothing but a classic case of projection. You don't like the spotlight so you assumed that was the reason I didn't want to sit under yours."

She didn't so much as flinch. "Then what is the reason you went to such great lengths to get me out of the office?"

The shrewd glint in the depths of those chocolaty irises tipped him off that he hadn't been as slick with the schedule-clearing as he believed. Odds were, she'd also figured out that she'd hit a couple of nerves yesterday and lunch was designed to prevent that from happening again.

"That's your turf." He waved at the crowd of tables, people and ambiance. "This is mine."

"And I'm on it, with nary a peep. Cut me some slack. Tell me what your ideal mate brings to the relationship."

"A lack of interest in what's behind the curtain," he said instantly as if the answer had been there all along. Though he'd never so much as thought about the question, not once, and certainly wouldn't have told her if she hadn't made the excellent point about the turf change.

But lack of interest wasn't quite right. It was more the ability to turn a blind eye. Someone who saw through the curtain and didn't care that backstage resembled post-tornado wreckage.

Was that why he broke up with women after the standard four weeks—none thus far had that X-ray-vision-slash-blind-eye quality?

"Good." Elise scribbled in her ever-present notebook. "Now tell me what you bring to her."

When she'd called the questions intensive, she wasn't kidding. "What, presents aren't enough?"

"Don't be flip. Unless you want me to assume you bring nothing to a relationship and that's why you shy away from them." A light dawned in her eyes. "Oh. That's it, isn't it? You don't think you have anything to offer."

"Wait a minute. That's not what I said." This conversation had veered way too far off the rails for comfort.

He'd agreed to this ridiculous idea of being matched only because he never thought it would work. Instead, Elise challenged his deep-seated beliefs at every turn with a series of below-the-belt hits. That was not supposed to happen.

"Then say what you mean," she suggested quietly. "For once. If you found that woman, the one who didn't care what was behind your curtain, what do you have to offer her in return?"

"I don't know." It was the most honest answer he could give. And the most unsettling.

He shoveled food in his mouth in case she asked a follow-up question.

What *did* he have to offer in a relationship? He'd never considered it important to examine, largely because he never intended to have a relationship. But he felt deficient all at once.

"Fair enough. I get that these questions are designed to help people who are looking for love. You're not. So we'll move on to the lightning round." Her sunny tone said she knew she was letting him off the hook and it was okay.

Oddly grateful, he nodded and relaxed. "I rule at lightning rounds."

"We'll see, Mr. Wakefield. Glass half-full, or half-empty?"

"Technically, it's always full of both air and water." Her

laugh rumbled through him and he breathed a little easier. Things were clicking along at a much safer level now, and eating held more appeal.

"That's a good one. Apple or banana?"

"What is that, a Freudian question? Apple, of course."

"Actually, apples have biblical connotations. I might interpret it as you can't stay away from the tree of knowledge," she said with a smirk. "What relieves stress?"

"Sex."

She rolled her eyes. "I probably didn't need to ask that one. Do you believe in karma?"

These were easy, surface-level questions. She should have started with them. "No way. Lots of people never get what's coming to them."

"That is *so* true." She chuckled with appreciation and shook her head.

"Don't freak out but I do believe you're enjoying this after all."

Her smile slipped but she didn't look away. This might not be a date, but he couldn't deny that lunch with Elise was the most interesting experience he'd had with a woman, period. Even ones he was dating.

The longer this went on, the harder it was going to be to denounce her publicly. She was good—much better than he'd prepared for—and to criticize her abilities would likely reflect just as poorly on him as it did her.

Worse, he was afraid he'd started to like her. He should probably do something about that before she got too far under his skin.

By one o'clock, Elise's side hurt from laughing. Wine at lunch should be banned. Or required. She couldn't decide which.

"I have to get back to the office," she said reluctantly.

Reluctantly? She had a ton of things to do. And this

was lunch with Dax. Whom she hated…or rather didn't like very much. Actually, he was pretty funny and maybe a little charming. Of course he was—he had lots of practice wooing women.

Dax made a face. "Yeah. Duty calls."

He stood and gallantly took her hand, while simultaneously pulling her chair away. It was amazingly well-coordinated. Probably because he'd done it a million times.

They strolled to the car and she pretended that she didn't notice how slowly, and she didn't immediately fish her keys from her bag. Dax put his palm on the driver's-side door, leaning against it casually, so she couldn't have opened it anyway. Deliberately on his part, she was sure.

She should call him on it.

"Tomorrow, then?" he asked.

Elise shook her head. "I'm out of the office tomorrow. I have a thing with my mother."

Brenna had an appointment with a plastic surgeon in Dallas because the ones in L.A. stopped living up to her expectations. Apparently she couldn't find one who could make her look thirty again.

"All day?" Dax seemed disappointed. "You can't squeeze in an hour for me?"

No way was he disappointed. She shook her head. The wine was affecting her more than she'd thought.

"I have to pick her up from the airport and then take her to the doctor." Oh, that might have been too much information. "I need to ask for your discretion. She wouldn't like it if she knew I was talking to others about her private affairs."

"Because your mother is famous or something?"

Elise heaved a sigh. "I assumed you checked up on me and therefore already knew I was Brenna Burke's daughter. I should have kept my mouth shut."

Stupid wine.

"Brenna Burke is your mother?" Dax whistled. "I had a poster of her above my bed when I was a teenager. The one where she wore the bikini made of leaves. Good times."

"Thanks, I needed the image in my head of you fantasizing about my mother." That's precisely why she never mentioned Brenna. Not only because of the ick factor, but also because no one ever whistled over Elise. It was demoralizing. "You know she was thirty-five in that photo, right?"

Elise called it her mother's I'm-not-old stage, when the hot runway models were closer to her nine-year-old daughter's age than Brenna's, and the offers of work had all but dried up.

I should have waited to have kids, Brenna had told her. *Mistake Number One talked me into it. Being pregnant and off the circuit ruined me.*

Bitter, aging supermodels took out their frustration on those around them, including Elise's father, dubbed Mistake Number One when he grew tired of Brenna's attitude and left. Adult Elise knew all this from her psychology classes. Still hurt, even years later.

"So?" Dax sighed lustily. "I didn't care. She was smoking hot."

"Yeah. So I've been told." She feigned sudden interest in her manicure, unable to take the appreciation for her mother in Dax's expression.

"Elise." His voice held a note of…warmth. Compassion.

Somehow, he'd steered her around, spine against the car, and then he was right there, sandwiching her between his masculine presence and the Vette.

He tipped her head up with a fist and locked those smoky irises on hers and she couldn't breathe. "Tastes change. I like to think I've evolved since I was fourteen. Older women aren't so appealing anymore."

She shrugged. "Whatever. It hardly matters."

"It does." The screeches and hums of the parking lot

and chatter of other diners faded away as he cocked his head and focused on her. "I hurt your feelings. I'm sorry."

How in the world had he figured that out? Somehow, that fact alone made it easy to admit the truth. She probably couldn't have hidden it anyway. "It's hard to have a mother known for her looks when you're so average, you know?"

He shifted closer, though she would have sworn there wasn't much space between them in the first place.

"You're the least average woman I've ever met, and you know what else? Beauty fades. That's why it's important to use what's up here." He circled an index finger around her temple, oh so slowly, and the electrified feel of his touch on her skin spread through her entire body.

"That's my line," she murmured. "I went to college and started my own business because I never wanted a life where my looks mattered."

After watching her mother crash and burn with Mistake Number Two and then Three without finding the happiness she seemed to want so desperately, Elise learned early on that a relationship built on physical attraction didn't work. It also taught her that outward appearance hardly factored in matters of the heart.

Compatibility and striving to find someone who made you better were the keys to a relationship. She'd built EA International on those principles, and it hadn't failed yet.

Dax was so close; she inhaled his exotic scent on her next breath. It screamed *male—and how.*

"Me, too. Unlike your mother, I never wanted to make a career out of modeling." When her eyebrows shot up, he chuckled. "Figured you checked up on me and knew that Calvin Klein put me through college. Guess you'll be looking me up when you get home."

A lit stick of dynamite between her and the laptop couldn't stop that from happening. "My mother put me through college. Reluctantly, but I insisted."

Funny how they'd both paid for college with modeling dollars and then took similar paths to chart their own destinies. She never would have guessed they had anything in common, let alone such important guiding experiences.

Dax's gaze drifted lower and focused on her mouth. Because he was thinking about kissing her. She could read it all over his expression.

Emergency. This wasn't a date. She'd led him on somehow. They didn't like each other, and worse, he shied away from everything she desired—love, marriage, a soul mate. She was supposed to be matching him with one of her clients.

First and foremost, she'd given him permission to *ruin her business* if he didn't find the love of his life. And she was compromising the entire thing.

All of it swirled into a big black burst of panic. Had she lost her mind?

Ducking clumsily out of his semi-embrace, she smiled brightly. "So I'll call you to schedule the next session. Ready to go?"

His expression shuttered and he nodded. "Sure. I'll leave you my card with my number."

In awkward silence, they rode back to EA International where Dax's car was parked.

Despite knowing he thought happily ever after was a myth, despite knowing he faked interest in her as a method of distraction, despite knowing he stood to lose $500,000 and pretended to misunderstand her questions or refused to answer them strictly to prevent it—despite all that, she'd wanted him to kiss her.

Dax Wakefield was better at seducing a woman than she'd credited.

When Elise got to her office, she locked the door and sank into the chair. Her head fell forward into her cupped palms, too wined-and-Daxed to stay upright any longer. If he flipped her out this much without laying those gorgeously defined lips on hers, how much worse would it be if he'd actually done it?

She couldn't take another session with him.

Match him now.

She had enough information. Dax might have thought he was being sneaky by probing her for answers to the questions in kind but he'd revealed more about himself in the getting there than he likely realized.

While the match program booted up, Elise stuck a stick of gum in her mouth in hopes it would stave off the intense desire for chocolate. She always craved chocolate, but it was worse when she was under stress.

Maybe she should take a page from Dax and relieve her stress with sex.

But not with him. No sir.

Almost of their own accord, her fingers keyed his name into the browser. Provocative photos spilled onto the screen of a younger Dax with washboard abs and formfitting briefs scarcely covering the good parts. Her mouth went dry. The man was a former underwear model with a psychology degree, a wicked sense of humor and a multibillion-dollar media empire.

Who in the world did she have in her system to match *that?*

Usually she had a pretty good idea who the match would be ahead of time. One of the benefits of administering the profile sessions herself—she knew her clients very well.

A slice of fear ripped through her. What if the program couldn't find a match? It happened occasionally. The algorithms were so precise that sometimes clients had to wait a few months, until she entered new clients.

Dax would never accept that excuse. He'd call foul and claim victory right then and there. Either he'd crow about proving Elise a sham or worse, claim she'd withheld the name on purpose to avoid the fallout when the match wasn't the love of his life.

Newly determined, she shut down the almost-naked pictures of Dax and flipped to the profile screen. She flew through the personal information section and consulted her notes before starting on the personality questions.

That went easily, too. In fact, she didn't even have to glance at the scribbled words in her notebook.

Do you want to be in love? She typed yes. He did, he just hadn't found the right person yet, or he wouldn't have agreed to be matched. Plus, she'd watched his face when he described a woman who didn't care about whatever he hid behind his curtain. That man wanted to connect really, really badly with someone who got him.

How do you sabotage relationships? She snorted and typed "by only dating women he has no chance of falling in love with."

When she reached the last question, she breathed a sigh of relief. Not so bad. Thank goodness she wouldn't have to see him again. A quick phone call to set up his first meet with the match and she'd be done with Dax Wakefield.

She hit Save and ran the match algorithm. Results came back instantly. Fantastic. She might even treat herself to half a carton of Chunky Monkey as a reward. She clicked on the pop-up link and Dax's match was...*Elise Arundel*.

No! She blinked, but the letters didn't change.

That was so wrong, she couldn't even put words together to say how wrong.

She ran the compiler again. *Elise Arundel*.

Stomach cramping with dread, she vised her temples. That's what she got for not asking him all the questions. For letting her professional ethics slide away in the wake of the whirlwind named Dax.

He'd think she did it on purpose—because she'd started

to fall for his slick charm. If she actually told him she was his match, he'd smirk with that knowing glint in his eyes and…

She'd skewed the results. That had to be it. Talk about your Freudian slipups—she'd been thinking about the almost-kiss and the almost-naked pictures and his laugh and thus answered the questions incorrectly.

Besides, the short, fat girl inside could never be enough to change Dax Wakefield's mind about love. She had to match him with someone else.

Her fingers shook and she could hardly type, but those answers had to change. He didn't want to be in love. Total projection on her part to say that he did, exactly as he'd accused her of earlier. She fixed that one, then the next one and eventually worked her way back through the profile

There. She clicked Run and shut her eyes.

This time, the pop-up opened to reveal…Candace Waters.

Perfect. Candy was a gorgeous blonde with a high-school education. Dax would love running intellectual circles around her and Candy liked football. They'd get along famously.

No one ever had to know Elise had nearly screwed up.

Four

When an unrecognized number flashed on Dax's phone, he almost didn't answer it.

Instead of working, as he should be, he'd been watching his phone, hoping Elise might call today.

He couldn't get that moment against the car out of his head, that brief flicker in her gaze that said she didn't hate him anymore and better yet, didn't see him as a match to be pawned off on some other female. Before he'd had time to explore what she did feel, she'd bolted, leaving him to wonder if he'd imagined it.

He should call her already. It was only a conversation to schedule the next session, which would likely be the last. What was the big deal about calling? It wasn't as if she'd answer the main line at EA International anyway. He could schedule the appointment through Angie and go on with his day.

The quicker they finished the sessions, the closer Elise would be to be finding him a match, at which point he'd prove beyond a shadow of a doubt that Elise's matchmaking service fronted as a school for gold diggers. Then, the cold place inside that had developed during the rift with Leo could be warmed nicely by the flames of EA International roasting on the morning news.

A prospect that held less and less appeal the more time he spent with Elise.

The dilemma ate at him, and if he didn't see her again, he didn't have to think about it. That's why he didn't call.

But Dax answered his phone, mentally preparing to spiel off a contract's status or sales figures—pending the caller's identification. "Wakefield."

"It's Elise Arundel." The smooth syllables hit him in all the right places. "Do you have a few minutes?"

He should have called her. Elise had a sexy phone voice.

Grinning like a loon for who knew what reason, Dax settled back in his chair and put his feet out. "Depends on what for. If it's lightning round two, yes."

Elise's chuckle was a little on the nervous side. "I'm afraid that's not the reason for my call. Actually, I have good news on that front. More sessions aren't required after all. I've got your match."

Oh, wow. This thing had just become nauseatingly real.

"Already? That is good news," Dax said heartily. It *was* good news. The best. He didn't have to see Elise again, exactly as he wanted.

And a little voice inside was singing, *Liar, liar, pants on fire.*

"So," Elise chimed in quickly, "I'm calling to set up your first meet with your match, Candace. She prefers to be called Candy, though."

"Candy." That was something you ate, not someone you dated, and sounded suspiciously like a name for a coed. "She's legal, right?"

"You mean is she over the age of eighteen?" Elise's withering tone put the grin back on his face. "What kind of matchmaker do you take me for? She's twenty-eight and works as a paralegal for Browne and Morgan."

"Just checking. What's the drill? I'm supposed to call her and set up a date or something?"

"That's up to you. I've emailed her picture to you, and

I've sent yours to her. If you're both agreeable to meeting, I'd be happy to coordinate or you can go it alone from here."

Curiosity got the best of him and he shouldered the phone to his ear so he could click through his email. There it was—"Sender: Elise Arundel, Subject: Candace Waters." He opened it and a picture of Candy popped onto the screen.

Holy hell. She was *gorgeous*. Like men-falling-over-themselves-to-get-her-a-drink gorgeous. Not at all what he was expecting. "Is she one of your makeover success stories?"

If so, Elise might have a bit more magic in her wand than he'd credited.

"Not everyone is in need of a makeover. Candy came to me as is."

Nice. Not a gold digger then. He took a closer look. She was blonde-with-a-capital-B, wearing a wicked smile that promised she had the moves to back it up. He would have noticed her across the room in a heartbeat.

For the first time, he got an inkling that this whole deal might be legitimate. "She'll do."

Then he returned to planet earth. There was a much greater chance that Candy had something really wrong with her if she'd resorted to a matchmaker to find a date.

"I had a feeling you'd like her," Elise said wryly. "She's perfect for you."

Because something was really wrong with him too?

Elise was obviously running around wielding her psychology degree like a blunt instrument. She'd probably come up with all kinds of bogus analyses about his inability to commit and his mama issues—bogus because he didn't have a problem committing as long as the thing had Wakefield Media stamped on it. Females were a different story. He'd die before letting a woman down the way his mother had let down his father, and he'd never met someone worth making that kind of promise to.

No doubt Elise had warned Candy about what she'd gotten herself into. Maybe she'd given Candy hints about how to get under his skin. Elise certainly had figured out how to do that well enough. And of course Elise had a vested interest in making sure Candy made him happy. This woman he'd been matched with might even be a plant. Some actress Elise had paid to get him to fall in love with her.

That…*schemer*.

Thank God he never had to see Elise again. A paralegal sounded like a blessed reprieve from razor-sharp matchmakers with great legs.

"I'll call her. Then I expect you'll want a full report afterward, right?"

The line went dead silent.

"Still there, Elise?"

"Not a *full* report."

"About whether she's my soul mate. Get your mind out of the gutter."

For some reason, that made Elise laugh and muscles he hadn't realized were tense relaxed.

"Yeah, I do want that report. I guess we never really laid down the ground rules of how this deal was going to go. Do we need an unbiased third party to verify the results?"

A judge? Suddenly, he felt like a bug pinned to cork. "The fewer people involved in this, the better. I'll call you afterward and we'll go from there. How's that?"

"Uncomplicated. I can get on board with that. Have a good time with Candy. Talk to you later."

The line went dead for the second time and Dax immediately saved Elise's number to his contacts. It gave him a dark little kick to have the matchmaker's phone number when she'd been so adamantly against giving it to him.

Then he dialed Candy's number, which Elise had included with the picture. His perverse gene wanted to find out if Candy was on the up-and-up. If Elise had hired someone to date him, he'd cry foul so fast it would make her head spin. And he'd never admit it was exactly what he'd have done.

Dax handed the valet his Audi's key fob and strolled into the wine bar Candy had selected for their first meet. She wasn't difficult to find—every eye in the room was on the sultry blonde perched on a bar stool.

Then every eye in the room turned to fixate on him as he moved forward to buss Candy on the cheek. "Hi. Nice place."

They'd conversed on the phone a couple of times. She had a pleasant voice and seemed sane, so here they were.

She peered up at him out of china doll–blue eyes that were a little less electric in person than they'd been on his laptop screen. No big deal. Her sensual vibe definitely worked for his Pleasure Principle—she'd feel good, all right, and better the second time.

"You look exactly like your picture," she said, her voice a touch breathier than it had been on the phone. "I thought you'd swiped it from a magazine and you'd turn out to be average-looking. I'm glad I was wrong."

Dax knew what reflected back at him in the mirror; he wasn't blind, and time had been kind to his features. It was stupid to be disappointed that she'd commented on his looks first. But why did his cheekbones have to be the first thing women noticed about him?

Most women. He could have been wearing a paper bag over his head for all the notice Elise had taken of his outward appearance. One of the first things she'd said to him was that he was lonely.

And as Candy blinked at him with a hint of coquettishness, he experienced an odd sense of what Elise meant. Until a woman ripped that curtain back and saw the man underneath the skin, it was all just going through the motions. And Dax dated women incapable of penetrating his cynical hide.

How had he just realized that?

And how *dare* Elise make him question his dating philosophy? If she was so smart, why hadn't she figured out he was dating the wrong women?

Besides, he wasn't. The women he dated were fine. Ms. Arundel was *not* ruining this date with her psychobabble.

He slid into the vacant bar stool next to Candy, swiveled it toward her and gave her his best, most practiced smile. It always knocked 'em dead. "You look like your picture, too. Have you ever modeled?"

Dax signaled to the bartender to bring a wine menu and tapped the Chilean red without glancing at it for more than a moment. Ordering wine was a necessary skill and he'd had plenty of opportunity to develop it. Regardless of whether this woman was his soul mate or Elise's accomplice, she'd appreciate his taste.

She nodded. "Since I was fourteen. Regional print mostly, department stores, catalogs, that kind of thing. Celebrities took over cosmetics so I never had a chance there, but eventually all the offers stopped. My mom made me get a job with benefits when I turned twenty-five."

It had been a throwaway question, one you asked a woman as a compliment, but she'd taken it seriously, reeking of sincerity as she'd talked. "So you're a paralegal now?"

She wrinkled her nose and laughed. The combination was cute. Not perky cheerleader let-me-make-you-a-cupcake cute. Actually, it wasn't so cute at all, in retrospect.

"Yes, I research legal briefs all day," she said. "It's not what I imagined myself doing, but it was so hard to find a job. If a woman interviewed me, I got shown the door immediately. Men were worse. You can bet they made it clear the job was mine if I agreed to 'after hours' work."

Candy shuddered delicately and Dax had no problem interpreting what "after hours" meant. "Discrimination at its finest."

"Most people think it's a nice problem to have. It's not. I get so beat down by people who judge me by my looks." Crossing her legs casually, Candy leaned forward and rested an elbow on the bar to casually dangle her hand an inch above Dax's knee. "That's why I signed up with EA International. I can't meet men the traditional way."

Her body language screamed *I'm into you*. The benefit of understanding human psychology—people rarely surprised him. And Candy was legit. He'd stake his life on it.

"I get that. Who wants to meet someone in a crowded bar, knowing they only came up and talked to you because of your face?" Dax sipped his wine and realized somewhere along the way, he'd actually relaxed. He was on a date with a nice, attractive woman and they had several things in common. It was comfortable ground. "You like football?"

"Sure. It's mindless, you know? Easy to follow."

He did know. That was why he liked it, too. Wakefield Media took 99 percent of his gray matter on a regular basis; it was fantastic to veg out on Sundays, the one day a week he didn't focus on work. "We should catch a game sometime."

Elise might very well be legit, too. Candy was exactly his type, almost to the letter. Dax's neck went a little hot. Wasn't that an interesting turnabout? People in general might not surprise him, but Elise almost never failed to.

"I'd like that." Candy smiled widely enough to display a mouthful of expensively capped teeth. "Tailgating is my favorite part. It's like a six-hour party every Saturday and Sunday."

Dax liked a good party. But *six-hour* parties…every Saturday *and* Sunday? "You watch college ball too?"

"I guess. Is that who plays on Sundays? I forget which one is which. I, um, actually don't watch the game most of the time." Laughing, she shook her head carefully so that strands of hair brushed her bare shoulders and drew attention to her cleavage simultaneously. It was impressive. And it was his turn to give her some signals in kind. He knew this dance well.

Candy's phone beeped. His was on silent, which he considered an unbreakable date rule. Obviously she didn't subscribe to it.

"Oh, pardon me," she tittered in that fake way designed to make it seem like an accident her phone wasn't off, when it was anything but. "I have to check in with my friend so she knows you didn't slip something in my drink and drag me ino a dark alley."

"No problem."

Okay, she got a pass on that one. It did make sense to be safe.

As she thumbed back a reply and then another one, Dax glanced at his own phone while his date texted with her girlfriend.

He had a couple of texts himself. As Candy was still facedown in her phone—likely sending messages to her female posse about Dax with the words "delish" and "rich" in all caps—he glanced at his own messages. They were both from Elise and, for some reason, that made him grin.

How's it going?

Must be going well since you're not answering.

His smile widened as he responded: She's great.

And left it at that. Elise could wait for her full report. While Candy finished texting what must be half the female population of Dallas, Dax sipped his wine and amused himself by imagining a certain matchmaker cooling her jets as she waited for additional details. Which he wasn't going to give her until he was good and ready.

* * *

Elise sat on her hands so she couldn't tap out a reply. Dax was on a date with Candy and she had no business bothering him with inane text messages.

But there was so much riding on this. Of all the women in her database, Candace Waters had the best shot at keeping Dax from vilifying Elise's company. Well, and obviously she wanted Candy to find the love of her life too. Dax was charming, sinfully hot even with his clothes on, and quick on the draw with that intelligent sense of humor. What wasn't to like? If you were into that kind of man, which Candy totally should be.

But what if Dax didn't like Candy? "She's great" didn't really say a whole lot, but then they'd only just met. Elise had to give them both a chance to find out more about each other and trust the process that she herself had created.

To keep her hands busy, she tried typing up copy for an ad campaign that needed to go out immediately. January was just around the corner, which was traditionally a demanding time for EA International. The one-two punch of Christmas and then Valentine's Day got people motivated to find someone special.

Once Dax grilled Candy for all her personal history and figured out what she'd like, what kind of Christmas gift would he buy her?

Yeah, the ad copy wasn't working as a distraction either.

She grabbed her phone and texted Dax back: That's it? Great? Do you like her?

In agony, she stared at the phone waiting for the reply. Nothing.

Dax was ignoring her. On purpose. Not sending a message was as pointed a message as actually sending one.

Butt out, her blank screen said.

Now she really had to stop obsessing. She pushed the

button to power off the phone and tossed it on the couch where she couldn't see it.

Maybe she should comb through some applications for her makeover program. Juliet had been such a challenge and then such a triumph, Elise hadn't taken on a new project yet. There were so many deserving applicants, from the one who'd been caring for her three younger brothers after the death of their parents, to another who'd been in the foster care system her whole life and just wanted to find someone who would love her forever.

Decision made, Elise sat down in her home office to contact them both. These two women had stayed on her mind for a reason, and she could handle two houseguests at the same time. Dannie would help out with the hair and makeup sessions, and after the infusion of cash from Prince Alain's match fee, Elise could afford to feed and clothe two women for a couple of months.

She never charged for her makeover services, instead choosing to gift these destitute women with new lives. Elise's magic wand might be the only opportunity they would have to succeed.

Done. She glanced at the time as she saved the women's information to EA International's database using a remote connection. Eight whole minutes had passed.

Why was she so *antsy?*

Because she'd butchered Dax's profile questions the first time. What if she'd messed it up the second time and Candy wasn't really his soul mate?

Armed with a bowl of grapes and a tall glass of ice water, she opened the algorithm code, grimly determined to sort through how it had arrived at the original match so she could reasonably conclude if it had completed the second match correctly.

After fifteen minutes of wishing the grapes were chocolate and staring at code until her eyes crossed, she couldn't stand it. Retrieving her phone from its place of banishment, she powered it on. And powered it off before it fully booted up.

What was she doing? She might as well drive to the restaurant and peer through the window like a stalker. And worse, she had a feeling she might have done exactly that if she had a clue where Dax and Candy had met.

Ridiculous. She'd check for text messages once and then find a movie or something to watch.

She powered on the phone. Nothing.

That…*man*. She couldn't think of a bad enough word to encapsulate how infuriating Dax Wakefield was. He knew how much this meant to her. Knew she was on pins and needles. How hard would it have been to type, "She's beautiful and fun. I like her a lot"?

Not hard. He wasn't doing it because ignoring Elise was part of the game, to make her think the date was going from bad to worse, so she'd sit here and stew about losing.

In reality, he was laughing it up with Candy, having an awesome time drinking red wine and talking about their similar interests. Right now, he was probably watching her over his wineglass with those smoky bedroom eyes and somehow getting Candy to admit things she'd never told anyone before.

Maybe they'd moved to the parking lot and Dax had Candy cornered against her car, breathless and…that was going too far for a first date. They should be taking things slowly, not jumping right into something physical, the way Dax most assuredly did with all his previous women.

Immediately, Elise pulled up the text app: Candy doesn't go all the way on a first date.

She groaned. Dax had officially fried her brain. She hit the delete button.

Oh, God, had she just hit Send? *Please, please, please,* she prayed, hoping against hope she'd deleted the message as she'd meant to, and scoured her phone's folders for the answer.

Which she instead got in the form of a message from Dax: Speaking from personal experience?

Her stomach flopped at the same time she laughed, quite against her will. He'd made the faux pas okay and comical in one shot. How did he *do* that?

At least she'd gotten him to respond. She replied: You specified no one-night stands. She's in it for the long haul.

Dax: I wouldn't have called her otherwise.

That flopped her stomach in a different way. If this worked, Dax and Candy might very well get married. Most of the couples she matched did. She was in the business of introducing soul mates, after all.

Why did the thought of Dax and Candy falling blissfully in love make Elise want to cry?

The prospect of another round of holidays alone coupled with the stress of dealing with Dax—that was it. They were both killing her. Slowly.

And…if someone as cynical about relationships as Dax found his happily ever after, what did it say that she couldn't find hers?

Five

Candy laughed again and launched into another convoluted story about her dog. Dax was more than a little sorry he'd asked if she had any hobbies. Who knew a dog could be a hobby? Or that a grown woman would actually shop for outfits for said dog?

He signaled the bartender for another round and not for the first time, his attention wandered.

She finally wrapped up her monologue and leaned forward to give him an eyeful of her strategically exposed cleavage, which meant he wasn't paying enough attention to her. It was the fourth time she'd done it in thirty minutes, not that he was counting. Her signals were just so uncomplicated and easy to read.

Despite Elise's warning to the contrary, Candy was most definitely open to ending the night skin-on-skin. She would be energetic and creative in bed and yeah, it would be pleasurable.

But in the morning, she'd wake up intending to pursue a long-term, very serious relationship. Big difference from his usual dates. Regardless, he should embrace the spirit of what Elise had set up here, so when it failed, his conscience was clear.

Time to pay attention to his date. After all, she was supposed to be his soul mate. She certainly had a distinct lack of interest in what was going on behind his curtain. Likely she hadn't noticed he had one.

Giving Candy another practiced smile, he nodded to the door and stood, palm extended. "Shall we find a place to have a bite to eat?"

It was how these things worked—if drinks went well, you asked the woman to dinner. If not, you said you'd call her and escaped. Not that he'd claim drinks had gone particularly well, but maybe over dinner Candy would reveal some hidden depths he couldn't resist.

Without bothering to play coy, she took his hand and slid off the bar stool, rising to her full height. "I'd love to."

Jeez, her legs were long. Too long. She was almost as tall as Dax.

"Pardon me while I powder my nose," she said, and turned to sway across the room with a one-two gait.

Dax was meant to think it was sexy. He *should* think it was sexy. But, all at once, nothing about Candy seemed sexy. The lady had moves and a clear interest in demonstrating them. She was exactly the type of woman he went for in a big way. Something was broken here.

His phone vibrated in his pocket, distracting him totally from Candy's departure. His lips curled up involuntarily. He pulled it out, expecting to see another text from Elise. Which it was.

I hope you're not checking your messages in front of Candy. Because that would be rude.

He laughed, painfully aware it was the first genuine amusement he'd felt all evening. He hit Reply: Then stop texting me.

Elise: .

He groaned through another laugh. A blank message. Her sense of humor slayed him.

Candy materialized in front of him far sooner than expected. "Ready?" she said.

"Sure." He pocketed his phone and followed his date out into the chilly night. She didn't have a coat, deliberately of course, so Dax could offer her his. Then she'd accidentally-on-purpose leave something in the pocket—lipstick, an earring; it varied from woman to woman—so she'd have an excuse to call him.

He shrugged out of his jacket anyway and handed it to her, earning a grateful smile as she slung it around her shoulders.

That's what he had to offer in a relationship—a coat. Nothing more. And it wasn't fair to Candy, who came into this date thinking there might be a possibility of something magical. The back of his neck heated. If Candy was his soul mate, she deserved better.

This was jacked up. He never should have called her. But how else could he have handled this? To prove Elise ran a sham business, he had to go on the date. Who knew said date would be exactly like every other date he'd ever been on, which had worked quite well for a long time, and yet not feel right?

As they walked to the valet stand, Candy stumbled, just a little and with practiced grace. Dax rolled his eyes even as he slung a steadying arm around her waist. She peered up at him in invitation. *Kiss me and let's get this party started,* she said without saying a word.

He could have scripted this date ahead of time and not missed a trick. Wearily, he eyed Candy's plumped lips, knew how good it would feel when she melted into him. On paper, they made sense together, for the short term anyway.

And he had no interest in her whatsoever. The perfect woman wasn't so perfect. What was *wrong* with him?

Elise was wrong with him. She'd set him up on a date with a woman who had all these long-term, soul-mate, mumbo-jumbo expectations and it was seriously cramping his style.

And okay, it pricked at his conscience too. Which had picked a fine time to surface.

Elise had ruined his ability to have fun on a date. She'd pay for that.

"I'm sorry, Candy, but this isn't going to work out."

"Oh." Candy straightened, her face hardening. "But we were matched. By Elise. I was really happy with her choice. But you're not?"

Obviously she'd not been clued in that this date was also part of an experiment. And a wager. Yet another mark against Elise.

"She did a great job matching us. You're exactly the kind of woman I like."

"Then what's the problem?"

"I'm not interested in a relationship, and it would be unfair to you for us to continue." The standard excuse rolled from his tongue.

"You forgot to say it's not you, it's me." Candy had obviously heard the excuse before too. She flung his jacket at him with surprising force. "Thanks for the drinks. Have a nice life."

She flounced to the valet and tapped her foot while the uniformed kid raced to get her car. Then she roared out of the parking lot with a screech.

Not only had Elise ruined him, she'd set him up in a catch-22. There was no way he could have fallen for Candy, not when it meant he'd lose the wager. Plus, all of Elise's profile questions kept getting in the way, making him think about his intentions. *That* was the problem, not the sound bite he'd spieled off to Candy.

The valet pulled Dax's car into the lane and hopped out. Dax slipped him a folded bill and got behind the wheel. The closer he drove to his loft, the deeper his blood boiled. Thanks to a certain matchmaker, he'd be spending yet another night alone, his least favorite thing to do.

He pulled onto a side street and hit the call button on his phone before checking the time. Almost nine.

Elise answered on the first ring, so he didn't worry about interrupting her plans too much.

"Expecting my call?" he said with as much irony as he could. She must have been sitting there watching her phone like a hawk. On a Friday night. Looked like Elise could use a bit of her own magic to find a date.

"Um, yeah," she said, her voice husky as though she'd been running laps, and it sent heat to his blood in a whole different way. "You said you'd give me the full report. Isn't this it?"

He'd totally forgotten about that, but it was absolutely the reason for his call now. "Text me your address. It's an in-person kind of report."

He ended the call and an instant later, the message appeared.

Who said I was at home?

She was *not* allowed to make him laugh when he was still so furious with her.

The address came through a moment later and the grin popped out before he'd realized it. *Let's rock and roll, Ms. Arundel.*

Looked like he wouldn't be returning to his empty loft just yet after all.

Elise answered the door of her uptown condo wearing jeans and a soft yellow sweater, all perky and cupcake-y though she'd only had a few minutes' warning before Dax appeared on her front porch. He tried really hard to not notice how the sweater brought out gold highlights in her eyes. He was mad at her for…something.

"That was fast," she said and raised her eyebrows in that cool, infuriating way that said she had his number. "Did you observe the speed limit at any point on your way here?"

"Gonna give me a ticket?" He crossed his arms and leaned a shoulder on the door frame, because she'd very pointedly not invited him in. That was okay. The view was pretty good from here.

"No, a guess. The date must not have gone well if you were in that much of a hurry to get here."

"You think I wanted to see you instead?"

How had she arrived at that conclusion?

But then hadn't he compared Candy to Elise all night and never found a thing in Candy's favor? Hadn't he anticipated this showdown with Elise during the drive over and looked forward to it far more than he'd anticipated having a naked Candy in his arms?

Well, it was stupid to pretend otherwise, regardless of how ridiculous it sounded. The facts spoke for themselves. He'd wanted to see Elise. He liked baiting her.

She stared at him as if he'd grown an extra nose. "No, ding-dong. Because you wanted to lord it over me that I didn't match you with your soul mate."

"Yeah." He nodded by rote and mentally kicked himself. *Ding-dong.* It might be funny if it wasn't so true. "That's why I sped over here. To tell you Candy was perfect, but it didn't work out."

Perfect for the man he'd shown Elise, anyway. She'd failed to dig beneath the surface and find the perfect woman for the man behind the curtain. *Not as good as you think you are, huh, Ms. Hocus-Pocus?*

Elise cocked her head, contemplating him. "I know she's perfect. I matched you with her. But you never really gave it a chance, did you?"

No point in pretending on that front. "What do you want me to say, Elise? I never made any bones about the fact that I'm not interested in a relationship."

No, that wasn't entirely true. He wasn't interested in a relationship with anyone he'd ever met and part of him was disappointed Elise hadn't pulled someone out of her hat who could change his mind.

But that would have been impossible because she didn't exist.

Dax sighed, weary all of a sudden. "Look, the idea of true love is as bogus as the idea of feeding a bunch of data into a program and expecting something magical to come out."

The porch light highlighted a strange shadow in her expression. "It's not magic. The algorithm is incredibly complex."

"I'm sure the software company told you that when they sold it to you but there's no way a developer can be that precise with intangibles. Admit it, you're—"

"I wrote the program," she interrupted, so softly he had strain to hear her.

Then the words sank in and he forgot all about getting her to admit the matches were actually just random pairings. "*You* wrote the program? You have a psychology degree."

The shadows deepened in her expression and he felt like crap for opening his mouth without censor. He'd hurt her feelings, not once but twice. At what point had she started to care what he thought of her?

"I do have a psychology degree. A master's. My bachelor's degree is in computer science."

"A *master's?*"

"That's right." Her jaw tightened. "I almost went on for the PhD in psychology but decided to take the plunge with EA International instead. I can always go back to school later."

"But…you wrote the program?"

She might very well be the sharpest woman he'd ever met. And not just because she'd earned an advanced degree. Because she defied his expectations in ways he'd only begun to appreciate.

Her slight form held a wealth of secrets, things he'd never imagined might lie beneath the surface. Things he'd never dreamed would be so stimulating—intellectually *and* physically. After an incredibly frustrating night in the company of an inane woman who dressed dogs for fun, he wanted to uncover every fascinating bit of Elise Arundel.

"Is it *really* so hard to believe?" She crossed her arms, closing herself off from him. It was way past time for a heartfelt apology.

"It's not that I don't believe it, it's just so incredibly sexy." That was not even close to an apology and he needed to shut up, like yesterday. "I mean, I wasn't kidding. Brains turn me on."

Her eyebrows drew together. "Really? Because I have one in a jar on my kitchen counter. I've never found it particularly attractive but to each his own."

In a spectacularly unappealing combo, he snorted and laughed at the same time. "Wait. You're kidding, right?"

She rolled her eyes, but a suspicious tug at her lips told him she was having a hard time not laughing. "I do not now, nor have I ever, had a pickled brain in my possession."

"It was worth the clarification." A host of things unsaid passed between them, most of them indecipherable. He wanted to unscramble her in the worst way. "How bad is to admit that a conversation about pickled brains is the most scintillating one I've had this evening?"

With a sigh, Elise butted the door all the way open with the flat of her hand. "You better come in. I have a feeling I need to be sitting down for the full report."

Inside—exactly where he wanted to be, but not to discuss Candy. Dax trailed the matchmaker through a classically decorated condo with rich, jewel-toned accents. "So this is where all the magic happens?"

"The women who go through my makeover program stay here, yes." Elise flopped on the sofa, clearly unconcerned about appearing graceful.

She had no pretense. It was almost as if she didn't care whether he found her attractive. She wasn't even wearing lipstick. The only time he'd ever seen a woman without lipstick was after he'd kissed it off. Women of his acquaintance always put their best face forward.

But Elise hadn't invited him in for any sort of behind-closed-doors activities. She wanted the lowdown on his date with another woman. This was like sailing through uncharted waters during a hurricane.

Slightly off stride, he sank into the plush armchair near the couch.

"Tell me what happened with Candy," she instructed without preamble. "Every last detail. I have to know precisely what didn't work, if anything did work, more abou—"

"Whoa. Why do you have to know all that?" That bug-on-cork feeling was back and on a Friday night in the company of an interesting woman, no variation of this conversation sounded like it would lead to the kind of fun he'd rather be having.

Her stare was nothing short of withering. "So I can get it right the second time."

"What second time?"

"I promised to match you with the love of your life. Admittedly, I like to get it right the first time, but I'm okay with one mistake. Two is unacceptable. So I need details."

Another date? He almost groaned. Somehow he'd thought they could let that lie, at least for a blessed hour or two. The wager was over. She'd lost. Didn't she realize that?

"Elise…"

She gazed across the coffee table separating them, and he couldn't do it. Couldn't denounce her as a fraud, couldn't tell her flat out that she wasn't the fairy godmother she seemed to think she was, couldn't stand the thought of hurting her feelings again.

Then there was the whole problem of this strange draw he felt every time he thought about Elise. Without this mission of hers to match him with his mythical soul mate, he'd have no excuse to see her again, and the thought made him twitchy.

She held up her hand in protest. "I know what you're going to say. You don't kiss and tell. I'm not asking you to."

"I didn't kiss Candy. And that wasn't what I was going to say."

"You didn't kiss her?" Elise looked a little shocked. "Why not?"

"Because I didn't like her. I only kiss women I like."

"But the other day at the bistro, you almost kissed *me*. I know you were about to. Don't bother to deny it."

As Dax did actually know the value of silence on occasion, he crossed his arms and waited until all the columns in her head added up. A blush rose on her cheeks. Really, he shouldn't enjoy that so much.

And he probably shouldn't have admitted he liked her. Not even to himself, but definitely not to her. Too late now.

"Stop being ridiculous," she said. "All this talk about how I'm sexy because I wrote a computer program and trying to throw me off balance with cryptic comments designed to make me believe you like me—it's not going to work."

She thought he was lying. Better yet, she thought he'd told her those things for nefarious purposes, as a way to manipulate her, and she wanted to be clear there was no chance of her falling for it. If he hadn't liked her already, that alone would have clinched it, and hell if he knew why.

Thoroughly intrigued, he leaned forward, elbows on his knees. "What exactly am I working here?"

"The same thing you've been working since moment

one. Distraction. If I'm all flustered and thinking about you kissing me, I'll mess up and match you with the wrong woman. Then I lose. It's brilliant, actually."

And instantly, he hit his stride. The wager, the full report he'd come to deliver, soul mates and matches—all of it got shoved to the back burner in favor of the gem buried in Elise's statement.

He zeroed right in on the kicker. "You're thinking about kissing me?"

Kissing Dax was, in fact, *all* Elise had been thinking about.

Did they make human muzzles? Because she needed one. "I said you were *trying* to get me to think about it. So I'd be distracted. It doesn't work."

Because she didn't need to think about kissing him to be distracted. That had happened the moment she'd opened the door to all that solid masculinity encased in a well-cut body. She didn't know for sure that he still had the washboard abs. But it was a safe bet. And it was easy to fantasize about when she already had a handy image emblazoned across her mind's eye of him half-naked.

Casually, Dax pulled at the sleeve of his date-night suit, which shouldn't have looked so different on him than what he'd worn all the other times she'd seen him. But it was clearly custom-made from gorgeous silk, and in it, he somehow he managed to look delicious and dangerous at the same time.

"Really," he said. It was a statement, not a question, as though he didn't believe her.

Probably because he knew she was skirting the truth. Why had she invited him in? Or given him her address in the first place? This was her sanctuary, and she rarely allowed anyone to intrude.

Dax got a pass because she *had* messed up. "You can't

distract me. I've got a one-track mind and it's set on finding the perfect woman for you. Candy wasn't it. I get that.
But her name came up due to the unorthodox profile sessions. We have to do the last one and do it the right way."

For all the good it would do. Who else did she have
in her database to match with Dax? Mentally, she sorted
through the candidates and tried to do some of the percent-
ages in her head.

And forgot how to add as a slow smile spread across his
face, heavy with promise and a side of wicked. "Shall we
put that to the test?"

"Um…" Her brain went a little fuzzy as he pierced her
with those smoky eyes and raked heat through her abdomen
without moving an inch. "Put what to the test?"

Then he stirred and she wished he'd stayed still.

He flowed to his feet and resettled next to her on the
couch. "Whether I can distract you or not."

Barely a finger width separated them and she held her
breath because oh my God, he smelled like sin and salvation and she had the worst urge to nuzzle behind his ear.

This was not part of the deal. She was *not* attracted
to Dax Wakefield. It was unthinkable, unacceptable. She
had no experience with a predatory man who had a new
woman in his bed more often than he replaced his tube of
toothpaste.

How could this have happened? Did her previously co-
matose libido not understand what a player this man was?
How greatly he disdained long-term commitment and true
love?

The man was her lonely heart's worst nightmare
wrapped in a delectable package. She might as well hand
him a mallet and lie down at his feet so he could get to
smashing her insides flat right away.

He was meant for his true soul mate, who would be the
right woman to change his mind about love. Elise was not it.

Pulse hammering, she stared him down, praying he couldn't actually see her panic swirling. Now would be a great time for some pithy comeback to materialize in her fuzzy brain, but then he slipped his hand under hers and raised it to his lips.

Her fingertips grazed his mouth and his eyelids drifted lower, as if he found it pleasurable. Fascinating. Little old Elise Arundel could make a walking deity like Dax feel pleasure. Who would have thought?

Watching her intently, he pursed his lips and sucked, ever so slightly, on her index finger, and the answering tug between her legs wasn't so slight. Honeyed warmth radiated outward, flushing over her skin, and a hitch in her lungs made it hard to catch a breath.

"What are you doing?" she asked hoarsely.

"Seeing what you taste like," he murmured and slid her hand across his stubbly jaw, holding it against his skin. "And it was good enough to want more."

Before she could blink, his head inclined and his lips trailed across hers, nibbling lightly, exploring, teasing, until he found what must have been the angle he sought. Instantly, their mouths fused into a ragingly hot kiss.

Elise's long-dormant body thundered to life and broke into a rousing rendition of the Hallelujah Chorus.

His hands cupped her neck, tilting her head back so he could take it deeper. Hot and rough, his tongue slicked across hers, and she felt strong responding licks deep in her core. A cry rose up in her throat and came out as a moan.

Those strong and deft hands drifted lower on her back, dipping under the hem of her sweater, spreading across her bare skin at the arch of her waist.

Stop right there.

He did.

She really wished he'd kept going.

They both shifted closer, twining like vines. Then he

pushed with his palm against the small of her back and shoved her torso into his. Oh, my, it was hard against the roused tips of her breasts, which were sensitive enough to feel him through layers of cloth.

This wasn't the PG-rated kiss she'd been thinking about since the almost-kiss of the parking lot. This one had *rated R* slapped all over it. Fisting great wads of his shirt in her hands, she clung to him as he kissed her, shamelessly reveling in it, soaking up every second.

Until she remembered this was all designed as a distraction.

Pulling away was harder than it should have been. Chest rising and falling rapidly, she put a foot of couch between them. Not enough. She hit the floor and kept going, whirling only when the coffee table was between her and the hot-tongued man on the couch.

"Good kisser," she said breathlessly and cursed her fragmented voice. "I'll note it on your profile."

His heavy-lidded gaze tracked her closely. "I wasn't finished. Come back and see what else I'm good at. You want to be thorough on the profile, don't you?"

"I can't do that." If he triggered such a severe reaction with merely a kiss, what would her body do with more?

"Scared?"

"Of you? Not hardly." The scoff was delivered so convincingly, she almost believed it herself.

A light dawned in his expression and she had the distinct impression he'd just figured out exactly how much he scared her. That sent another round of panic into the abyss of her stomach.

"There's just no need," she clarified, desperately trying to counter the effects of being kissed senseless. "We put it to the test, and while the kiss was pleasant, it certainly didn't distract me from the next steps. When do you want to schedule the last session?"

Dax groaned the way someone does when you tell them they have to get a root canal followed by a tax audit. "I'd rather kiss you some more. Why are you all the way over there?"

"We're not doing this, Dax. Hear me now, because I can't stress this enough. You and I are not happening." She held up a finger as he started to speak. "No. Not any variation of you and I. We have a deal, a wager, and nothing more. I have to do my job. It's my life, my business. Let me do it."

He contemplated her for a long moment. "This is important to you."

"Of course it is! You threatened to destroy my reputation, which will effectively ruin the company I've built over the last seven years. How would you like it if I had the power to do that to you and then spent all my time trying to seduce you into losing?"

"Elise." He waited until she glanced at him to continue. "I'm sorry. That was not my intent. I like kissing you. That's all. If you want to do another session, I'll be there. Name the time."

Oh, how *dare* he be all understanding and apologetic and smoky-eyed? "How about if I call you?"

She needed Dax gone before she did anything else stupid, like set off on an exploratory mission to see if he still had underwear-model abs under that suit.

"Sure. I can give you some space. Call me when you're ready to pick up where we left off."

Of course he'd seen right through her and then dumped a heck of a double entendre in her lap. Pick up where they left off with the sessions—or with the kiss? And which way would he interpret it?

Which way would she mean it?

She'd just realized something painful and ridiculous. The text messages during his date, letting him kiss her, the supreme sadness of imagining him blissfully in love with his soul mate; it all rolled up into an undeniable truth—she didn't want Dax to be with anyone else.

And she couldn't let herself be with him, even for what would undoubtedly be the best night of her life. It was the morning after when she woke up alone, knowing she hadn't been enough to keep him, and all the mornings alone from then on, that she couldn't do.

That was the best reason of all to get him matched with someone else in a big hurry.

Six

At precisely seven-thirty the next evening, Elise's doorbell rang. And yes, Dax was exactly who she expected to see grinning at her on the other side of the door, both hands behind his back.

"I said I'd call you."

Not that she'd really thought he'd wait around for the phone to ring, but he could have given her at least twenty-four hours to figure out how to call him without creating the impression she wanted him to pick up *exactly* where that kiss had left off.

Which would be really difficult to convey, when truthfully, she did. And now her house was spotless because every time she considered picking up the phone, she cleaned something instead.

"I know. But I'm taking this seriously. For real. Your office isn't the best place to get answers to your questions. So we're going to do it here."

"Here? At my house?" *Bad, bad idea.* "You want to do the profile session on a Saturday night?"

Didn't he have a new woman lined up already? Candy hadn't worked out, but a man like Dax surely wouldn't wait around for Elise to find him some action. Saturday night equaled hot date, didn't it?

"I don't think you fully appreciated the point I made about getting to know me best while on a date." With a flourish, he pulled something from behind his back. A DVD she didn't recognize. "So we're going to watch a movie."

"The profile session is going to be a date?" *She* was his hot date. How in the world had she not seen this coming?

It was straight out of Psych 101—to get the cheese, she had to complete the maze. But why? What was his motivation for forcing her to navigate a date in the first place?

"More of a compromise," he allowed with a nod. "This is not anything close to what I've ever done on a date. But the setting is innocuous and we can both relax. I don't feel like you're grilling me, you don't feel like it's work."

That sounded remarkably like the excuse he'd used to get her to go to lunch, which had proved to be rather effective, in retrospect. "What if I'm busy?"

"Cancel your plans. You want to know what makes me tick?" His eyebrows lifted in invitation. "I'm offering you a shot. Watch the movie. Drink some wine. If you do that for me, I'll answer any question you ask honestly."

Dax gestured with his other hand, which clutched a bottle of cabernet sporting a label she'd only ever seen behind glass at a pricey restaurant.

She shook her head. "This is a thinly veiled attempt to seduce me again."

The sizzling once-over he treated her to should not have curled her toes. Of course, if he'd given her a warning before he showed up, she could have put on shoes.

"I'm not trying to tilt the scales by coming on to you," he insisted. "Trust me, if I wanted you naked, this is not how I would go about it."

As she well knew his seduction routine, she opted to keep her mouth shut. For once.

"I, Daxton Wakefield, will not touch you one single time this whole evening." He marked the statement by crossing his heart solemnly with the DVD case. "Unless you ask me to."

"You're safe on that front. Not that I'm agreeing to this, but what did you bring?" She nodded at the movie against her better judgment.

He shrugged. "An advanced screening copy of *Stardate 2215*. It's that big-budget sci-fi flick coming out Christmas day."

She eyed him. "That's not in theaters yet. How did you get a copy?"

"I have friends in low places." He grinned mischievously. "One of the benefits of being in the media business. I called in a few favors. You like sci-fi and I wanted to pick something I knew you hadn't seen."

Speechless, she held on to the door so she didn't end up in a heap at his feet. She'd never told him what kind of movies she liked, but somehow he'd figured it out, and then went to great lengths to get one. Her heart knocked up against her principles and it was not cool.

Not a seduction, my foot.

But she really wanted to see that movie. And she really wanted to get Dax Wakefield matched to someone else so she could stop thinking about kissing him.

"Truce?" He held out the DVD and the wine with a conciliatory smile and he looked so freaking gorgeous in his $400 jeans and long-sleeved V-neck, she wanted to lap him up like whipped cream.

If that bit of absurdity didn't decide against this idea for her, nothing would.

"I haven't eaten dinner yet."

"Jeez, Elise." He huffed out a noise of disgust. "You're the most difficult woman to not have a date with in the entire United States. Order a pizza. Order twelve. You may have free rein with my credit card if that's what it takes to get me over your threshold."

"Why are you so dead-set on this? Honestly."

He dropped his arms, wine and DVD falling to his sides.

"Believe it or not, this is me leveling the field. You deserve a genuine chance at doing your thing with the questions and the algorithm. This is an atmosphere conducive to giving you that."

Sincerity laced his words, but to clarify, she said, "Because you don't like my office."

Something flitted through his expression and whatever it was scared her a great deal more than the kiss. "Because I have an extremely full week ahead and daylight hours are scarce. I want to give you my undivided attention, without watching the clock."

Her heart knocked again.

"You've just won an evening with a matchmaker." She stepped out of the door frame and allowed Dax passage into the foyer for the second time in two days.

She should have her head examined.

True to his word, he strolled past her without touching, went to the living room and set the wine on the coffee table.

She fetched wineglasses and he ordered the pizza. They settled onto the couch and three sips in, she finally relaxed. "This cabernet is amazing. Where did you find it?"

"In my wine rack." He handed her the remote without grazing her fingers. It was carefully done. "I was saving it for a special occasion."

"Right. Pizza and a movie is special."

He didn't move, didn't touch her at all, but she felt the look he gave her in all the places his kiss had warmed the night before. "The company is the occasion, Elise."

Prickles swept across her cheeks. The curse of the fair-skinned Irish. She might as well take out a billboard proclaiming her innermost thoughts. "We'll get through the profile session much faster if you quit detouring to flatter me with platitudes."

His head tilted as if he'd stopped to contemplate a particularly intriguing Picasso. "Why do you find it so hard to believe that I like you?"

Because he made a habit of working emotions to his advantage. Because he was a swan and she was not. Because to believe would be akin to trusting him.

But she ignored all that in favor of the most important reason. "You don't ruin the reputation of someone you hold in fond regard. If you really like me, prove it. Let's end this now."

"To be fair, I didn't know I was going to like you when I made that deal. But if you do your job, you've got nothing to worry about, do you?" He lifted his glass in a mock toast.

A part of her had hoped he'd take the opportunity to call it off, and she shouldn't be so disappointed he hadn't. Why—because she'd internalized his pretty words? Thought maybe he'd realized she was actually a very nice person and hadn't deliberately set out to ruin his friendship with Leo?

"Hey."

"Hey, what?" she said a touch defensively, pretty sure she had no call to be snippy.

"It's a compliment that I'm holding fast to our deal. You're a smart, savvy woman and if I didn't respect the hell out of you, I'd have let you bow out long before now."

"Bow out? You mean give up and quit? No way."

When he grinned, she deflated a little. He'd phrased it like that on purpose to get her dander up and allow him to slide the nice stuff by her. How did he know how to handle her so well?

"That's why I like you," he said decisively. "We're both fighters. Why else would I be here to put myself through your profile wringer? I can't claim the matchmaking process is bogus unless I submit to it wholly. Then we both know the victor deserves to win."

Now he'd dragged ethics into this mess. She shook her head in disbelief. Against all odds, she liked him too.

Somehow he'd stripped everything away and laid out

some very profound truths. Of all the ways he could have convinced her he really liked her, how had he done it by *not* calling off their deal?

He respected her skills, respected her as a business woman, and she'd been on the defensive since moment one. It was okay to let her guard down. Dax had more than earned it.

"It's hard for me to trust people," she said slowly, watching him to see if he had a clue how difficult a confession this was. "That's why I give you so much grief."

He nodded once without taking his eyes off her. "I wasn't confused. And for the record, same goes."

He stretched his hand out in invitation and she didn't hesitate to take it. Palm to palm, silent mutual agreement passed between them. Warmth filled her as the intensity of the moment unfolded into something that felt like kinship.

Neither of them trusted easily, but each of them had found a safe place here in this circle of two. At least for tonight.

Dax stopped paying the slightest bit of attention to the movie about fifteen minutes in. Watching Elise was much more fun.

She got into the movie the same way she did everything else—with passion. And it was beautiful. He particularly liked the part where she forgot they were holding hands.

There was nothing sexual about it. He didn't use it as an excuse to slide a suggestive fingertip across her knuckle. He didn't yank on her hand and let her spill into his lap, even though nothing short of amnesia was going to get that hot kiss out of his head.

Far be it from him to disrupt the status quo. The status quo was surprisingly pleasant. He'd agreed not to come on to her, and he'd stick to it, no matter how many more times she gave him a hard-on just by looking at him.

Promises meant something to him and he wanted Elise to understand that.

And oddly enough, when he knew there wasn't a snowball's chance for anything above pizza and a movie, it was liberating in a way he'd never expected.

It was new. And interesting. Instead of practicing his exit strategy, he relaxed and enjoyed the company of a beautiful woman who made him laugh. He couldn't wait to find out what happened next.

The pizza arrived, and he let her hand slip from his without protest, but his palm cooled far too quickly.

Elise set the box on the coffee table and handed Dax a bright red ceramic plate. The savory, meaty smell of pepperoni and cheese melded with the fresh-baked crust and his stomach rumbled. Neither of them hesitated to dig in.

Dax couldn't remember ever eating with a woman in front of the TV. It was something couples did. And he'd never been part of one. Never wanted to be, and furthermore, never wanted to give someone the impression there'd be more couple-like things to come.

But this wasn't a date and Elise wasn't going to get the wrong idea. It was nice.

"Thanks for the pizza," she said around a mouthful, which she couldn't seem to get down her throat fast enough. "I never eat it and I forgot how good it is. You do amazing things with a credit card."

She'd meant it as a joke but it hit him strangely and he had a hard time swallowing the suddenly tasteless bite in his own mouth.

Yes, his bank account could finance a small country, and he made sure the women he dated benefited from his hard work, usually in the form of jewelry or the occasional surprise overnight trip to New York or San Francisco. He'd never given it much thought.

Until now. What *did* he have to offer a woman in a relationship? A coat and a credit card. Thanks to his friendly neighborhood matchmaker, it seemed shallow and not... enough. What if Elise did the impossible and introduced him to his soul mate? She was smart and had a good track record. She could actually pull it off.

By definition, his soul mate would be that woman worth making lifelong promises to.

Did he really want to meet her and be so inadequately prepared?

"You're supposed to be asking me questions." Dax gave up on the pizza and opted to drown his sudden bout of relationship scruples with more wine.

Eyebrows raised, Elise chewed faster.

"I suppose I am," she said and washed down the last of her pizza with a healthy swallow of cabernet, then shot him a sideways glance. "Say, you're pretty good. I did forget about work, just like you predicted."

He crossed his arms so he didn't reach for her hand again. It bothered him that he wanted to in the same breath as bringing up the profile questions designed to match him with another woman. "Yeah, yeah, I'm a genius. Ask me a question."

After pausing the movie, Elise sat back against the sofa cushion, peering at him over the rim of her glass. "What does contentment look like?"

This. His brain spit out the answer unchecked. Thankfully, he kept it from spilling out of his mouth. "I spend my day chasing success. I've never strived for contentment."

Which didn't necessarily mean he hadn't found it.

"What if Wakefield Media collapsed tomorrow but you had that woman next to you, the one who doesn't care about what's behind your curtain? Would you still be able to find a way to be content as long as you had her?"

No surprise that Elise remembered what he'd said at

lunch the other day. How long would it take her to figure out he actually *wanted* someone to care?

Nothing was going to happen to Wakefield Media. It was hypothetical, just like the soul mate. So if this was all theoretical, why not have both?

"What if having the woman *and* success makes me content? Is that allowed?"

Somehow, the idea buried itself in his chest and he imagined that woman snuggled into his bed at the end of a long day, not because he'd brought her home, but because she lived there. And they were together but it wasn't strictly for sex—it was about emotional support and understanding—and making love heightened all of that.

Dax could trust she'd stick around. Forever.

"If that's what contentment looks like to you, then of course."

Her catlike smile drove the point home. She'd gotten a response out of him even though he'd have sworn he'd never so much as thought about how to define contentment.

He had to chuckle. "Well played."

Now that he'd defined it, the image of that woman wouldn't dissolve. She didn't have a face or a body type, but the blurred shape was there in his mind and he couldn't shake it.

What was he supposed to do with that?

With a nod at his concession, Elise sipped her wine and contemplated him. "What do you do with your free time?"

Dax grinned and opted to bite back the inappropriate comment about his after-hours activities. "Should I pick something that makes it sound like I have an interesting hobby?"

"No, you should say what you like."

"I like to people-watch," he said.

"Tell me more about that. What's great about people-watching?"

"Spoken in true therapist fashion." He meant it as a joke and she took it as one. He liked amusing her, and it was easy to do so. "People-watching is the best way to figure out what motivates the masses. And it never gets old."

She was really, really good at this, especially when he wasn't trying to weasel his way out of having his psyche split open. Actually, she had a knack for yanking things out of his brain even when he *was* looking for a way to avoid answering her questions.

So there was no point in being anything less than honest. Plus, this environment, this bubble with only the two of them, created a sort of haven, where it didn't seem so terrible to say whatever he felt.

"Go on," she encouraged with a small wave. "Why do you have to figure out what motivates people?"

"Wakefield Media isn't just a top-grossing media company. It's a top-grossing company, period. That's not an accident. I got a degree in psychology instead of business because it's crucial to have a keen understanding of what brings people back for more, especially in the entertainment space."

Wine and pizza totally forgotten, she listened with rapt attention as if he'd been outlining the secrets of the universe, which she couldn't get enough of. "And people-watching helps?"

For a woman who'd moaned so appreciatively over the pizza, she had amazing willpower. She'd only eaten one piece. She was so interested in what he said, food took a backseat. It was a little heady to be worthy of so much focus.

"People can be notoriously loyal to certain shows, and conversely, very fickle. You'd be shocked at how much you can pick up about why when you just sit and observe how people interact."

Her soft smile punched him in the gut. "Your insights must be something else."

"I bet yours would be as good. Do it with me some time."

Now why had he gone and said that? Hadn't he gotten a big enough clue that she didn't want to hang out with him? Look how hard it had been to get her to agree to pizza and a movie.

The wine must be messing with his head.

"I'd like that. It's a date," she said without a trace of sarcasm and he did a double take.

The wine was messing with her head too, obviously.

"A date that's not a date because we're not dating?" She'd been undeniably clear about that last night. Otherwise, he'd never have agreed to keep his hands off of her.

And look what that promise had netted him—this was bar none the most enjoyable evening he'd had in ages, including the ones that did involve sex.

"Right. We're not dating. We're...friends?" she offered hesitantly.

A denial sprang to his lips and then died. *Friends.* Is that what was happening here? Did that explain why he felt as though he could tell Elise anything?

"I don't know. I've never been friends with a woman. Aren't there rules?"

She made a face. "Like we're not supposed to cancel our plans with each other when someone we *are* dating calls?"

"Like I'm not supposed to fantasize about kissing you again." The answering heat in her expression told him volumes about her own fantasies. "Because if that's against the rules, I can't be friends with you."

She looked down, that gorgeous blush staining her cheeks. "You're not supposed to be doing that anyway. Regardless."

He tipped up her chin and forced her to meet his eyes

again because that heat in hers liquefied him. And he craved that feeling only she could produce. "I can't stop."

As he'd just broken his promise not to touch her, he tore his hand away from her creamy skin with reluctance and shoved it under his thigh.

Elise messed with his head. No wine required.

She blinked, banking all the sexy behind a blank wall. "You'll find it surprisingly easy to stop as soon as I match you with someone else. She'll help you forget all about that kiss, which never should have happened in the first place."

There it was again, slapping him in the face. Elise wasn't interested in him. Her main goal was to get him paired off with someone else as soon as possible.

And that was the problem. He didn't want to be matched with another Candy. The thought of another date with another woman who was perfect for him on paper but not quite right in reality...he couldn't do it.

He wanted that blurred woman snuggled into his bed, ready to offer companionship, understanding. Contentment. Instantly, she snapped into focus, dark hair swinging and wearing nothing but a gorgeous smile.

Elise.

Yes. He wanted Elise, and when Dax Wakefield wanted something, he got it.

But if he pursued her, would this easiness between them fall apart? After all, she wasn't his soul mate and that in and of itself meant she couldn't be that woman in his imagination, with whom he could envision a future.

What a paradox. He'd finally arrived at a place in his life where he could admit he'd grown weary of the endless revolving door of his bedroom. And the woman he pictured taking a longer-term spot in his bed wanted to be *friends,* right after she hooked him up with someone else. Whom he did not want to meet.

Where did that leave the wager between them?

Seven

Bright and early Monday morning, Elise sat in her office and plugged the last of the data into the system. Dax had answered every single question and she firmly believed he'd been honest, or at least as honest as he knew how to be when the content involved elements a perpetual player hardly contemplated. But they'd stayed on track Saturday night—mostly—and finished the profile. Finally.

This would be her hour of victory. She'd built a thriving business using nothing but her belief in true love and her brain. Not one thin dime had come from Brenna, and Elise had fought hard to keep herself afloat during the lean years. She would not let all her work crumble.

She was good at helping people find happiness. Matching Dax with someone who could give him that would be her crowning achievement.

She hit Run on the compiler.

Elise Arundel.

Her forehead dropped to the keyboard with a spectacular crash. She couldn't decide whether to laugh or cry.

Of course her name had come up again. The almost-kiss had been enough to skew the results the first time. Now she had a much bigger mess on her hands because she couldn't get the *oh-my-God* real kiss off her mind. Or the not-a-date with Dax, which should have only been about completing the profile, but instead had eclipsed every evening Elise had ever spent with a man. Which were admittedly few.

They'd bonded over pizza and mutual distrust. And—major points—he'd never made a single move on her. When he confessed he still thought about kissing her, it had been delivered with such heartbreaking honesty, she couldn't chastise him for it.

But his admission served as a healthy reminder. Dax liked women and was practiced at getting them. That's why it felt so genuine—because it was. And once he got her, she'd start dreaming of white dresses while he steadily lost interest. They were *not* a good match.

It didn't stop her from thinking about kissing him in return.

Her mixed feelings about Dax had so thoroughly compromised her matchmaking abilities she might as well give up here and now. It wasn't as though she could fiddle around with the results this time, not when it was so clear she couldn't be impartial. Not after Dax had made such a big deal about ethics.

She groaned and banged her head a couple more times on the keyboard. He was going to have a field day with this. Even if she explained that matchmaking was as much an art as a science, which was why she administered the profile sessions herself, he'd cross his arms and wait for her to confess this matchmaking business was bogus.

But it wasn't, not for all her other clients. Just this one.

The truth was, she abhorred the idea of Dax being matched with another woman so much, she'd subconsciously made sure he wouldn't be. It was unfair to his soul mate—who was still out there somewhere—and unfair to Dax. He was surprisingly sweet and funny and he deserved to be with a woman he could fall in love with. He deserved to be happy.

And she was screwing with his future. Not to mention

the future of EA International, which would be short-lived after Dax crucified her matchmaking skills. That would be exactly what *she* deserved.

How in the world could she get out of this?

A brisk knock on her open door startled her into sitting up. Angie poked her head in, and the smirk on her assistant's face did not help matters.

"Mr. Wakefield is here," she said, her gaze cutting to the lobby suggestively.

"Here?" Automatically, Elise smoothed hair off her forehead and cursed. Little square indentations in the shape of keys lined her skin. "As in, here in the office?"

Maybe she could pretend to be out. At least until the imprint of the keyboard vanished and she figured out what she was going to tell him about his match. Because of course that was why he'd jetted over here without calling. He wanted a name.

"I've yet to develop hologram technology," Dax said smoothly as he strolled right past Angie, filling the room instantly. "But I'm working on it. In the meantime, I still come in person."

Hiding a smile but not very well, Angie made herself scarce.

Elise took a small private moment to gorge herself on the visual panorama of male perfection before her. She'd been so wrong. His everyday suit was anything but ordinary and he was as lickable in it as he was in everything else. And then her traitorous brain reminded her he was most lickable *out* of everything else.

Her mouth incredibly dry, she croaked, "I thought you were busy this week. That's what pizza was all about, right?"

He didn't bother with the chair intended for guests. Instead, he rounded the desk and stopped not a foot from her, casually leaning against the wood as if he owned it.

"I am. Busy," he clarified, his gaze avidly raking over her, as if he'd stumbled over a Van Gogh mural amid street graffiti and couldn't quite believe his luck. "I left several people in a conference room, who are this very minute hashing out an important deal without me. I got up and walked out."

For a man who claimed his company was more important than anything, even contentment, it seemed an odd thing to do. "Why?"

His smoky irises captured hers and she fell into a long, sizzling miasma of delicious tension and awareness.

"I wanted to see you," he said simply.

Her heart thumped once and settled back into a new rhythm where small things like finding his real soul mate didn't matter. The wager didn't matter. The rest of her life alone didn't matter. Only the man mattered.

And he wanted to be with her.

"Oh. Well, here I am. Now what?"

He extended his hand in invitation. "I haven't been able to think about anything other than sitting on a park bench with you and watching the world go by. Come with me."

Her chair crashed against the back wall as she leaped up. She didn't glance at the clock or shut her computer down, just took his hand and followed him.

Most men took her hints and left her alone, more than happy to let her stew in her trust issues. Not this one. Thank goodness. She could worry about how wrong they were for each other and how she had to find someone right for him later.

Fall nipped the air and Elise shivered as she and Dax exited the building. Her brain damage apparently extended to braving the elements in a lightweight wool dress and boots.

"Hang on a sec. I need to go back and get my coat."

She turned when Dax spun her back. "Wait. Wear mine."

Shrugging out of his suit jacket, he draped it around her

shoulders and took great care in guiding her arms through the sleeves. Then he stood there with the lapels gripped in his fists, staring down at her as if the act of sharing his warmth had great significance.

"You didn't have to do that," she said as she rolled up the sleeves self-consciously. But she had to do something with her hands besides put them square on his pectorals as she wanted to. "My coat is right in—"

"Humor me. It's the first time I've given a woman my coat because she needed it. I like it on you."

"I like it on me, too." She hunched down in it, stirring up that delicious blend of scent that was Dax, danger and decadence all rolled into one. She could live in this jacket, sleep in it, walk around naked with the silk liner brushing her skin...

Too bad she'd have to give it back.

They strolled down the block to the small urban park across the street from EA International's office building. Dax told her a funny story about a loose dog wreaking havoc at one of his news station studios and she laughed through the whole thing. Their hands brushed occasionally and she pretended she didn't notice, which was difficult considering her pulse shot into the stratosphere with every accidental touch.

She kept expecting him to casually take her hand, as he'd done Saturday night. Just two people holding hands, no big deal. But he didn't.

No wonder her feelings were so mixed. She could never figure out what to expect. For a long time, she'd convinced herself he only came on to her so she'd lose the wager. Now she wasn't so sure.

Dax indicated an unoccupied bench in the central area of the park, dappled by sunlight and perfectly situated to view a square block of office buildings. People streamed to and from the revolving doors, talking to each other, checking their phones, eyeing the traffic to dart across the street.

She'd opted to sit close, but not too close, to Dax. At least until she understood what this was all about. They might have bonded over the fact that neither of them trusted easily, but that didn't mean she'd developed any better ability to do so.

"How does this people-watching deal go?" She nodded at the beehive of activity around them.

He shrugged. "Mostly I let my mind wander and impressions come to me. Like that couple."

She followed his pointed finger to the youngish boy and girl engaged in a passionate kiss against the brick wall of a freestanding Starbucks.

"Eighteen to twenty-five," he mused. "Likely attending the art school around the corner. They both own smartphones but not tablets, have cable TV but not the premium channels, read Yahoo news but not the financial pages, and can tell me the titles of at least five songs on Billboard's Top 100, but not the names of any politicians currently in office except the president."

Mouth slightly agape, she laughed. "You made all that up."

Dax focused his smoky eyes on her instead of the couple and the temperature inside his jacket neared thermonuclear. "He has a bag with the art school logo and they both have phones in their back pockets. The rest is solid market research for that age group. The details might be slightly off, but not the entertainment habits."

"Impressive. Do you ever try to find out if you're right?"

He gave her a look and stretched his arm across the back of the bench, behind Elise's shoulders. "I'm not wrong. But feel free to go ask them yourself."

Carefully, she avoided accidentally leaning back against his arm. Because she wanted to. And didn't have any clue how to navigate this unexpected interval with Dax, or what to think, what to feel.

"Uh…" The couple didn't appear too interested in being interrupted and all at once, she longed to be that into someone, where the passing world faded from existence. "That's okay."

His answering smile relaxed her. Marginally.

Unfortunately, she had a strong suspicion she could get that into Dax.

"Your turn," he said. "What do you see in those two?"

Without censor, she spit out thoughts as they came to her.

"They're at an age where love is still exciting but has the potential to be that much more painful because they're throwing themselves into it without reservation. They're not living together yet, but headed in that direction. He's met her parents but she hasn't met his, because he's from out of state, so it's too expensive to go home with a girl unless it's serious. Next Christmas he'll invite her," she allowed. "And he'll propose on New Year's because it's less predictable than Christmas Eve."

Dax's lips pursed. "That's entirely conjecture."

He was going to make her work for it, just as she'd done to him.

"Is not. He has on a Choctaw Casino T-shirt, which is in Oklahoma, and if they lived together, they'd be at home, kissing each other in private. The rest is years of studying couples and what drives them to fall in love." She recoiled at the smirk on his face. "So, you can cite research but I can't?"

"Cite research all you want. *Validated* research." As he talked, he grew more animated and angled toward her. "You can't study how people fall in love. Emotions are not quantifiable."

"Says the guy with a psychology degree. How did Skinner determine that mice responded more favorably to partial reinforcement? Not by asking them whether they prefer Yahoo or Google news."

A grin flashed on his face and hit her with the force of a floodlight.

She fought a smile of her own and lost. "You study, you make a hypothesis, you test it and *voilà*. You have a certified conclusion."

Only with Dax could she enjoy a heated argument about her first and only love, the science of the heart.

"So tell me, Dr. Arundel." His gaze swept her with some of that heat in a pointed way she couldn't pretend to miss. "What's your hypothesis about me? Break me down the way you did that couple."

The honks and chattering people filled the sudden silence as she searched his face for some clue to what he was after. Besides the obvious. Clearly he was still thinking about kissing her.

And she was pretty sure she wouldn't utter one single peep in protest.

Great. If she couldn't trust him and she couldn't trust herself to remember why they wouldn't work, why was she still sitting here in the presence of a master at seduction?

"Honestly?" He nodded but she still chose her words carefully. "You don't like to be alone, and women fill that gap. You want her to challenge you, to make it worth your while to stick around, which never happens, so you break it off before she gets too attached. It's a kindness, because you don't really want to hurt her. It's not her fault she's not the one."

His expression didn't change but something unsettled flowed through the depths of his eyes.

"What makes you think I'm looking for the one?" he said lightly. But she wasn't fooled. His frame vibrated with tension.

She'd hit a nerve. So she pressed it, hard.

"You never would have agreed to be matched if you weren't. And you certainly wouldn't keep coming back, especially after it didn't work out with Candy."

He shifted and their knees nested together suggestively. Slowly, he reached out and traced the line of her jaw, tucking an errant lock of hair behind her ear, watching her the entire time.

"I came for the match and stayed for the matchmaker."

"Dax, about that—"

"Relax."

His fingers slid through her hair, threading it until he'd reached the back of her neck. She was supposed to *relax* when he touched her like that?

"You're off the hook," he murmured. "I'm officially calling off our wager. Don't be disappointed."

He'd read her mind. Again.

Relief coursed through her body, flooding her so swiftly, she almost cried. She didn't have to confess that she'd skewed the results. He'd never have to know she'd abandoned her ethics.

But without the wager in place, she had no shield against the onslaught of Dax. No excuse to hold him at arm's length. Much, *much* worse, she had no excuse to continue their association.

"You don't think I can match you?"

"I think you can sell ice to Eskimos. But the fact of the matter is I don't want to meet any more women."

"But you have to," she blurted out. If he didn't, how would he ever meet the love of his life? She might have abandoned her ethics, but not the belief that everyone deserved to be deliriously happy.

Calmly, Dax shook his head. "I *don't* have to. I've already met the one I want. You."

A thousand nonverbal sentiments pinged between them, immobilizing her.

She wasn't right for him. He wasn't right for her. They didn't make sense together and she couldn't let herself think otherwise. Not even for a moment.

The best way to stop wishing for things that couldn't be was to match him with someone else, wager or no wager. Then he could be happy.

Elise froze and forcibly removed his hand from her silky hair.

Now that was a shame. He liked the feel of her.

"Me?" she squeaked.

"Come on. Where did you think I was headed?" Apparently, telling a woman you wanted to see her wasn't enough of a clue that you were into her. "It would be a travesty to continue this matchmaking deal when it's not going to happen."

"What's not going to happen? Finding you a match?" Indignation laced her question.

But then he'd known she wouldn't go down without a fight. He'd have been disappointed otherwise. It had taken him most of Sunday to figure out how to maneuver past all her roadblocks. He still wasn't sure if he'd hit on the right plan. Chances were, she'd drop a few more unanticipated blockades.

That's what made it great.

"The concept was flawed from the beginning. And we both know it. Why not call a spade a spade and move on? We've got something between us." He held up a finger to stem the flow of protests from her mouth. "We do. You can't deny it. Let's see what happens if we focus on that instead of this ridiculous wager."

"I already know what's going to happen." A couple of suits walked by and she lowered her voice. "You'll take me to bed, it'll be glorious and you'll be insufferably smug about it. Hit repeat the next night and the next, for what… about three weeks?"

He bit back a grin. "Or four. So what's the problem?"

His grin slipped as she sighed painfully. "That's not what I want."

"You'd rather I fumble around with no clue how to find your G-spot and then act like it's okay when I come before you? Because I grew out of that before I hit my twenties. The smug part might be a little insufferable, but…" He winked. "I think you'll forgive me."

"You know what I'm saying, Dax. Don't be difficult."

He was being difficult?

"You want promises right out of the gate?" His temper flared and he reined it in. "I don't operate like that. No one does."

"Not promises. Just an understanding that we have the same basic goals for a relationship."

He groaned. "This is not a computer program where you get to see the code before executing it. Why can't we take it day by day? Why can't it be like it was Saturday night?" His thumb found the hollow of her ear again. He spread his fingers against her warm neck and she didn't slap his hand away. "Today is pretty good, too. Isn't it?"

Her eyes shut for a brief moment. "Yeah. It's nice. But we want different things and it's not smart to start something when that hasn't changed. Am I supposed to give up the hope for a committed, loving relationship in exchange for a few weeks of great sex?"

"Who said you have to give up anything? Maybe you're going to gain something." A lot of something if he had his way. He waggled his brows. "What have you got against great sex?"

"I'm a fan of great sex, actually." She crossed her legs, pulling herself in tighter. "It's especially great when I can count on it to be great for a long time instead of wondering when the end is coming."

"Let's break down precisely what it is that you want, shall we?" His head tilted as he contemplated the slight woman who'd had him on the edge of his seat since day one. "You want desperately to find your soul mate but when a guy isn't exactly what you envisioned, you run screaming in the other direction. There's no middle ground."

Her fair skin flushed red. "That's not true."

It was, and she needed someone real to get her over her hang-ups and visions of fantasy lovers dancing in her head. "You have check boxes in your mind, profile questions that you want answered a certain way before you'll go for it. No guy could ever perfectly fit the mold. So you stay home on Saturday nights and bury yourself in futuristic worlds to avoid finding out your soul mate doesn't exist."

"Soul mates do exist! I've seen it."

"For some people." It was a huge reversal for him to admit that much, and she didn't miss it. "But maybe not for me, or for you. Did you ever think of that?"

"Never. Every male I've ever met, that's the first thing I wonder. Is he my soul mate?"

Every male? Even him? "But you don't take that first step toward finding out."

"Just as you evaluate every woman to see if she's the one, decide she can't be, and then don't stick around long enough to let her disappoint you."

Deflection. They were both pretty well versed in it when the subject material grew too hot, and digging into the fact that no one ever measured up—for either of them—was smoking. Escaping unsinged seemed more and more unlikely. But neither of them had jumped out of the fire yet.

She was scared. He got that. It squeezed his chest, and what was he supposed to do with that? After all, *he* was the one who scared her.

"Yeah," he allowed. "But I'm willing to admit it. Are you?"

She slumped down in his jacket, which almost swallowed her. Her wry smile warmed him tremendously. She looked so sweet and delectable sitting there wearing a jacket she hadn't tried to manipulate her way into, and an urgent desire to strip her out of it built with alarming speed.

"It's not fair, you know," she complained. "Why can't you be just a little stupid?"

He laughed long and hard at that and didn't mind that she'd evaded his challenge. He already knew the answer anyway.

"I should ask you the same thing. If you'd relax your brain for a minute, we could avoid all this."

"Avoid what? Psychoanalyzing each other under the table?"

"Hell no. That's the part about us that turns me on the most."

"There's no us," she said and looked away. Her cheeks flushed again, planting the strangest desire to put his lips on that pink spot. "What happened to being friends?"

"Would it make things easier for you to stick a label on this thing between us? I'm okay with calling us friends if you are. But be prepared for an extra dose of friendliness."

She snorted. "Let's skip the labels."

"Agreed. With all the labels off the table, let's just see what happens if I do this."

He tipped her chin up and drew her lips close, a hairbreadth from his, letting her get used to the idea before committing.

Her whole body stilled.

He wanted Elise-on-Fire, as she'd been on the couch the first time he'd kissed her, before she freaked out. And he felt not one iota of remorse in pushing her buttons in order to get her there.

"Scared?" he murmured against her lips. "Wanna go home and watch *Blade Runner* for the four-thousandth time?"

"Not with you," she shot back, grazing his mouth as she enunciated, and it was such a deliberate tease, it shouldn't have sent a long, dark spike of lust through his gut.

He pulled back a fraction, gratified when she swayed after him. "Rather do something else with me? All you have to do is ask."

Her irises flared, and he fell into the chocolaty depths. The expanse between them was an ocean, an eternity, the length of the universe, and he wanted to close the gap in the worst way. Holding back hurt. Badly. But he wanted to see if she'd take the plunge.

"Dax," she murmured and her breath fanned his face as she slid both hands on either side of his jaw. "There is something I want to do with you. Something I've been thinking about for a long time."

Whatever it was, he'd do it. This not-quite-a-kiss had him so thoroughly hot it was a wonder he didn't spontaneously combust. "What's that, sweetheart?"

"I want to beat you at your own game," she whispered and the gap vanished.

Hungrily, she devoured him, tongue slick against his, claiming it masterfully. Her hands guided his head to angle against her mouth more deeply, and fire shot through his groin, nearly triggering a premature release the likes of which he'd not had to fight back in almost two decades.

Groaning, he tried to gain some control, but she eased him backward, hands gliding along his chest like poetry, fingers working beneath the hem to feel him up, and he couldn't stand it.

"Elise," he growled as she nipped at his ear. At the same moment, her fingernails scraped down his abs. White-hot lust zigzagged through the southern hemisphere.

They were in public. On purpose—to prevent anything too out-of-control from happening. Of course Elise had smashed that idea to smithereens.

He firmed his mouth and slowed it down. Way down. Languorously, he tasted her as he would fine wine and she softened under his kiss.

Emboldened now that he had the upper hand, he palmed the small of her back and hefted her torso against his. She moaned and angled her head to suck him in deeper, and he nearly lost his balance. Shifting to the back of the bench, he gripped her tighter, losing himself in the wave of sensations until he hardly knew which way was up.

They either needed to stop right now or take this behind closed doors. He pulled back reluctantly with a butterfly caress of his mouth against her temple.

It had to be the former. It was the middle of the day; he had to get back to work and see about the mess he'd left behind. She probably needed time to assess. Analyze. Work through her checklists and talk herself off the ledge.

Breathing hard, she pursed kiss-stung lips and peered at him under seductively lowered lashes. "Did I win?"

Eight

They held hands as they strolled back to Elise's office and she reveled in every moment of it. Dax didn't pause by his car, clearly intending to walk her all the way back inside. Maybe he was caught up in the rush and reluctant to part ways, too.

Wouldn't that be something? Dax Wakefield affected by Elise Arundel.

What was she *doing* with him?

For once, she had no idea and furthermore, didn't care. Or at least she didn't right now. Dax had a magic mouth, capable of altering her brain activity.

"Don't make plans for tonight," Dax said as they mounted the steps to her office. "I'll bring dinner to your house and we'll stay in."

That worked, and she refused to worry about lingering questions such as whether he intended to seduce her after dinner or if it would be a hands-off night. Maybe she'd seduce him before dinner instead.

She grinned, unable to keep the bubble of sheer bliss inside. This was her turn, her opportunity to get the guy.

"A date that's really a date because we're dating now?" she asked.

Insisting she still had to find him a different match had been an excuse, one contrived to avoid wanting him for herself—and to deny that the whole idea scared her. It still did. But it was her turn to be happy and hopefully make Dax happy at the same time. What could it hurt to try?

He scowled without any real heat. "Dating sounds like a label."

"I'm biting my tongue as we speak."

Unfortunately, she suspected she'd be doing a lot of that in the coming weeks. Somehow Dax had made it seem possible to forgo not only labels, but also guarantees about the future. But that didn't mean her personality had changed. She still wanted a happily ever after. She still wanted Dax to find true love.

The park-bench confessional had revealed more than either of them intended, of that she was sure. It was the only thing she was sure of. But she desperately wanted to believe that the raw revelations had opened them both up to trying something new in a relationship. Sticking around for Dax and day-by-day for her.

It required an extreme level of trust she wasn't sure she had in her. Day-by-day might be a blessing in disguise—it gave her time to figure out if she could trust Dax without wholly committing her fragile heart.

Dax opened the door to EA International and uttered an extremely profane word. She followed his gaze to see four women crowded around Angie's reception desk, all of whom turned in unison at the sound of the door. He dropped her hand without comment.

The park-bench kiss euphoria drained when she recognized Candy. The other three women, a brunette, a blonde and a redhead, weren't familiar but they all had a similar look about them as if they shared a hair stylist. And, like Candy, they all could have stepped from the pages of a magazine.

New clients referred by Candy? That seemed unlikely considering things hadn't worked out with Dax. And Elise had yet to find Candy's soul mate. Guiltily, she made a mental note to go through Candy's profile again to see if she could fix that.

"Is this an ambush?" Dax asked and she did a double take at his granite expression.

"An ambush?" Elise repeated with a half laugh.

That was no way to speak to potential customers. She skirted him and approached the women with a smile. "I'm Elise Arundel. Can I help you?"

"We're here to protest." The redhead stepped to the front and gestured to the other ladies to show she spoke for the group. Not only did these women have similar styles, they also wore identical glowers.

Elise took a tiny step backward in her boots and wished she'd bought the Gucci ones with the higher heel.

"Protest?" Automatically, she shook her head because the word had no context. "I don't understand."

Angie shot to her feet, straightening her wool skirt several times with nervous fingers. "I'm sorry, Elise. I was about to ask them to leave."

Dax took Elise's elbow, his fingers firm against the sleeve of his jacket, and nodded to the redhead. "Elise, this is Jenna Crisp, a former girlfriend. You know Candy. Angelica Moreau is the one on the left and Sherilyn McCarthy is on the right. Also former girlfriends."

These were some of Dax's ex-girlfriends. She couldn't help but study the women with a more critical eye. It seemed Dax had been totally honest when he claimed to have no preference when it came to a woman's physical attributes. The women, though all beautiful and poised and polished, were as different as night and day.

Hard evidence of how truthfully Dax had answered at least one of the profile questions led her to wonder if he'd been forthright on all of them from the very beginning.

Which meant he really did think love was pure fiction.

A funny little flutter beat through Elise's stomach. Dax's hand on her arm was meant to comfort her—or hold her back—and she honestly didn't know which one she needed. "What exactly are you here to protest?"

Had Dax texted them with the news that he was interested in Elise or posted it to his Facebook timeline? He'd have to be very slick to have done so without Elise noticing and besides, why would he? None of this made any sense. It might be upsetting for a former girlfriend to find out Dax had moved on, but surely not surprising—the man was still underwear-model worthy, even fifteen years later, and could give Casanova *and* Don Juan kissing lessons.

Jenna crossed her arms and addressed Elise without glancing at Dax. "We're here in the best interest of your female clients. We're protesting you taking him on as a potential match. Don't foist him off on another unsuspecting woman."

Unable to stop blinking, Elise gaped at Jenna, extremely aware of the other women's hardened gazes. Those lined and mascaraed eyes might as well be spotlights.

"I'm sorry, what?"

A hot flush swept up from her neck to spread across her cheekbones. All those eyes on her, including Dax's and Angie's, had done their job to make her uncomfortable. After all, she was wearing Dax's huge jacket, which told its own story, but also turned her figure blocky, like a stout oak tree in a forest of willows.

"He's not interested in a relationship." Candy cleared her throat. "He told me. Flat out. I thought it was so strange. Why would he go to a matchmaker? Then Jenna and I met by accident at Turtle Creek Salon and I found out he's only in your system as part of some wager the two of you made."

The other ladies nodded and the brunette said, "That's where we met Jenna and Candy too, at the salon."

They *did* share a hairdresser. Elise would congratulate herself on the good eye if it made one bit of difference. Her knees shook and she locked them.

Jenna waved at Dax. "He's a cold, heartless SOB who'll screw you over without a scrap of remorse. No woman deserves that in a match. You have to drop him as a client."

Dax's jacket gained about fifty pounds, weighing heavily on her shoulders. These women had no idea Elise had been kissing Dax not ten minutes ago and making plans to have dinner. But Jenna wasn't talking to her directly. Dax wasn't going to screw Elise over.

"This has gone on long enough." Dax stepped in front of Elise to position himself between her and the ex-girlfriends. "Say anything you like about me, but don't involve Elise in your grievances. She has a right to take on whomever she pleases as a client and you have no call to be here."

Dax's staunch defense hit her in the heart and spread. He was a gentleman underneath his gorgeous exterior, and she appreciated the inside *and* the outside equally.

This was a really bad time to discover she might care about him more than she'd realized.

Jenna glared at Dax, fairly vibrating with animosity. "We were still together when you agreed to be a client. Did you tell her that? One would assume your matchmaker might like to know you weren't actually single."

The bottom dropped out of Elise's stomach. Surely that wasn't true. Jenna was spewing half truths in retaliation for Dax's imagined transgressions. That's what all of this was about—scorned women spewing their fury.

The blonde—Sherilyn, if Elise's beleaguered brain recalled correctly—flipped her curls behind her back and put a well-manicured comforting hand on Jenna's shoulder.

"We were dating, yes." Dax's eyes glittered. "But I was very much single. I did not promise you anything beyond our last date. If you chose to read a commitment into it, that's unfortunate, but it has nothing to do with my business at EA International. Nothing to do with Elise. You're using her to exact revenge on me and it won't work."

Let's take things day by day.

It was almost the same as saying no promises past the last date. Elise suspected Dax gave that speech often.

No, Dax was definitely not a liar. He was a player, exactly as advertised. None of these women had been able to change that and Elise couldn't either, whether she took it day by day or not. Her burden was deciding if she could live with no promises and the likelihood he'd be giving that speech to another woman in a few weeks, after he'd moved on from Elise.

Her fragile heart was already closer to the edge of that cliff on Heartbreak Ridge than she'd like.

All the eyes were back on her, burning into her skin. Jenna's were the hottest as she swept Elise with a pointed look that clearly indicated she found her lacking.

"It has everything to do with what kind of company this is. Are you a matchmaker or a gambler? Do women like Candy come in here expecting to meet a compatible man who's also looking for love, only to be disappointed and out a substantial sum of money?"

It was the TV interview all over again, except this time she wasn't naive enough to offer her matchmaking services to Jenna as a way to prove her skills. She had a hunch that woman ate men alive and then let them beg for more. Except for Dax. He'd truly hurt her.

Elise shook her head, hardly sure where to start slashing and burning Jenna's incorrect and provoking statements.

"I'm a matchmaker. Only. I care about helping people find love, even someone like Dax."

"Someone like Dax?" he repeated silkily as he focused his attention on Elise instead of Jenna. "What's that supposed to mean?"

And now everyone had turned against her, even the one person who'd been on her side. Who *should* have been on her side. She and Dax were embarking on something with no label, but which she'd wanted to explore. Or she had before she walked into this confrontation, this *ambush*.

The room started closing in. "It means you don't believe in love, and I naively thought I could show you how wrong you are. But I can't."

Her heart hurt to admit failure. Not only had she failed to accomplish a reversal in Dax's stance with a soul-mate match, she had almost set herself up for a more spectacular disaster by giving in to his day-by-day seduction routine.

She met the gaze of each ex-girlfriend in succession. It wasn't their fault they weren't the one and she held no hostility toward them.

"Dax is no longer a client as of today. So your protest is poorly timed. Candy, I'll refund your money. Expect the credit to appear on your statement within two days. Please see yourselves out."

She fled to her office and shut the door with an unsatisfying click. Slamming it would have been unprofessional and wouldn't have made her feel any less embarrassed. But it might have covered the sob in her throat.

The door immediately opened and Dax ended up on her side of it. He leaned against the closed door. "I'm sorry. I had no idea they were waiting around to pounce on you. It was uncalled for and entirely my fault."

She let her head drop into her hands so she didn't have to look at him. "It's not your fault. And I was talking to you, too, when I said see yourself out."

"I wanted to make sure you were okay."

The evident concern in his voice softened her. And it pissed her off that he could do that.

"I'm not. And you're the last person who can fix it."

"Elise." His hand on her shoulder shouldn't have felt so right, so warm and like the exact thing she needed. "I have to get back to the office, but I'll make it up to you tonight."

Why did he have to be so sweet and sexy and so hard to pin down?

She shrugged it off—the hand, the man, the disappointment. "I can't do this with you."

"Do what? Have dinner with me? We've eaten plenty of meals together and you never had any trouble chewing before."

That was the problem. He wanted it to be dinner with nothing meaningful attached. In a few weeks, she'd end up like Jenna.

"Dinner isn't just dinner and you know it. It's a start and we have different ideas about what we're starting."

"That's completely untrue. Dinner is about spending time together. Making each other feel good. Conversation."

"Sex," she said flatly.

"Of course. I like sex. What's wrong with that?"

"Because I want to get married! I want to be in love. Not right away, but some day, and I need the possibility of that. I need the man I'm with to want those things too," she shouted.

Shouting seemed to be the only way to get through to him. This was not going to work and he kept coming up with reasons why she should feel differently, as though there was something wrong with her because she didn't want to get in line behind the ex-girlfriends.

He swiveled her chair around to face him. "Maybe I will want that. And maybe you want those things but you'll realize you don't want them with me, and you'll think that's okay. Neither of us knows for sure what's going to happen. Nobody does."

No, but she had a pretty good idea what would happen, and it didn't lead to happily ever after. "Did you imagine yourself marrying Jenna while you were dating her?"

He flinched. "Don't let a few disgruntled women spook you."

The flinch answered the question as well as if he'd flat out said *no*.

"I'm not." That might have been the genesis, but the gang of ex-girlfriends had only brought suppressed issues to the surface. "This was a problem yesterday and the day before that. I let a few hot kisses on a park bench turn my brain off."

"So that's it then. You're done here?"

She didn't want to be. God help her, she couldn't let him walk away forever.

"I have more fun with you than with anyone else I've ever spent time with. If we can't be lovers, what's wrong with continuing to be friends?"

He let his hands fall to his sides. "That's what you want?"

"No, Dax. It's not what I want. But it's what I can offer you." She met his slightly wounded gaze without flinching, though her insides hurt to be so harsh. But what choice did she have? "Go back to work and if you still want to hang out *as friends,* you know where to find me."

Friends.

The word stuck in Dax's craw and put him in a foul mood for the remainder of the day. Which dragged on until it surely had lasted at least thirty-nine hours.

What did Elise want, a frigging engagement ring before they could have a simple *dinner* together? He'd never had so much trouble getting a woman to go on a date, let alone getting her between the sheets. He must be slipping.

"Dax?"

"What?" he growled and sighed as his admin scurried backward over the threshold of his office door. "I'm sorry. I'm distracted."

It wasn't just Elise. The Stiletto Brigade of Former Girlfriends had been brutal, digging barbs into him with military precision. He treated women well while dating them, with intricately planned evenings at expensive venues, gifting them with presents. A woman never left his bed unsatisfied. So why all the animosity?

"You don't have to tell me. I needed those purchase orders approved by five o'clock." Patricia pointed at her watch. "Past five o'clock."

"Why can't Roy sign them? He's the CFO," he grumbled and logged in to the purchase order system so he could affix his digital approval to the documents. Why have a chief financial officer if the man couldn't sign a couple of purchase orders?

"Because they're over five hundred thousand dollars and Roy doesn't have that level of purchasing approval. Only the CEO does. As you know, since you put the policy in place," she reminded him with raised eyebrows. "Are you okay?"

"Fine."

He *was* fine. Why wouldn't he be fine? It wasn't as if he'd lost anything with Elise. They hadn't even slept together yet. A couple of really amazing kisses weren't worth getting worked up over.

Actually, to be precise, he and Elise had shared a couple of amazing kisses and a few good conversations. More than a few. Several.

"Why don't you go home?" Patricia asked.

To his lonely, industrial-size loft? Sure, that would fix everything. "Thanks, I will in a few minutes. You're welcome to leave. You don't have to wait on me."

She nodded, backing away from him as if she expected a surprise attack any second, and finally disappeared.

Dax messed around until well after six o'clock, accomplishing exactly zero in the process, and tried not to think about the Vietnamese place where he'd intended to pick up dinner before going to Elise's house. Vietnamese food warmed up well and he'd fully expected to let it get good and cold before eating.

So Elise hadn't been on board with taking their whatever-it-was-with-no-label to the next level after the run-in with the Stiletto Brigade. They'd freaked her out, right when he'd gotten her panic spooled up and put away.

Fine. He was fine with it.

Elise wanted all her check boxes checked before she'd commit to dinner. It was crazy. She'd rather be alone than spend a little time with a man who thought she was funny and amazing and wanted to get her naked.

Actually, that wasn't true. She was perfectly fine with being friends. As long as he kept his hands to himself and didn't complain when she made astute, painful observations about his relationship track record.

He fumed about it as he got into his car and gunned the engine. He fumed about it some more as he drove aimlessly around Dallas, his destination unclear.

Dax shook his off morose mood and focused on his surroundings. The side-street names were vaguely familiar but he couldn't place the neighborhood. He drove to the next stoplight, saw the name of the intersection, and suddenly it hit him.

He was a block from Leo's house.

House, fortress, same thing when it came to his former friend. Leo had excelled at keeping the world out, excelled at keeping his focus where it belonged—on success. Dax slowed as the car rolled toward the winding, gated drive. The huge manor skulked behind a forest of oaks, bits of light beaming between the branches stripped of leaves by the fall wind.

Was Leo at home? Hard to tell; the house was too far from the street. Once upon a time, Dax would have put money on the answer being no. For as long as he'd known Leo, the man worked until he nearly dropped with exhaustion. Occasionally, when Dax found himself between women, he'd coax his friend out from behind his desk and they'd tie one on at a bar in Uptown.

Case in point—Dax had no woman on call. No plans. It would have been a great night to meet up with a friend who didn't ask him pointed questions about why he never stuck it out with a woman longer than a few weeks.

He didn't call Leo. He didn't drive up to the security

camera at the gate, which was equipped with facial recognition software, and would admit him instantly.

Leo wasn't that friend, not any more. Leo had a new playmate locked away inside his fortress, one he'd paid a hefty chunk of change to meet.

Well, not really a playmate since he'd married Daniella. *Married.* That was a whole lot of forever with the same woman. If Elise could be believed, Leo and Daniella were soul mates.

For the first time, Dax wondered if Leo was happy. Because wasn't that the point of a soul mate? You had someone you wanted to be locked away with, someone you could be with all the time and never care if the world spun on without either of you.

If Dax's soul mate existed, she would care very much what was behind his curtain and furthermore, he'd trust her with the backstage mess—the doubts about whether he actually had something to offer a woman in a relationship. The anxiety over whether he'd find out he had more in common with his mother than he'd like. The fear that he actually lacked the capacity to be with one person for the rest of his life. The suspicion that he was broken and that was why he'd never found someone worthy of promising forever to.

Five hundred thousand dollars seemed like a bargain if it bought a woman who stilled his restlessness. Dax had just spent twice that with the click of a mouse, and barely glanced at the description of the goods Wakefield Media had purchased. Whatever it was—likely cameras or other studio equipment—would either wear out or be replaced with better technology in a few years.

A soul mate was forever. How could that be possible for someone like Dax? What if he'd already met her and didn't realize it? That was the very definition of being broken, and it was exactly what Elise had meant when she'd said "someone like Dax."

Before he did something foolish, such as drive up to Leo's house and demand an explanation for how Leo had known Daniella was his soul mate, Dax hit the gas and drove until the low fuel light blinked on in the dash. He filled up the tank and went home, where he did not sleep well and his mood did not improve.

The next day dragged even worse than the day before. Everyone, including Patricia, steered clear, and while he appreciated their wisdom, it only pissed him off. He needed a big-time distraction.

Because he was in that perverse of a mood, he pulled out his phone and texted Elise.

Have a nice evening by yourself?

Well, that was stupid. Either she'd ignore him, tell him what a fabulous evening she had without him or make a joke that gave him zero information about whether she was in as bad of a mood as he was. And he wanted her to be. He wanted her to suffer for…

Beep. No. It sucked. I miss you.

His heart gave a funny lurch and the phone slipped from his nerveless fingers. God, what was he supposed to do with that?

Nothing. She was trying to manipulate him. She knew he didn't like to be alone and wanted him to crack first. That wasn't happening. He wasn't texting her back with some cheesy message about how he was miserable too. She was probably sitting there on that champagne-colored couch in her condo, phone in hand, waiting for his reply.

They weren't dating. Elise wasn't his lover. It shouldn't be this difficult.

He set the phone off to the side of his desk and proceeded to ignore it for the next thirteen minutes while he read the same paragraph of a marketing proposal over and over again.

The phone sat there, silently condemning him.

"Stop looking at me," he growled at the offending device and turned it over.

Elise wanted him to be some fairy-tale guy who swept her off her feet with promises of undying love, and it was so far from who he was, he couldn't even fathom it. So that was it. Nothing more to say or do.

The phone rang.

Elise. Of course she wasn't going to put up with his stupid text embargo. His heart did that funny dance again as he flipped the phone over to hit the answer button.

"Hey, Dax," a female voice purred in his ear. It was not Elise.

Dang it. He should have at least glanced at the caller ID. "Hey…you."

He winced. He had no idea who she was.

"I've been thinking a lot about you since yesterday," she said.

Sherilyn. He recognized her voice now and if he hadn't been moping around like a lovesick teenager with an atrophied brain, he'd never have answered her call. "Yesterday when you and the rest of your wrecking crew stormed into a place of business and started telling the proprietor how to run it?"

Which wasn't too far off from what he'd done to Elise, but he'd staged his showdown over EA International's formula for success on TV. He swallowed and it went down his throat like razor blades. In his defense, at the time he hadn't known how much she hated being in the spotlight. She'd handled herself admirably, then and yesterday. Because she was amazing.

"Oh, I wasn't really a part of that." Sherilyn *tsk*ed. "I went along because I had a vested interest in seeing that you no longer had a shot at getting matched. I'm in the mood for round two with you."

What a mercenary.

"I'm sorry, Sherilyn, but I'm not interested in a relationship with anyone right now. You heard Candy. It would be unfair to you."

He did not want to have this conversation. Not with Sherilyn, not with Candy, not with any woman. He was sick of the merry-go-round.

"Come on. Remember how good it was?" Sherilyn laughed throatily. "I'm not asking for a commitment, Dax. Just one night."

Her words reverberated in his head, but he heard them in his voice, as he said them to Elise. And of course the idea had seemed as repugnant to Elise when it came from him as it did now to Dax coming from Sherilyn.

Why hadn't Elise slapped him? Instead, she'd offered him friendship, which he'd thrown back in her face because he'd wanted things his way, not hers. And he'd lost something valuable in the process.

Dax sighed. "No, actually, I don't remember. Thanks for calling, but please forget about me. We're not going to happen again."

He hung up and stared out the window of his office. He might as well go ahead and admit he missed Elise, too, and had no idea how to fix it.

The Stiletto Brigade hadn't caused his problem with her. The problem had been there from the beginning, as she'd said. He'd discounted Elise's hopes and dreams because they were based on something he considered absurd and improbable—true love. Yeah, he'd done the profile and gone along, but only to win the wager fairly, not because he believed she had some special ability to prove something that was impossible to prove. Yet she'd built an entire business on the concept, and if someone as smart as Leo bought into Daniella being his soul mate, maybe there was more to the idea than Dax had credited.

Maybe he should give Elise's way a chance.

Or…

Love was a myth and now that some time had passed, the new marriage smell had worn off, but Leo was too embarrassed to admit he'd made a mistake. If Dax gave in to Elise without more information, he could be setting himself up for a world of hurt. After all, he didn't trust easily for a reason. Look what had happened to his friendship with Leo.

Besides, Elise wanted to meet her soul mate and Dax was not it. Their vastly different approaches to relationships—and to life as a whole—proved that. So why pretend?

There was nothing wrong with two consenting adults having fun together. They didn't have to swear undying devotion to take their relationship to the next level.

Why was she being so *stubborn* about this?

Leo might be too ashamed to come clean about how disastrous his relationship had become with Daniella, but Elise had lots of other clients. Surely several of EA International's former matches hadn't lasted. An unhappily ever after was a better way to attest that love was a myth than being matched with another Candy, anyway.

All he needed was one couple who hadn't ended up with their soul mate as advertised. Then he could take the evidence to Elise. She needed to understand how the real world worked, and what better way to convince her? He'd have hard proof that even when people started out wanting a lifelong commitment, sometimes it still didn't happen. Sure, she might be a little upset at first to learn she'd held out for something that didn't exist, but then she'd see his point. She wanted him as much as he wanted her, and it was time to let things between them take their natural course.

Guarantees were for products, not people. By this time tomorrow, he could have Elise naked and moaning under his mouth.

Nine

Saturday night, Elise finally stopped carrying her phone around in her hand. Dax hadn't called, hadn't texted, hadn't dropped by. He wasn't going to. The line had been drawn, and instead of doing something uncomfortable like stepping over it, Dax had hightailed it in the other direction. His loss.

And hers, unfortunately. She couldn't shake a slight sense of despondency, as though she hadn't seen the sun in weeks and the forecast called for more rain.

It was a good thing she'd put on the brakes when she had—imagine how hurt she'd be if things had gone any further. Regardless, she was undeniably disappointed he didn't even want to stay friends, which she had to get over.

She needed to focus on Blanca and Carrie, the two new applicants in her makeover program. They were both due to arrive in a couple of weeks and Elise had done almost nothing to prepare.

She tapped out a quick email to Dannie, who helped Elise with makeup and hair lessons when needed. After years at the knee of a supermodel, Elise had enough fashion and cosmetic tips to fill an ocean liner, but Dannie liked the work and by now, the two women were fast friends.

Elise confirmed the dates and attached a copy of a contract for Dannie's temporary employment. Normally, it wouldn't be a question of whether Dannie would say yes, but she and Leo had just returned from an extended vacation to Bora Bora in hopes Dannie would come home pregnant.

Elise would be thrilled if that was the reason Dannie said no.

Then she made a grocery list as two extra mouths required a great deal of planning, especially to ensure the meals were healthy but not too difficult to prepare. Few of the women in her program came to her with great culinary skills. It was one of the many aspects of training she offered, and after a lifelong love-hate relationship with food, Elise brought plenty to the literal and figurative table.

The remainder of the evening stretched ahead of her, long and lonely. She flipped on a movie, but her mind wandered.

The doorbell startled her and she glanced at the clock. Good grief, it was nearly midnight. It could only be Dax. A peek through the window confirmed it. Despite the shadows, she'd recognize the broad set of his shoulders and lean figure anywhere.

Her heart lightened. She'd missed him, fiercely.

She took a half second to fortify herself. He could be here for any number of reasons. Better to find out straight from the horse's mouth than get her hopes up.

"I wasn't expecting you," she said needlessly as she opened the door and cursed the jumpy ripples in her stomach. He was just so masculine and gorgeous. Then she got a good look at his face. The sheer darkness in his gaze tore through her. "What's wrong?"

Tension vibrated through the air as he contemplated her. "I don't know why I'm here."

"Bored? Lonely? Can't find anyone else who wants to play?" She crossed her arms over her middle. Something was up and it was far more chilling than the frigid fall night.

"On the contrary," he said smoothly, his voice like pure honey. "Women seem to be coming out of the woodwork. Except for the one I really want."

Her?

Why was that so affecting in places better left unaffected? It should irritate her to be thought of as an object of lust. The idea shouldn't feel so powerful and raw. But a week's worth of being on edge and missing their verbal swordplay and dreaming about his abs culminated in a heated hum in her core.

"I…" *Want you too.* "…hoped you'd call."

"Did you?" He hooked his thumbs in the front pockets of his jeans, but the lethal glint in his eye belied the casual pose. "What did you hope I'd say? Let's be friends? Let's paint each other's nails and shop for shoes together?"

She should shut the door. She should tell him to go away and forget she'd ever mentioned being friends.

"I hoped you'd unbend enough to admit there's a possibility you might fall in love one day. Barring that, I hoped you'd still want to have lunch occasionally or—"

"Elise. I don't want to be your friend."

"Not worth it to you?" she snapped.

"It's not enough." His hands fisted against his pockets and she realized he was trying to keep himself under control. "I wasn't going to call. I wasn't going to come over. I found myself within a block of your house five times this week all the same."

"But you kept driving."

He nodded once. "I kept driving. Until tonight."

After a long pause, she voiced the question he obviously wanted her to ask. "What was special about tonight?"

"I can't—I don't know how to give you what you want," he bit out. "And I don't know how to stay away."

Her heart stuttered and shoved all her suppressed feelings to the surface. That's why she'd missed him—when he showed her glimpses of his soul, it was more beautiful than the ocean at sunset.

"I never asked you to stay away. You shouldn't have."

"Yes. I should have. I absolutely should not be here on your doorstep." His chest shuddered with his next deep breath. "But I can't sleep. I can't concentrate. All I can think about is you naked, wrapped around me, and that brain of yours firing away on all cylinders as you come up with more inventive ways to challenge me."

The image of her unclothed body twined with his sprang into her consciousness, sparked through her abdomen, raised goose bumps on her skin. She swallowed against the sudden burn in her throat.

"You say that like it's a bad thing," she joked and nearly bit her tongue as fire licked through his expression.

"It's ridiculous. And I'm furious about it, so stop being so smug."

His glare could have melted ice. All at once, his strange mood made sense. Normally when he wanted a woman, he seduced all her reservations away. But he respected Elise too much to do that to her and he was incredibly conflicted about it. The effect of that realization was as powerful as being the object of his desire.

Combined, it nearly took her breath.

"Poor thing," she crooned. "Did that bad Elise tie you up in knots?"

One brow lifted and every trace of his ire disappeared, exactly as she'd intended. "Don't you dare make a suggestion like that unless you plan to follow through."

"Uh-uh." She shook her head. "This conversation is not devolving into foreplay."

"Not yet." Lazily, he swept her with a half-lidded smoky once-over. "But I appreciate the confirmation that talking dirty to you counts as foreplay."

Now she should slam the door in his cocky face. Except she'd shifted the mood on purpose, to give him a reprieve for confessing more than he'd probably intended. And the last thing she wanted was for him to leave.

But did she want him to stay? This wasn't some random drive-by; it was a showdown.

Between his mercurial mood and the hum in her core, this night could end up only one of two ways—either she'd let him into her bed and into her heart, or she'd give him that final push away.

Dax was still on the porch. Waiting for her to make the decision. And Dax would never let her forget she'd made the choice.

Who was tying whom up in knots here?

"Why are you here, Dax?" She took a tiny step behind the door, in case she needed to slam it after all. Of course there was a good chance he'd slam it for her, once he crossed the threshold and backed her up against it in a tango too urgent and wild to make it past the foyer. "And don't feed me another line. You know exactly why you got out of the car this time."

His reckless smile put her back on edge. "Why do I find it so flipping sexy when you call me on my crap?"

He thought her no-filter personality was sexy. He really did. She could see the truth of it in his expression. The wager was over and there was no reason for him to say something like that unless he meant it.

"Because you're neurotic and deranged, obviously." When his smile softened, she couldn't help but return it, along with a shrug. "We both must be. If you want the real answer, you said it yourself. You like that I challenge you. If it's easy, you don't value it as much."

His irises flashed, reflecting the bright porch light. "I would definitely classify this as not easy."

"And you still haven't told me why you're here."

He crossed his arms and leaned on the door frame. "Have you ever followed up with any of the couples you've matched?"

"Of course. I use them as referrals and I throw parties every few months for both former and current clients as a thank-you for being customers. Many become friends."

"They're all happy. All of them. They've all found their soul mates and say you were one hundred percent responsible." He said it as if Elise had single-handedly wiped out a small village in Africa with a virus.

"You talked to my former clients?"

The shock wasn't that he'd done so, but that he'd *just* done so. Why hadn't he had those conversations at the very beginning, when they were still operating under the terms of the wager?

"Not the recent ones, only those matched over five years ago. They should be miserable by now. Happily ever after doesn't exist." His rock-hard expression dared her to argue with his perfunctory statement.

Except he'd learned otherwise, and clearly it was throwing him for a loop.

He hadn't talked to her clients before now because he'd assumed he didn't need to. That he'd only be told what he already believed to be true.

It was hard to be handed back your arrogance on a silver platter.

"I offer a guarantee, Dax," she reminded him gently. "No one's ever asked for their money back."

Instead of bowing and scraping with apology, he stared at her. "Aren't you going to invite me in?"

"Why would I do that?"

His gaze burned through her. "Because you want to know what else I learned when I talked to your clients."

He'd learned *more* than happily ever after happened to people on a regular basis? Oh, yes, he had and he was going to make her work to find out what, running her through his maze until she dropped with exhaustion. Or solved it and won the prize. It was a ludicrous challenge. And it was working.

But she didn't for a moment believe he only wanted to

tell her about his findings. The prize wasn't simply information and they both knew it.

She held the door open wide in silent invitation and prayed she wasn't going to be sorry.

She shouldn't have answered the bell. But now she had to know if talking to happy couples had somehow opened his eyes. Maybe gotten him to a place where he could see a future with one woman.

What if she *could* be that woman? She didn't want to send him on his way before finding out.

"Dax?"

He met her gaze as he stepped over the threshold. "Elise."

Searching his beautiful face for some small scrap of reassurance, she put it all on the line.

"Please don't do this unless you mean it."

Dax shut the door behind him and leaned back against it, both hands flat against the wood.

The click reverberated in the silent foyer.

Elise's eyes were shiny and huge and he didn't mistake the look for anything other than vulnerability, which just about did him in where the last week of awfulness hadn't.

Why had he stayed away so long?

It didn't matter now. He was surrounded by Elise and everything finally made sense again. He breathed her in before he hauled her into his arms right there in the foyer.

Tonight wasn't about slaking his thirst in the well of Elise, though he'd be lying if he said he wasn't hopeful they'd eventually get there. He'd have sworn this was all about taking pleasure where pleasure was due. But now that he was here…it wasn't. He still wasn't sure *what* tonight was about, what he truly wanted—or what she wanted— but the fragile quality to her demeanor wasn't doing his own brittle psyche any favors.

Don't do this unless you mean it.

He didn't pretend to misunderstand. Her voice broke as she'd said it and it echoed in his head, demanding an answer—which he didn't have.

They needed to shake off the heaviness.

"Don't do what?" he asked lightly. "Tell you about the nineteen conversations I had with blissfully happy couples? It was nauseating."

Her quick smile set off an explosion of warmth in his midsection.

"Nineteen? That's a lot of conversations about true love. What I don't get is why you'd subject yourself to that."

He shrugged. "Seek-and-destroy mission. I was sure I'd find at least one couple embroiled in a bitter divorce settlement. Needless to say, no one was. On the heels of that estrogen ambush in your office, I needed to figure out some things."

Guilt flickered across Elise's face. "I'm sorry that happened. Some of that must have been really hard to stomach, especially coming from women you were formerly intimate with. I was selfishly caught up in my own reaction and didn't think about how you must have felt."

"Uh…" He'd been about to brush it away. But this was Elise. She'd see through him in a second. How had she known the whole thing had bothered him so much?

So much for lightening the mood.

"I was more worried about you than me," he said gruffly. "But thanks."

Such a small word to encompass the full generosity of Elise's apology. A lot of women—most women—would have said he'd gotten what was coming to him. And maybe he had. He'd treated Jenna pretty shabbily. He sighed. There was a possibility all of the women had genuine grievances. Relationships were not his forte.

But he wanted that to be different.

Elise motioned him out of the foyer and walked into the living room. "So while talking with my clients, what did you figure out?"

He followed, caught up with her in a couple of steps and grasped her hand to swing her around to face him in front of a gas-log fireplace, the flame lowered to a romantic glow.

Don't do this unless you mean it.

But that was exactly it. He *wanted* meaning, wanted something to finally click.

"I figured out *I'm* the one missing something." And only Elise held the answer. "I got out of the car tonight because I want to know what it is. You're the relationship expert. Tell me."

Her skin was luminous in the firelight and he wanted to trace the line of her throat with his lips, then keep going to discover the delights of the trim body waiting for him under her off-white sweater. But he wanted to hear her response just as much.

She looked up, hand still in his. Flesh to flesh, it sparked and the answering awareness leaped into her expression. Something powerful that was part chemistry and part something else passed between them. He let it, embraced it, refused to disrupt the moment simply because he'd been off balance since the moment this woman insisted he call her Ms. Arundel.

He tightened his grip. He wasn't about to let her step away, either.

"Tell me what I'm missing, Elise."

"What if I show you?" Her voice scraped at him, raw and low.

"What if you did?" he murmured. "What does that look like?"

"It looks like two people connecting on a fundamental level." Without breaking eye contact, she slid her free hand up his chest and let it rest over his heart, which sped up under her fingers. "It looks like the start of a long kiss that you can't bear to end. It looks like a friendship that's made more beautiful because you've opened your soul along with your body. Have you ever had that before?"

"No," he said, shocked at the catch in his throat. Shocked at how much he suddenly wanted something he'd had no clue existed.

"Me, either."

The wistful note of her admission settled over him heavily, binding them together in mutual desire for something meaningful and special.

"How do we get it?"

"It's right here," she whispered, tapping the place over his heart once with an index finger, then touching her own heart. "For both of us. All we have to do is reach out at the same time. That's what makes it wonderful."

Everything inside woke up at once, begging to dive into not just the sensations, but the swirl of the intangible. He'd called off the wager strictly because he'd begun to suspect he was about to lose. Spectacularly. And as he looked into her soul, it was done.

He was lost.

"Elise." He palmed her chin and lifted those luscious lips to his and hovered above them in a promise of pleasures to come. "I mean it."

And then he fell into that long kiss he hoped would never end and wrapped Elise in his arms. When his knees buckled, he took her to the carpet with him, twisting to break her fall, sliding into a chasm of pure joy.

She found the hem of his shirt and spread her palms hot against his back. He groaned and angled his head to take the kiss deeper, to explore her with his tongue, to taste the beauty of her.

This wasn't an urgent coupling, a slaking of mutual

thirst. It was more. Much more. Profound and meaning-ful. And he couldn't have stopped if his life depended on it.

He wanted Elise. Wanted it all, everything she'd offered, especially the emotional connection.

She lifted her head a fraction. "Dax?"

"Hmm?" He took the opportunity to run his lips down the column of her neck, exactly as he'd envisioned, and yes, it was sweet. She moaned, letting her head fall back to give him better access.

"Don't you want to go upstairs?" she asked after a good long minute of letting him taste her.

Upstairs was far away and required too much effort to get there.

"Not especially. I don't think I can wait that long." That gorgeous blush rose up in her cheeks. Mystified, he ran the pad of his thumb over the coloring. "What's this all about?"

"We're in the living room," she whispered.

"I know," he whispered back and snaked a hand under her sweater to feel the curve of her waist in an intense ca-ress. "I'm becoming very fond of your living room. The fireplace is a nice touch."

"I just…you know. The living room is for watching TV. The bed is for…lying down. In the dark."

More blushing. Despite the rock-hard bulge in his pants and the near-breathless state of desire she'd thrown him into, he recognized a woman in the midst of uncertainty. But over what?

"I'm not a particular fan of darkness. I want to see you."

"There's uh…not much to see." She wiggled a little until his hand fell from her waist, and then she yanked the hem of her sweater down over her exposed skin with a little too much force.

Sitting back on the carpet a bit to give her space, he reached out and took her hand gently. The last thing he wanted was for her to be uncomfortable. "What happened to opening yourself body and soul? Isn't that what this is about?"

"Easier said than done." She made a face. "Especially when I'm up against such stiff competition."

Competition?

Then it dawned on him. The Stiletto Brigade. They'd not only spooked her, they'd given Elise a complex about her appearance. His heart flipped over painfully but when it faded, a strange sort of tenderness replaced it.

"Look at me." When she complied, the earlier vulnerability was back tenfold. "There's not a way to say this without sounding arrogant, but roll with it for a minute. Don't you think I could be in the bed of any woman I chose?"

Her brows furrowed. "Yeah, but that wasn't really in question."

He gave her a minute but her anxiety didn't fade. A smart woman was still susceptible to being deceived by her own self-consciousness, apparently. "Then wouldn't it be safe to assume I'm with the woman I want? And that I think you're beautiful beyond compare?"

Except he'd done almost nothing to convince her of that because their relationship had evolved in such an out-of-the-norm manner. He'd never sent her flowers, never bought her jewelry, and certainly never spent an evening flattering her over dinner.

But he didn't want to do those things with her. He'd done them with other women. A lot. And it had never amounted to more than a shallow bit of nothingness designed to get a woman in bed.

Elise deserved better.

He slid a hand through her hair and smoothed it away from her face. "Instead of telling you how I feel about you, how about if I show you?"

Ten

The corners of Elise's mouth lifted. "What does that look like?"

Obviously she'd recognized her own words as he repeated them back to her.

"It looks like something so stunning, I can hardly breathe." Watching her intently, he fingered the hem of her sweater and lifted it slowly until her stomach was bared. Then he stopped. "Do you trust me with the rest?"

Surprise flitted through her expression. "I…I never thought about this being about trust."

"Of course it is. We're reaching out at the same time, but doing so requires a measure of faith. On both sides."

She stilled, taking it all in, and in a flash, he got the distinct sense she had a lot less experience with men and sex in general than the majority of women he knew. She talked such a good game he'd missed it, but with all the discussion around competition and being embarrassed about the locale he'd chosen, not to mention how often he found her home alone on the weekends…it all fit.

Then she nodded and lifted her arms, silently offering him access to completely remove her top—and placing utter trust in him at the same time. It just about broke him. Sucking in oxygen, which did not settle his racing pulse, he took his time unveiling her, inch by creamy, gorgeous inch.

She wasn't wearing a bra. And her breasts were perfect,

topped by peaks that went rigid under his heated gaze. He muttered a curse as his hands involuntarily balled up, aching to stroke her from neck to belly button. *Take it slow, Wakefield.*

"You're exquisite," he ground out through a throat gone frozen, and tossed the sweater aside, unable to tear his attention from her half-naked form. Nonsense spilled from his mouth, murmured words of praise and awe. So maybe he'd tell her how much he liked her body in addition to showing her.

"Your turn," she whispered.

Immediately he complied, whipping his shirt off as fast as humanly possible because there was no way he was letting fabric block his ability to drink in the sight of gorgeous, uncovered Elise.

"Look your fill," he advised her. "Here in the light."

Look her fill she did, hesitantly at first but then with a hungry boldness that somehow turned erotic instantly. As her gaze traveled over his bare torso, heat flushed across his skin and coalesced at the base of his spine. All the blood in his head rushed south, leaving him slightly dizzy and enormously turned on.

She was going to kill him.

"Get used to me without clothes," he continued. "I'm about to be a whole lot more naked. I want you to see how much you affect me when I look at you. How much I want you, how gorgeous you are to me."

No time like the present to shed his jeans. He stood and with the heat of the fire at his back and the heat of Elise at his front, he flipped the button. She watched, silently, her head tipped up and her lips parted, hands clasped in her lap tightly.

He should have opened with a striptease because she'd totally forgotten her own nakedness. Win-win.

Then he was fully undressed and she huffed out a strangled gasp. It was potent to render a woman with such a quick wit speechless.

"See this?" he pointed at the obvious erection straining toward her. "This is all you, honey. You're not even touching me and I'm about to bust."

He wasn't kidding. Show and Tell was turning into his favorite foreplay game ever.

"What if I wanted to touch you?" she asked coyly. "Is that allowed?"

He strangled over a gasp of his own. "That's more than allowed. In fact, it's encouraged."

Crawling to him, she wiggled out of the remainder of her clothes unprompted and knelt at his feet.

With incredible care, she ran her hands up his legs, fingering the muscles of his thighs, breezing by his erection. She grazed it and his eyelids fluttered with the answering spike of unadulterated pleasure.

She climbed to her feet to continue her exploration and he fought to stay still. Every nerve vibrated on full alert, poised to pounce at the first opportune moment.

"You still have gorgeous abs," she murmured as her fingertips read the muscles of his torso like braille. "They feel like warm, velvet stone."

"Looked me up on Google, did you?" He grinned, pleased for some ridiculous reason. Millions of people had seen those ads and he'd never given it a moment's thought. But the idea of Elise taking secret pleasure in looking at pictures of him—it was hot. "Put your hands a little south of my abs and you'll find something else that feels like velvet stone."

There came the blush again and he should totally be chagrined that he'd provoked it on purpose. But he wasn't.

Glancing at the real estate in question and back up again quickly, she gave a little sigh of appreciation that sang right through him. "I do that to you? Really?"

He groaned in disbelief and frustration. "You have been for weeks and weeks. Years. For an eternity. And now I'm moving on to the 'show' part of this demonstration."

Catching her up in his arms, he fitted hungry lips to her mouth and let all the pent-up desire guide the kiss. Instantly, she melted against him and he took full advantage, winding his embrace tighter to fit her luscious little body against him.

She felt amazing, warm and soft, and he wanted to touch. So he did, running his hands down her back, along the sweet curve of her rear, and he nearly cried out when she responded in kind. Her hands were bold and a bit clumsy with eagerness and combined, it swirled into a vortex of need more powerful than any he'd ever felt before.

This was so far beyond simply taking pleasure and returning it, he couldn't fathom it.

The urge to make this cataclysmic for her became more important than breathing.

He picked her up easily and laid her out on the couch where he could focus on loving every inch of her. Kneeling between her amazing legs, he inched over her until they were skin to skin, but his full weight rested on his elbows on either side of her.

"Talk to me," he murmured as he nuzzled her neck.

"Talk to you about what?" she asked.

He lifted his head so he could speak to her directly.

"Tell me what you like, Elise."

As passionate as she was about connection and relationships, she'd probably be incredibly responsive to anything he did, but he'd prefer to start out educated.

She bit her lip, contemplating. "Shoes. And this is a horrible thing to admit, but I really, really like chocolate."

He couldn't even laugh. She truly had no clue he'd meant for her to tell him what she liked sexually. Probably no one had ever asked her before or she had less experience than

he'd assumed. The seriousness of the trust she'd shown hit
him in a place inside he'd never realized was there.

"Why is it horrible to like chocolate?"

"Because it goes straight to my hips. I gain weight easily."

"That's impossible." Because he wanted to and he could,
he shifted onto his side and ran the back of his hand down
the curve of her waist, over the not-chunky hip and around
her thigh, and it was nice indeed. "You're so thin you'd have
to run around in the shower to get wet."

She snorted. "Thanks, but I didn't always look like this."

The small slice of pizza, the unfinished lunches, came
back to him suddenly. She really didn't eat much. And
somehow, this fear of gaining weight was tied to her self-
image issues.

"You'd be beautiful to me even if you weighed more."
In fact, she could stand to gain a few pounds.

"I thought we were doing the show part," she said pertly
and slid her leg along his, opening herself without seem-
ing to realize it. It was so unconsciously sexy, he let her
change the subject. Plus, the new subject was one he happened to approve of.

"Yeah?" he growled. "You like it when I show you how
much you turn me on? Let's begin with exhibit A."

And then he mouthed his way down her stomach to the
juncture of her thighs, parting them easily, and she gasped
as he tasted her sweet spot, laving it lightly to give her time
to adjust to such an intimate kiss.

Her hips rolled, shoving his lips deeper against her wet
center, and he sucked. She moaned on a long note and that
was it—she pulsed against his tongue with a little cry that
he felt clear to his toes. His own release almost transpired
right then and there. It took all he had to keep it together.

He couldn't wait to be inside her any longer.

Slipping on a condom with quick fingers, he rose up over

her and caught her gaze, communicating without words, letting all his desire for her spill from his expression. She stared back, eyes luminous with satisfaction.

Slowly, so slowly, he bent one of her gorgeous legs up and nestled between her thighs to complete their connection. She sighed lustily as he pushed. When he'd entered her fully, a wash of pleasure slammed his eyelids shut and he groaned in harmony with her.

It was a dazzling thing to be joined with Elise, and he couldn't hold back. Her name tumbled from his lips, over and over, as he spiraled them both higher. Nearly mindless, he sought to touch her, to caress her, to make her come again before he did…because there were rules. But she shifted, and the angle was so sweet, he lost complete control. Splintering into oblivion, he cried out as answering ripples of her climax sharpened his. The powerful orgasm sucked him under for a long moment, blinding him to everything but the release.

With the fireplace crackling merrily and the warmth of an amazing afterglow engulfing him, he lay there, unable to move. Elise cradled his spent body, both of their chests heaving as one, and he experienced the most profound sense of bliss.

That's what he'd missed.

Happily ever after just might begin with one day of happiness that you found so amazing and wonderful, you woke up the next day aching to repeat it. And didn't let anything stop you.

Elise finally coaxed Dax into bed and they thoroughly christened it in what was the most monumentally earth-shattering experience of her admittedly short list of sexual encounters. So far, she'd managed to keep her total cluelessness from him, but she couldn't let this particular first slide.

She snuggled up against his absolutely delicious body and waited until he'd pulled the sheet up around them to spill it. "You're the first man I've had in this bed."

"Ever?" His voice was soft with a hint of wonderment. As if she'd given him a special gift he'd always wanted but never received.

Was she *that* far gone over a couple of orgasms? She was assigning all kinds of emotions to Dax that she had no business assigning. Her head needed to be plucked out of the clouds really fast, before she got ideas about what was going on here that would only lead to disappointment.

She'd consented to sleep with him, but not to fall for him.

She nodded against his shoulder and opted for candor. "I bought this set about a year ago and I didn't want to sleep here night after night with memories of a past relationship gone wrong still haunting it."

The hand intimately caressing her waist stilled. "Guess that means you figured out how to exorcise the ghosts of past lovers. Or you think I'll be in your bed for the rest of its life."

The post-orgasm high vanished as the heaviness of his real question weighted the atmosphere.

"Um…" Well, she really hadn't thought through how that particular confession was going to go, had she? "Door number three. I thought you were worth it regardless."

He slid a hand up to her jaw and guided her head up so he could look at her. Something misty and tender sprang from his gaze. "That's the best thing anyone's ever said to me."

How could that be? Surely someone had told him he had value before. But his expression said otherwise.

She couldn't look away as a powerful and intangible current arced between them. It was more than the connection she'd told him was possible. More than the deepening of their friendship that she'd sought.

Then he laid his lips on hers in a sweet kiss that went on and on and sent her into the throes of a whole different kind of high. So what if her head was firmly in the clouds?

She was in bed with Dax and he was beautiful and precious and it was the most amazing night in her memory.

And it didn't appear to be ending anytime soon.

"Lay here with me." He spooned her against his warm torso and held her as if he'd never let go, as if it was the most natural thing in the world.

"So are you...staying?" She bit her lip and left it at that, though the question was so much bigger.

"What, you mean overnight?" he mumbled. "Since it's nearly two a.m., I assumed that was pretty much a given. Do you want me to leave?"

"No!" Horrified, she snuggled deeper into him in apology and his arms tightened. The last thing she wanted was to wake up alone. "Just checking. I'm happy with you where you are."

No man had ever slept in this bed, either, and she wasn't sorry she'd waited for Dax to be the first. He fit into it perfectly and if he wasn't careful, she would invite him to spend a good long while in it.

That was actually what she'd hoped to establish by asking whether he planned to stay. Not just overnight, but when tomorrow came, then what? Was it too soon to talk about it? Was it implied that this was the start of a relationship in every sense?

Or was she supposed to know this was one night only?

"Good. Get some sleep. You're going to need it. And Elise," he whispered in her ear. "I might stay tomorrow night, too."

Apparently he'd read her thoughts.

Whether she'd given herself permission or not, it was too late to pretend she wasn't falling for him. She tucked the feeling away and held it close to her heart.

She fell asleep with a smile on her face and woke up with the same smile. Dax made her happy and she wanted to do the same for him. But he wasn't in the bed. Covers thrown back, his side was already cool. Frowning, she strained to hear the shower. Nothing.

He wasn't downstairs either. She sighed and pulled the sash on her robe tighter, cursing herself for thinking…well, it didn't matter. Dax was free to leave. She'd just hoped he wouldn't. He hadn't made promises—false or otherwise—and she hadn't requested any.

But she'd put a lot of faith in him based on his insistence that he meant it and his pretty speech about trust. Perhaps she should have established a better understanding of his definition of "I mean it."

When the front door swung open and Dax called out cheerily, she nearly dropped her freshly brewed cup of coffee.

Dax sauntered into the kitchen all windblown and smiley. It shouldn't be possible to look that delicious after only a few hours of sleep. She didn't bother to hide her openmouthed gaping.

He dropped a kiss on her temple and handed her a bag. "Hey, gorgeous. Bagels. I hope that's okay. Breakfast is the most important meal of the day, after all." He grinned and eyed her robe. "But now I'm wondering what's underneath there. Breakfast can wait a few minutes, can't it?"

"Maybe. Depends on how good the bagels are." She smiled as he glared at her in mock dismay. Then she noticed the other bag, hanging from his shoulder. "That, um, looks like a suitcase. Taking a trip?"

He shrugged. "Picked up a few things while I was out. I don't live far. Figured I'd like to be dressed in an actual suit Monday morning when I show up for work."

Oh, my. Obviously he'd decided to spend Sunday with her. And the whole of Sunday night too. Dare she hope he'd undergone such a miraculous conversion that he was ready to spend every waking second with her?

Or was this blissful weekend the beginning of the end?

"So what are we doing here?" she blurted out, suddenly panicked and quite unable to pinpoint why. "You're staying all day, tonight and then what? I'm sorry, I can't just go with it. I need some parameters here."

The bag dropped to the floor and he leaned against the kitchen counter, his expression blank. "What kind of parameters do you want? I thought this was a pretty good compromise, bringing some stuff over. It's not day by day, but no one's made any promises they can't keep. Were you expecting me to show up with more stuff?"

She'd been expecting *less* stuff, far less. She had no idea what to do with all the stuff he'd unloaded. Relationships were supposed to be structured, predictable. Weren't they? Why hadn't she practiced a whole lot more before this one? The two relationships she'd been in before were vastly inadequate preparation for Dax Wakefield.

"I wasn't actually expecting you to show up at all," she confessed. "I thought you'd bailed."

"I sent you a text. Isn't that our thing?" He grinned. "I thought you slept with your phone in your hand, pining for a message from me. That takes me down a few notches."

Frowning, she scouted about for her phone and finally found it in the side pocket of her purse. On silent. She thumbed up the message.

Don't eat. I'll be back asap with breakfast. Can't wait to see you.

All righty then. She blew out a breath and it turned into a long sigh. She kept looking for reasons not to trust him and he hadn't disappointed her yet. What was her *problem?*

"Hey." He pulled her into his arms and rested his head on top of hers. "You really thought I wasn't coming back? You don't do one-night stands. I respect that. I wouldn't have come here last night if I didn't."

"Sorry," she mumbled into his shirt in case she'd offended him. In truth, he didn't sound anything other than concerned but she'd somehow lost the ability to read him. That scared her. "I'll shut up now."

"I don't want you to shut up." Pulling back slightly, he peered down at her. "Your mouth is the sexiest thing on you."

With that, the tension mostly blew over. Or rather she chose to ignore the lingering questions so she could enjoy spending the day with a man she liked, who liked her back. It *was* a good compromise—for now. She didn't like not knowing the plan or what to expect. But for today, she knew Dax would be in her bed at the end of it and that was something she readily looked forward to.

They had fun giggling together over a couple of Netflix movies and ate Chinese delivery for lunch.

"Let me take you someplace really great for dinner," he suggested as he collected the cartons to dispose of them. "If you'll actually eat, that is."

He hefted her half-full takeout carton in deliberate emphasis.

"I'm not all that hungry," she said out of habit, and then made the mistake of glancing up into his slightly narrowed gaze, which was evaluating her coolly. Of course he hadn't bought that excuse.

Instead of taking the trash to the kitchen as he should have, Dax set the cartons back on the coffee table and eased onto the cushion next to her. "Elise—"

"I ate most of it. There's no crime in not being hungry." Her defensive tone didn't do much for her case.

"No, there's not." He contemplated her for a few long moments. "Except you're never hungry. I didn't press you on it last night when you told me you gain weight easily because, well, I was a little busy, but I can't ignore it forever. Do you have a problem I should know about?"

"Like anorexia?" The half laugh slipped out before she could catch it. This was not funny *at all* but he'd caught her by surprise. "I like food far too much to starve myself entirely, thanks."

How had the conversation turned heavy so fast? And when precisely had they reached a point in their relationship where it was okay to throw it all out there, no censor, no taboos?

"Maybe not *entirely*," he stressed. "But you don't like yourself enough to have a healthy relationship with food either."

Gently, he took her hand and she let him. His concern was evident. But he could stop with all the psychobabble any time now. She didn't have a problem other than an intense desire to never be fat again. Nothing wrong with that.

"Thanks for checking in, but it's okay. My health *is* my concern." She glanced away. He saw too much but it was the price for opening up to him. "This will be hard for you to sympathize with, I realize, but I was an ugly duckling for a long time. A fat girl. When I finally lost all the weight, I vowed never to gain it back. Portion control is my friend."

"Elise." He stroked her knuckles with his thumb in a comforting caress. "I don't know what it's like to be fat. But it's not fair to frame your struggles as if no one else can comprehend them. To deliberately shut me out solely because I have a few strands of DNA that put my face together like this."

He circled an index finger over his cheekbones, and the darkness underneath the motion, in his expression, startled her.

"I'm not trying to shut you out." Was she?

The alternative meant she'd have to let him glimpse her innermost secrets, her deepest fears. It would mean trusting him with far more than her body. It would mean trusting him with her soul.

But hadn't she already done that when she invited him into her bed?

"You may not be consciously trying to. But you are," he said mildly. "And not only that, you're making an assumption about me based on my appearance. Like I can't possibly know what it feels like to have disappointments or pain because of the way I look."

Speechless, she stared into his snapping, smoky eyes. She'd hurt him with her thoughtless comments.

She *had* made assumptions and drawn her fat-girl self around her like a familiar, impenetrable blanket.

Dax had called it during their discussion on the park bench. She ran screaming in the other direction before a man could get close enough to hurt her.

Had she already screwed this up—whatever *this* was— before it started?

"I'm sorry," she said sincerely and squeezed his hand. He squeezed back and her heart lightened a little. "I'm sensitive about food and about being fat. It's an ugly part of me. I'm not used to sharing it with anyone."

"There's nothing ugly about you," he shot right back. "Why in the world would you think a few pounds makes you ugly?"

She debated. It was so much easier to make a joke. But she'd been patiently explaining the components of happily ever after to Dax for weeks, which had everything to do with honesty, vulnerability and trust. Was she really going to balk when it was her turn to lay it all out?

"You've seen my mother. You've been in that world. Surely the pursuit of thinness is not so mysterious an ideal."

He shrugged. "But you're not a model. Neither are you your mother. So your weight is not a requirement for your job."

Easy for him to say. It was different for boys no matter what they looked like.

"It's not that simple. I grew up surrounded by swans and constantly aware I wasn't one of them. In case I didn't feel bad enough about being overweight, my mother made sure I didn't forget it for a moment."

"She's the one who made you self-conscious about being fat?" Dax scowled. "That's horrible."

His unconditional support squeezed her heart sweetly. "It turned out okay. I buried myself in algorithms and computer code instead of hanging out in the spotlight, which was, and still is, cruel. I built a business born out of the desire to shut myself away from all the negativity. Only EA International could have gotten me in front of those cameras where we met. Even now, I give deserving women makeovers because I know how it feels to be in the middle of all those swans, with no one on your side."

"I'm glad you found the fortitude to venture onto my set." Dax smiled. "And I like that you made something positive out of a bad experience."

"There's more." And it was the really important part. "That's why my profile questions dig into the heart of who you are. So my clients can find someone to love them for what's underneath, not what they look like."

Which was not-so-coincidentally what she wanted too—someone to love her forever, no matter what. She'd never had that before.

The smile slipped from his face and he gazed at her solemnly. "I get that."

Of course he did. She'd made sweeping generalizations about him because of his appearance and she'd bet it wasn't the first time someone had done that. Not only did he understand the point about loving someone's insides; of all the people she'd shared her philosophy with, he had the singular distinction of being the only one who'd seen the pain that had created it.

And she was terrified of what he'd do with all this insight.

Eleven

Dax took Elise to eat at the top of Reunion Tower, a place she'd never been despite having lived in Dallas for years. They dined while overlooking the downtown area as the room revolved 360 degrees inside the ball. It should have been a wildly romantic evening.

It *was*. But Elise couldn't quite relax.

When they returned to her house from dinner, Dax took her keys and opened the front door for her, then swept her up in his arms to carry her over the threshold. Solid and strong, he maneuvered through the door frame without hesitation, and it was undeniably sexy.

"What's this all about?" she asked as soon as she unstuck her tongue from the roof of her mouth.

"I seem to have a lot of trouble getting past your front door. This way, I'm guaranteed entrance." He grinned at her cockeyed stare. "Plus, I've got a very special treat planned and thought I'd start it off with a bang."

"Really?" Her curiosity was piqued as her tension lessened. "What is it?"

He let her slide to the ground braced against his gorgeous body and took her hand. "Follow me, Ms. Arundel, and see for yourself."

That made her grin, dispelling more of her strange mood. She trailed him upstairs and the second she entered the bedroom, he whirled her into a mind-numbing kiss.

Her brain emptied as his lips devoured her and heat tunneled into every last crevice of her body. *Oh, yes.*

Bright, white-hot desire flared in a sunburst at her core, soaking her in need and flooding her with Dax, and she couldn't catch her breath. She wanted him to love her exactly as he had last night, perfectly, completely.

Slowly, he backed her to the bed and when she would have stumbled, he tightened his arms. Then he sat her down and drew off her boots, one zipper at a time, and kissed her uncovered calves, all the way to her heels.

She watched him through heavy eyelids, a little unable to process the sight of such a beautiful man at her feet, all his attention on her. He glanced up, his gaze full of dark, sinful promise, and she shuddered as he centered himself between her legs.

With deft, strong fingers, he gathered the hem of her dress and slowly worked it up over her thighs, caressing her bare skin as he went, following the fabric with his mouth and tongue.

A moan rose in her throat and she strangled on it as he licked at her nub through her damp panties.

"I want to see you, Elise," he murmured and slipped off her dress with skill. Quick-like-fox, he had her bra and panties in the same pile as her dress.

As he raked her with a smoldering, hungry once-over, she fought the urge to crawl under the covers.

"You are so beautiful," he croaked, as though he might be coming down with something. Or she'd affected him enough to clog his throat.

Wasn't that amazing? *She* affected *him*.

He stared down at her as he lowered himself to the bed next to her, still fully clothed. "I want to make you feel beautiful."

"You do," she said automatically. Well, actually, he made her feel good. Beautiful was a little more difficult to come by.

His brows arched. "Maybe. But I can do better. Much better. So tonight is about that."

He reached under a pillow and withdrew a bag of Ghirardelli chocolate chips. She'd recognize the bag a mile away. Her mouth started watering. And then her brain caught up. "Why is that instrument of torture in my bed?"

Dax grinned and winked. "You told me you liked chocolate. *Voilà*. We'll get to the shoes another time."

The wall her insides had thrown up crumbled and everything went liquid. "You were paying attention to what I said?"

"Of course." He scowled in confusion. "Why would I have asked if I didn't want to know the answer?"

Heat flamed through her cheeks and she shut her eyes. "I thought you were being polite."

Laughing, he kissed both of her shut eyelids in succession until she opened them. "One thing I am not is polite. But I am interested in giving you an amazing experience. Starting now."

With a wicked smile, he laid her back and tore open the bag, spilling chocolate chips all over her bare stomach.

The chips rolled everywhere, and she jackknifed automatically to catch them, but he stopped her with a gentle hand to her shoulder. Then he grasped a piece of chocolate between his fingertips and traced it between her breasts, up her throat and to her lips, teasing her with it.

The rich, sweet smell of chocolate drugged her senses. She wanted to eat that bite of heaven in the worst way. But she couldn't. A moment on the lips…and it went straight to her hips. She didn't keep chocolate in the house for a reason.

"Open," he instructed. "None of these calories count because honey, I promise you're about to burn them all."

The temptation was humongous. She wrestled with it. And lost.

How could she do anything else but eat it? Chocolate burst on her tongue and a moment later, his tongue twined with hers, tasting the chocolate along with her in a delicious kiss.

The twin sensations of Dax and chocolate nearly pushed her over the edge. She moaned in appreciation. Desire. Surrender.

Trailing chocolate kisses back down her throat, he paused to line up several chips around her nipple and proceeded to lick each one, smearing more chocolate on her breasts than he got in his mouth. He proceeded to suck off the sweetness, sending her into a taut spiral of need that could only be salved one way.

As if he'd read her mind again, he lowered himself between her thighs, opened them and kissed each one. Muscles tight with anticipation, she choked on a breath, waiting for the sweet fire of his intimate kiss.

He didn't disappoint her. She felt a chip graze her nub and then Dax's tongue followed it, and her eyelids slammed closed as her senses pulsed with pleasure.

"You taste delicious," he rasped and stuck another chip under his tongue, laving so hard, she came instantly in a starburst of sparkles that bowed her back and ripped a cry from her throat.

Immediately, he rose up and treated her to a chocolate, musky kiss, twining all the flavors together into an overwhelming, sensual bouquet.

"See how delicious you taste?" he murmured and cupped her with his hand, sliding fingers through her folds and into her damp center, yanking yet another climax from deep inside.

Still in the throes of a chocolate orgasm, she couldn't sort one sensation from the other and didn't want to. Finally the ripples faded, leaving her gasping and nearly blind as dots crowded her vision.

"Delicious," he repeated. "Beautiful."

Then he put the icing on it.

"By the way," he said casually. "In case it wasn't crystal clear, this was me showing you how gorgeous you are. Remember this every time you put chocolate in your mouth, which better be a lot. Because I don't want you to ever, ever forget that you're beautiful or that the sight of you eating chocolate is so hot, I'm about to lose it."

She blinked and focused on his wolfish smile. He'd been trying to psychoanalyze her with this little stunt?

So now every time she thought about chocolate, she'd make all kinds of associations that it should never have, like unbelievable pleasure, a gorgeous man's mouth tasting of sin and sugar, and the pièce de résistance, that watching her eat chocolate turned him on.

It was...brilliant. The benefits of sleeping with a man who understood both psychology and a woman's body couldn't be overstated.

And she wasn't simply falling for him; it was more like being dropped off a cliff, straight into a mess of emotion she had no idea how to handle.

She would have thought herself capable of understanding love, if indeed that's what was going on. Certainly she would have said she could recognize it. And it did not resemble this crazy, upside-down thing inside that was half thrilling, half terrifying and 100 percent Dax.

What if this *wasn't* love but an orgasm-induced hallucination? Worse, what if she went with it, straight into a broken heart? Her fat-girl blanket usually kept that from happening, but she'd lost it.

Or rather, Dax had stolen it from her with chocolate.

And he'd completely piqued her curiosity as to what he planned to do with shoes.

Dax picked up Elise and took her to the bathroom, where he filled the tub and spent a long time washing the chocolate from her body. He wanted to sink into the steaming water and sink into Elise, but he was too busy breathing her in to stop.

She smelled like chocolate and well-loved woman and home, all rolled into one bundle he could not get enough of. He'd only meant to worship her gorgeous body and enable her to eat something she liked at the same time. He had *not* intended to forever alter his perception of chocolate, but he'd never taste it again without getting a hard-on.

Which wasn't necessarily a bad thing.

Finally he couldn't stand being separated from her any longer and stripped to slide into the tub. She watched him unashamedly, ravenous gaze flickering to his rigid erection as he bared it. Last night she'd had a hard time with that, as if nakedness were shocking.

Not so tonight. But he didn't dare say he was proud of her lest he frighten her back into that shell. Besides, the heat in her eyes sent such a shaft of desire spiking through him, he couldn't do anything other than slide into the tub, gather her against his chest and dive in.

He kissed her, openmouthed, sloppy and so very raw. She melted into him, fitting her lithe body into his. Water sloshed out of the tub, which she didn't notice and he didn't point out.

He needed her. Now.

After an eternity of fumbling due to wet fingers and wet body parts and far too much "help" from Elise that nearly set off what would be a nuclear explosion of a release, Dax got the condom in place.

He never had this much trouble. But his fingers were still shaking as he slid into her with a groan and then he simply clung, hands gripping Elise's shoulders. Flinging his head back, he let the sensations bleed through him and only some of them were physical.

That profound sense of what he could only label as *happiness* saturated the experience, lighting him up inside. It felt as if it would burst from his skin and pour out in a river. He savored the harmony, the rightness of it.

Elise, clearly impatient with all the savoring, planted her knees on either side of him and took over the rhythm, and he let her because it was amazing. The faster she moved, the higher he soared, and a growl ripped from his mouth unrestrained as she pushed him to the edge.

Nearly incoherent and almost numb with the effort to hold back, he fingered her in an intimate caress, silently begging her to let go. Instantly, she tightened around him in an answering pulse that triggered his release, and he came in a fountain of blessed relief.

She slumped on his chest, cheek to his skin, and he shut his eyes, reveling in the boneless bliss that he'd only ever experienced at the hands of Elise.

Being with her evoked so many things he had no way to describe, things he hoped never went away. But since he didn't know how it had happened in the first place, what guarantee did he have he wouldn't wake up tomorrow and find himself back in the real world where Elise wasn't "the one"?

Because here in this alternate reality he'd somehow fallen into, it felt an awful lot as though she was a...soul mate.

Against all odds, he wanted to believe the concept existed, that it might be possible for him. For them.

After they dried off and got comfortably snugged together in bed he murmured, "Elise, you have to promise me something."

"Anything. After the chocolate, you name it." She sighed, her breath teasing the hair on his torso.

"Don't stop. Keep doing whatever you're doing and don't stop. Even if I tell you to."

She stirred and raised her head to peer at him in the darkened room, lit only by the moonlight pouring in through the opened blinds. "Why would you tell me to?"

"Because…"

I'm broken.

That's why he'd never found a woman worth promising forever to. Why Elise's matchmaking efforts had failed, despite participating in her profile sessions to the best of his ability. Not because there was something wrong with the women he'd dated, or even Candy, but because something was wrong with him. How could he explain that he pushed women away on purpose, before things got complicated?

But then, he didn't have to explain. Elise knew that already. She had spelled it out in painful detail on the park bench. If he was being honest, that had been the tipping point, the moment he knew she'd snared an unrecoverable piece of him he'd never meant to give up.

He tried again. "Because I'm…"

Falling for you.

His eyelids slammed shut in frustration and fear and God knew what else. What was wrong with him that he couldn't voice a simple sentence to tell this amazing woman how she made him feel? Or at least confess that she made him want to be better than he'd ever dreamed possible?

He wanted to be the man she deserved. For the first time in his life, he didn't want to push her away.

But he knew he was going to anyway.

He couldn't say all those things because Elise wasn't *his* soul mate. She was someone else's and he was in the way. For her sake, he would have to end things eventually.

That realization nearly split him in two. Appropriate to be as broken on the outside as he was on the inside.

"Hey." Her soft hand cupped his jaw and her thumb rested near his eyes, brushing the lashes until he opened them. "What's going on? You're never at a loss for words."

He laughed in spite of himself. She'd been tying him up in knots from day one. Why should this be any different?

"Yeah, this is all kinds of abnormal."

"Start with that. What's abnormal, being in bed together?" She cocked her head and smoothed the sheets over them. "Are you about to tell me your reputation with women is vastly inflated? Because I won't believe you. The things you do to me can only be the result of years of careful study."

"I've had a lot of sex, Elise. Make no mistake," he said without apology. "But it wasn't anything like this. What's different is you. I can't explain it. It feels…bigger. Stronger. I don't know what to do with it."

She stared at him, wide-eyed. "Really? It's not like this with other women?"

"Not even close. I didn't know it *could* be different."

If he had, he would have hunted down Elise Arundel about a decade ago. Maybe if he had, before he'd become so irrevocably damaged, things might have worked out between them.

He could have actually *been* the man she needed instead of merely wanting to be.

Wanting wasn't good enough. She deserved someone unbroken and he needed to give her space to find that guy.

But it didn't have to be now. He could wait a few days, or maybe longer.

"But I'm just me." Bewilderment crept over her face. "I'm not doing anything special."

"You don't have to do anything special. It just is. You don't feel it, too?"

Slowly, she nodded and a sense of relief burst through his gut. Relief that this wasn't all one-sided. Guilt because it might already be too late to get out without hurting her.

"I feel it. It scares me and I don't know why." She gripped his hand. "It's not supposed to be like this, all mixed up, and like I can't breathe if you're gone. Like I can't breathe when you're here."

Exactly. That's how he'd felt all week as he'd talked to the couples Elise had matched and then drove around aimlessly, out of sorts, with no clue how to absolve the riot of stuff seething under his skin. Elise was his affliction. And his deliverance.

Maybe she was the answer, the only woman in existence who could fix him. If he wasn't broken anymore, maybe he could find a way to be with Elise forever. Maybe he *could* have her, without pushing her away. But only if he could finally let her behind his curtain.

"I have to tell you something," he said before he lost his nerve. "Your mother made you feel bad about your weight. Well, I understand how mothers can shape your entire outlook on life. Because mine left. When I was seven."

Tears pricked at his eyelids. He'd never spoken of his mother's abandonment and somehow, saying it aloud made it An Issue.

"Oh, honey, I'm so sorry." Elise pressed her lips to his temple and just held him without another word. The odd, bright happiness she evoked filled him.

"It's stupid to still let it affect me. I know that," he muttered and let his muscles relax. He wouldn't flee into the night and not talk about this.

Elise, of all people, understood the twisted, sometimes warped pathways of his mind, often when he didn't get it himself. He could trust her.

"Dax." She gave him time to collect himself and that small act meant a lot to him. "If you don't want to let it affect you, then stop."

"Oh, sure. I'll wave my magic wand and everything will be fine. Better yet, why don't you wave yours?" he said magnanimously. She didn't laugh.

Instead, she leaned forward and pierced him with a somber gaze. "That's exactly what I've been trying to do. By matching you with your soul mate, so you could be happy with someone. I want that for you."

"What if I said I want that too?"

Twelve

She froze, confusion flitting through her expression. "You do?"

"Yeah. Maybe."

She blinked and swallowed several times in a row before speaking. "You mean commitment, emotions, forever?"

Hope shone in her eyes.

For a brief moment, he felt an answering tug of hope in his heart. Forever sounded amazing.

And then reality took over and squelched everything good inside. These feelings would change—or fade—and he'd prove he was just like his mother by walking out the door.

He was wrong for Elise. She had all these visions of true love he could never measure up to. Being with her made him want things he couldn't have, and it wasn't her job to fix him.

That was the final nail. Just because he wanted to be unbroken didn't make it so. Why hadn't he kept his mouth shut and his curtain closed? He couldn't continue this charade, as though there was a future for them.

For once, he'd thought about trying. That's why he'd shared the truth with her. That's why he'd gotten out of the car.

He shouldn't have. And he had a hundred reasons why he should walk out right now before it was too late. He wasn't cut out for this, for relationships. He had to get out now, before he hurt her even more later.

Ruthlessly, he shut off everything inside, especially the part that had started to believe.

"Why do you sound so stunned?" he said instead of answering her question as he scrambled for a way to let her down easy. "This is your area of expertise. Didn't you set out to change my mind about love?"

"I'm not that good," she blurted out and bit her lip.

"Of course you are. The couples you matched think you're every bit the magical fairy godmother you claimed. Take credit where credit is due."

A grin spilled onto her face. "Does that mean I won the wager?"

His chest had the weight of a skyscraper on it and all Elise could think about was the wager? "The wager is over."

"Sorry." Her confusion wrapped around him, increasing the tension unbearably. "What about marriage? Are you on board with that, too?"

The longer he dragged this out, the more hope she'd gather. Heart bleeding, he shrugged and looked away. "Maybe someday. With the right woman."

"Wait a minute." Unease flitting over her face, she sat up, clutching the covers to her bare breasts. "I thought you were talking about having a relationship with *me*."

Carefully, he composed his expression as if this was no more than a negotiation gone wrong and both parties just needed to walk away amicably.

It nearly killed him.

"Come on, Elise. You and I both know we won't work. I got out of the car because I knew I was missing something and I needed you to tell me what. So thanks. I'm good."

She wasn't buying it. Elise was far too sharp to be put off by half truths. That's why it never paid to let anyone behind the curtain.

"Dax, we have something good. Don't you want to see if we work before giving up?"

Her warm hand on his arm shouldn't have felt so right, as though his skin had been crafted specifically for her touch.

"It doesn't matter what I want. I can't make long-term promises. To anyone," he stressed. "I'm all about keeping my word because my mother didn't. I can't stand the thought of caring about someone and then figuring out I don't have what it takes to stick around."

Nothing like the whole truth to make the point. She needed to understand that this was for her own good, so she could move on and find her Mr. Forever, and he could go back to his empty loft.

"But you can make promises to me because I'm your soul mate."

The soft whisper penetrated his misery. "What did you say?"

"*I'm* your soul mate. Your perfect woman. The computer matched us."

Something dark whirled through his chest, squeezing it even tighter, pushing air from his lungs. "That's not true. It matched me with Candy."

She shook her head. "My name came up first. But I thought I'd made a mistake due to the unorthodox profile sessions. So I messed around with the responses until Candy's name came up instead."

Blood rushed to his head and the back of his neck heated. "You did *what?*"

"It was the ethical thing to do. I thought I'd compromised the results because of how I felt about you."

Ethical. He'd been told Candy was his soul mate and therefore he'd believed Elise was meant for someone else. But it had never felt right, never fit…because he'd thought *he* was the problem.

Instead, it was all a lie.

Letting him think he couldn't do happily ever after, letting him think he was broken—that was her definition of *ethical?*

"Let me get this straight." He pinched the bridge of his nose and reeled his temper back. "You had such deep feelings for me it compelled you to match me with someone who isn't my soul mate?"

"I hoped you'd hit it off. Because I do want you to be happy. Candy just wasn't right for you."

"And who is, you?"

The question was delivered so scathingly, she flinched and didn't respond. Fortunately. His mood had degenerated to the point where he was genuinely afraid of what he might say.

He rolled from the bed and scouted around until he found his pants, and then jerked them on, but stood staring at the wall, fists clenched until he thought he could speak rationally.

"Why tell me now? Why didn't you tell me from the beginning?"

The wager. She'd been trying to win and altered the results in order to do so. It was the only explanation. That's why she'd asked if she'd won earlier. Rage boiled up again, clouding his vision.

"It wasn't a secret," she said defensively. "I thought you'd laugh and make some smarmy joke about how I couldn't possibly resist you. Plus, I wanted you to have a shot at finding your real soul mate."

"Who isn't you."

She couldn't be. His real soul mate wouldn't have let him believe all this time that he was the problem. That he was the broken one and that's why Elise's algorithm couldn't find his perfect match.

He'd trusted her. In vain, apparently.

If she'd just told him the truth, everything might be different. But she'd stolen that chance and thoroughly destroyed his fledgling belief in the possibility of happily ever after.

"I am," she corrected softly. "My match process just realized it before I did."

"Pardon me for questioning the results when it seems your process is a little, shall we say, subjective. In fact, I'd say this whole wager was slanted from the beginning. So save the sales pitch, babe."

Oh, he'd been so blind. From the very first moment, all she'd cared about was proving to everyone that she could change his mind about relationships. She didn't want true love, or at least not with him. It had all been an act to gain the upper hand. If Dax had one talent, it was recognizing a good show when he saw one.

"Slanted? What are you talking about?"

"Admit it. This was all an attempt to bring me to my knees, wasn't it? You planned for it to happen this way." He shook his head and laughed contemptuously. "You're far, far better at this than I ever dreamed. To think I almost fell for it."

She'd dug into his psyche with no other intent than to uncover his deepest longings and use them against him. It was unforgivable.

The only bright spot in this nightmare was that he no longer had to worry about how to push her away or whether he'd eventually walk out the door. She'd destroyed their relationship all on her own.

Thankfully, he'd found out the truth before it was too late.

His mistake had been starting to trust her, even a little.

"Fell for what? Dax, you're not making any sense."

Pulse hammering, Elise sorted through the conversation to figure out where this had gotten so mixed up. What had she missed? Up until now, she'd always been able to sort his fact from fiction, especially when he tried to throw up smoke screens, but that ability had disappeared long about midnight yesterday.

She was losing him, losing all the ground she'd gained—

or imagined she'd gained. Clearly, he'd done some kind of about-face but apparently not in her direction. That couldn't be right. She couldn't be this close to getting a man like Dax for her own and not figure out how to get her happily ever after.

He shook his head and laughed again without any humor. "All this time I thought *you* were looking for a relationship and I *wasn't*. You sat right there on that park bench and told me exactly what you wanted. I ignored it." He crossed the room and poked a rigid finger in her face. "'I want to beat you at your own game,' you said. And you know what, you almost did."

She flinched automatically. Oh, God. She had said that. But the way he'd twisted it around...unbelievable. As if she'd cold-bloodedly planned this to hurt him, playing dirty, fast and loose.

"Listen, this wasn't the game I was trying to win."

Except she'd been pretty focused on winning. From the beginning. Maybe she'd been more compromised than she'd assumed. She'd developed feelings for him without really understanding how to love him.

Maybe she didn't really understand male/female dynamics unless they were other people's.

"What game *were* you trying to win, then? Why is this a game at all?" A dangerous glint in his eye warned her to let him finish before she leaped on the defensive again. "Tread carefully, Elise. You clearly have no idea what you're playing around with here."

"This isn't a game," she cried. "When my name came up as your match, I wanted it to be true. I wanted you for myself and I thought those feelings compromised my integrity."

"You're lying." The harsh lines of his face convicted her further. "If that was true, you wouldn't have played so hard to get."

She couldn't fault his logic. Except he was drawing the wrong conclusion. "The truth is I didn't believe I was enough to change your mind about happily ever after."

"Enough?" he spat. "Enough what?"

"Pretty enough, good enough, thin enough. Take your pick," she whispered.

He laughed again and the sound skated down her spine. "I get it now. You said you don't trust easily, but in reality, you don't trust at all. You didn't ever intend to give me a real chance, did you? That's the game you wanted to beat me at. Get me to confess my feelings and then take my legs out from under me. Good job."

"I *did* want to give you a chance. You said we wouldn't work."

He threw his hands up. "This is why I don't do relationships. This conversation is like a vicious circle. With teeth."

She cursed as she realized her mistake. Misdirection was his forte and he was such a master, she'd almost missed it. He *had* developed feelings for her and they scared him. That's what all this was. Smoke and mirrors to deflect from what was going on back stage.

This was the part where she needed to tread carefully.

"Last night," she whispered. "Before you kissed me. You said you meant it. What did you mean?"

The raw vulnerability in his expression took her breath. And when her lungs finally filled, they ached with the effort.

"I meant I was falling in love with you." His expression darkened as her heart tripped dangerously. "I—forget it. It's too late to have that conversation now."

Dax was falling in love with her? The revelation pinged through her mind, through her heart—painfully—because he'd finally laid it all out there while also telling her to forget it. As if she could.

She'd done it. She'd reversed his stance on love and happily ever after. Shannon Elise Arundel *was* that good. Her match program was foolproof. The algorithm had matched them because she had a unique ability to understand him, to see the real him, just as he did her.

Why hadn't she realized it sooner?

"It's not too late." She crawled to her knees, begging him without words for something she had no idea how to express. "Let's figure this out."

"I don't want to figure it out!" He huffed out a frustrated breath. "Elise, I thought I was *broken*. That the reason you couldn't find my soul mate was because there was something wrong with me. I felt guilty for wanting you when your soul mate was supposed to be someone else, someone better. Instead, you were lying all along. You never trusted me."

In one shot, he'd blown all the smoke away and told her the absolute unvarnished truth. While she'd been pushing him away, he'd filed the rejection under *it's not her, it's me.*

Speechless, she stared at the pain-carved lines in his beautiful face. "I didn't know that's how you'd take it when I told you I was your match. There's nothing wrong with you. This is all about me and my issues."

"I get that you have a problem believing I think you're beautiful." He snorted. "You want to find true love but you won't let anyone in long enough to trust that they love you. That's why you've never had a connection with anyone."

"I've been holding out for someone to love me. The real me, underneath."

I've been holding out for you.

He swept her with an angry look. "Yet you're completely hung up on whether you're beautiful enough. If someone loves you solely for what you look like, that's not true love. Neither is it love to refuse to trust. You have a lot of nerve preaching to me about something you know nothing about."

"You're right." Head bowed, she admitted the absolute,

unvarnished truth in kind. "I didn't fully trust you. I don't know how."

"I bought into what you were selling." His bleak voice scored her heart. "Hook, line and sinker. I wanted something more than sex. Understanding. Support. A connection."

Everything she'd hoped for. For both of them. But somehow she'd messed up. "I want those things, too."

A tear tracked down her cheek and he watched it. As it fell to the bed, he shook his head. "You're not capable of giving me those things. This is over, if it ever started in the first place. I can't do this."

Then he stormed from the room, snagging his bag on the way out. She let him go, too numb to figure out how to fix it. Some relationship expert she was.

Dax's ex-girlfriends had been wrong. He wasn't cold and heartless and he hadn't screwed Elise over. She'd done it to him, smashing his fragile feelings into unrecoverable pieces because at the end of the day, she hadn't trusted Dax enough to believe he could really love her. She hadn't trusted herself enough to tell him they'd been matched. And now it was too late to do it all over.

Happily ever after might very well be a myth after all. And if that was true, where did that leave her and Dax? Or her company?

The sound of the front door slamming reverberated in her frozen heart.

Dax nearly took out a row of mailboxes in his haste to speed away from the mistake in his rearview mirror. Astounding how he'd assumed he was the broken one in their relationship. Only to discover she was far more broken.

While he'd naively been trying to get out without hurting her, she'd actually been one step ahead of him the entire time, determined to break him. And she'd done a hell of a job. She'd matched him with the perfect woman all right—the only one capable of getting under his skin and destroying everything in her path.

It was late, but Wakefield Media did not sleep. He drove to the office, determined not to think. Or to feel. He closed it all off through sheer will until the only thing left was a strange hardness in his chest that made it impossible to catch a deep breath.

Shutting himself off behind his desk, Dax dove into the business he loved, the only thing he could really depend on. This company he'd built from the ground up was his happily ever after, the only one available to him. If he put his head down, maybe he'd come out the other side with some semblance of normality. Dawn came and went but the hardness in his chest didn't fade.

At noon, he'd had no human contact other than a brief nod to Patricia as she dropped off a cup of coffee several hours ago. Fatigue dragged at him. Well, that and a heavy heart.

His phone beeped and he checked it automatically. Elise. He deleted the text message without reading it, just as he'd done with the other three. There was nothing she could say that he wanted to hear.

Morosely, he swiveled his chair to stare out over the Dallas skyline and almost involuntarily, his eye was drawn to the building directly across from him, where Reynolds Capital Management used to reside. Dax had heard that Leo left the venture capital game and had gone into business with Tommy Garrett, a whiz kid inventor.

It was crazy and so unlike Leo. They'd been friends for a long time—until Daniella had come along and upset the status quo.

Bad, bad subject. The hardness in his chest started to hurt and the urge to punch something grew until he couldn't physically sit at his desk any longer.

He sent Patricia an instant message asking for the address of Garrett-Reynolds Engineering and the second he got it, he strode to his car. It was time to have it out with Leo once and for all.

Except Leo wasn't at the office. Dax eyed Tommy Garrett, whom he'd met at a party an eon ago. The kid still looked as though he belonged on a surfboard instead of in a boardroom.

"Sorry, dude," Tommy said and stuck a Doritos chip in his mouth. "Leo's still on vacation. But I'm pretty sure he's at home now if you want to catch him there."

"Thanks." Dax went back to his car, still shaking his head. Leo—at home in the middle of the day on a Monday. His affliction with Daniella was even worse than Dax had imagined.

By the time he hit Leo's driveway, Dax was good and worked up. This time, he didn't hesitate, but drove right up to the gate and rolled down his window so the security system could grant him entrance.

Leo was waiting for him on the front steps as Dax swung out of the Audi. Of course the state-of-the-art security system had alerted the Reynoldses that they had a visitor, and clearly Leo was as primed for a throw down as Dax was. Dax meant to give it to him.

"Dax." Leo smiled warmly, looking well-rested, tan and not wearing a suit. "It's good to see you. I'm glad you came by."

Dax did a double take.

Who was this guy? Because he didn't resemble the Leo Dax knew.

"Hi," Dax muttered, and tried to orient. Leo wasn't supposed to be happy. And he wasn't supposed to be nice. They weren't friends anymore.

"Please, come in." Leo jerked his head behind him toward the house. "Dannie's pouring us some iced tea."

"This isn't a social call," he fairly snarled and then heard himself. Where were his manners?

Leo didn't flinch. "I didn't assume that it was. But this is my home, and my wife wanted to serve you a drink. It's what civilized people do when someone comes by without an invitation."

My wife. The dividing line couldn't have been clearer. But then, Leo had drawn that line back in his office when he'd told Dax in no uncertain terms that Daniella was more important to him than anything, including money, the deal between Leo and Dax, and even their friendship.

All at once, Dax wanted to know why.

"I'm sorry," Dax said sincerely. "Tea is great. Thanks."

He followed Leo into a dappled sunroom with a view of the windswept back acreage of the property. The branches were bare of leaves this late into the season, save a few evergreens dotting the landscape.

Daniella bustled in with a tray, smiled at Dax and set a glass full of amber liquid in front of each man. "Nice to see you, Dax. Enjoy. I'll make myself scarce."

Gracious as always. Even to a man who made no secret of his intense dislike and mistrust of her.

Dax watched her drop a kiss on Leo's head. He snagged her hand to keep her in place, then returned the kiss on her lips, exchanging a private smile that seemed like a language all its own. They were so obviously in love, it poleaxed Dax right in the heart.

Because he didn't have that. Nor did he hold any hope of having it.

Against everything he'd ever believed about himself, the world and how he fit into it, he wanted what Leo and Daniella had.

The floodgates had been opened and then shut so swiftly, he'd barely had time to acclimate, to figure out what he was going to do with all the emotions he'd never felt before.

Then *bam!* Betrayal at its finest. The two people he'd let himself care about had *both* betrayed him. And one of them would answer for it right now.

After Daniella disappeared, Dax faced Leo squarely. "I suppose you're wondering why I'm here."

"Not really." Leo grinned at Dax's raised eyebrows. "Dannie and Elise are very good friends. I'm guessing you didn't know that."

Elise. Her name pierced that hard place in his chest and nearly finished what the lovey-dovey scene between Leo and Daniella had started. Death by emotion. It seemed fitting somehow.

And no, he hadn't realized Daniella and Elise were friends. Daniella had probably been treated to an earful already this morning. "And your wife tells you everything, right?"

"Yep."

Dax sank down in the wicker chair, but it didn't swallow him as he would have preferred. If he'd known his spectacular flameout at the hands of Elise had been trotted out for everyone's amusement, he might have gone someplace else, like Timbuktu.

"Last night was really messed up," Dax allowed without really meaning to. It just came out.

"I sympathize." Leo cleared his throat. "Which is more than you did for me when I was going through something similar, I might add."

That hurt. "Is this what you were going through? Because I don't see how that's possible."

Leo and Daniella had an effortless relationship, as if they'd been born for each other and never questioned whether they trusted the other.

"No, it's not the same because we're different people in love with very different women."

"I'm not in love with Elise," Dax broke in.

He might have been entertaining the notion, but she'd killed it. Somehow it was worse to finally embrace the idea that love wasn't just a fairy tale only to have your heart smashed.

Leo just looked at him and smirked. "And that's your problem right there. Denial. That, plus an inability to give someone a chance."

"That's not true," he burst out. "She's the one who didn't give me a chance. She lied to me. I can't trust anyone."

And that was the really painful part. There wasn't one single person in existence he could fully trust. If it could have been anyone, he'd have put his money on Elise, the one person who understood the man behind the curtain. He *had* put his money on Elise—five hundred thousand dollars—and she'd never lost sight of the prize. He should take a lesson.

"I can give you relationship advice all day long if that's what you're after. But you didn't really come here to find out that you guard yourself by pushing people away? You already know that."

Yeah, he did. He ended relationships before he got invested. He left women before they could hurt him. No mystery there. The question was why he'd let his guard down with Elise in the first place.

Dax sipped his tea and decided to go for broke with Leo. "I came to find out why Daniella was such a big deal. I know you married her. But why her? What was special about her?"

Leo's face lit up. "I love her. That alone makes her special. But I love her because she makes me whole. She allows me to be me. She *enables* me to be me. And I wake up every day wanting to do the same for her. That's why Elise matched us. Because we're soul mates."

Dax nearly snorted but caught himself. The evidence stood for itself and there was no need to act cynical about it any longer. No one in this room was confused about whether he believed in it. But believing in soul mates and allowing a woman who professed to be yours to take a fillet knife to your heart were two different things.

"And that was worth ending a friendship over?" Dax asked.

Stupid question. Clearly Leo thought so and at that particular moment, Dax almost didn't blame him. Look what Leo had gotten in return.

"Dax." Leo sat forward in his chair. "I didn't end our friendship. You did. You weren't being a friend when you said disparaging things about my wife. You weren't being a friend when you demanded I choose you over her. I was messed up, wondering how I could love my wife and still maintain the workaholic life I thought I wanted. I needed a friend. Where were you?"

There was no censure in Leo's tone. But there should have been. Hearing it spelled out like that sheared a new layer of skin off Dax's already-raw wounds. He'd been a crappy friend yet Leo had welcomed Dax into his home without question.

"I was wallowing in my own selfishness," Dax muttered. "I was a jerk. I'm sorry."

"It's okay. It was okay as soon as you rolled up the driveway. I've been waiting for you to come by." Leo held out his hand for Dax to shake, which he did without hesitation.

The hardness in his chest lifted a bit. "Thanks for not barring the gate."

"No problem. I had a feeling you'd need a friend after what happened with Elise. It sounded rough. I'd like to hear about it from you, though."

Dax watched a bird hop from branch to bare branch outside the sunroom's glass walls. "Her computer program matched us. But she wasn't interested in me or finding the love of her life. Or professional ethics. Just winning."

"I watched the interview," Leo said quietly. "You were ruthless. Can you blame her for bringing her A game?"

The interview. It felt like a lifetime ago, back when he'd been smugly certain he couldn't lose the bet because love didn't exist. He almost preferred it when he'd still believed that.

"She screwed me over. I can't forget that."

"You reap what you sow. You started out going head-to-head and that's where you ended up. Change it if that's not what you want."

Leo sipped his tea as Dax shifted uncomfortably. "You say that like I had some fault in this, too."

"Don't you?" Leo tilted his head in way that told Dax the question was rhetorical. "I went into my marriage with Dannie assuming I wanted a wife who took care of my house and left me alone. And that's what I got until I realized it wasn't what I really wanted. Fortunately, she was waiting for me to wake up and see what I had. You didn't give Elise that chance. You ended it."

Of course he'd ended it. "I don't make promises I can't keep."

It was an automatic response, one he'd always said was the reason he didn't do relationships. But that wasn't why he'd walked out on Elise.

The problem was greater than the fear of learning he was like his mother, faithless and unable to make promises to one person forever.

He also feared being like his father—pathetic. Mooning over a woman who didn't actually care about him, waiting in vain for her to come back.

Elise hadn't told him the truth and he could never trust her to stay. And if he let himself love her, and she didn't stay, he'd be doomed to a lifetime of pain and an eternity of solitude because he'd never get over losing his soul mate.

Thirteen

When the doorbell rang, Elise's pulse sprang into double time as she flew to answer it.

Dax.

He'd come to apologize, talk, yell at her. She didn't care. Anything was fine as long as he was here. Hungry to see him again after three miserable days, she swung open the door.

Her heart plummeted.

It was Dannie, dressed to the nines in a gorgeous winter-white cashmere coat, matching skirt and heels. Next to her stood Juliet, the new princess of Delamer, wearing a T-shirt and jeans, of course.

"What are you doing here?" Elise glowered at Juliet. "You're supposed to be on your honeymoon."

The princess shrugged delicately and waved a hand full of bitten-off nails. "It was a working honeymoon and you need me more than His Royal Highness. I left my husband in New York with a host of boring European diplomats. I miss him already, but I owe you more than I can ever repay for giving me back the love of my life."

"I need you?" Elise glanced at Dannie. "You called Juliet and told her I needed her?"

"Yes, yes I did." Dannie bustled Juliet into the house, followed her and shut the door, then held up two bags. "This is an intervention. We brought wine and chocolate since you never keep them in the house."

The heaviness Elise had carried since Dax left returned tenfold. "No chocolate for me. But wine sounds pretty good."

The silence had been deafening. He'd ignored her text messages, even the funny ones. He hadn't called. At first she'd thought it was merely pride, which was why she kept reaching out. But he really didn't want to talk to her.

"Come on, Elise. Live a little. When a man acts like an ass, chocolate is the only cure," Dannie called from the kitchen where she'd gone to fetch wineglasses and a corkscrew.

Tears welled up and the ugly-cry faucet let loose. Dannie flew into the living room and enfolded Elise in a comforting embrace while Juliet looked on helplessly.

Murmuring, Dannie smoothed Elise's hair and let her cry. Sobs wrenched Elise's chest, seizing her lungs until suffocation seemed more likely than a cease-fire of emotions.

Her life had fallen apart. But her friends were here when she needed them.

"It's okay, cry all you want," Dannie suggested. "The endorphins are good for you. It'll help you feel better."

"I know." Dabbing at her eyes ineffectively with a sleeve, Elise sniffled and gave up. "But they don't seem to be working."

"Maybe because Dax is more of an ass than regular men?" Juliet suggested sweetly.

Dannie bit back a snort and Elise choked on an involuntary laugh, which led to a fit of coughing. By the time she recovered, the tears had mostly dried up.

"It wasn't working because it's my fault. I'm the problem, not Dax," Elise confessed.

They might be soul mates, but obviously there was more

to it than that. Happily ever after didn't magically happen, and being matched was the beginning of the journey, not the end. And she had no clue how to get where she wanted to be. That's why she couldn't hold on to Dax, no matter how much she loved him.

Everything he'd accused her of was true.

"That's ridiculous." Dannie *tsk*ed.

"I'm not buying that," Juliet said at the same time. "It's always the man's fault."

Elise smiled at the staunch support. She'd had a hand in these two women's becoming the best they could be, in finding happiness with the men they'd married, and it had been enough for so long to be on the sidelines of love, looking in from outside, nose pressed to the glass.

At least then she hadn't known what she was missing.

"Dax has a hard time trusting people," she explained. "I knew that. Yet I didn't tell him we were matched and he took it as a betrayal."

More than a betrayal. She hadn't trusted that he could love the real her. He'd been gradually warming up to the idea of soul mates, putting his faith in her, and she'd forgotten to do the same.

"So what? When you love someone, you forgive them when they mess up," Juliet declared. "People mess up a lot. It's what makes us human."

"And sometimes, you have to figure out what's best for them, even when they don't know themselves," Dannie advised. "That's part of love, too. Seeing beneath the surface to what a man really wants, instead of what he tells you he wants."

"And sometimes," Elise said quietly, "love isn't enough. Sometimes, you hurt the person you love too much and you can't undo it. That's the lesson here for me."

She'd had a shot at being deliriously in love and ruined

it. She'd always believed that if her soul mate existed, then love *would* be enough.

Juliet and Dannie glanced at each other and a long look passed between them.

"You get the wine." Dannie shooed Juliet toward the kitchen and then extracted a jewelry box from her purse.

Juliet returned with the wineglasses, passed them out and perched on the edge of the couch. "Open it, Elise."

After handing the box to Elise, Dannie sat next to Juliet and held her glass of wine in her lap without drinking it.

Carefully, Elise cracked the hinged lid to reveal a silver necklace. A heart-within-a-heart charm hung from the chain. Surprised, she eyed the two women. "Thank you. But what's this about?"

Dannie unclasped the necklace and drew it around Elise's neck. The cool metal warmed instantly against her skin.

"You gave us necklaces during our makeovers," Dannie said and nodded at Juliet. "We were about to embark on the greatest adventure of our lives. We had your guidance from the first moment we met our matches and it stayed with us every day, right here in silver."

"Open heart." Juliet pointed at Dannie's necklace and then at her own. "Hearts holding each other. Simple but profound messages about love. We wanted to return the favor."

"I had no idea those necklaces meant so much to you." Tears threatened again and Elise blinked them back. "What does mine mean?"

Juliet shook her head with a small smile. "That's for you to figure out at the right time. That's how it works."

"We can't tell you. Just like you didn't tell us." Dannie put a comforting hand on Elise's arm. "I wish I could make it easier for you because honestly, working through the issues I had with Leo was the hardest thing I ever did."

Nodding, Juliet chimed in. "Finn and I are so much alike,

it was nearly impossible to compromise. But we found a way and it was so worth it."

Elise fingered the larger heart with the smaller one nestled inside. Her match was a disaster, not like Dannie's and Juliet's. She'd known their matches were solid from the beginning. Of course, it was easier to see such things from the outside.

What was it about matters of your own heart that were so difficult?

That was it. A heart within a heart.

The necklace's meaning came to her on a whisper, growing louder as her consciousness worked through it, embraced it. The large heart was the love between a man and a woman, which had the capacity to be huge and wonderful, eclipsing everything else.

But inside the larger heart lay a smaller heart.

I have to love myself too.

The fat girl inside hadn't vanished when Dax poured chocolate chips over her. Or when he admitted he was falling in love with her. Because it wasn't enough.

She had to be enough, all by herself, with or without a man by her side.

Until she believed she was worthy of loving a man like Dax and allowing him to love her in return, she wasn't his soul mate. She wasn't his perfect match.

Not yet. But she could be.

"I get it. The necklace," Elise clarified, and took the other women's hands in hers, forming a circle. "I know how to get my happily ever after, or at least how to shoot for it. Will you help me?"

"Yes," they said simultaneously.

"You have a plan," Dannie guessed.

Elise nodded slowly as it formed. "Wakefield Media has a box suite at AT&T Stadium, but Dax never goes. He hates the Cowboys." She didn't recall when he'd shared that information. During one of their marathon profile sessions, likely. "But I need him there on Sunday. Can you have Leo make up some reason why they both need to go to a game?"

"Of course." Dannie smiled mischievously. "Leo will do anything I ask. I finally got two pink lines this morning."

"You're pregnant?" Elise gasped as Juliet smiled and kissed Dannie's cheek. "No wonder you told Juliet to get the wine."

"We're not announcing it. I'm only telling you two because I had to tell *someone*." The glow only made Dannie more beautiful. "But enough about me. I'll get Leo and Dax there."

"Thanks." Elise squeezed both of their hands. "You are the finest ladies I've ever had the privilege of meeting."

The last thing Dax wanted to do was go to a Cowboys game. But Leo insisted and they'd only recently resurrected their friendship. How could he say no and not offend Leo?

Dax would much rather spend the day asleep, but that wasn't an option. He hadn't slept well since that last night with Elise. Spending the day alone held even less appeal. So he went.

The stadium teemed with blue and silver and stars aplenty. The world's fourth-largest high-definition video screen hung from the roof, from the twenty-yard line to the opposing twenty-yard line, and only someone in the media business could fully appreciate the glory of it.

The retractable roof was closed today in deference to the late season weather, which boosted the crowd noise to a new level of loud. Once he and Leo arrived in the luxurious box suite, blessed silence cloaked them both as they ordered beer from the efficient waitstaff and then slid into the high-backed suede stools overlooking the field.

Leo held out his longneck bottle and waited for Dax to clink his to it. They both took a long pull of beer.

After swallowing, Leo said, "Thanks for doing this. I thought we should hang out, just us."

"Sure." Dax shrugged, a little misty himself at the catch in Leo's voice. "No one was using the suite today and the Cowboys are playing the Redskins. It'll be worth it if the 'Skins trounce the homeboys."

The spectacle of the teams taking the field began, and they settled in to watch the game. They sat companionably until halftime, when Leo cleared his throat.

"We've been friends a long time. But some major changes have happened in my life. I've changed. I hope you can respect who I am now and it won't affect our friendship going forward." Leo stared out over the field. "On that note, I have to tell you something. It's huge."

Dax's gut clenched. Leo was about to announce he had two months to live. Or Daniella did.

Fate couldn't be so unkind to such genuine people. And Dax had wasted so much time, time Leo may not have, being stupid and prideful.

"I've been hard on Daniella and on you about her. I'm over it." Over his pettiness, over his inability to be happy for his friend. But not over the slight jealousy that Leo had figured out how to navigate relationship waters with such stellar success. "It's great that you found her. She's amazing and obviously good for you."

"She is. And that's good to hear, because—" Leo grinned and punched Dax on the arm "—I'm going to be a father."

"That's what this bro-date was about?" Dax grinned back as his nerves relaxed. "Congrats. I'm glad if you're glad."

Leo was going to have a family.

Jealousy flared again, brighter, hotter. Shock of all shocks. Dax had never once thought about having a family. Never thought he'd want one. Never dreamed he'd instantly imagine a tiny, beautiful face with dark hair and a sharp wit. A little girl who took after her mother.

"Of course I'm glad! It's the second-best thing that's happened to me after marrying Dannie." Leo swallowed the last of his beer and set it down with a flourish. "And no. That's not why I insisted we come to the game. That is."

Leo pointed at the jumbo screen in the middle of the stadium. A woman's face filled it. A familiar, dark-haired woman. *Elise*.

Dax's pulse pounded in his throat. "What's going on?"

Audio piped into the suite quite clearly.

"Thanks for giving me thirty seconds, Ed," she said, her voice ringing in Dax's ears, filling the stadium as the crowd murmured and craned their necks to watch. "My name is Elise Arundel and I'm a matchmaker."

What was this all about—advertising? Or much more? He glared at Leo. "You had something to do with this?"

"All her," Leo replied mildly. "I'm just the delivery boy."

Dax's gaze flew back to the screen where Elise was addressing the entire stadium full of Sunday afternoon football fanatics. *Elise* was addressing *80,000 people* voluntarily. If he weren't so raw, he might be proud of her. It must have been difficult for her, given that she didn't like to be the center of attention.

"Some of you saw me on the *Morning Show* a few weeks ago, being interviewed by Dax Wakefield. We struck a deal. If I matched Dax to the love of his life, he'd agree to sing my praises at the Super Bowl. Which is in February and unfortunately, I lost the wager."

Lost? She'd been quite gleeful over the fact that she'd won the last time he'd seen her. His mind kicked into high gear. She was up to something.

"So," she continued. "Congratulations, Dax. You win. You get to put me out of the business of happily ever after. I'm such a good loser, I'm going to let you do it at a football game. All you have to do is join me on camera. Tell these people I didn't change your mind about true love and that you still don't believe soul mates exist."

"How can I do that?" Dax muttered. "I don't know where you are."

"I'm here," Elise said. But in the flesh, not through the stadium's sound system.

He whirled. And there she was, gorgeous and real, and her presence bled through the air, raising heat along his neck. She was within touching distance. He'd missed her, missed her smile, her quirky sense of humor. The way she made him feel.

And then he remembered. She was a liar, a manipulator. She cared only about winning.

Except she'd just announced to 80,000 people that she'd lost. And she'd told him in no uncertain terms that only promoting EA International could get her in front of a camera. Obviously she'd found another motivator, but what?

A cameraman followed her into the suite, lens on Dax. He couldn't even muster a fake grin, let alone his "camera" smile, not when Elise had effectively pinned him to a piece of cork after all. "What is this all about, Elise?"

"I told you. This is your shining moment. It's your chance to ruin me. Go ahead." She nodded to the stadium, where this nightmare was playing out on the screen.

Thousands of eyes were riveted to the drama unfolding and it needed to be over. Now.

He opened his mouth. And closed it. Not only was he pinned to a cork, on display for everyone to examine, she was daring him to lie in public.

He wasn't a liar.

So he didn't lie.

"My soul mate doesn't exist."

Something sharp and wounded glinted in the depths of her eyes.

"Tell them I didn't match you to the love of your life," she suggested clearly, as if the stadium deserved to hear every word regardless of what was going on inside her. "That I'm a fraud and my match software doesn't work."

Obviously, this was not going to end until he gave her what she was asking for.

"True love doesn't exist for me and your match process is flawed," he growled as his pulse spiked and sweat broke out across the back of his heated neck, though both statements were true. "Is that what you wanted me to say?"

It was done. He'd set out to ruin her and now everyone in the stadium, as well as those watching at home, heard him say it. His comments would be broadcast far and wide on social media, he had no doubt.

His stomach churned. The victory was more hollow than his insides.

All at once, he realized why. He'd called off the wager and meant it. But only because he refused to lose and calling it off was the only way to ensure that would never happen.

He and Elise were put together with remarkable similarity. Was he really going to blame her because she didn't like to lose either?

Leo might have had a small point about Elise bringing her A game.

Too bad the wager was the only real thing they'd ever had between them.

Vulnerability in her expression, she stared at him without blinking. "Is that all? There's nothing more you have to say?"

"I'm done."

Wasn't what he'd already said enough? His heart felt as if it were being squeezed from its mooring through a straw. Did she not realize how painful this was?

She crossed the suite, closing the few yards between

them, barging right into his personal space. Finger extended, she pointed right at the area of his torso that hurt the worst.

"You need to tell them the *whole* truth. You not only admitted love does happen to others, you started to believe in it for yourself. In the possibility of soul mates," she said. "Because I matched you with the perfect woman. And you fell in love with her, didn't you?"

He groaned. She'd seen right through his carefully worded statements. Right through him. The curtain didn't exist to her.

He crossed his arms over the ache in his chest. "It would be unfair to say either of us won when in reality, we both lost."

Tenderness and grief welled in her eyes. "Yes. We both lost something precious due to my lack of trust in you. But not because you were untrustworthy. Because I couldn't trust myself, couldn't trust that I was the right person to change your mind about true love. I was convinced you'd end our relationship after a couple of weeks and when I fell in love with you, I—"

"You're in love with me?" Something fluttered in his chest as he searched her face.

All her deepest emotions spilled from her gaze, spreading across her expression, winding through his heart.

It was true.

His pulse spiked and he fought it. What did that really change? Nothing.

"I'm afraid so," she said solemnly. "Nothing but the truth from here on out. I thought love conquered all. But without trust, someone can be perfect for you and still screw it up."

She was talking to him. About him. She knew he'd let his own issues cloud their relationship, just as she had. He'd let his fears about turning out like his parents taint his life, never giving anyone a chance to betray his trust.

He'd let anger blind him to the truth.

This had never been about winning the wager, for either of them.

"How do you know if you can trust someone forever? That's a long time."

"Fear of the unknown is a particular expertise of mine," she allowed with a small smile. "I like to know what's going to happen, that I can depend on someone. Especially when he promises something so big as to love me for the rest of my life. That's scary. What if he changes his mind? What if—"

"I'm not going to change my mind."

The instant it was out of his mouth, he realized what she'd gotten him to concede. And the significance of it.

"And by the way, same goes," he said. "How do I know you're not going to change yours?"

How had he not seen they were alike even in this? Neither of them trusted easily, yet he'd crucified her over her inability, while tucking his own lack of trust away like a favored treasure. She hadn't been trying to bring him to his knees. Just trying to navigate something unexpected and making mistakes in the process.

"Let's take it day by day. As long as you're in this relationship fully today, that's the only guarantee I need. I love you." She nodded to the stadium. "I'm not afraid to stand up in front of all these people and tell you how I feel. Are you?"

It was a challenge. A public challenge. If he said he loved her, it would be the equivalent of admitting she'd won. Of admitting she'd done everything she said she would in the interview.

"What are you trying to accomplish here?" he asked.

"I believe this is more commonly known as me calling you on your crap."

Against his will, the corners of his lips turned up. "Is that so?"

Only Elise knew exactly how to do that. Because she got him in a way no one else ever could.

She nodded. "But I had to wade through my own first. When my algorithm matched me with you, it wasn't wrong. But I was. I'm sorry I didn't tell you I was your match. I wasn't ready to trust you. I am now."

And she'd proved it by declaring her flaws to the world on the big screen, publicly. The one place she said she'd go only for her business. But she'd done it for him because *he* was her motivator. Because she loved him.

Somehow, that made it easier to confess his own sins.

"I...messed up, too. I wasn't about to stick around and find out I couldn't trust you to stay, so I didn't. I'm sorry I didn't give you that chance."

The exact accusation he'd flung at her. His relationship philosophy might as well be Do Unto Others Before They Do Unto You. That ended today. If he loved Elise and knew beyond a doubt he wasn't going to change his mind, he wasn't broken. Just incomplete.

His soul needed a mate to be whole.

Her smile belied the sudden tears falling onto her cheeks. "You didn't meet your soul mate because your soul mate wasn't ready to meet you. But I am ready now." She held out her hand as if they'd just been introduced for the first time. "My name is Shannon Elise Arundel, but you can call me Elise."

He didn't hesitate but immediately grasped her fingers and yanked her into a kiss. As his mouth met hers and fused, his heart opened up and out spilled the purest form of happiness.

He'd found his soul mate, and it turned out he didn't want a woman who didn't care what was behind his curtain. He wanted this woman, who'd invited herself backstage and taken up residence in the exact spot where she belonged.

She'd been one step ahead of him the entire time. She

was the only woman alive who could outthink, outsmart and out-love him.

Lifting his head slightly, he murmured against her lips, "I love you too. And for the record, I'd rather call you mine."

An "aww" went up from the spectators and without taking his attention off the woman in his arms, Dax reached out to cover the lens with his palm. Some things weren't meant to be televised.

Epilogue

Elise's first Super Bowl party was in full swing and surprisingly, she'd loved every minute of it. It had been her idea and Dax let her plan the whole thing. And he didn't mind that she spent more time in the kitchen with Dannie and a host of female guests cooing over baby talk now that Dannie was in her second trimester.

"Hon," Dax called from the living room. "I think you'd better come see this."

Immediately, Elise set down her wine and moved to comply. The other women snickered but that didn't slow her down.

"What?" she called over her shoulder. "If any of you had a gorgeous man like that in your bed every night, you'd jump when he said jump, too."

She sailed out of the kitchen to join Dax on the couch in front of the sixty-five-inch LED TV that now dominated her—their—living room. It was the only thing Dax had requested they keep from his loft when he moved in with her at Christmas.

How could she say no? They hardly ever watched it anyway. Neither football nor science fiction movies held a candle to doing everything together—going to the grocery store, dinner and sometimes even to work with each other. It was heaven on earth and it could not possibly get any better.

"I like what I see so far," she told him as her gaze lit on his beautiful face.

Dax grinned and took her hand, nodding at the TV. "You can look at me anytime. That's what you should be focusing on."

The game had cut to a commercial break. A Coca-Cola polar bear faded away as one commercial ended and another began. A familiar logo materialized on the screen. *Her* logo. EA International's, to be precise.

"What did you do?" she sputtered around a startled laugh.

"I owed you the match fee. Watch," Dax advised her and she did, fingers to her numb lips.

A montage of clips from her confessional at the Cowboys game flashed, interspersed with snippets of former clients espousing her praises in five-second sound bites. The whole commercial was cleverly edited to allow Elise's speech about true love to play out in real time in the form of happy couples. Then the last scene snapped into focus and it was Dax.

"EA International specializes in soul mates," the digital version of Dax said sincerely, his charisma so crisp and dazzling on the sixty-five-inch screen she nearly wept. "That's where I found mine. Elise, I love you. Will you marry me?"

Her pulse stopped, but her brain kept going, echoing with the sound of Dax's smooth voice.

The screen faded to a car commercial and the house full of people went dead silent as Dax dropped to his knees in front of her, his expression earnest. "I'm sorry, but I can't call you Ms. Arundel any longer."

And then he winked, setting her heart in motion again as she laughed through the tears that had sprung up after all. "You can call me Mrs. Wakefield. I insist."

Applause broke out and Elise was gratified to feel absolutely no heat in her cheeks. Dax lived in the spotlight, and she'd deal with it gladly because she wanted to stand next to him for the rest of her life.

The crowd shifted their attention to other things, leaving Dax and Elise blessedly alone. Or at least as alone as they could be with thirty people in the house.

Without a lot of fanfare, Dax pulled a box out of his pocket and produced a beautiful, shiny diamond ring, eclipsed only by the wattage of his smile. "I'm assuming that's a yes."

She nodded, shaking loose a couple of the tears. "Though I'm intrigued to find out what you'd planned as a backup to that commercial if I said no."

How could he come up with anything more effective than *that?* He'd declared his love for her, asked her to marry him and endorsed her business in the most inarguable way possible. He was brilliant and all hers.

It was better than a fairy tale. Better than Cinderella because he saw *her*, the real her, underneath. No makeover, no fancy dresses. If she gained a few pounds, he wouldn't care.

"No backup," he said smugly and slipped the ring on her finger, which fit precisely right, of course. Dax Wakefield never missed a trick. "I knew you'd say yes since I proposed during the Super Bowl. You know, because it's less predictable than Valentine's Day."

Her heart caught on an erratic, crazy beat. He remembered what she'd said on that park bench a season ago. That alone made him her perfect match. The rest was icing on the cake.

"I thought being with you couldn't get any better. How like you to prove me wrong," she teased and then sobered, taking his jaw between both of hands. His ring winked back at her from its place on her third finger, perfect and right. "Don't stop, even if I tell you to, okay?"

"Deal." He leaned forward to kiss her sweetly, and against her lips, mouthed, "I love you."

"I love you, too."

Happily ever after had finally arrived. For both of them.

* * * * *

MILLS & BOON®

Want to get more from Mills & Boon?

Here's what's available to you if you join the
exclusive **Mills & Boon eBook Club** today:

✦ *Convenience – choose your books each month*
✦ *Exclusive – receive your books a month before
   anywhere else*
✦ *Flexibility – change your subscription at any time*
✦ *Variety – gain access to eBook-only series*
✦ *Value – subscriptions from just £1.99 a month*

So visit **www.millsandboon.co.uk/esubs** today
to be a part of this exclusive eBook Club!

EBOOK_SUBS_2014

MILLS & BOON®

Maybe This Christmas

* cover in development

Let Sarah Morgan sweep you away to a perfect winter wonderland with this wonderful Christmas tale filled with unforgettable characters, wit, charm and heart-melting romance!
Pick up your copy today!

www.millsandboon.co.uk/xmas

MILLS & BOON®

The Little Shop of Hopes & Dreams

* cover in development

Much loved author Fiona Harper brings you the
story of Nicole, a born organiser and true romantic,
whose life is spent making the dream proposals of
others come true. All is well until she is enlisted
to plan the proposal of gorgeous photographer
Alex Black—the same Alex Black with whom
Nicole shared a New Year's kiss that she is
unable to forget…

**Get your copy today at
www.millsandboon.co.uk/dreams**

0914_ST_2

MILLS & BOON®

Why shop at millsandboon.co.uk?

Each year, thousands of romance readers find their perfect read at millsandboon.co.uk. That's because we're passionate about bringing you the very best romantic fiction. Here are some of the advantages of shopping at www.millsandboon.co.uk:

* **Get new books first**—you'll be able to buy your favourite books one month before they hit the shops

* **Get exclusive discounts**—you'll also be able to buy our specially created monthly collections, with up to 50% off the RRP

* **Find your favourite authors**—latest news, interviews and new releases for all your favourite authors and series on our website, plus ideas for what to try next

* **Join in**—once you've bought your favourite books, don't forget to register with us to rate, review and join in the discussions

Visit **www.millsandboon.co.uk**
for all this and more today!

LS_WEB